The History of Liberalism in Russia

Pitt Series in Russian and East European Studies
Jonathan Harris, Editor

THE HISTORY
OF LIBERALISM
IN RUSSIA

VICTOR LEONTOVITSCH

Translated by
PARMEN LEONTOVITSCH

With a foreword by Aleksandr Solzhenitsyn

UNIVERSITY OF PITTSBURGH PRESS

Published by the University of Pittsburgh Press, Pittsburgh, Pa., 15260
Manufactured in the United States of America
Printed on acid-free paper
10 9 8 7 6 5 4 3 2 1
Victor Leontovitsch, *Geschichte des Liberalismus in Russland,* © Vittoria Klostermann, Frankfurt am Main, 1957
© Vittorio Klostermann Frankfurt am Main; Geschichte des Liberalismus in Russland, 1957, 2nd edition 1974
© Alexander Solzhenitsyn for the Preface to the YMCA Press, Russian Edition, 1979

Library of Congress Cataloging-in-Publication Data

Leontovitsch, Victor, author.

   [Geschichte des Liberalismus in Russland. English]

   The history of liberalism in Russia / Victor Leontovitsch ; translated by Parmen Leontovitsch with a foreword by Aleksandr Solzhenitsyn.

       p.   cm. — (Pitt series in Russian and East European studies)

   Includes bibliographical references and index.

   ISBN 978-0-8229-4415-7 (hardcover : alkaline paper)

   1. Russia—Politics and government—1689–1801. 2. Liberalism—Russia—History.
3. Russia—Politics and government—1801–1917. I. Leontovitsch, Parmen, translator.
II. Solzhenitsyn, Aleksandr Isaevich, 1918–2008, writer of added commentary. III. Title.
IV. Series: Series in Russian and East European studies.

   DK62.9.L4613 2012

   320.510947—dc23   2011039625

CONTENTS

Foreword by Aleksandr Solzhenitsyn   *vii*

Preface   *ix*

Notes on the Translation   *xi*

Introduction   *1*

PART 1: THE HISTORY OF LIBERALISM, 1762–1855

Chapter 1: Catherine II   *17*

Chapter 2: Alexander I   *31*

Chapter 3: Speransky   *38*

Chapter 4: Karamzin   *56*

Chapter 5: The Codification of the Law   *69*

Chapter 6: Nicholas I   *79*

Chapter 7: Nicholas I (continued)   *89*

PART 2: THE DEVELOPMENT OF CIVIL LIBERTY, 1856–1914

Chapter 8: The Emancipation of the Serfs   *107*

Chapter 9: The Emancipation Laws and Their Later Interpretation   *115*

Chapter 10: Peasant Law   *124*

Chapter 11: The Peasant Question in the Reign of Alexander III   *133*

Chapter 12: The Peasant Question in the Reign of Nicholas II before 1905   *143*

Chapter 13: The Agrarian Program of the Left-Wing Parties   *155*

Chapter 14: The Peasant Question after 1905   *164*

Chapter 15: The Peasant Question after 1905 (continued)   *175*

PART 3: THE DEVELOPMENT OF POLITICAL LIBERTY, 1856–1914

Chapter 16: The History of Political Liberalism in the Reign of
Alexander II   *189*

Chapter 17: The Period from 1881 to 1902   *203*

Chapter 18: The Liberation Movement   *220*

Chapter 19: Liberalism in 1904   *227*

Chapter 20: The *Zemstvo* Congresses   *242*

Chapter 21: Further *Zemstvo* Congresses and the Aggravation of the
Revolutionary Situation   *254*

Chapter 22: The Manifesto of October 17, 1905, and the Constitution of
April 23, 1906   *269*

Chapter 23: Witte and Public Opinion   *283*

Chapter 24: The Constitutional-Democratic Party and the Union of
October 17   *292*

Chapter 25: The First Duma   *300*

Chapter 26: The Second Duma   *311*

Chapter 27: The Coup of June 3, 1907, and the Third and Fourth Dumas   *321*

Notes   *331*

Index of Names   *371*

FOREWORD

Aleksandr Solzhenitsyn

The present book has suffered the bitter fate of works written in emigration: first published only in a foreign language, it is only appearing now, twenty years later, in its native tongue and twenty years after the death of its author—for all that time remaining inaccessible to the readers of its native land. Yet this book is needed most by Russian readers, as it deals only with Russian history and ideas that more than anything are waiting to be explained and assimilated by Russian society.

Here is a rigorous exposition of a number of ideas of the utmost importance about the nature of liberalism and its manifestations in Russia. This results in a markedly clearer definition of liberalism and helps to bring closer a comprehensive understanding of this concept. On reading, one gains the impression that this concept was used in Russia in a way that was far from exact for over a hundred years or more (and is still used by us today). Particularly instructive for us is the author's systematic distinction between liberalism and radicalism; too often during the nineteenth and twentieth centuries in Russia the latter became synonymous with the former and as such accepted by us—and radicalism triumphed over liberalism to the great detriment of our progress. The author also presents examples of other possible corruptions of liberalism that, to use his terminology, lead to democratic absolutism and imperialist democracy. Today when, even in the West, liberalism has retreated everywhere under devastating pressure from socialism, the author's warnings resonate all the more. This, for example: liberalism only remains a vital force as long as it keeps changing existing structures through evolution; each time it tries to impose an external readymade blueprint, it will be immediately overtaken and defeated by socialism. Alternatively, take another example: without property rights there can be no real individual freedom, and it is for this reason that no form of socialism would be able to make people free. In addition, this makes us wonder whether we do not overestimate the importance of political liberty compared to that which gives us civil rights.

The author takes a fresh look at numerous figures and events in Russian history and helps us to do likewise: from Radishchev, Pugachev, Catherine II, and

Karamzin, to the Decembrists (the last, already radical, were in the author's view fateful for the development of liberalism in Russia). He continues on to Stolypin's resolute liberalism, the breadth of the civil liberties granted by the 1906 Constitution, and the depth of Russian political thinking at the beginning of the twentieth century. Moreover, in our troubled and distorted present day, like an appeal and a warning, the old choice reappears: first a constitution and then the emancipation of the serfs (Speransky) or first civil rights for the peasants and only then political liberty (Stolypin).

This book has that elegant quality of successful works that, while elucidating a specific subject, throw light in passing on other questions that are sometimes of greater significance. Thus, we find in this history of liberalism a profound analysis of some of the key factors that made revolution possible in Russia.

Nevertheless, the approach rigorously followed by the author, namely, that of legal formalism, sometimes restricts his vision and interpretation of history—a history that cannot be kept within these bounds. Thus, exemption from state service granted to the gentry in the second half of the eighteenth century is presented as progress toward liberty and hence as a victory for liberalism. However, one's feelings protest against such an interpretation, for it is precisely this exemption, granted only to the gentry, that reinforced their corrupt idea of land ownership, which for a long time stood in the way of the emancipation of the peasantry. By defining liberalism's method as the removal of all that restricts the freedom of the individual, the author does not tell us whether or not one would encounter religious interdictions along the way. He attributes a determining role to legal consciousness and concepts in the course of events and even sees a similarity between legal norms and liturgical texts (hence an almost hostile attitude to those we call "Slavophiles," with the exception of D. N. Shipov, cited frequently and sympathetically). Nowhere does he mention—or even appear to admit the idea—that when one is studying the historical process, the juristic method cannot be adequate and does not provide the best viewpoint when looking at the whole.

Today, when our country is so anxious to understand our recent history—recent but completely lost—many will find Professor Leontovitsch's synoptic work illuminating and useful.

PREFACE

On reading De Ruggiero's famous *Storia del Liberalismo Europeo,* I was disappointed that in recounting the history of liberalism in Italy, France, England, and Germany, it left out the history of liberalism in Spain and Russia. It thus seemed desirable to sketch out the history of liberalism in Russia in a longer article. This book came from that attempt to add a chapter to someone else's book.

It became apparent, however, in the course of my work, that the history of liberalism in Russia was quite different from the history of Western European liberalism. This was because liberalism in Russia had to confront problems whose resolution preceded the advent of liberalism in Western Europe. This process was prolonged over centuries of Western European history, while the conditions making it possible had already matured during the Middle Ages.

I deliberately chose the title "The History of Liberalism in Russia" in contrast to "The History of Russian Liberalism." Although liberalism in Russia was faced with other tasks, and consequently took on different forms than in the West, it was largely derived from Western European liberal ideas. In addition, I have written a history of liberalism, not of liberals. I am not so interested in individuals who saw themselves as liberals or were considered as such by others. I am only interested in those who made a real contribution to the spread of liberal ideas or to the creation of liberal institutions in Russia. Some of them would no doubt be very surprised to find their names in a history of liberalism, while others, certainly greater in number, would surely be dismayed that they have not been given the place in the history of liberalism in Russia that they feel is theirs.

This approach, as well as the fact that the concept of liberalism is in general very contentious, has led me to begin my historical study with an introduction setting out my understanding of liberalism. I am quite prepared to acknowledge that I have defined liberalism somewhat narrowly, although that is not my own view. This approach allowed me, as a historian, to write an account of a specific and clearly defined political current, not a collection of phenomena that are only rather haphazardly called liberal.

Furthermore, I thought it necessary to describe in detail the institutions and political ideas that liberalism opposed. This is because I believe this is essential for a correct understanding of the nature of liberalism.

I intentionally included many quotations, as I did not think it advisable to refrain from quoting the sources, even where this might have been possible. These sources are not easily accessible, and it is surely useful for the reader to gain a direct insight into them.

Regrettably, it was not possible to include in this work the influence of liberal ideas and principles on reform of the law courts and legal procedures or the setbacks that this development suffered. This could only have been done at the expense of the detailed treatment of the main issues—that is, the development of civil and political freedom in Russia—something I wanted to avoid at all costs. Furthermore, I have chosen to end the history of liberalism not in 1917, but in 1914, as normal life in Russia was profoundly disrupted by the First World War. Even such an event as the formation of the "Progressive Block" in the Duma, which in itself deserves to be considered as part of the history of liberalism in Russia, came about largely as a result of the course of the war. To do it justice, I would have had to deal with the history of the war, something that lies well beyond the scope of this book.

In references to works in Russian, I have mostly only given the Russian title once and from then on used only the translated title (often abbreviated) to make it easier for the reader, who does not have command of the language to see from which work the citation was taken.

At this point, I wish to express my gratitude to all who read the manuscript and thus paved the way for its publication: Professors Mathias Gelzer, Otto Vossler, Paul Kirn, Hermann Mosler, David Footman, Hugh Seton-Watson, Leonard Shapiro, and Dr. George Katkov. I am also greatly indebted to the Frankfurt Scientific Society and the publisher Vittorio Klostermann, which made publication of this book possible. I would like to convey my sincere thanks to the Institute for Social Research and its director, Max Horkheimer, for their generous support of my initial research trips, which enabled me to consult extensively the library of the British Museum. I also cordially wish to thank Dr. Helmut Neubauer, who undertook the heavy burden of checking the proofs, and finally, but by no means least, Dr. Witte, head of the Slavic Department of the West German Library, and his deputy, Mr. Palissen, whose kind cooperation made it easier to access a number of books.

NOTES ON THE TRANSLATION

Regarding the transliteration of Russian terms and names, I have followed the U.S. Library of Congress system, with the notable exception of proper names, where I have preferred to use the -*sky* ending rather than -*skii*. On the other hand, I have retained the palatalization marker ('). I have tried to use this system consistently, but where there are mistakes or discrepancies, these are entirely my own. One idiosyncrasy is the transliteration of the name of the Kadet journal *Reč* (Speech), in my view avoiding the ungainly *Rech* or *Riech*.

As explained in his preface, Victor Leontovitsch quoted at length from his sources, and so to make things easier for the reader I have isolated longer quotations from the main text. Another feature of the book is a significant number of quotations in French, as well as a sprinkling in Latin and Italian. I have retained these as in the original but have provided translations in the text or in the footnotes.

Victor Leontovitsch embedded a number of Russian terms in parentheses in the text, in both his own material and in quotations, particularly in the section on the emancipation of the serfs, where he was not always sure the German translation rendered the exact meaning, allowing the specialist reader to cross-check. I have retained these to give a flavor of the original text. A number of key Russian terms were used by the author throughout, and I have kept these—for example, *duma, ukaz, volost', zemstvo*. Regarding the last of these, I have, however, used *zemstvos* for the plural rather than *zemstva*. Similarly, I have used *desiatin* uninflected to stand for both the singular and the plural. Bracketed interpolations are my own.

I have referred to the *Dictionary of Russian Historical Terms from the Eleventh Century to 1917*, by S. G. Pushkarev and G. Vernadsky (Yale University Press 1970), to find the best English equivalent of specialist words, but a number of leading books on Russian history have also proved invaluable in this respect. As there can be some variation among the English versions, I have sometimes had to make a choice—for example, whether to use "editing commission" or "editorial commission" when discussing the emancipation of the serfs. I have also chosen "legislative commission" over "law code commission" when discussing Catherine the Great's reign.

The nonspecialist reader may be unfamiliar with the use of the term *estate* to mean a social class with a political or legal status—a system that persisted in Russia into the early twentieth century. As this book deals with issues of land ownership, the term *estate* is also used to mean a large landholding, mainly owned by the gentry. Occasionally, I have qualified *estate* with *landed* or *social* to make clear which meaning is intended.

Regarding citations, Victor Leontovitsch in many instances gave the Russian title only once and then used a German version in subsequent references. I have largely followed this, except that I have substituted an English version for the German. Most citations appear in footnotes, but where there are a large number of references from one source, the author embedded these in the text. The author's footnotes and my additional translator footnotes are numbered sequentially in each chapter, with my notes clearly marked as such.

This translation includes the author's original preface and an index of names based on the German version.

Finally, I wish to thank a number of people for their help and encouragement: Denis Briggs, for his patient perseverance in checking the translation; Julia Oswalt, for her help with specialist terms and the translation in general; Maria Manley, for her help and her corrections of my transliteration and general proofreading; Peggy Troupin and Sylvia Juran, for their invaluable advice and assistance; and last but not least, the Solzhenitsyn Estate for its permission to translate Aleksander Solzhenitsyn's foreword to the Russian edition.

I would welcome any feedback regarding the translation. Please send any comments by email to parmen.leontovitsch@gmail.com.

PARMEN LEONTOVITSCH

The History of Liberalism in Russia

Introduction

Historical sources of liberalism—Nature of
liberalism—Civil society—The administrative
state—Constitutional government—Political
radicalism—The antirevolutionary nature of
liberalism

The fundamental idea of liberalism—as the name itself indicates—is to make
freedom, the freedom of the individual, a reality. Liberalism's basic approach
is not creation, but negation, that is, the elimination of all that threatens the survival of individual freedom and impedes its development. It is precisely because
of this approach that liberalism, compared to other programs, finds it difficult to
attract support. It does not appeal to those so aptly called "activists" in modern
parlance, but who are surely an eternal psychological type, turning up repeatedly
throughout history, although perhaps not to the same extent as today.

As is well known, liberalism, as a developed system, superseded the absolutist police state. The term *police*, however, had a much broader meaning in the
seventeenth and eighteenth centuries than later. The term was taken to mean the
entire bureaucratic apparatus, all the administrative government that had developed vigorously within the centralized eighteenth-century state, discharging an
extremely varied range of functions. Liberal movements, therefore, naturally as-
pired to reduce this administrative system with its regulations and organizations.
This is precisely what justifies, at least from a historical perspective, the assertion
that liberalism works by negation and not creation.

Liberalism is the product of Western European culture and before that, in
essence, of the Greco-Roman world of the Mediterranean. Already known in an-
tiquity, clearly defined concepts such as the *Rechtssubjekt* [legal subject] and rights

(especially private property), as well as institutions that provided a framework for the citizen to participate in the exercise of state power, primarily legislative power, belonged to liberalism's core ideas.[1] This foundation was rediscovered by modern Western European nations and supplemented by a number of new ideas.

The history of liberalism in the West lies outside the scope of this book, although it is essential to highlight two historical sources of Western European liberalism: feudalism and the independence of spiritual from secular power during the Middle Ages. De Ruggiero begins his *History of European Liberalism* with a quotation from Mme de Staël, who makes the comment, "In France, liberty is an old, traditional value, whereas tyranny is a recent phenomenon." He comments, "These words of Mme de Staël are historically well founded, for liberty is rooted in medieval society and thus predates the absolutism of the new monarchy." In fact, from a historical perspective, the balance of power that had developed between king and feudal barons formed the basis for liberties in Western European states. The first example of the establishment of such a balance, such a separation of powers even, was the creation of the Magnum Concilium in England. Initially, then, in Western Europe political liberty took on an aristocratic form, something the French constitutional law expert Hauriou also highlighted. He writes: "It is important to distinguish a historical law regarding states that came into existence and developed normally. These states go from aristocracy over to democracy. The political liberty that exists there takes on two successive forms—first aristocratic, then democratic freedom."[2] In the West, an equally important source of liberty was the independence of the pope vis-à-vis the holders of secular power, as this allowed the formation of a sphere of spiritual autonomy in relation to the state.

The reason I felt the need to highlight these roots of Western European liberalism is that neither of them existed in Russia. Russian church leaders never enjoyed the status of sovereign rulers, while feudalism did not exist in Russia.

Although liberalism in Russia in essence corresponded exactly to liberalism in Western Europe, including the need to defeat and replace the absolutist, bureaucratic police state, nevertheless it is important to be clear that Russian liberalism did not have these historical roots. Liberalism in Russia, as both an idea and a practical program, was effectively derivative in nature. In addition, the Russian variant of the police state, as embodied in serfdom, stood in even starker contradiction to all the principles of liberalism, compared with the Western European absolutist state, in both its political and its social structure.

Liberalism is an individualistic system, giving precedence to the individual and his rights. This liberal individualism, however, is not absolute, but relative. Liberalism does not assume that man is always virtuous and motivated to strive for what is good. On the contrary, liberalism knows well that man, with a relatively free moral sense and possessing a relatively free will, can choose either good or evil. Liberalism therefore requires, in contrast to anarchism (certain variants of which can be seen as a form of absolute individualism), the creation of a positive system of law and government opposed to and binding the will of the individual. It is therefore in favor of institutions or social structures that subsume and discipline the individual. Nevertheless, liberalism is an individualistic system, because man, as an individual, is given priority. Social structures or institutions can only be valued insofar as they can be justified from the point of view of the interests and rights of the individual and help the individual subject to achieve his aims. Thus, the basic task of the state and other social structures is to protect and secure these rights: "The aim of every political association is the preservation of the natural and imprescriptible rights of man."[3]

Liberalism sees the well-being, or quite simply the happiness, of the individual as its aim and therefore aspires to extend the possibilities for each to develop his or her personality freely in all its variety and richness. Accordingly, liberalism regards individual initiative and enterprise as the ultimate foundation of society. For this reason, a distinct feature of liberalism, as we have seen, is the reduction to a minimum of all rules and organizations that, as elements of an objective order, stand in the way of individual enterprise and initiative, forming a barrier to the energy of the individual.

All the other demands of liberalism flow from the fundamental principle that society is based on personal initiative and enterprise and justified by the protection it gives to the rights of the individual. Liberalism affirms the security and inviolability of private property vis-à-vis the state, because it sees that the unhindered possession of goods by individuals is the most effective guarantee that the individual should be able to pursue his aims and develop his potential without hindrance. The individual freed, at least to a certain degree, from the pressure of material need is able to devote himself to creating his personal happiness. According to liberalism, *beati possedentes* [blessed are those who possess]. As property is regarded as something positive, liberalism defends the freedom of those activities that are directed at acquiring and augmenting private property. Liberalism advocates the removal of all barriers hindering private initiative and enterprise that have the acquisition of property as their aim. It must be added, however, that liberalism does not just favor money-making enterprises. It supports all initiatives and forms of social enterprise, welcoming them because they are an expression and enrichment of the human personality and develop the energy and talents of the individual.

On the basis of the same fundamental principles, liberalism favors making penal law more humane. A criminal nonetheless remains an individual human being, someone who as such retains his value as a person. The task of penal law cannot consist in merely rendering this person harmless for the sake of society as a whole, even if he has shown himself to have a criminal bent and to be a danger to the public. On the contrary, the powers and means available to society, to which the criminal belongs, must serve to put him in a position to improve and reeducate himself. Liberalism considers punishment above all as a means for improvement and rehabilitation. Thus, the welfare of the individual represents the starting point for all provisions in the liberal penal system. The demand that anyone arrested should be brought before a proper, that is, legally constituted court—and not before an extraordinary tribunal—in the shortest possible time, or at least within a period laid down in law, as well as further legal safeguards for the remainder of the process, are based on the same basic principles.

Overall, the fundamental principles of the liberal, individualistic social order are set out very precisely and succinctly (in agreeable contrast to modern attempts at declarations of rights) in the 1789 French *Déclaration des droits de l'homme et du citoyen*. This declaration identifies four fundamental rights that form the basis of this liberal order. These are the rights of (1) liberty, (2) property, (3) security, and (4) resistance to oppression (Article 2).

The rights specified here—private property, personal security, and finally the right to resist oppression—constitute what is called civil liberty. Personal freedom has two aspects: first, the rejection of private legal subordination in all its forms, and second, the upholding of the unimpeded expression of individual initiative in enterprises of all kinds—in other words, the autonomy of private initiative even in the face of the power of the state.

Insofar as these particular human rights are described as natural law, they apply in equal measure to all. De Ruggiero writes, "Natural law represents a fundamental rejection of all privilege, especially because it is based on the oldest and best-founded of all privileges, namely the privilege of being human"—which (self-evidently) applies equally to all persons.[4] The demand for equality before the law derives from the recognition that human rights or the individual's fundamental rights are based on natural law. Article 1 of the declaration states, "Men are born and remain free and equal in rights."

A clear distinction between civil liberty and political freedom has to be made. Political freedom consists in the right of the citizen to participate in the exercise of political power. Article 6 of the declaration states, "All citizens have the right, either personally or through their representatives, to participate in the formation of the law." Civil liberty—that is, the basic rights that, when recognized and applied, are the foundation of civil society—constitutes the supreme value in the state and its first principle. Accordingly, political freedom is regarded only as an extension of civil or civic liberty, being required only as the guarantee, albeit the sole effective one, for civil liberty and its necessary complement.[5] Hauriou writes, "It is no exaggeration to say that the whole apparatus of the state is constructed to ensure that civil society is maintained."[6]

Civil society must be seen as the foundation of civilization, because it creates the conditions required for the birth of cultural values.[7] Hauriou continues:

> Civic life, that is, life in the context and under the conditions of civil society, consists in the utilization of property. In a sense, this is a life of ease in which a person, no longer beset by economic worries thanks to the advantages and security derived from the assets he has acquired, can think of other things besides his daily needs. He can then devote himself to intel-

lectual pursuits or the free professions, turn to matters of general interest, form ideas about the state, and in general become a citizen.

Private property can thus afford the owner a certain degree of leisure. As a life of ease, however, is the prerequisite for creative concentration (it is no coincidence that the Greeks called a place of intellectual activity a *schole,* meaning "leisure"), it is correct to describe private property as the basis of, or at any rate a necessary condition for, intellectual creativity. Consequently, civil society based on private property can be regarded as the foundation of civilization. This is the real justification for this social order and confirms Hauriou's assertion that the ultimate goal of the state must be to safeguard civil society.

Aristocratic regimes too have certainly secured for their ruling elite the leisure required for creative cultural activity. These regimes, however, have permitted, or rather imposed, legally established systems of extreme harshness and brutality, namely slavery and serfdom, that are unacceptable to the humane conscience. The actual difference between the haves and the have-nots in the context of civil society is often no less than that between the master and serf in an aristocratic regime. There is nevertheless a significant difference between the two: in civil society, both haves and have-nots are equal in the eyes of the law—here there is no legal barrier to improving one's lot or status.

What is more, the state has resources at its disposal that can reduce the disadvantages resulting from this real inequality, which admittedly is associated with the nature of civil society based on private property. These resources, taken as a whole, can be found in the structure of an administrative system, a *régime administratif,* organized in parallel to civil society. In essence, the administrative system consists in the state taking over a range of practical services that were either previously performed through private enterprise or not undertaken at all. In providing these services, the proceeds that might be earned from them are of only secondary interest to the state; it is above all concerned that these services should be universally and regularly available. The fact that these services are regular and universal allows the government departments tasked with delivering them to offer to all a whole range of public provision, so neatly called *commodités publiques* in French, free of charge or for very little. In this fashion, the multiple needs of the "have-nots" can be met even better and more easily with the help of such public services than was the case before the development of administrative government, when the same needs of the "haves" were met through private enterprise. Overall, this results in a significant improvement in the living standards of the broad mass of the population without property. These are the undoubted benefits of administrative government and in fact largely justify the formidable growth of the administrative state.

If, however, meeting the individual's numerous needs is taken over by the state's administrative structure, if private enterprise is replaced by state bureaucracy, this means (as far as the present day is concerned) a return to the police state of the absolute monarchy of the seventeenth and eighteenth centuries. At the same time, it also signifies the establishment of what is called socialism (leaving aside the mystical aura surrounding this word) and what is, from a constitutional point of view, nothing other than an extreme development of the *régime administratif,* a bureaucratization of society and, in a sense, ultimately the rebirth of the old police state. The two aspects of this evolution are thus largely two sides of the same coin.

Although, as previously stated, the development of the administrative system and the provision of numerous services by the bureaucratic apparatus doubtless initially yielded positive outcomes, these changes become negative and dangerous if excessive, resulting in administrative overproduction. The administrative departments even begin offering services to the public that it neither demands nor expects. "It is in the nature of public administration," writes Hauriou, "once begun, perpetually to seek to extend itself and therefore to increase the number of public services." This process takes on various forms: thus, for example, when the free professions, always fertile ground for liberal aspirations, if not liberal ideas as such, are superseded by the bureaucracy or even partly bureaucratized themselves; above all, however, when free private enterprise is replaced by state-run companies. This administrative hypertrophy or excessive socialism threatens to stifle the very principles on which the free modern state is founded, namely civil society based on individual freedom, and thus in effect to destroy the model of the state developed in Western Europe. In particular, this administrative hypertrophy is a threat to civil liberty because each government agency has, or is able to create, a monopoly in its own field, that is, to eliminate any private initiative, which, in general, is also in its interest. The agencies use administrative regulation to this end, a weapon against which the private citizen is completely powerless. In general, this results in a proliferation of the public at the expense of private law and in the crowding out of civil law through administrative law, leading to a more or less general restriction of the sphere of civil liberty.

Finally, excessive administrative development can also be a threat to political freedom, which is based, specifically, on various forms of the separation of powers. The growth of bureaucracy, however, always leads to centralization and to an extreme concentration of power, with the result that these forms of the separation of powers either go into complete decline or remain in place as mere empty shells devoid of their true substance. The freedom of public opinion too is stifled over time by the excessive burgeoning of the bureaucracy.[8]

Nevertheless, the state is, as Hauriou states, one of the institutions with the most potential. Just as the administrative system (kept within sensible limits) is an effective agency for remedying the shortcomings of an inequitable civil society, so a counterweight can be found to offset the dangers of an overdeveloped bureaucracy. This counterbalance is constitutional government. There is a marked difference between centralized bureaucratic systems and constitutional law aimed at realizing political freedom (*régime administratif* or *régime constitution-*

nel).[9] The former is based on centralization and the concentration of power, the latter on decentralization and the separation of powers. Article 16 of the *Décla-ration des droits* is quite clear on this: "A society in which the observance of the law is not assured, nor the separation of powers defined, has no constitution at all." One should note that decentralization, even when it only occurs in the context of restructuring administrative functions, as for example with the replacement of centralized bureaucracy by local administration, already constitutes an expression of constitutional thinking.[10] In fact, states came to introduce constitutional government either to overcome an excessive expansion of administration in the bureaucratic monarchies with their police apparatus, as was the case with continental states, or to thwart its development, as was the case with England.[11] Thus, in principle, the constitution aims to reclaim liberty from the oppression of concentrated state power and centralized bureaucracy. Above all, therefore, it is the legal and political safeguard for civil society, the individualistic principles on which it rests, and the individualistic basic rights that it embodies.

Because of the establishment of representative constitutional government, the structure of the state becomes differentiated and enhanced. One can distinguish in it three systems or structural features:

A. Civil society: the sphere of individual rights, liberty, and private autonomy

B. The administrative system: the sphere of the centralization and concentration of state power, state welfare provision, and authoritative control

C. Constitutional government: the constitution; the sphere of the self-limitation of state power accomplished through the balance among the different organs of the state (or, preferably, *pouvoirs publics*) helped by the decentralization of sovereignty—in other words, the separation of powers

In its classic form, the separation of powers was expounded by Montesquieu in his *Esprit des lois*. This is the relative independence and juxtaposition of legislative power vis-à-vis, on the one hand, the governing power, rather loosely called the executive (I say loosely as its functions are by no means restricted to the execution of legislation), and, on the other hand, the judicial power. All these powers are constitutional and fit in the framework of the constitutional system. It should be emphasized, however, that each of these three branches is at the same time more closely associated with one of the three systems or structural features of the state mentioned above. The representative assembly, the legislative institution, is the primary organ of constitutional government. The administrative and executive branches are inextricably linked. Finally, the judiciary is especially closely associated with civil society. The courts are there, above all, to protect the rights of the individual, in the first instance from infringements by other citizens, but also from infringements by the state.

Protection of the individual's rights from infringement by the state has not been developed to the same extent and in the same form in all countries with established constitutional systems. In most countries, this is limited to protecting the individual's rights from violation by the administrative branch of government. Only in the United States does the judiciary have the task not only of protecting the justly acquired rights of the citizen against the illegal actions of government agencies, but also of safeguarding the whole of civil society and the individualistic legal principles on which it rests against attack from the legislature. The courts in the United States have the authority to refuse to apply new laws passed by the legislature, if these contradict the basic principles of individualistic civil society and are incompatible with the Bill of Rights, which is regarded as the basis of the nation's constitution. It means that the rights included in the declaration and the basic principles of an individualistic liberal social order proclaimed through it are regarded as inviolable natural law. Consequently, the legislature may only pass laws that are compatible with these fundamental principles, which acquire the significance of a constitutional superlegality. Here, where the power of the judiciary is accorded such preeminence in the constitutional framework, what emerges more clearly than elsewhere is that one of the most important tasks of constitutional government is to serve as a guarantee for civil society.[12]

The relationship between constitutional government and civil society, just discussed by us above, following the modern constitutional lawyer Hauriou, is a confirmation of classical liberalism's view, based primarily on the teachings of Montesquieu, that political rights are principally an extension of civil rights and that political liberty above all constitutes a guarantee of civil liberty.[13]

This relationship between civil society and the constitution, between civil and political liberty, results in a fundamental limitation of legislative power, essentially binding that power to the principles of the individualistic civil order even where there are no legal guarantees to back it up. Furthermore, this bond exists even if these principles are not explicitly set out in constitutional law.[14]

It is possible, however, to consider the political rights or liberty of members of the body politic as an unqualified, even absolute value. One can therefore assume that the legislative or, at any rate, constitutive power in the state is not bound by any inviolable legal principles, that there is in the state an institution with this power, through whose will, irrespective of such ties, true law is always crafted when legislation is decided. In this case, it matters little to what extent the content of new legislation accords with the fundamental principles of the individualistic legal order or how far decisions enacted by government or legislature in the form of legislation are in fact law, because it is assumed a priori that is what they are. According to this view, legislative acts must always be regarded as law, because it is assumed that law is the product of the will of the people and that there exists an institution in the state that precisely articulates this.

The primary source for this point of view is Rousseau's *Du contrat social*.[15] Rousseau doubtless concedes (Book II, chapter IV) that besides the *personne publique*, private individuals (*personnes privées*) also need to be taken into consideration and that their life and liberty are by nature independent of the *personne publique*. He also discusses natural law, which characterizes the citizen as a human being. Yet Rousseau develops a complete doctrine of the general will that is always right and always in the common interest. Accordingly, this general will, the will of the *communauté* or the people, is the source of true laws. These laws can thus never be unjust, "for no one is unjust to himself." It is the essence of the *volonté générale*, and the *contrat social* it establishes, that "so long as the subjects have to submit only to conventions of this sort, they obey no one but their own will" (Book II, chapter IV). Logically it follows that "the sovereign, being formed wholly of the individuals who compose it, neither has nor can have any interest contrary to theirs; and consequently the sovereign power need give no guarantee to its subjects" (Book I, chapter VII). In general, the *contrat social* removes any necessity for a particular guarantee of the rights of the individual vis-à-vis the society of which he has become a member. All the clauses of the *contrat social* can be reduced to a single one, namely "the total alienation of each associate, together with all his rights, to the whole community" (Book I, chapter VI). This alienation is "without reserve; the union is as perfect as it can be, and no associate has anything more to demand" (Book I, chapter VI). The difficulty that arises, which certainly did not escape Rousseau's attention, is how to be certain in each specific instance that whoever wields the sovereign power (of the people) "acts as sovereign and not as magistrate," that is, that he really does represent the general will (Book II, chapter IV). Rousseau skates over this problem rather than resolving it.[16] Nevertheless, Rousseau's doctrines were enough to persuade his optimistic followers that they could presume that democratic representation would fundamentally reflect the general will through its laws and that vis-à-vis the former there would be no need to guarantee either the rights of the individual or the basic principles of the individualistic legal order.

Consequently, the principle of the separation of powers would largely lose its significance. If the legislature, the democratic assembly, is the real locus of the *volonté générale*, then the other powers, the executive and the judiciary, should not be seen as factors of equal importance. They must be regarded, rather, as delegated powers derived from the legislature. It thus becomes impossible to speak of the separation of powers in its original meaning, but merely of an allocation of functions among different institutions. The separation of powers as understood by Montesquieu, of course, includes an allocation of function. Essentially, however, the separation of powers includes the idea that a real social force stands behind each power and acts through it. Furthermore, the separation of powers can exist without a division of function. Thus, the separation of powers between two consuls in Rome was a genuine separation of powers even though there was no division of function. Equally, the creation in 1215 in England of the Magnum Concilium that later developed into the English Parliament amounted to a separation of powers. An element of the power of the throne, which was wrested from the king, was transferred to the council. It would be wrong, however, to think of this division or decentralization of power as a mere distribution of function. What counted here was not the division of function, but the fact that both the power of the king and the power of the aristocracy as represented in the Magnum Concilium constituted two independent forces.[17]

Rousseau's doctrine, therefore, makes law and the legislator all powerful. The old adage "Quod principi placuit, legis habet vigorem" [What pleases the ruler has the force of law] seems to apply here, although the word *princeps* should be replaced by "parliamentary democracy," the majority in a democratic assembly elected on the basis of universal, direct, equal, and secret suffrage. Inviolable legal principles cannot apply or be upheld against such a law decided by this majority. Legislation is law because it embodies the general will. Interestingly enough, this notion was even retained after the doctrine of the general will had largely been abandoned. All that was needed to make this possible was to substitute for the *volonté générale* the will of the state understood as a legal person.

Over time, interest in the question of the separation of powers declined even further. This is quite natural, insofar as there was no longer any interest in the inviolability of the individualistic legal principles that acted as a sort of social premise and created a foundation, so to speak, for the political constitution. The purpose of the separation of powers is to limit and moderate the impact of one power through another, all in the name of the individualistic principles of the legal order. What is the point of the separation of powers if one no longer attaches any decisive importance to these principles? Thus, the sense is lost of Montesquieu's statement, reiterated in the *Déclaration des droits* (Article 16), namely, "A society in which the observance of the law is not assured, nor the separation of powers defined, has no constitution at all." This leads to a new and fundamentally different concept of the constitution. Constitutions begin to develop in such a way that they soon can become internal parliamentary rules of procedure, whose purpose is to make it easy for a particular majority to implement its program with as little resistance as possible. This political and legal approach can no longer be qualified as liberalism, but rather as radicalism. This contrasts with liberalism, which has as its aim the preservation, once in place, of the individualistic legal order, as well as the existing acquired rights of the individual.

In fact, no social program or legal principles stand behind political freedom seen as an end in itself. All possibilities are open. In this fashion, the individualistic legal order of the liberal social constitution can be replaced by the resurrection of the most extreme interventionism and bureaucracy, indeed even pure collectivism. The replacement of the individualistic legal order through collectivism signifies much more than the adoption of a few legal principles. It means the dissolution of a complete civilization, a profound rupture in an entire cultural tradition. This is what Stolypin, one of the last significant representatives of the old Russia, sensed and expressed in a speech to the Second Duma in 1907. He said that the destruction of the existing legal order in Russia in the name of socialism meant that later, out of its ruins, a new and unfamiliar fatherland would have to be constructed.

This evolution in constitutional ideas bears with it the seeds of the destruction, or better still the self-destruction, of the modern Western European constitutional state. If a purely formal or absolute democracy or democratic absolutism supersedes liberal democracy, that is, a state in whose constitution the fundamental principles of the individualistic social order are incorporated in the form of basic rights as a form of superlegality, then the way is open for the development of the imperial form of democracy.[18] In fact, all the aspects of the development discussed above prepare the way for the emergence of imperial democracy. If laws no longer take account of the basic legal principles of the individualistic social order and the existing rights that are embedded in it, but merely embody the legislator's will, subject to certain formal conditions, it no longer matters whether this legislator is an elected representative of the holders of individual rights, that is, the citizens, or a ruler who, regardless of any election, sees himself called upon to express the legislative will of the nation. Furthermore, if the principle of the true separation of powers is destroyed, and the government considers itself to be merely the executor of the legislature or a sort of executive board of the legislature, the latter will acquiesce much more easily in the growth of administration, the concentration of bureaucratic power. It is quite clear, however, that the existence of a strongly developed, centralized bureaucratic apparatus is advantageous for the development of an imperial form of government. Ultimately, it becomes particularly easy for this tendency to win the day, if the development of administrative government has passed a certain threshold, and nationalization, that is, the displacement of civil society, has consequently reached a certain level. After all, this eliminates one of the most important and fundamental separations of power, namely the division between political and economic power.[19]

The extensive destruction of civil society, as well as the concentration of economic power in the hands of the state, puts virtually unlimited power at the state's disposal. Who could seriously dispute that such a huge increase in the power of government favors the formation of dictatorial governments and tyrannical state power? In my article "Abhängigkeit und Selbständigkeit bei der Gewaltenteilung," I paid particular attention to this division between economic and political power.[20] I pointed out that while economic power is in the hands of capitalists in the private enterprise system, in a socialist state, by contrast, it is combined with political power in the hands of the state, in effect the bureaucracy. This, however, eliminates a separation of powers, which had been, and had to be, advantageous not just, as is self-evident, for the independence of the middle class but also for the freedom of the working class, because the separation of powers always has liberating results for the individual. By way of a greater justification for this assertion, I quote in extenso a passage from Hauriou's *Principes de droit public*, a work that has still not received enough attention in Germany:

> Economic power has the capacity to secure the means of subsistence in its sphere. Economic power is exercised by someone, whether the owner of a modern industrial concern, the proprietor of a large estate, or the leader of

a military force, who, in one form or another, possesses a stock of essential goods that he can distribute as he wishes among his servants, dependents, and clients. Political power has the potential to create valuable positions in the legal system, thus providing these post-holders access to the means of subsistence. In a sense, therefore, power boils down to satisfying these needs, a concern that is universal, except that economic power can affect subsistence more directly than political power.

. . . In most state systems, political and economic powers can be separate and usually are. In the context of a free-market economy, wealth is accumulated, and as a result, wealthy people emerge with property and money at their disposal; they provide work and reward it; through their wages, thousands depend on it for their living. In a word, capitalists emerge whose power can be exercised ruthlessly. Nevertheless, capitalists do not necessarily have to wield political power; others can come to power through the mechanisms of the constitution. These will occupy high office in the state and be able to distribute benefits and titles. In addition, having the power to create posts in the legal system, they will make use of it, not to consolidate the actual power of the wealthy but rather to restrict it. A state of equilibrium will result from the separation of these two forms of power to the benefit of the mass of individuals. Some will benefit from capitalists, others from politicians, the rest from general measures or from laws to protect the many various interests. In this state of equilibrium a certain freedom for the majority of individuals can be established; a middle class can be formed.

Outside such a state system, by contrast, in both the patrimonial institutions that preceded it and the collectivist societies that threaten to succeed it, these guarantees of liberty disappear because political and economic powers fall into the same hands. Under feudalism, it has been classically observed, property and power were joined together. It is the same for collectivist societies. The administrative personnel in such a society would have a firm grip on the keys of state warehouses from which everyone would be expected to obtain their subsistence; the same officials would also have the legal power to create advantageous jobs; they would have the most complete power that ever existed. It is hard to imagine what could act as an effective counterweight to such power.[21]

Human willpower can of course counteract this development. If it cannot be completely halted, at least it can be slowed down considerably through deliberate resistance. In Hauriou's opinion, the recognition of the way things can develop does not absolve us of the intellectual duty to commit ourselves to the preservation of political liberty. "We know quite well," Hauriou concludes, "that we are going to die, and yet we make the effort to survive."[22] Consistently upholding the individualistic principles of civil society, above all the principle of private property, can certainly prolong the survival of political freedom and democracy, because it is one of the few effective means of resisting the excessive growth in bureaucracy and the evisceration of constitutional powers.

As we have seen, liberalism's approach is abolition. This ought not to take the form of a violent upheaval or, indeed, destruction. There is always something in the status quo that should be retained and that can be stimulated to develop through the removal of external barriers or perfected and made fruitful through restructuring. Furthermore, liberalism does not seek abolition in every area. According to the liberal point of view, what have to be abolished are primarily the unrestricted powers of the state, which enable it to place itself above the law and allow it either to disregard the existing order or to alter it through arbitrary legislation as it sees fit. Equally, it would abolish the excessive accumulation of regulation, planning rules, and administrative authorities that hamper the individual's economic and cultural freedom of action. On the other hand, liberalism is especially concerned with defending the rights of the individual. Liberalism regards the protection of existing rights and their unhindered exercise as the basic duty of the state. In general, oppressive intervention in the individual's actual circumstances and the destruction of traditional ways of life are completely alien to the liberal state. An authentically liberal state would never agree to the expulsion of a population, not even from a defeated and conquered country, or the resettlement within a state of individual ethnic groups, whatever political or economic motives lay behind it.

There is, however, a further consequence arising from this. Liberalism must act with the utmost prudence even when taking steps to abolish components of the administrative apparatus that it believes to be superfluous or even detrimental. Traditional forms of administration are always bound closely to some particular interest or other. The interests and positions of individuals (e.g., of personnel) connected with the administrative structures to be abolished should not be violated so abruptly or ruthlessly that it has a destructive effect on the sphere of these individuals' civil rights.

In addition, even those historical forms of government predating liberalism should not be overthrown by revolution, but reformed. Liberalism knows that violent revolution often only destroys the more valuable aspects of the old regime, while, on the other hand, the primary substance of any state, naked power, remains in place. Consequently, the conditions are created for government rule to take on an even more brutal form, not alleviated by anything, not even by old traditions. Furthermore, from a liberal perspective, the fact that a form of government, albeit not as perfect as a liberal state with a constitution, can often survive over a long period proves that the conditions are still absent in the nation or the people for a transition to liberal constitutional government and a liberal social order. Such conditions are not created, of course, by violent action.

This antirevolutionary position taken by liberalism derives essentially from the following consideration: if a state, not constructed on liberal principles but also not completely dictatorial or despotic, survives for a lengthy period, then this long existence helps traditions to emerge that can moderate the way power is exercised. It also leads to this type of state acquiring and consolidating some of the positive characteristics of states in general. This observation is rooted in turn in the conservative theory of progress, related to liberalism, namely the theory that "la force de fixation est la force progressive," that is, the theory according to which progress consists in establishing a model, and developing and perfecting its features, and not in the evolutionary substitution of one model for another.[23] From a historical point of view, and considering all these points, liberalism would unhesitatingly prefer enlightened absolutism to revolutionary dictatorship.

These considerations compel me to distinguish rigorously between liberalism and radicalism and to regard conservative liberalism as true liberalism.

PART 1

THE HISTORY OF LIBERALISM, 1762–1855

Chapter 1

Catherine II

Catherine's liberal program—Liberal economic
ideas—Property rights of the gentry—Plans
concerning the property rights of serfs—Situation
of the serfs—Affirmation of absolutism and
rejection of the French Revolution—Catherine's
concept of law

L iberal ideas became more significant in Russia during the reign of Catherine II. Certainly some of the individual laws or measures enacted by Catherine's predecessors could be seen as liberal, insofar as they confirmed or extended the rights of the subjects of Russia's rulers and thus served to develop their freedom. First, there was Peter III's famous *ukaz* [decree] of February 18, 1762, on the "Freedom of the Nobility." This was followed by an *ukaz* proclaimed by the Empress Anna on March 17, 1731 (P.S.Z. no. 5717),[1] which essentially abolished the distinction between patrimonial estates [*votchiny* landholdings] and estates granted in return for state service [*pomestie'* land], thus extending the property rights of the gentry belonging to the latter group.[2] These laws, however, were not based on any conscious intention to put liberal principles into practice. In one sense, Empress Elizabeth's entire reign can be seen as a liberal age. In this case, however, liberty did not derive from a conscious wish to promote it, but simply sprang from, and was guaranteed by, the sovereign's joie de vivre and easygoing personality.

By contrast, Catherine's reform agenda was underpinned by the principles of Western European liberalism, especially Montesquieu's ideas. Catherine endeavored to establish a legal basis for religious tolerance, to make the criminal law more humane, to allow freedom for private enterprise in economic life, to consolidate the gentry's and townspeople's personal freedom, to extend the property rights of these two estates, and to protect them from abuses of state power. She further undertook to improve the condition of the peasantry by allowing the social estates' self-governing bodies a significant role in the development of the administrative system and to introduce systematically the principle of the separation of powers in local administration and government. This extensive liberal program was set out, above all, in the empress's own Instruction to the legislative commission that she had convened. It was expressed too in a series of publications written either by herself or at her request. Important elements of this program became the law of the land through various pieces of legislation during the course of her long reign.

Catherine held liberal opinions in the field of economic policy. Her views are expounded most fully in a memorandum called "Reflections on the Manufactures."[3] It is not certain whether the empress herself was the author of this memorandum. However, insofar as Catherine made clear her complete agreement with the ideas in the memorandum, the question as to her authorship is of no real significance. Moreover, Catherine wrote a set of ninety-six comments ("Remarki") about the problems addressed in the memorandum. These too represent an important source by which to judge her approach to basic economic issues.[4]

Catherine sent the memorandum to the College of Manufactures and, in the decree of March 18, 1767, ordered it to be studied closely, as in her opinion the memorandum would serve as a useful basis for the work of the college's representatives on the legislative commission. Florovsky has put forward the conjecture that Catherine's comments were written in response to a report from the college, which has since disappeared, but which it presented to the empress after studying her memorandum. What the report of the College of Manufactures was about is no longer known. In any case, it could not have contained a rejection of the ideas of the memorandum, since the college appended the complete memorandum as the best source of information and guidance for its representatives. It is thus apparent that not only the empress herself but also the representatives of one of the foremost economic bodies shared the views contained in the memorandum.

A belief in the natural and spontaneous nature of all healthy economic development was the basis for the opinions set out in the memorandum and the empress's comments. "All things," Catherine writes in her comments, "naturally adopt a form that is characteristic for them" (Points 1, 2, 3). "The best outcome arises from the nature of things" (Point 83). This is why she resolutely rejected any regulation. "Nothing is more dangerous than drawing up regulations for everything," the empress stresses. Which spheres of economic activity develop and where they develop depend on the needs of the population—indeed, must be based exclusively on them (Point 49). One should not fear the excessive development of individual industries. "One need not worry about too many factories, as insufficient demand will stop their development" (Point 6). "If there is no profit in a thing, it will not get done" (Point 47; see also Point 61). On the other hand, she explains, profitable enterprises will multiply. The government has no need to concern itself with this. People will establish these on their own; "one must not impede them in this" (Point 35; see also Point 27). "Neither forbid nor compel" is the phrase that recurs in several places in the comments (Point 69; see Points 58, 72, 78) and that Florovsky correctly considers as the empress's motto. "We do nothing better than that which we undertake voluntarily, without compulsion," writes Catherine, repeating in Point 19 of her comments the words of her memorandum (Art. 75). Therefore, the basic rule of the College of Manufactures must be, she writes, "to erect no barriers that impede anyone earning an honest living. Each will understand what he has to do" (Point 63; see Point 31). "I hold all other controls (for the protection of legitimate interests) to be superfluous," the empress continues. "The College was not established to repress industry, which would certainly be the result of interfering in all the affairs of entrepreneurs. I'd like to ask the members of the College how they would feel if I ordered their homes to be visited each month to rummage through their worldly goods. . . . Then they too would no longer demand that they should be allowed to rummage through the houses of those who earn a living from their craft." On the contrary, "the less the College gets involved, the better" (Point 4). Indeed, the empress expresses the hope that the college would actually "be left without work" (Point 93), which did apparently happen, as it was closed down in 1779. The abolition of the College of Manufactures was also consistent with Catherine's principal demand: do not interfere with entrepreneurs, and do not set up too much bureaucracy (Point 75). Catherine thus considers unified planning for the whole country senseless. "You must never entertain the idea," writes the empress, "that wealth could be distributed evenly across sections of society, much as bread is handed out to monks in a refectory" (Point 5). Catherine also rejects granting monopolies to some companies: the methods that the state should use to develop industry and the economy are subsidy (Point 19) and education (Point 21).[5]

Catherine's ideas are also reflected in the memorandum of the College of Manufactures to its representatives, in which, for example, the advantages of free labor over the labor of serfs is stressed.[6] You again find Catherine's ideas in the draft of the legal statute for the middle classes (the "Proekt Zakonov o Pravakh Zhitelei" or "Liudei Sredniego Roda") and in the commentary on this draft that dates from about the same time.[7] Thus, "if one has to ask permission for everything, it means that there are no longer any rights." It is possible that those who expressed this thought in Catherine's time were not aware of its full theoretical implications. Yet this sentence has profound meaning from the standpoint of the philosophy of law: enjoying a right means precisely not having to ask permission for it. Needing permission in all matters signifies having no human rights at all, which in turn entails a complete lack of justice. Making rights completely dependent on government action amounts to their negation.[8]

Catherine not only supported the freedom of economic activity and the liberation of private initiative; she was also firmly in favor of the liberal principle of private property and, accordingly, the precedence of civil law over statute law in specific areas. This is shown especially in the recognition of the principle of state compensation in cases of expropriation. The following passage from the documents relating to the memorandum published by Chechulin was then also included in the memorandum to the procurator general: "If the state needs an individual's property, it must not act with the full force of political law, but this is where civil law must triumph, which looks at each individual with the same maternal care as as for society as a whole. If a state official would like to erect some public building or new road, he must offer compensation."[9]

Here Catherine anticipates the liberal principle of compensation, in which the recognition of private property by the state is given the highest priority, a principle later taken up in the 1789 *Déclaration de droits de l'homme* (Art. 17) and in the Napoleonic Code. It is only possible to appreciate the full significance of this recognition if one recalls the fact that the famous "otpisat' na gosudaria" (i.e., the confiscation by the state of privately owned land) [literally, "to transfer to the sovereign"] had been more or less common practice in the recent past. It is only in light of this fact that one can measure the importance of the recognition of land as the private property of the gentry in the Charter to the Nobility of 1785.[10] It was only by this act that the consequences of Ivan IV's revolution were reversed, while at the same time the foundations were laid for the assertion of the liberal principle of private property and thus for the dawn of the liberal era in Russia. This charter laid down, as is well known, that a member of the gentry could not be deprived of his or her property without due process (Arts. 11, 24) and that they could dispose of it freely with the exception of inherited property (Art. 22).

Catherine not only confirmed the existing property rights of the gentry, endowing them with the features of genuine private ownership, but also went further and enlarged their scope. She enacted two laws in 1782 that extended the rights of the gentry and nonnoble landowners to own mineral deposits and stretches of water. Restrictions on the right of disposal of forests (introduced in the interests of the admiralty) were also lifted.[11] In support of these measures, it was pointed out that they were another step in the implementation of the liberal program set out at the start of her reign. This is a crucial point. The measures had been included in the Charter to the Nobility and largely taken from the charter itself. However, as the charter did not state why they were needed, they are mostly regarded as privileges for the gentry and not as measures forming part of a liberal program.

In fact the Manifesto of June 28, 1782, states: "From the very beginning of our reign we adopted the firm principle of abolishing the restrictions on all trades, on the contrary indeed, to stimulate them and to help them flourish." However, the intention to guarantee complete freedom of trade for all could not be carried out at that time as far as the exploitation of mineral deposits was concerned. Nevertheless, "after having learned much from experience, which has confirmed the principles we held," Catherine decided on the twentieth anniversary of her reign to extend the property rights of landowners to include mineral rights and to grant them the freedom to prospect for such deposits and to set up private companies to exploit them. Article 16 of the same law forbade the fiscal authorities and other government offices from interfering in the affairs of these private companies. Article 4 granted landowners the right to sell the minerals extracted from their own estates to state enterprises at market rates. Article 15 states that none of these companies would be allowed to claim a monopoly position.

These laws, enacted in 1782, and the measures contained in them, represent proof, in my opinion, that Catherine consistently held on to her liberal principles throughout her long reign and not just during the early years after her accession to the throne.[12] This important question bears closer examination, as it helps to explain Catherine's views on a series of basic issues and will be dealt with again below.

Private ownership of land was first introduced in Russia in the form of a privilege for the gentry. This was determined by Russian legal history—especially by the legacy of two hundred years of serfdom, a system that had encompassed all classes and had shaped the entire social and political structure of the Russian state. To facilitate the transition to a free, or at any rate freer, system, or to a system whose subjects are accorded civil liberty and where individuals have civil rights—in other words, to a civil society—one had to find such elements in Russia within the framework of the old, existing system of serfdom. These were the components for the construction of the new civil order. One had to establish a form of legal status, which included the recognition of civil rights, for specific categories of subjects or estates. Incidentally, Catherine may have originally contemplated creating a new middle class in Russia, which would only have been loosely connected to the old estates and would have been granted just such a legal status. The draft "Prav Sredniago Roda Liudej" [Legal Statute for the Middle Class] was certainly prepared with this in mind. That her ideas took this direction is not unnatural, as in the West the middle class and the towns where it developed were the foundation of civil society. However, she must have soon noticed that in Russia some of the key conditions for the development of towns and thus the creation of such a middle class were missing. Thus, it turned out that the only solution for her was to grant civil freedom—civil rights—to the gentry, which in fact she did in the Charter to the Nobility. Subsequent developments proved Catherine right. Here, too, her outstanding realism and the sureness of her sense of history paid off. Zaitsev writes: "If in the West it was the 'townsman' who became the epitome of the free citizen, who in the general process of the abolition of privileges and the assertion of freedom was followed by all others, so in our country a similar role fell to the 'nobleman' (*dvorianin*)."[13] Thus, the Charter to the Nobility of 1785 granted civil freedom throughout Russia to a social class whose members then enjoyed civil rights. From then on, the task consisted in extending these rights to more and more sections of the population. One of the main aims of this book is to chart the process of extending civil liberty and civil rights to each of the other social strata.

Catherine's intention to issue in the same year as the 1785 charters a decree by which every person born after that year would be born free demonstrates what she had in mind for the next stage. She regarded granting civil liberty to the gentry not as—or rather, not purely as—a privilege for the members of this estate and saw the Charter to the Nobility of 1785 (and to a lesser extent the Charter to the Towns) as laying the foundations of a civil society in Russia.[14] Thus, she considered the charters as forming the basis for the status of free citizen and intended its gradual extension to all the subjects of the Russian Empire as a result of the natural disappearance over time of all those who were not born free.

Catherine's codification and thus affirmation of the rights and freedoms of the gentry in her charter do not mean in any way that she was indifferent to the interests of the peasantry. There is no doubt that the only reason Catherine did not openly declare her support for the abolition of serfdom was that she was only too aware how much opposition such a proposal would arouse. Pressure from those opposed to this step in the end forced parts of her memorandum to be cut. These had been intended "to alleviate the fate of these subjects too, as far as sound reason allows" (Art. 252). Just from the wording of Article 260 of the memorandum—"one must not free a large number of serfs all at once and by general legislation"—it is apparent that the empress had considered measures setting in motion the gradual process of emancipating the serfs.[15] In any case, Catherine certainly considered extending and securing the property rights of the serfs. "To alleviate the peasants' servitude,"[16] she recommended following one nobleman's proposal: "to regard the serf's goods and chattels and especially the fruits of their labor as their own."[17] Furthermore, "the various contributions of the serfs should be fixed and in proportion to their means."[18] Even more significantly, she thought it desirable to consolidate the land made available for the serfs' own use so that it essentially became their permanent property. She writes: "If in certain states some raison d'état or some private interest prevents the liberation of the serfs, because of the fear that land would be abandoned, one could find the means to tie, in a manner of speaking, the serfs to the land by handing over their land to them and their children to cultivate. This would be in accordance with a contract concluded with them for money or payment in kind in proportion to the produce of this land."[19] This program clearly reveals the following aims:

1. To replace the ties to the soil based on legal regulation with ties based on economic interest;

2. To reduce the amount of farming on the landowners' estates based on labor service and conversely to increase the cultivation undertaken independently by the serfs (in this case they would only be obliged to pay dues).

Without doubt, this was a step to loosen the ties between the serfs and their masters. In comparison to labor service, the dues paid in money or in kind represented a milder form of dependency. Catherine's proposed legislation, by which the level of dues was to be set in proportion to the output of the land and laid down in a contract, would have unmistakably signified an even greater improvement in the situation of the peasants. Even more important was the suggestion that relations between serf and master should be based on a contract at all. This clearly points to the intention to provide a legal basis for these relations. If Catherine's words, as quoted above, can be taken to mean that these contracts were to be indissoluble, provided the serfs cultivated the land in accordance with their contract, then the transformation of the land left to the peasants for their own exploitation into a kind of private property would have been an established fact.[20]

Naturally, the fact that during Catherine's time the serfs became even more subordinated to their masters must not be overlooked. Some have tried to explain the fact that under Catherine the condition of the serfs worsened still further by noting her basic sympathy for the institution of serfdom and that all her proposals leading to the eventual abolition of serfdom were mere hypocrisy, merely a public relations exercise to please opinion in the West. To see Catherine's intentions as hypocritical and self-serving is too superficial in my view. Neither does the pressure on her from the gentry get to the heart of the matter. It may sound paradoxical, but the intensification of the dependency of the serfs on the gentry was a direct and necessary consequence of granting liberty to the gentry, the partial replacement of the system of serfdom by a civil society, and the nature of these two systems. If the power of the gentry over their serfs had certain limits under the classic form of serfdom, this was not because the serfs had any recognized rights vis-à-vis their masters, but only because the gentry themselves were completely subordinated to the power of the state. They were always under its control in every respect, including in their relations to the serfs.[21]

Thus, it is clear that the removal of these controls, the liberation of the gentry from the all-embracing supervision of the state, inevitably led to the extension of their power over the peasants.

The following is also noteworthy: the difficulty, indeed the insolubility, of the problem of the emancipation of the serfs in the eighteenth century lay in the fact that liberation meant creating free men. The status of the free citizen did not exist at all in Russia before Catherine. Even the nobleman was—albeit in a different form from the serf, but exactly like him—a dependent of the state, no different from the members of other social estates. Before Catherine, the liberated serf could never have become a free citizen. He could have become either a townsman or a state peasant—a peasant directly owned by the state. Finally, he could have been ennobled; that is, he could have exchanged the burden of the *tiaglo* (labor service) for the burden of "gentry service." Wherever he went, he remained bound by the chains of the old regime of serfdom. It was consequently difficult for landowners to release peasants, insofar as the dependence of those belonging to the gentry in the context of the old system of serfdom was in the interest of the state and constituted a relationship assured and controlled by the state under public law. How complicated and uncertain the legal position of freed serfs in the eighteenth century was is already apparent from the laws of the Empress

Elizabeth demanding the return of freed peasants to their status as serfs, as well as the laws of Catherine, which, on the contrary, aimed to prevent such a return to serfdom by emancipated peasants. A series of laws was enacted whose intention was to secure the legal status of the liberated serf (e.g., the 1775 Manifesto and subsequent decrees). By granting the rights to the gentry that are inherently those of the free citizen, Catherine first created the conditions for the liberation of all—for the emancipation not just of serfs but other social estates too. In doing so, she laid only the first foundation stone for a civil society in Russia. This had to be consolidated before the liberation of the serfs could begin.

One can conclude from the above that revolutionary attempts to abolish serfdom at a stroke have to be viewed with justifiable skepticism. As is well known, Pugachev proclaimed the liberation of the serfs in a manifesto on June 31, 1774. In this manifesto, he promised not only to free the peasants from "noble evil-doers" and "corrupt judges" but also to abolish forced conscription, the poll tax, and other taxes. He further held out the prospect that they would become "the faithful and humble subjects of our crown (i.e., Pugachev's)." It is doubtful whether a victorious Pugachev would have brought the peasants much happiness—*on ne détruit qu'en remplaçant* [you only destroy something by replacing it]. Pugachev had no other political ideas except those that he could take from the existing reality of Russia at the time, that is, absolute monarchy and serfdom. He passed himself off as the murdered Tsar Peter III (he even went so far as to call Catherine his wife), and his companions adopted the names of the empress's famous collaborators—Panin, Orlov, and so on. Of course, after his victory, Pugachev would have been indebted to his collaborators and, in order to reward them, would have fallen back, just as certainly, on the old tried and trusted methods, the only ones he knew: sharing out estates together with the peasants (serfs) who came with them among his comrades. Pugachev wanted to declare the peasants subjects of his rule, and as tsar, he would have had the power to dispose of them as he wished. It is more than doubtful whether the peasants would have benefited from replacing their former landowners—among whom there were still many, like Karamzin and General Suvorov, who in the traditional way felt morally obliged to care for their serfs paternalistically in the best sense of the word—with the sadists and murderers in Pugachev's train (even if they did belong to the same social estate). On the contrary, if you bear in mind the sadistic mass murders that can be laid at their door, you would be justified in thinking that they, as the new masters, would have put the infamously cruel landowner Saltykova in the shade. (At least Saltykova was condemned to life imprisonment, if somewhat late in the day.) The mere destruction of the existing order necessarily leads to its resurrection, but in a more brutal and unjust form, not having been refined over time.

Many have held the view, as mentioned above, that Catherine was only influenced by liberal ideas in the first years of her reign (assuming that even then her liberalism was more than mere hypocrisy and an attempt to woo Western public opinion) and that she later broke with her liberal past. An example of someone holding this view in Germany was Stählin, as can be seen just by glancing at the chapter headings on Catherine in his *History of Russia*. The first chapter is called "Last Battle for the Throne" and the final one "Realistic Development and Reactionary End." The basis for this view is, essentially, that Catherine was convinced that absolute monarchy was the right sort of government for Russia; that during her reign the situation of the serfs had deteriorated even further; that right from the start she was implacably hostile to the French Revolution; that she broke with Novikov and persecuted Radishchev, the author of the famous book *Journey from St. Petersburg to Moscow*. I take the view that all these reasons are insufficient to deny the liberal character of Catherine's reign, not just at the beginning but also toward the end of her rule.

Doubtless Catherine did not intend to restrict absolutism in Russia. Yet it is undeniable that absolutism can be reactionary or progressive, liberal or antiliberal. Had this not been the case, then the liberal reforms of the 1860s introduced by Alexander II, who was just as much of an absolute monarch, would not have deserved to be described as such, something that has been universally accepted. Of course, Catherine's legislation did not pursue the goal of establishing political freedom;[22] rather, the goal was the recognition and guarantee of civil freedoms and the construction of a civil society in Russia, in particular, and at first almost exclusively, with regard to the gentry. However, this fact does not allow us to deny the liberal character of Catherine's legislation and the political philosophy that underpinned it. One could perhaps with justification reproach those times, the era of enlightened despotism, with neglecting the significance of political freedom and concentrating exclusively on personal, civil freedom. It must be remembered, however, that in the eighteenth century the historical priority for Russia consisted above all in abolishing serfdom, that is, a regime that fundamentally excluded any notion of civil rights, indeed human rights altogether. In addition, it is certain that this regime could only be superseded by a civil regime, by a system based on human rights. Besides, one would be even more justified in asking the question of our own times as to whether the importance of political freedom has not been overestimated, whether today an understanding of the fundamental importance of civil freedom and civil society has not been lost to a dangerous degree. Benjamin Constant, a typical representative of liberalism and of a later generation with a much greater interest in the issue of political freedom, maintains that in contrast to the ancient world, where freedom consisted above all in "participation in the general exercise of government," the essence of freedom in his time lay first and foremost in the "enjoyment of personal autonomy."[23] This was assured above all by civil rights and the guarantees of those rights that are inherent in a civil society. Constant adds: "Our innovators believed that everything should be subordinated to collective force and all restrictions on the rights of the individual would be compensated by participation in the power of society."[24] At this point, I would also like to recall Napoleon's terse statement, quoted by Mme de Staël, "La liberté, c'est un bon code civil."[25]

The question as to whether the situation of the peasants deteriorated during Catherine's reign has been dealt with above.

Radical circles in the nineteenth century held the view that the surest way of distinguishing progressive people from reactionaries was through their attitude to the French Revolution, an event that, in Maklakov's phrase, became a myth dominating the consciousness of progressive society for the whole of the nineteenth century.[26] Catherine rejected the French Revolution from the outset and remained antagonistic to the last. This has led people to conclude that Catherine was reactionary or at least had progressively abandoned liberalism. It is evident from Catherine's statements, however, that her hostile attitude to the revolution did not derive from opposition to the idea of freedom, but rather from her view of the revolution not as establishing freedom, but as an expression of anarchic tyranny and the road to despotic dictatorship.[27] She felt offended when Voltaire, whom she regarded as the representative of the idea of true freedom, was identified with the revolution. In judging the French Revolution, Catherine evidently agreed with Burke, who rejected the revolution from the point of view of English constitutional thought. Burke, whose writings the empress knew and appreciated, made an appeal to her in a letter.[28]

It is also significant that the liberal La Harpe remained Alexander's tutor. The two princes, Alexander and Constantine, were not taught about the dark side of the ancien régime without her complicity, and she herself read and commented on the French constitution, especially the *Déclaration des droits,* with Alexander, who was fifteen years old at the time. Perhaps it was precisely his grandmother's influence that lay behind Tsar Alexander's later warnings to Louis XVIII against taking a reactionary course. This influence may also explain the unmistakable contrast between his basic outlook and Metternich's.

At first sight, the measures that Catherine took against Radishchev seem inexplicable, if one assumes that she had not rejected her earlier ideas, as both she and Radishchev had expressed similar views on a range of extremely important issues. There is no essential difference between Catherine's and Radishchev's views regarding religious toleration or their views regarding making criminal trials and punishments more humane. Both perceived the principle of private property and the peasant question in more or less the same way.[29] They shared in the general admiration for liberty. Radishchev writes, "You are great, spirit of liberty, creative like God himself."[30] Moreover, Catherine calls liberty "the soul of all things."[31]

Yet in respect to the established order—*l'ordre établi*—Catherine's position is utterly different from Radishchev's, so that her rejection of Radishchev's views appears well founded. In his *Journey from St. Petersburg to Moscow,* Radishchev, while not claiming to put forward any system, nevertheless set out a genuinely radical system in literary terms. In this, he anticipated many aspects of the ideology of the nineteenth-century Russian intelligentsia. Here he sketches out a "project for the future," a future order in which his ideals, his theories, would be put into practice. This future order is the one and only object of his interest. In its name, he resolutely rejects the existing order, to which he is mostly hostile. As Pushkin noted, the whole of Enlightenment philosophy is reflected in the *Journey from St. Petersburg to Moscow* as if in a distorting mirror. In any case, the general outlook of the Enlightenment is expressed in Radishchev's work, an outlook that is aptly described by Savigny:

> At this time, a wholly unenlightened thirst for knowledge emerged all over Europe: an understanding and feeling for the greatness and uniqueness of other times, as well as for the natural development of peoples and their constitutions, in other words for everything that should make history valuable and fruitful, were lost. In their place came a boundless optimism about the present, which, it was believed, was destined to be nothing less than the embodiment of absolute perfection.[32]

In particular, there was a very negative view in Enlightenment circles in the West vis-à-vis Russia's history. The whole of Russia's past was considered nothing more than a state of barbarism, which had to be brought to an end as quickly and radically as possible. "Mon cher Abbé," wrote De La Rivière to Abbé Raynal, "tout est à faire dans ce pays. Pour parler mieux encore, il faudrait dire tout est à défaire et à refaire" [Everything remains to be done—or better still, to be undone and redone]. In the whole of Russian history, only Peter the Great was accorded any admiration. He was applauded as a ruler who broke with his people's past, who was very serious about *défaire* and *refaire*.

Catherine II had a lengthy correspondence with Voltaire and Diderot. She especially admired Voltaire, whom she often described as her teacher. There can be no doubt that she was, to a certain extent, influenced by the ideas of the Enlightenment. It has long since been established, however, that besides ideas of reform, typical of the Enlightenment, a positive assessment of existing society and a favorable view of the historical legacy were equally important factors in Catherine's outlook. This fact has been particularly stressed by the St. Petersburg historian of law V. Sergeevich. He considers Montesquieu to be the key influence on this aspect of Catherine's thinking: "Besides the Encyclopaedists, Catherine the Great studied Montesquieu enthusiastically. From his works, she became familiar with ideas such as the notion that laws should be nonarbitrary and in harmony with the character of a people and its country and other factors relating to human society."[33]

In fact, Montesquieu's teachings on law and constitutions, which Catherine valued so much, must have convinced her that new laws should not introduce a break with *l'ordre établi,* but should aim to improve the existing order and to perfect its longstanding institutions. Furthermore, one can find statements made by Catherine exactly along those lines. In one of her notes to the legislative commission, which was comprised of elected representatives of nearly all the estates and which was charged with drafting a codex applying to all law, the empress writes:

"The commission cannot proceed to undertake its duties until it is fully informed of the current situation in our state, as any amendment must be made not for its own arbitrary sake, but for the purpose of improving any deficiencies, as far as they have been discovered. What is good and useful should be excluded from change, because it must remain in force." There is an even clearer example of her approval of the existing order in a note she wrote in the margin of Radishchev's book: "If something of all that had been instituted and established today on the basis of past experience and the requirements of the past, and not by blind arbitrary action, were changed, it would lead to a deterioration, because what is better is the enemy of what is already good. It is also preferable to keep to what is familiar, rather than to open the way for the unknown." This conviction also forms the basis for her view that "making new law has the greatest drawbacks."[34] In general, Catherine was clear in her own mind that there were definite limits to legislation. She was aware that some circumstances could not, indeed should not, be regulated by law at all. She states this clearly in Articles 59 and 60 of the Instruction:[35] "Laws are particular and precise products of the legislator. Customs and tradition are institutions of the nation as a whole. Thus, when it is a question of making great changes in a nation for its greater benefit, one must reform by law what is established in law and change by custom what has become established in custom. It is bad policy to want to change by law what must be changed by custom."[36]

As all aspects in the life of the people are closely connected, laws have to take into account not just the customs and manners of the people, but also the common law that is in force; that is, it must be harmonized with law that was developed earlier in history and that can thus be regarded as the prevailing law. In fact, this type of law is closely linked to customs, to aspects of life that cannot be successfully affected by legislation. Therefore, legislative regulation must also only be undertaken with extreme caution, even in those areas with which it does not in essence stand in contradiction. The existing order must be guaranteed protection against arbitrary rule. It is thus always preferable to keep an old law that is in harmony with the other existing laws and that, because of the way it is subsequently interpreted and applied, in the course of time has become an organic element in the established order. In her Instruction, Catherine also suggests specific measures to prevent new laws from conflicting with existing ones and thus to protect subjects from the arbitrary actions of a ruler, even if the new law is an expression of his will.[37] She writes, "Laws must have a repository (*khranilishche*)" (Art. 22). "This repository can only be found in the courts of the imperial state,[38] which acquaint the people with new laws and remind them of those that have been forgotten" (Art. 23).[39] The general purpose of this institution is to "ensure that the will of the monarch is exercised in accordance with the basic law and constitution of the empire" (Art. 28) and that the people will be protected from "capricious and unbridled acts" (Art. 29) by making "the constitution fixed and unalterable" (Art. 21). In order to achieve this overall aim, the courts are invested with the right carefully to scrutinize legislation enacted by the monarch. Should they find something in the legislation that stands in contradiction to the statute book, that is, the fundamental law, or is "damaging, obscure and impractical" (Art. 21), they could make representations; indeed, this institution should be given the competence to refuse to incorporate those laws "contrary to the existing order in the state" (Arts. 24 and 25).[40]

Radishchev holds a completely different point of view in this area. In *Journey* he writes, "Never dare to go by a tradition when it contradicts the law. The law, however bad, holds society together. Moreover, should the ruler order you to break the law, do not obey him, for he is mistaken, doing harm to himself and society. Let him annul the law if he gives the order to break it; then you can obey him, for in Russia the monarch is the originator of the law."[41]

This is extremely significant. Here are two of the principles that are characteristic of all revolutionary and radical thinking. First, there is the precedence of statute over custom and practice, and thus over common law, which clearly shows a belief in the omnipotence of the law so typical of revolutionary thinking. Second, Radishchev conceives of the law purely and simply as the expression of the will of the holder of power, the legislator. As a consequence of these principles— a voluntarist conception of law on the one hand and an underestimation of the customary roots of existing law on the other—Radishchev sees no essential difference between new laws, new pieces of legislation, and old laws that have been sanctified by the passage of time and tradition and that are the embodiment of prevailing law. Thus, the problem, which concerned the empress, of scrutinizing new laws as to whether they are in harmony with existing law (*l'ordre établi*) is completely foreign to Radishchev. On the contrary, the assumption, characteristic of revolutionary thought, that new law, new statutes enacted by the will of the legislator, takes precedence over existing law is self-evident to him. In fact, this idea follows logically from the basic principle according to which statute law is superior to custom and common law. Existing law taking precedence over newly enacted legislation can only be justified if the precedence of common law over law enacted by the state is acknowledged, that is, by recognizing the adage of medieval canon-law philosophy: "Law will conform to the customs of a country."[42] This is complemented by the perception that, as Hauriou has shown, existing law, even if it starts off as statute law, over time takes on, or at least may take on, the character of common law.[43]

The basic positions of both radicalism and liberalism emerge clearly from this analysis of comments made by the empress and Radishchev. From the standpoint of radicalism, new laws are the means to create a better order, that is, a generally accepted and desired situation. Naturally, liberalism also regards new laws as the way to reform and improve the existing order. Yet the optimism that is typical of radicalism is foreign to liberalism. It is concerned about guarantees that safeguard the existing legal order, as well as, within the framework of this order, the hard-won rights of the individual, which are recognized and protected from the exercise of arbitrary power by the lawmaker. Because freedom is unthinkable without protecting existing law from arbitrary state power, one has to acknowledge that in this area too, in her rejection of Radishchev's position, Catherine did not abandon the terrain of liberalism.

Chapter 2

Alexander I

Reaction under Paul I—Constitutional ideas in the
reign of Alexander I—Mordvinov

That Catherine's reflections on issues of law were significant not merely from
a theoretical point of view, but also from a practical one, was shown by her
son Paul I's reign, which must be seen as a period of radical reaction. Paul I was
convinced that his patriarchal power was unlimited. He endeavored to regulate
every sphere of life, even going so far as to lay down rules for his subjects on
their use of language. Severe punishments were meted out to those who were in
breach of them. He did not see himself as duty bound to respect the rights of his
subjects. Thus, he decreed the repeal of Article 15 of the Charter to the Nobility,
by which members of the gentry were no longer subject to corporal punishment.
On the other hand, measures that he took to rescue noblemen from ruin (Paul
I set up a bank especially for this purpose) were based on what Waliszewski has
aptly called "the phantasm of the universally provident state."[1] That this reactionary phase was brought to a relatively quick end by Paul's violent elimination can
only be seen as a positive development from a liberal perspective. Alexander I,
who succeeded to the throne, had been introduced at a young age to liberal ideas
by his grandmother Catherine.

As Karamzin put it, Paul I did for absolute monarchy what the Jacobins had
done for the republic: he turned the abuse of unlimited power into an object of
loathing.[2] It is natural, therefore, that Alexander and those around him were interested in the question of a constitution. This problem had concerned Alexander

even before his ascension to the throne, indeed, while Catherine was still alive. In a letter to Count Kochubei of May 10, 1796, which was thus written six months before Catherine's death, in which he complains about chaos in the affairs of state, Alexander asked, "Can a single person govern the state, and more especially can they remove its ingrained defects?"[3]

It is well known that the question of a constitution in Russia was not resolved under Alexander I, although during his reign a number of constitutional projects were drafted. Speransky's draft constitution will be dealt with in the chapter on that statesman. Novosil'tsev's draft will also be described below. At this point, I shall just refer to plans that were proposed immediately after the succession to the throne and the following years. These plans embodied liberal ideas or at least bore some relation to them, even if one cannot describe these plans as constitutional projects in the true sense of the term.

First, there was a plan to promulgate an affirmation of the basic rights of the subject in conjunction with the manifesto that formed part of the coronation celebrations. This was not about constitutional institutions or the establishment of a constitutional system, but about something like a *Déclaration des droits*.[4]

This declaration contained some of liberalism's basic tenets: it highlighted the necessity for clear legislation to guarantee the inviolability of the individual and private property, as well as to moderate the penal code. Further articles ceremonially ratified Catherine's legislation afresh, especially the charters, and reenacted those laws that Paul I had revoked. The basic direction of this draft declaration was, above all, to go back to Catherine's legislative program, back to the spirit of her government. This was only natural in that the idea of writing the *gramota* (charter) came from Count A. Vorontsov, one of the old liberals from Catherine's era. In his opinion, Catherine's legislative program contained a series of provisions reflecting liberal ideas. As, however, they had attracted little attention, he went on to explain, it was of the upmost importance to reaffirm them and thereby give them a new emphasis. In the abovementioned observations accompanying the articles,[5] Vorontsov stressed (in the observations to Arts. 4, 5, and 6) that guarantees for trade and industry, entrepreneurial initiative, and private property were nothing new. They could be found in Catherine's Instruction, as well as in her legislation. Up to then, however, "they had had no more effect than any of the fine phrases of a Socrates, Marcus Aurelius, Cicero and many more." In order to become effective, they had to be gathered together in a charter (*corps de privilèges*). Furthermore, this declaration should not just restate the liberal measures of earlier legislation, but should also take up liberal ideas that could be borrowed from legislation enacted in other states, while taking into account Russia's unique character.

This trend of adopting law from abroad, in particular liberal measures from foreign legislation, was common among the old statesmen from Catherine's era. This is not surprising, if one considers how extensively Catherine herself had drawn on Montesquieu and other foreign sources. Count Zavadovsky, for example, who was appointed by Alexander I as head of the commission drafting new legislation, expressed a similar point of view in a memorandum, which is also very interesting in other respects, in April 1802.[6]

In January 1804, Rosenkampf, the secretary of the commission for framing new legislation (which was reorganized that year), was given the task of working out draft fundamental laws for the Russian Empire. This draft contains some clauses embodying the liberal principles of the inviolability of the person and private property (§35) and highlighting the freedom of private enterprise (§42). Furthermore, in line with liberal ideas, a clear distinction was drawn between the state finances and the personal wealth of the monarch (§§119, 121). On the other hand, there were no provisions in this draft granting political freedom. The draft contained no mention of a representative assembly, be it only consultative. On the contrary, in §11 it emphasized the fact that not only the executive power but also all legislative power would be concentrated in the hands of the monarch. As A. Makarov has rightly pointed out, this draft was not of a constitution, but rather represented a draft of the basic laws of an absolute monarchy.[7] This one was not adopted either.

Overall, as far as the application of liberal principles during Alexander I's reign is concerned, what was achieved was, if not too little, certainly less than could have been expected. On the one hand, this can be explained by the Napoleonic Wars, on the other hand by the fact that Alexander I's political gifts lay primarily in the sphere of foreign policy and not in the field of domestic politics, which was not as dear to him as diplomacy. One should also not forget the role played by developments in domestic politics, which I shall analyze below. Therefore, Alexander I's reign would remain above all a time when liberal ideas were circulated in Russia, a time when the liberal consciousness of the elite gradually matured.

This section of my book will consist primarily of a study of the world of ideas of a number of significant liberal thinkers. Particular laws and measures that contributed to the implementation of liberal principles will only be mentioned in this section insofar as they are connected with the theoretical development of the liberal program.

One of the most significant liberal figures in Russia was N. S. Mordvinov (born in 1754). He came to court to be educated together with the heir to the throne, Paul, after Catherine ascended the throne. In 1774, he was sent to England to study navigation (at the instigation of Grand Duke Paul) and spent three years there. During this time, he went on several sea voyages, which presented him with the opportunity to visit America as well. His biographer Ikonnikov writes, "The stay in England, however, was significant for Mordvinov in another respect: heavily influenced by English scientific ideas, he also became an admirer of the English political system."[8]

Adam Smith's "Inquiry into the Causes of the Wealth of Nations" (1776) appeared just at the time of his stay. The influence that this work had on Mordvinov's views on matters of finance is even evident in memoranda that he wrote at the end of his long life. Adam Smith had become well known in Russia at an even earlier date. Two students from Moscow University, Desnitsky and Tretiakov, had been sent to Glasgow, where he was teaching moral philosophy, in 1761, staying there until 1767.[9] Desnitsky became a professor of the Faculty of Law in Moscow. In Korkunov's opinion, Desnitsky did not allow his Glasgow teacher to influence the issues he dealt with. On the other hand, he was indebted to Smith for his general approach to the subject. One should bear in mind, in particular, his dislike of the abstract rationalist teaching that was predominant in the universities in Russia during Desnitsky's own student days. Furthermore, we also know that Prince Dashkov too was among Smith's students; that Smith's theories were taught at the court by Storch, a member of the Academy of Sciences; that Professor Balugiansky gave lectures about these theories;[10] and that the government itself paid for the translation of Smith's principal work. Politkovsky, the translator, was paid five thousand rubles by the state treasury. Extracts from this translation regularly appeared in the official journal of the Interior Ministry, the *St. Peterburgsky Zhurnal*.

Extracts from the works of Bentham, Bacon, Ferguson, and others also appeared in the same journal.[11] Bentham, especially, was admired. From 1805 to 1806, Alexander himself commissioned the publication of the Russian translation of two volumes of Bentham's work. Among the earliest of Bentham's devotees in Russia was Mordvinov, who, incidentally, was an acquaintance of Samuel, Jeremy Bentham's brother. Mordvinov began his civil-service career in the administration of the Black Sea fleet under Potemkin, while at the same time Samuel Bentham was the manager of Potemkin's estates in White Russia. If, on the one hand, Ikonnikov maintains that Mordvinov was the only genuine admirer of Bentham in government circles, so, on the other hand, one could counter that Bentham was, in any event, one of the authors who were widely read in Russia. Dumont in particular, who translated his works into French, undertook to disseminate Bentham's ideas in Europe. He repeatedly visited Russia for this purpose. He most likely came to St. Petersburg for the first time in 1802. In 1808, he reported that as many copies of Bentham's books (certainly in translation) were sold in St. Petersburg as in London. Pushkin too (in *Eugene Onegin*) confirms that Bentham, Say, and Smith were fashionable reading in Russia.

Mordvinov was in personal contact not only with Bentham but also with Smith and Say, as well as a number of other Western European thinkers. He sent the French translation of his work on banks (*Réflexions sur les banques*) to Ganihl, Say, de Laborde, and Gioja. He made efforts to interest Speransky in Ganihl's work, sending him the latter's books. In general, Mordvinov was familiar with many liberal works from Western Europe. We know that he sent Bentham, through his brother Samuel, a French translation of the work of the Spanish liberal thinker and politician Caspar Melchior de Chovellanos, in particular *L'identité de l'intérêt général avec l'intérêt individuel*. This book was published in St. Petersburg in 1806 at the request of Prince Kochubei, the minister of the interior. It is not surprising that Kochubei wanted to make this book available to the Russian reader, as it contains a critique of communal property and a defense of the private ownership of land.

During Catherine's and then Paul's reign, Mordvinov's official duties were restricted to the navy. Under Alexander I, too, Mordvinov initially worked as a specialist in naval affairs. However, his advice was soon sought on other matters too by the "unofficial committee" and by its individual members, above all Stroganov.[12]

At a meeting of the committee held on November 4, 1801, Count Stroganov reported that in discussions about the peasant question, many people, especially La Harpe and Count Mordvinov, had drawn the emperor's attention to the necessity of doing something to help the peasants. Their situation was extremely wretched, as they had no "civil existence" (*grazhdanskogo sushchestvovania*)—that is, they had neither civil liberty nor any civil rights. He added that this could only be improved progressively and gradually, and the first step in this direction, in Mordvinov's view, was to grant the right to purchase land to peasants who were not serfs.[13] Mordvinov's view, supported by others, was immediately put into effect through legislation: the decree of December 12, 1801, gave merchants, townspeople, and state peasants the right to buy land.[14]

Mordvinov did not campaign with great energy just for civil rights, especially the right to own and to buy land, for other classes besides the nobility, but also for the consolidation of the rights of the nobility to own land and for government recognition of the inviolability of these rights. His efforts were reflected, for example, in the arguments he put forward in the Nepremennyi Soviet regarding the dispute between counts Saltykov and Kutaisov about coastal fishing in the Caspian Sea (at the mouth of the River Emba).[15] In particular, one can find a number of statements from which Mordvinov's fundamental view on the question of a civil society can easily be deduced. It will be useful to bear in mind Mordvinov's statements when we come to Speransky's views about the question of civil society: "If one only considers the whole matter from the point of view of absolute power, the solution presents no difficulties. In addition, these waters were given to a private individual by the unlimited power of the sovereign. Another ruler with unlimited power, who is equal to the first, can take it back, and it depends again entirely on them to judge whether or not (more or less) compensation should be paid." However, "taking property away . . . means taking over the property of the owner without his consent, which amounts to breaking the first principle distinguishing a well-ordered government from a ruthless one." "Therefore, should it emerge that the exclusive (private) ownership of an estate is in conflict with the general good, that must not be a reason to take this property into public ownership. . . . The general good can never be based on the ruin of an individual." "If property law (the right to property) is inviolable in Russia, then Count Kutaisov's property must also be sacrosanct."[16] He was no less resolute in his support for private property in another memorandum. He wrote, "Property is the cornerstone. Without it, without the permanence of the rights that guarantee it, neither laws nor the fatherland nor the state can be of use to anyone." Guarantees of ownership became more important in Russia, particularly after December 12, 1801, that is, "since that famous day, on which the right to own land was extended to the lower orders."

After the creation of the State Council on January 1, 1810,[17] Mordvinov was appointed as head of the Department of State Economic Affairs.[18] He was convinced that the most urgent priority was to remove all obstacles to the development of private credit and to free internal trade from those restrictions that had previously hampered it.[19] He said it was fundamental that the rights of the individual should never be sacrificed for the short-term political interests of the state, as the general good was inseparably linked to the well-being of all. England was the best evidence for this. England owed its prosperity to respect for private property, specifically to the fiscal policy by which the state's income was not derived from private capital as such, but was only taken from the profit earned from it. Mordvinov proposed paying off the national debt in order to bolster trust in state finances, that is, to convince more people that the state would not abuse its power over individuals to harm their interests.[20] He also wanted to introduce courts of arbitration to decide legal disputes between private individuals and the state. As far as exports were concerned, Mordvinov was not an unalloyed supporter of free trade. He considered that import tariffs were necessary to protect the development of Russian industry.[21]

Mordvinov was convinced that the principles of civil liberty and private property—that is, the recognition by the state of the inviolability of an individual's property and the freedom of individual enterprise—and a corresponding fiscal policy, or rather economic policy, were not sufficiently guaranteed purely through the goodwill of the sovereign. This made him a supporter of the transition to constitutional government in Russia. However, as far as I am aware, nowhere does he express this as clearly as Speransky (as shall be seen below).[22] Mordvinov's firm view was that Russia needed political freedom above all. The fact that, at the time, parliamentary representation would have been nothing more than an assembly of the gentry did not deter him at all. On the contrary, he saw in the aristocratic composition of the parliament—a feature that would be accentuated even further by the establishment of an aristocratic second chamber—a guarantee that the former would commit itself genuinely and effectively to political freedom and rights as well as to civil liberty, to a civil society.[23]

Mordvinov was—and here too he was in agreement with Speransky—against the sudden, complete abolition of serfdom.[24] In his plan for the liberation of the serfs that he presented in 1818, in which he advocated their gradual emancipation, he wrote: "In nature, we can see that the quiet and gradual passage of time always entails life, prosperity, and fruitfulness, and that on the other hand, sharp and sudden events lead to destruction. It might be possible to grant civil liberties on the orders of the sovereign to the people, who have lived for centuries unaware of them. However, it is impossible by means of a law to give them the ability to enjoy this freedom for their own and the general good."[25]

The emancipation of the serfs, he thought, had to be preceded by the consolidation of a civil society in Russia. The status of the free individual, the citizen, had first to be created. Only then could one consider the gradual liberation of the serfs, that is, move progressively toward granting the peasant the status of a free property owner. In general, the consolidation of the status of free citizen, of civil society, could only be assured through political freedom, through Russia's transition to a constitutional state.

That is why the change to constitutional government was at this time the first and most important priority for Mordvinov and many other liberal figures. This was pointed out by Gradovsky, who saw it as a political error: "At that time, only a few understood that social evolution in Russia was only possible if preceded by the emancipation of the peasants. The majority of liberals under Alexander I, on the other hand, aimed above all for political freedom for the upper classes."[26]

Later in the twentieth century, Gradovsky's view was echoed by Witte, as well as Stolypin—by the latter even after the constitution was brought in. It is quite remarkable that, on the other hand, the supporters of the immediate abolition of serfdom under Alexander I (and under Alexander II) thought the introduction of a constitution in Russia was undesirable and supported the retention of the absolute monarchy. Nicolai Turgenev, for example, recalled his difference of opinion on this question with Mordvinov in his book, published in French, *Russia and the Russians* (vol. 1, p. 93):[27] "He (Mordvinov) wanted political freedom and the upper chamber. He denounced all arbitrary power with noble and passionate selflessness. I, on the other hand, sympathized with unlimited power and defended the necessity of freeing the country from the horrific exploitation of man by man."[28] Various foreigners also expressed the same sentiment, such as, for example, John Stuart Mill in 1861, just before the emancipation of the serfs.

Chapter 3

Speransky

The 1809 memorandum—The State Council—
The 1803 memorandum—*K Poznaniiu Zakonov*—
The evolution of Speransky's views

Speransky, the man who codified Russian law, held views—as indicated above —that were very close to those of his older contemporary Mordvinov. The most extensive exposition of his ideas is probably contained in the paper called "Introduction to the Codification (Ulozhenie) of the Laws of the State," presented to Alexander I in 1809.[1] Here Speransky not only deals with specific, concrete problems of the structure of the state and the law, but bases his views on the theory and philosophy of law.

Speransky points out that the vital forces in the state—in the final analysis the intellectual and physical powers of human beings ("Introduction," pp. 4ff)— can occur either in a concentrated, centralized form or be divided among individuals. In the first situation, he says, they create the power of the state and its political authority, in the second the rights of the subject: "If the authority of the state were unlimited, were the powers of the state to be centralized to such a degree (i.e., absorbed to such an extent by the state) that its subjects were left without rights, then the nation would be in servitude and the government despotic" (ibid., p. 5). In his view, this servitude can have two forms or exist on two levels. The first, worse form not only excludes the subject from any role in the state but also robs him of his rights regarding individual freedom and property (ibid., p. 6). The second, milder form also excludes the subject from a role in the state, but does confer rights as regards subjects' individual freedom and property. In this milder case, while the subject does not therefore enjoy political rights, he is accorded civil rights (ibid., p. 6). The existence of individually held civil rights and an autonomous sphere of relations based on private law, that is, of a civil society, means that freedom, within certain limits, exists in the state. This freedom, however, is not sufficiently safeguarded and can easily be flouted: "Civil rights can no doubt exist without political rights, but in such circumstances the maintenance of these rights cannot be assured" (ibid., p. 6). Speransky goes on to explain that in order to protect these civil rights against violations by the state, it is necessary to embed them in a basic law, in a political constitution. Civil rights must be included in the state constitution "in the form of direct consequences for civil society arising from political rights." Citizens must be granted political rights, whose exercise enables them to protect their civil rights, their civil liberty (ibid., p. 6).

Thus, Speransky is convinced that civil rights, civil liberty, are not sufficiently protected by the existence of civil legislation (civil law). Civil laws without constitutional guarantees for civil rights and freedoms are impotent and therefore superfluous: "What purpose is served by laws regulating property relations between private individuals, if the concept of property itself (here surely meaning private property in a general sense) has nowhere been clearly set out? What is the point of civil laws if their 'tablets of stone' can break at any time on the rocks of the autocracy?" (ibid., p. 16). Also: "For example, a sales contract is a civil right. However, what security would this right have, if political legislation did not generally stipulate that all property is inviolable?" (ibid., p. 6, n. 2).

It was precisely this requirement to consolidate civil society that justified the necessity of putting the state on a firm constitutional basis, and this was precisely the inspiration for Speransky's plan for reforming the state. It also determined the basic premise behind the reform that now consisted of "establishing and basing the hitherto autocratic state on inviolable law" (ibid., p. 18)—that is, to enact a constitution, which would act as an absolute guarantee of civil liberty. Speransky's idea of basing political authority on lasting principles, of putting the state on a solid constitutional foundation and thereby giving it definite constitutional limits—that is, channeling the stream of its activity between the solid embankments of the law, comes from the desire to establish a secure basis for civil rights and liberty in the state's constitution, to anchor civil society safely within it. The history of Russian law also confirms that the idea of a constitutional state is inseparably bound up with the concept of a civil society.

Speransky goes on to add the following comment to justify the necessity of a state based on the rule of law, which in the end has to be a constitutional state: "Laws exist for the benefit and security of the people who are subject to them" (ibid., p. 4). According to Speransky, the general purpose of all laws "is the security of the individual and of property" (ibid., p. 3). This need for security is natural. "It would be contrary to human nature," writes Speransky, "if a person were prepared to live in a society in which his person and his property had no protection at all" (ibid., p. 29). The security of the person and of property is the first right given to each individual as a member of society and must not be taken away. It forms the substance of civil rights and civil liberty, which assumes two main forms: personal freedom and material freedom (ibid., p. 29).

Personal freedom includes:

1. No one can be punished without due process of law.

2. No one can be obliged to perform a personal service except in accordance with the law.

Material freedom includes:

3. Each can freely dispose of his property within the general framework of the law, and no one can be deprived of his property except by order of a court.

4. No one can be forced, except by law or contract, to provide material services, whether by paying taxes or by undertaking labor duties.

One can see that Speransky always considers the law as a protection for personal security and freedom.

Speransky, however, also sees that guarantees are needed not only against an arbitrary executive but also against an arbitrary legislature: "However, utility and security are vague concepts subject to the most varied changes. If laws needed to be amended to accommodate the various changes in these concepts, they would soon become muddled, which could even lead to them contradicting their original purpose. Therefore, in any well-ordered state there must be a permanent, positive basis for legislation with which all other laws must concur." Thus, Speransky arrives at the demand that the state must embody the principle of stability, that is, the principle that, ultimately, legislation enacted by government must be subordinate to existing law.[2]

Speransky, then, demands guarantees against arbitrary legislative power.[3] This constitutional limitation of power, this requirement that government take into account existing rights in carrying out its legislative functions, indeed, that it sees itself substantially bound by them, does not at all entail, according to Speransky, any weakening of the authority of the state. On the contrary, by realizing the aim of intentionally putting the autocracy on a foundation of immutable laws, "government power, supported by laws and institutions, is grounded on permanent principles, thus conferring on the exercise of this power greater stability, greater dignity, and more genuine authority."[4] For a solution to the problem of how to subordinate the government to law (to immutable law), Speransky considered the separation of powers necessary, along the lines of the dominant Western European ideas at that time. He writes, "Government cannot be based on law, if the same state authority drafts and then implements the law. This therefore necessitates establishing institutions, some of which deal with drafting laws and others with their implementation" (ibid., p. 18). As the discussion of draft laws requires the participation of a good number of people, assemblies or "dumas" must be set up (ibid., p. 37). In this connection, Speransky advocates extensive decentralization; that is, local dumas should be established as well as the central Duma. That these dumas should be made up of elected representatives is one of the most important prerequisites for genuine ministerial accountability, that is, an effective guarantee against an arbitrary executive (ibid., p. 47). It was, however, not just a question of subordinating the executive to the law, but of specific, fundamental legal principles binding the legislature.

The right to send representatives to a legislative assembly or to elect these assemblies cannot therefore be given to all in equal measure. Laws have to protect the individual and property, and it is thus natural that the more property a person owns, the more they are interested in the protection of property rights (ibid., p. 32). It follows that in general a property owner will be concerned more with the "justness of laws" and exercise better judgment about them. By contrast, why should a person without property be interested in, for example, moderating the provisions of land-tax law? (ibid., p. 32). This is the basis for the rule (a rule accepted even in revolutionary France) that those who possess neither property nor capital are, to a degree, excluded from elections. This rule is particularly important, as people without property would predominate in the assembly because of their large number, whereby the least mature would gain the most influence over legislation. "Without doubt this rule must be followed here in Russia," writes Speransky (ibid., p. 33). Thus, although the democratic principle of universal and equal suffrage (like all political rights) is alien to Speransky, he places all the more emphasis on the liberal principle of the separation of powers. The intended separation of powers was not just a matter of merely sharing out functions. Each branch of government had to possess true autonomy in relation to the other parts of the state.

Speransky emphasizes that this real autonomy of each branch of the state, that is, the introduction of a true division of powers, is evidence for the fact that it is a question of a genuine constitution and not a pseudo-constitution. He clearly recognizes the problem of pseudo-constitutions in light of his observation of Napoleonic France, at least as far as its political aspects are concerned. The passage in his memorandum dealing with this problem is in general very interesting and is quoted here at length:

> At first sight, two different approaches (in implementing these reforms) seem possible here: the first consists in endowing the autocratic regime with all the external trappings of legality (*zakona*), while in essence retaining the significance and extent of its power. The second approach consists in not only lending the autocracy the external features of legality but also restraining it through institutions with their own substantive power and basing the state's authority on law, not just in words but also in fact. One has to choose decisively one of these alternatives right at the start of the reform process. Whichever choice is made will determine its actual direction. In the case of the first approach, all institutions have to be set up to appear

effective in the eyes of public opinion, without being so in reality. The basic features of such a constitution would be as follows:

1. An institution would be established as a free legislature, but would in fact remain under the influence of and be completely dependent on the autocracy.
2. The executive would be set up to appear accountable according to the wording of the law, but remain essentially completely autonomous.
3. The judicial branch would retain all the advantages of apparent freedom. In reality, however, it would be bound by such restrictions as to remain dependent on the autocracy.

The present political constitution of France is based on these three main principles.

If, on the other hand, the second option is preferred, then the institutions have to be based on the following principles:

1. The legislative institution must be organized so that it cannot carry out its functions without the participation of the government, although it must have freedom of expression and represent the views of the people.
2. The judiciary must be selected through free elections, while only the oversight of the procedures of the courts and public security remain as responsibilities of the government.
3. The executive must be entrusted wholly and exclusively to the government. As, however, this power is able, under the guise of applying legislation, not just to deform it but to completely destroy it, it must be made accountable to the legislature.

The general approach of either of these two systems may be followed in drafting a constitution. If they are compared, there is no doubt that the first has only the appearance of legality, while only the second has it in reality; the former introduces total autocracy under the pretext of unifying political authority, but the latter in fact aims to restrain and moderate it. (Ibid., pp. 18f)

On the other hand, it is doubtful whether Speransky saw the problem of pseudo-constitutions as clearly in relation to the social constitution as he did in respect of the political constitution. Was it clear to him that not only legislation but also the constitution itself could destroy not only political but also civil liberty? As we have seen, Speransky was clear that political power could harm and even destroy civil liberty, but when Speransky talked about the tablets of civil rights breaking on the rock of autocracy, he had in mind, above all, arbitrary and unlawful acts of government, even the possibility that individual laws can embody despotic tendencies. He did not apparently foresee, however, the possibility that the constitution or fundamental laws could rob the citizens of their civil liberty. In my opinion, this can be explained in the first place by the fact that Speransky recognized the problem of pseudo-constitutions from his observation of Napoleonic France, but that, on the other hand, pseudo-constitutionalism in relation to the social sphere, that is, in respect to civil liberty, only became fully apparent later with socialist pseudo-constitutions.[5] Second, it can also be explained by the fact that he was convinced that the constitution, by its very nature, inevitably encompassed among its most important fundamental principles the recognition of civil rights, of civil liberty.

Speransky thought that Russia was ready to embark on the road to reform, to adopt a constitution that secured civil as well as political liberty. According to Speransky, history offers no example of an enlightened, economically advanced (*kommercheskii*) country remaining in servitude for long (ibid., p. 12). Since the reign of Peter the Great, education as well as industry had developed in Russia. Peter the Great, who had done nothing for political freedom in terms of the formal structures of government, did nevertheless open the door to it, insofar as he allowed the sciences and trade access to Russia (ibid., p. 13).

Speransky cites Bacon's saying "Time is the greatest innovator" (ibid., p. 11) and maintains that crises are to be expected if the structures of the state are not in harmony with the times.[6] Heads of state must therefore observe how the outlook of society develops and adapt the political system accordingly. This would avoid much harm and bloodletting (ibid., p. 12). It would be a great advantage for the development of Russia if the constitution were "the result not of the flaring up of passions and the pressure of circumstances but the benevolent inspiration of the sovereign" (ibid., p. 10).

In general, Russia was going through the same stages of development as other states, only at a much faster rate (ibid., p. 15, n. 3), and therefore, Speransky insists, the decision should not be delayed. There was sufficient evidence that "the present system of government is no longer in tune with the mood of society" (ibid., p. 17). According to Speransky, the first indicator had to be the weakening of government authority: "In the present situation, one can state with certainty that all government measures demanding not just physical but also moral subjugation must remain ineffective" (ibid., p. 16). Speransky continues that the second indicator is general dissatisfaction:

> Ultimately, this general dissatisfaction, this tendency to feel pessimistic about everything, is nothing more than a generalized feeling of satiation and boredom with the current state of affairs! Wars and political events no doubt play a certain part, but there have been difficulties and wars before, and yet the people's morale was never as low as it is now. Is it really possible to blame this dissatisfaction on increases in the price of coffee and sugar? Is there any less luxury as a result? Are people less well off now? Where are the cruel blows that have hit them? Everything is almost as it was before. Yet people are restless. How can this unrest be explained, other than by a

complete change in outlook, by a silent but powerful desire for a new order? (Ibid., p. 17)

Only a few points from Speransky's reform program, which had been presented in the memorandum analyzed above, were put into effect. The most significant of these was the establishment of the State Council in 1810. The State Council was made up of members appointed by the tsar, mostly high-ranking dignitaries of the state.[7] The most important function of the council was to express opinions on draft legislation proposed by the government, in the main by individual ministers.

In his reform plan of 1809, Speransky had not originally intended the State Council to be an institution concerned with the details of draft legislation. This role was to fall to a duma, whose members were supposed to be elected, not appointed, while the State Council was to have a different role. As each of the three basic branches of the state had to be granted genuine autonomy and genuine independence from the other two branches, the unity of the state could only be embodied in the person of the sovereign. This unity was thus only maintained by the fact that the monarch, as head of state and representative of the sovereignty of the state (*vozglavitel'*), remained the nominal holder and highest representative of all branches of the state. Because of this, Speransky believed that another institution had to be created to foster harmonious relations between the different branches of the state and give concrete institutional expression to the abstract embodiment, in the person of the sovereign, of the unity of the state, of state power. The State Council was to be such an institution. In addition, in Speransky's plan, the State Council, in contrast to the Duma, would consist of members appointed by the sovereign. In the area of legislation, the council would take the role of upper chamber in relation to the Duma. As, however, the Duma had not been created, the State Council, or rather its plenary sessions (*obshchee sobranie*), became a consultative body that mainly assisted in drafting the most important pieces of legislation.

The Manifesto of January 1, 1810 (written by Speransky), which set up the State Council, and the statute (*obrazovanie*) of the State Council enacted with it, laid down that all draft legislation had to be presented to the State Council and discussed in its plenary sessions (Arts. 1, 2; statute §29). The statute also contained regulations that gave decisions agreed on by a majority in the State Council a certain binding power, at least in the sense that the tsar could only ratify legislation that had been approved by a majority of the plenary session. This is shown just by the wording to be used by the tsar to ratify draft laws—"after hearing and accepting the opinion (*vniav mneniiu*) of the State Council we determine/ratify" (§73). It is only logical to assume that by "opinion of the State Council" is meant only the opinion of the majority and not of the minority. Another fact that confirms that the tsar could only ratify the opinion of the majority of the State Council is that in the journal (*zhurnal*) of the council, only the majority view is recorded, whereas the minority and other views are only appended (§54). Particularly important in this context is §55, in that according to this regulation, if the tsar regarded a minority view as worthy of interest, it could be presented at his request to the council for further consideration. Obviously, this excludes the ratification of such an opinion, that is, the passage of a minority legislative proposal into law.

Thus, an institution was created with the State Council that had a consultative function in drawing up legislation, even if it was made up of appointed and not elected members. There is no doubt that the State Council was able to influence legislation, which, to a degree, guaranteed that new laws were based on definite legal principles. The establishment of the council was, therefore, a factor in securing the rule of law and the application of law in public life. It has to be recognized that the birth of the State Council was definitely in the spirit, if not the letter, of Speransky's plan and represented another step in consolidating liberal principles of law in Russia.

Going into the detail of the history of the State Council would be to digress from the subject of this book, especially as later laws increasingly cut back its powers. Subsequent legislation, therefore, restricted rather than fostered the development of the liberal principles that Speransky had been able to incorporate into the manifesto and the statute of January 1, 1810. The 1842 statute on the State Council decreed that the tsar could also ratify a minority opinion and not solely a majority one, indeed would be able to make a decision that overrode all the views expressed in the council (Arts. 112, 116).[8] Furthermore, the practice of the tsar enacting a decree precisely in those cases where opposition from the State Council was expected became increasingly common. Such decrees were based on the personal reports of individual ministers or resolutions of the Committee of Ministers. Insofar as the distinction between laws and decrees is always vague in absolute monarchies (the will of the monarch also being the source of law), such decrees were laws too. It is just that these were laws enacted without the participation of the State Council, that is, by circumventing it, and in a less formal way than would otherwise have been the case.[9] To what extent there was a legal basis for this practice is a complicated question. It should not be forgotten that not only Article 24 of the 1842 decree but also §30 of the decree of January 1, 1810, can be seen to provide such a basis. It is certainly interesting to note that Gradovsky considers that this practice was not based on the articles of the 1810 and 1842 edicts, but on a decree enacted in the 1850s.

This tendency to bypass the State Council in the preparation of some draft legislation sprang from the recognition that the opinions as well as the criticisms expressed in the council by individual members on the subject of draft laws put forward by ministers attracted a degree of authority that was not to be underestimated. Speransky reports that these views and criticisms were heard in the State

Council by Alexander I with great tolerance (*s terpeniem*) and were based on the authority of experts, experienced former officials, ex-ministers, governors, senators, and so on. On the other hand, they were often an expression of opinion at the highest levels of Russian society, from which members of the State Council were almost exclusively drawn. At any rate, the members of the council were mostly individuals with considerable connections in the country, in the guards regiments and at court; their voice could not simply be ignored in society. Furthermore, they were often great figures, of independent character, who even in the presence of the tsar did not shy away from clearly expressing their opposition to his plans, still less from attacking ministers.[10]

As stated above, the history of legislation relating to the State Council cannot be explored here. It is important, however, to mention that the council often energetically insisted on respect for its authority, to the extent that over time certain traditions were established that were in tune with the ideas that Speransky had incorporated in the Manifesto of January 1, 1810. It is noteworthy that these traditions persisted even though later legislation did not give them a proper foundation and that the council then repeatedly attempted to protect this tradition. In his memoirs, Baron Korf recalls that the president of the State Council, Prince Vasil'chikov, forcefully insisted that all draft legislation should be laid before the council. In the 1840s, Bludov proposed measures to reduce the imperial household (*dvorovye liudi*). Bludov, the minister of justice, and Vasil'chikov, the president of the State Council, were given the task of preparing the text of the decree for the implementation of this measure, and no sooner had the draft been completed than Nicholas I immediately wanted to sign it, that is, to bring it into force. Vasil'chikov, however, raised the requirement of putting the draft before the State Council. There followed a lengthy argument between the prince and the tsar. Their respective principled positions are illustrated by the following exchange: "Is it really the case," asked the tsar, "that whenever I consider something to be useful or beneficial, I first have to seek the agreement of the council?" To which Vasil'chikov replied, "Not their agreement, but definitely their opinion, as that is what the council is for; either it has to be abolished (*unichtozhit'*), or the law, which you yourself enacted, must be followed (*ochraniat'*)."[11] Nicholas I did not concede immediately, but ordered a twelve-man committee to be set up to review the draft of the decree on the imperial household, as well as to take a view as to whether the draft decree should be laid before the State Council. It was only after the committee had expressed the view that this measure was necessary that Nicholas I agreed to lay the draft decree before a plenary session of the State Council. Korf also recalls another example in 1839 when Vasil'chikov prevented Kankrin, the finance minister, from nevertheless asking the tsar to ratify a draft decree previously rejected by the State Council. In this case, however, he was only partially successful. The draft was in fact laid before the State Council again, but the tsar then gave a direct order to the council to accept without dissent a compromise solution worked out by Kankrin as his own will.[12] It is interesting that

Kankrin set himself up as the defender of the principle of absolutism and that he was outraged at the suggestion to make the State Council into a kind of parliament (*kamer*) or power-sharing body (*mesto sotsarstvuiushchee*).[13]

Despite the fact that, according to the 1842 decree, the tsar was able to ratify a ministerial draft law even when the both the majority and the minority of the State Council opposed it, this only occurred in rare cases. The tsars in fact only reluctantly ratified the opinion of the minority, and then only if they thought it absolutely necessary. Prince Meshchersky in his memoirs recalls a case in which the tsar ignored all of the positions expressed in the State Council and the reaction that this provoked in the council. The occasion was the ratification of the draft law proposed by the minister of the interior, Tolstoy, on the "Zemskie Nachal'niki" [Land Captains] in 1889. The difference between the majority and minority positions was that the minority, while in general accepting the draft, which the majority totally rejected, insisted on retaining the office of justice of the peace in addition to the Zemskie Nachal'niki, which were to be created by the new law. In the opinion of the minority, the Zemskie Nachal'niki ought only to be administrative officials without combining any judicial role with their administrative function. This would preserve the principle of the separation of powers to which not only the majority of the council but also the minority attached great importance. The position of the State Council alarmed the supporters of the original ministerial draft law drawn up by Pazukhin. They could not accept the fact that the new law would create a post of responsibility lacking paternalistic power over the people and consequently unable to act as a sort of guardian over the peasants, in other words a mere police official.

Prince Meshchersky, who considered Pazukhin's draft to be the product of statesmanlike wisdom, succeeded through his connections in putting to the tsar a memorandum passed to him by the conservative senator Tatishchev (the authors of which preferred to remain anonymous and did so), with the recommendation that the draft law should be ratified without any amendment. Alexander III, influenced by this memorandum, in fact put forward a resolution regarding the "memoria" that the State Council had laid before him, to the effect that he agreed with the minority position, albeit in an amended form.[14] These amendments amounted to a complete restoration of Minister Tolstoy's original draft and the abandonment of all the amendments that had been adopted following a compromise agreement between the minority in the council and the minister. As a result of the tsar's decision, the office of justice of the peace, in particular, was to be abolished, whereas its retention had been precisely the main demand of the State Council. The tsar's intervention caused enormous consternation among the members of the council. Meshchersky writes:

> The entire world of St. Petersburg's dignitaries became greatly agitated, as if a revolution had broken out. . . . Secretary of State Polovtsov read out the tsar's resolution to the full State Council in a trembling voice.
> Virtually all the members of the council were convinced that such a

resolution was unprecedented, that "the tsar had for the first time departed from the custom of ratifying without amendment an opinion of the State Council."[15]

This was such a generally held and firm conviction that Polovtsov felt it was his duty to make representations to the tsar, pointing out that the members of the State Council were greatly bewildered and that there had never been an instance of "the tsar substituting his own opinion for that of the State Council."[16] At this Alexander III asked Polovtsov whether there was any law against the tsar amending the opinion of the State Council. The secretary of state answered that in fact there was no such law, but rather there was a tradition (*predanie*). After receiving this response, Alexander III asked Polovtsov to return the next day to discuss the issue in the presence of Tolstoy. When Tolstoy and Polovtsov were received the following day, Alexander III asked Tolstoy whether Polovtsov's view that he had contravened a "sacrosanct" tradition through his decision was justified. Tolstoy cited three similar examples from history. This soothed Alexander III's conscience, and he dismissed Polovtsov with these words: "You see, I was right." This incident shows, however, that, even if it was not "sacrosanct," there was nevertheless a strong tradition that the tsar hardly ever rejected or fundamentally altered the opinions put forward in the plenary sessions of the State Council. This tradition had in any case become so firmly established that neither the members of the council (with only a few exceptions) nor the secretary of state, who had to be particularly well informed about such matters, were able to recall any exceptions to this rule.[17]

Speransky's constitutional plans, analyzed above, culminated in his 1809 memorandum. Neither before nor after did he come out so decisively in favor of constitutionalism. Insofar as he did not even here achieve the desired clarity in respect of the constitutional principle of the separation of powers, it is important to recall Speransky's views on the subject from his earlier and later works. These writings could provide clues to establishing whether Karamzin's view is correct that, according to Speransky's system, the tsar would only be granted limited powers—those of supreme head of the executive—that would be counterbalanced and restrained by the other powers, especially the legislative power exercised by a parliament, or whether, as Speransky maintained in a letter of self-justification from Perm, this was just a slur.[18] There is no simple answer to this question on the basis of Speransky's plan as analyzed above. On the one hand, Speransky states that all powers culminate in the person of the monarch and stem from him. On the other hand, the relationship between the monarch and the legislative bodies is not made completely clear. Occasionally, one has the impression that this lack of clarity is intentional and serves to disguise the practical possibility of binding the will of the monarch through resolutions of the legislative body. The whole structure is even more impenetrable when one considers that in

Speransky's plan, the State Council is no purely legislative body, but the supreme body at the head of all three powers, above which the monarch himself stands. It is therefore necessary to refer to his other works, in particular *On the Organization of the Judicial and Administrative Systems in Russia [Zapiska ob ustroistve sudebnykh i pravitel'stvennykh uchrezhdenii v Rossii]* (1803) and *An Introduction to Law (K Poznaniiu Zakonov)* (1838).[19]

Even in the first work, that is, already by 1803, Speransky, quite in the spirit of liberalism, describes the actual goal of society as the security of the individual and property, which is guaranteed if order based on law remains undisturbed (*On the Organization*, p. 3). This goal can be achieved in an "authentic" (*pravil'noi*) monarchy.[20]

Speransky argues that in order to see which measures to take or which reforms to implement first, one has to start by describing the basic characteristics of an authentic monarchy, then investigate the actual form of the Russian state, and finally show how this differs from an authentic monarchy (ibid., p. 2). Then it has to be shown that the introduction of an authentic monarchy is impossible under the existing circumstances. At the same time, one has to explain how government in Russia could be reorganized in order to meet as far as possible, without the destruction of the existing order, the requirements arising from the nature of an authentic monarchy (ibid., p. 2).

Russia, says Speransky, is an autocracy, which at first sight appears to be an extremely simple type of state. Ultimate and supreme power resides with the autocrat. Legislative, executive, and judicial powers are all united in his person (ibid., p. 32). He is the sole legislator, judge, and executor of his laws. That seems the be-all and end-all of the nature of autocracy. It is debatable, however, whether this first impression can be upheld on closer inspection—particularly in the case of the Russian state (ibid., p. 31). Certainly there are no external limits (*veshchestvennye predely*) on the power of the autocrat, and yet there do exist some internal limits (*umstvennye granicy*), through trusted opinion (*mneniem*) and the customary ways of exercising power. As a result, power is exercised with a uniform regularity in which certain accepted conventions are observed. Speransky attaches great importance to the way autocratic power is bound by tradition, by customary law. He refers to Hume's view that the strength of the English constitution is due above all to tradition and the particular spirit of the people (ibid., p. 32, n. 2). Not just in England, but in general, these customary legal traditions form the basis, the essence even, of constitutions. Speransky writes: "What is called basic law or constitution is not written law, but real law, which is not on paper but works in reality. It is not so much particular structures of the state as the actual balance of power among the estates that is characteristic. It is based less on visible institutions (*soslovie*)[21] than on the traditions and the spirit of the people. It is a physical constitution, the temperament of the body politic" (ibid., p. 28, n. 1).[22]

It is precisely this view, and the value that Speransky attaches to tradition, which even in an autocratic state restricts the ruler, that explains why he held the opinion that the Russian state should only be reformed as long as this did not lead to the destruction of the existing order. It is tradition above all that lies at the heart of this order. It is, however, not through tradition alone that the primitive autocratic state becomes significantly more sophisticated. According to Speransky, Russia had a number of institutions that can be described as elements borrowed from an authentic, that is, a constitutional, monarchy. Examples of this are the Nepremnnyi Soviet (the Permanent Council, created by Alexander I in 1801), the Senate, the committee, and the ministries (ibid., p. 31). Of course, these cannot be seen as truly constitutional institutions, given the form they had in Russia. Yet to some extent, they were the germs of a constitutional order within the autocratic state, and their existence represented a further modification of this type of state.

For Speransky, the direction of future reforms follows logically from these facts. It is just a question of shaping the structures of the state so that they gradually but surely take on more and more the character of authentic constitutional institutions: "The state (in Russia) . . . must be based on the current autocratic constitution that lacks any separation of powers. . . . It must, however, include various institutions that, insofar as they evolve, pave the way for an authentic monarchy and prepare the people for it" (ibid., p. 35).

Speransky adds that although the two powers are still united in the person of monarch, progress therefore has to be made to separate the legislative from the executive power (ibid., p. 39). To achieve this, the Senate has to be divided into two institutions; that is, a legislative and an executive Senate must be set up. The latter must be further split into a judicial and an administrative senate (ibid., p. 40). The aim of this is to achieve the situation, typical for an authentic monarchy, in which administration is merely the application and implementation of legislation (ibid., p. 18), and the executive is accountable to the legislature (ibid., p. 22). This is one of the main reasons for the independence of the legislature from the executive and why it must be accorded an extremely high status in the state (ibid., p. 24). In the original draft Speransky also added, "Within certain limits all free estates must be brought into the legislative process" (ibid., p. 28). This sentence, however, was deleted by Speransky himself. His view at the time was that a legislative body could consist of people appointed by the sovereign (ibid., p. 41), because the decisive issue was not how one became a member of the legislative assembly, but how genuinely independent these institutions were from the executive. As a result of this independence, the establishment of these legislative institutions would in any case mark the first step away from despotism toward authentic monarchy (ibid., p. 25).

Public opinion is a further effective guarantee against infringements of the law by the executive. "Public opinion," he writes, "must be developed as soon as possible to put limits not on power as such, but on the way it works" (ibid., p. 35; see also p. 46). Thus, according to Speransky, public opinion can also exist in an autocracy. If this is true, it marks a significant difference between absolutist monarchies and modern totalitarian states, which not only suppress public opinion but also organize it, that is, falsify it and thereby annihilate it.

Work should be undertaken to complete and perfect the civil and criminal law to fulfill the demand for the executive to be confined to applying and implementing legislation. Speransky believed that achieving this ambition was hardly possible in the prevailing circumstances (ibid., p. 35). He writes: "At present, there is no good theory of either civil or criminal law in Russia or in the whole of Europe. . . . Jurists are still arguing about first principles" (ibid., pp. 35f). And: "As, however, this discipline has never attracted as much attention as now, it can justifiably be assumed that the best theories of civil and criminal law will soon emerge. . . . The current situation in Russia allows us to wait, for even if a good system of law in this field (i.e., in the field of civil and criminal law) became available in Europe, it could not be applied here straightaway" (ibid., p. 36).

This passage seems to me to be very important. In my opinion, it shows that Speransky was thinking of the widespread interest in Western European law, at any rate that he thought it necessary to make use of the scholarly work of Western jurists for the codification and further development of Russian law. In Speransky's opinion, however, it was not yet possible to embark on this task, and one had to restrict oneself to codifying existing laws. It was thus necessary to be content with improvements in the areas of policing and the economy, which would surely also result, of necessity, in certain improvements in legal processes.

The modesty of this program can be explained by the fact that Speransky rejects radical reforms that would destroy the legal and ethical traditions that existed in the autocratic state. The reason he does this is that in his opinion reforms that do not allow for the "contribution of time" and the "gradual evolution of all things toward their perfection" (ibid., pp. 33f) have no hope of succeeding. Furthermore, Speransky also emphasizes that the most basic elements for the establishment of an authentic monarchy, or a constitutional state, were missing in Russia. According to Speransky, the transition to constitutional institutions was clearly impossible, as long as half the population was in complete servitude. Furthermore, the fundamental laws, indeed law in general, had not been codified; the executive and the legislature had not been separated; there was no legislative institution based on public opinion; and the generally poor level of education hindered the development of public opinion (ibid., p. 34).

In his book *K Poznaniiu Zakonov,* Speransky begins by setting out the views on the philosophy of law that he held toward the end of his life.

The basis for moral order is found, in his view, in a conscience that is always truthful (*pravdiva*) (ibid., pp. 12, 17). Such a conscience can never judge as bad what is seen as good nor, conversely find good what is seen as evil. Thus, judgment based on conscience is *pravda* (ibid., p. 14). Conscience combined, however, with reason can err (ibid., p. 14), can be led astray by reason in telling good from evil, particularly in the quest for utilitarian ends (ibid., p. 19). Conscience must therefore be supported or bolstered by two forces, through religion and through positive law (*obshchezhitel'noe zakonodatel'stvo*) (ibid., p. 21).

One must therefore distinguish between the laws of conscience and the positive laws enacted by the state (ibid., pp. 24ff). The main difference between these two types of law is that the laws of conscience also relate to the inner stirrings of the will, while laws enacted by the state only govern behavior in society (ibid, p. 30). Otherwise, they both have the same end and the same content; they point to justice (*pravda*) and duty (*dolg*) (ibid., pp. 29ff). There can be no contradiction between the two, as "the social (*obshchezhitel'nyi*) order is part of the same moral order" (ibid., p. 39), and justice (*spravedlivost'*) is nothing less than *pravda* in its social aspect (ibid., p. 38). "The aim of society is to make moral laws prevail between people," writes Speransky. He essentially asserts that society (*obshchezhitie*) is the antechamber of eternal life, for which man must be educated and prepared (ibid., p. 26). Thus, "positive laws are invalid when they contradict natural law, in other words the demands of the moral order. Essentially, they must be nothing other than the firm application of this law through action taken by authority" (ibid., pp. 39f).

Speransky continues that there are four necessary institutions in society, or four types of key institutions: (1) freedom of the individual, (2) private property, (3) authority, and (4) the institutions of intellectual and spiritual life (religion, science, art). Social progress will result from extending and developing these institutions (ibid., p. 32).

Fundamental laws determine who in the state is invested with authority, as well as the norms that govern how the holder of supreme power in the state carries out his role as legislator and ruler (ibid., p. 48). According to Article 1 of Russia's 1832 "Fundamental Laws," the Russian emperor is an autocrat, an absolute monarch (ibid., p. 49); in other words, supreme power is exclusively in his hands. The word *autocrat* in the first place expresses sovereignty in foreign relations, while it also means that all state power and all the elements of public authority are invested completely and indivisibly in the sovereign (ibid., p. 50). This absolute power means that the supreme power of the Russian autocrat cannot be limited by any other power in the world and that the autocrat can never be brought to trial on earth. Nevertheless, the autocrat is answerable to God and to his own conscience. That is why the limits that he himself has set on his power, through international treaties on the one hand and by consent within the state on the other, are considered by him to be sacred and must be fully respected (ibid., pp. 56f). In general, absolute autocracy in no way amounts to untrammeled arbitrary power.

It is apparent just from the above quotations from Speransky that the holder of supreme power must try to act according to natural law, in other words, to meet the requirements of the God-given moral order (ibid., pp. 39f). This idea is even more clearly expressed in the following: "Supreme power is there to support conscience for the sake of justice. Without authority, neither individual freedom nor private property can exist" (ibid., p. 29)

In this sentence, Speransky takes the principles of liberalism, that is, the protection of individual freedom and private property, and makes them tenets of absolute monarchy. Thus, in his book *K Poznaniiu Zakonov*, Speransky not only discusses absolute monarchy but also postulates a liberal program, a liberal absolutism. Essentially this marks a return to the liberal absolutism of Catherine's Instruction, which, as we saw above, included only civil liberty, but not political freedom.

Speransky completely abandons his earlier conviction that political freedom is required to secure civil liberty. Civil liberty, he says, is safeguarded enough if it is expressed in clear, stable laws and becomes rooted in the customs and culture of the people (ibid., pp. 119f). At the same time, this would also secure the people's prosperity. Speransky then goes on to maintain that political freedom is purely the preserve of the aristocracy and, in general, only for the elites and serves to maintain their privileges (ibid., p. 116). However, Speransky continues, as the state must never try to protect the material advantages of specific estates and to promote the concentration of great wealth in the hands of one estate, its real aim must in fact be to lead all the people toward goodness and moral perfection, rather than affirming political freedom. It must also put the work and property of all citizens equally under the protection of the law (ibid., pp. 117f).

Thus, an aristocratic parliament, Speransky says, cannot serve the interests of the people, any more than a parliament elected by universal suffrage can bring good fortune to the people, as that would mean plebeian rule (*chern'*) (ibid., pp. 117 f). It is interesting to note that Speransky also rejects his earlier view that the best result or the best parliamentary composition could be achieved if the franchise had a property qualification: "Is it not remarkable to believe that someone with an income of 500 francs must love his fatherland more, must serve the general good better, and must be a better legislator than someone with 400 francs?" (ibid., p. 118). That Speransky cites an example using francs shows that he was thinking of France and the July Monarchy of 1830–48 in particular.

It is noteworthy and interesting that such different writers from such different periods as Ivan IV, Speransky, and some spokesmen for modern totalitarianism use the same antiaristocratic (or antibourgeois) arguments in defense of political absolutism. Absolute monarchy, that is, the concentration of all power in the hands of the sovereign, Speransky concludes, is the best guarantee of the freedom of the people, at any rate of the sort it really needs, that is, civil liberty. One cannot but help recall Napoleon's saying, "La liberté, c'est un bon code civil." Justinian had already demonstrated, however, that an absolute ruler could enact a good civil law code. Naturally, only if certain conditions were met would it be possible to achieve civil liberty in an absolutist state. First, the rules that lay down how supreme power is exercised must be strictly observed, and second, civil laws, and in fact all current law, must be exactly drafted and codified.

In this last book, Speransky combines the ideal of the Orthodox empire, lead-ing the people toward moral goodness (ibid., p. 117), with the basic premise of liberalism, putting the state at the service of individual freedom and private prop-erty. It is extremely characteristic that Speransky, in contrast to many Russian thinkers of later generations, neither sees conflict between these ideals nor finds them to be irreconcilable. On the contrary, he is also convinced that moral prog-ress in a Christian sense in society is only possible if and how liberal principles are applied in the life of the state and if the individual and property are regarded as sacred and inviolable by the state.

Speransky does not share the distinction between the inner moral *pravda* (truth) and the formal outer *pravo* (right) that the Slavophiles drew, one that is in fact already encountered in the dispute between Gogol and Belinsky, although here the terms themselves are not used, or at least the contrast between them is not emphasized.

It seems wrong to see Speransky's proclamation of the ideals of the Ortho-dox empire as merely a concession forced on him by changes in political circum-stances. First, as we have seen, he always, even in his earliest writings, greatly valued the political and ethical traditions in the life of the state. The political tra-ditions of Russia were all rooted in the ideal of the Orthodox empire and almost all linked to the idealized image of Orthodox autocracy. Second, Speransky was nothing if not open-minded and constantly inquisitive. It would thus be some-what unlikely for him not to be personally touched and influenced by the rise in conservative ideas in Russia and the West. The effect of these influences and the change in Speransky's outlook were initially exaggerated. Following Speransky's biographer, Korf, the "old" radical Speransky was contrasted with a "new" conser-vative one. It was only later that people began to question this view and to deny absolutely that a deep change had occurred in Speransky's ideas. It was then said that Speransky remained a partisan of radical reform in a liberal sense and that only circumstances had forced him to conceal his radical outlook.

I believe that there is some truth in both of these views, but they must be moderated on the one hand and supplemented on the other. In the first place, I believe that one should not exaggerate Speransky's radicalism, even before his banishment (1812). Even while he was working on liberal reform plans for Alex-ander I, he demonstrated a certain conservatism and a clear sense of history. On the other hand, even at the end of his life Speransky had not lost his belief in the principles of liberalism. Even then, he did not so much stand for the ideal of the Orthodox empire, as understood in the time of earlier tsars like Alexei Mikhailo-vich or Peter the Great, but rather dreamed of an empire that, while still Ortho-dox, had already been extensively liberalized—the liberal absolutism of Cathe-rine's Instruction. It should not be assumed, therefore, that there was a profound break in Speransky's political ideas, if the radicalism of the "old" Speransky is not exaggerated. On the other hand, it cannot be denied that a conservative tone in Speransky's political thought became more marked as time went on. What brought about this change? Was it the result of a rethinking, of the influence of the conservative tide? Was it the impression left by the defeat of revolutionary France and Napoleon, which could be seen at the time as conclusive? Was it his contact with provincial life in Russia, which was so different from life in St. Petersburg and which must have dampened the enthusiasm of anyone trying to initiate reform? Alternatively, was it a concession, a result of having to take account of political reality? No doubt, both of these are true. As I wrote above, I believe it is wrong to see this turn to conservatism as pure affectation or pure compromise. One must make allowances for his propensity as an administrator to adapt to the sentiments and views that dominated government "circles."[23] It is particularly difficult in Speransky's case to judge the impact of these different factors. It is hard to recall any figure in Russian history who was so reluctant to be frank with others and so guarded about his inner feelings.

In any case, Speransky had, in general, relatively little interest in ideas for their own sake or for their theoretical justification and dissemination. His whole interest lay in the practical application of principles he recognized as valid. He therefore concentrated all his attention on those aspects of liberalism that could apparently be implemented. Thus, the form and content of his arguments tended to depend on whom he was dealing with in any particular situation. It is interesting that these aspects of Speransky's character led some to deny that he had any real creativity. As early as the 1840s a certain Staroverov wrote to Pogodin in protest against including Speransky in the ranks of great Russian statesmen. "For heaven's sake," he exclaimed, "they were creative—Speransky was a bureaucrat (*te tvorili—Speransky svodil*)."[24] The theologian G. Florovsky also shared this opinion: "For all the audacity of his logical planning, Speransky had no original ideas of his own."[25] This judgment appears to me to be one-sided, even if partially correct. Practical work can consist in developing systems and structures creatively. If you accept that, you really have to admire Speransky's creative energy.

Speransky—and Tsar Alexander—faced a stream of conservative ideas from all sides, and in Russia, Karamzin was a brilliant exponent of these ideas. It has long been recognized and generally accepted that the codification of Russian law carried out by Speransky was based on Karamzin's ideas.[26] However, to my knowledge, no one has yet shown conclusively that Speransky's general ideas, as set out in his last work analyzed above, were inherently consistent with Karamzin's ideas or indeed, up to a point, simply reflected them. At the same time, it seems certain that in *K Poznaniiu Zakonov*, Speransky adopted the ideal of liberal absolutism as expounded by Karamzin. This underlines Karamzin's significance in Russian political history.

My categorization of Karamzin's ideal as liberal absolutism differs from the traditional view that Karamzin was a pure conservative, indeed a reactionary who was thoroughly hostile to any liberal trends. This assertion needs closer examination.

Chapter 4

Karamzin

Karamzin as the spokesman for liberal absolutism—
The "Eulogy to Catherine"—Karamzin and the
peasant question—Karamzin's traditionalism—The
poem "The Liberation of Europe"—Karamzin and
the Decembrist revolt—Significance of this revolt
for the development of liberalism in Russia—Last
years of Alexander I's reign

Including Karamzin in an account of the development of Russia toward liberalism runs counter to the way he is traditionally viewed. Yet on the other hand, his ideas, his general intellectual outlook, and his personality in general had a positive influence on Russia's progress in a liberal direction. In the first place, Karamzin did a great deal to build general intellectual links between Russia and the European West. He was effective in widening the channels through which liberal ideas were able to flow, and did indeed flow, into Russia. It has been generally acknowledged, in fact, that Karamzin played a key role in preparing the ground for the liberal era in Russia. It is often readily conceded that Karamzin, as the spokesman for a sort of sentimental humanism, helped articulate many of the premises, rooted in humanism, that underpinned liberalism. Any greater significance for Karamzin in the context of the spread of liberal ideas and for the progress of liberal institutions in Russia, however, is disputed. On the one hand, this is the result of his firm support for absolutism and his belief that liberal principles would only be put into practice in the context of an absolute monarchy. He rejected constitutionalism, that is, an attempt to limit the power of the autocrat. On the other hand, Karamzin's skeptical position on the emancipation of the serfs is perhaps an even greater reason why many deny his positive influence on

Russia's development toward liberalism. Furthermore, the fact that he supported the ideas of the Historical School and spoke for political and legal traditionalism is seen as incompatible with the aims of liberal ideology.

In my opinion, none of these objections is valid. I have already shown in the chapter on Catherine that essential elements of a liberal program could be implemented in the context of an absolute monarchy. This was also Karamzin's view.[1] It should therefore be acknowledged that Karamzin's position—namely that it would be possible for an absolute monarchy to adopt the basic aims of liberalism as a program of government, indeed even as the basis of the state, without at the same time abolishing itself—was a significant factor in encouraging Russian monarchs to embark on liberal reform. According to Karamzin, the adoption of liberal ideas by the absolute monarchy was not just one possibility among others, but a necessity. Implementing liberal reforms and adopting a liberal approach to government were required in the name of justice and thus a moral imperative. As such, this obligation was unconditionally binding on the autocrat. Karamzin was convinced that an absolute monarchy could remain an authentic monarchy and not turn into despotism, provided that it was based on the will of God and the demands of justice prevailed.

This conclusion brings us to one of the essential aspects of Karamzin's worldview. Karamzin can be seen as a political thinker, and his views on issues regarding the state and law only properly understood, if one does not overlook the critical importance he attached to the impact of ethical principles and moral imperatives on the state and on society in general. If Karamzin is in favor of absolute monarchy, of the unlimited power of the sovereign, it is not because he does not sufficiently value liberty or even because he is hostile to liberty in general.[2] In Article 13 of Catherine's Instruction she wrote, "Ultimately, what is the purpose of autocratic government (*samoderzhavnogo pravleniia*)? Not depriving people of their liberty, but rather leading the people to achieve the greatest good." Karamzin is convinced that absolute monarchy degenerates into tyranny much less often than other forms of government. In his opinion, history proves this. Over centuries, he says, Russia had only known two tyrants: Ivan IV and Paul I. In contrast, the attempt in France to abolish traditional monarchy and to go over to a republic had led directly to the triumph of tyrannical methods of government. In general, he comments:

> What else does the history of republics offer us? Can we perceive even one peaceful and happy island in the midst of this stormy sea? I am no less enthusiastic about the virtues of the great republicans—how short these brilliant periods of republican government are! How often has tyranny misused the name of freedom to clap its magnanimous friends in irons! Whose heart does not bleed when thinking of Miltiades in prison, Aristides, Themistocles in exile, Socrates and Phokion drinking hemlock, Cato taking his own life, Brutus who in his final moments no longer believed in virtue?[3]

Moreover, this is no coincidence. The legitimate sovereign is bound by moral imperatives to a particularly high degree and remains so if over the centuries these imperatives have taken on the form of deep-rooted traditions.[4]

For Karamzin, it is precisely these traditions and not the formal legal regulations or the official structures of the state that provide an effective guarantee that law, justice, and goodness prevail and its subjects are happy. If the sovereign rules virtuously according to these traditions, he does not just remain true to the ideal of virtue, the ideal of justice, but he also forces his successor to do the same. He writes:

> Our sovereign has at his disposal only one sure way of binding his successor and keeping him from abusing his power: he must rule virtuously! He should accustom his subjects to goodness! That will result in beneficial (*spasitel'nye*) customs, rules, and popular attitudes, which, better than any transitory arrangements, will make sure future rulers do not overstep the limits of power. And how would this happen? Through fear that introducing a contrary form of rule would provoke widespread hatred. From time to time, a tyrant may follow another and rule securely, but never after a wise ruler! (*Memorandum,* p. 499)

This explains the failure of Paul I:

> He wanted to be another Ivan IV, but Russia had already had Catherine, and Catherine's reign was the happiest for Russia's citizens. Paul I started to rule through general terror, to the utter astonishment of Russians. He knew no law but his own arbitrary power, regarded us not as subjects but as slaves, punished without the burden of guilt, without any justification. . . . He killed the noble spirit of the army, replacing it with a barrack room mentality (*dukh kapral'stva*). Every day he found new ways to intimidate people, while becoming increasingly afraid of himself; he thought he could build himself an impregnable fortress but only succeeded in building his own tomb. (Ibid., p. 496)

Karamzin is against the axiom coined by Speransky: "Place the law above the ruler." In his view, the sovereign can only be subject to the laws of God and conscience. The attempt to make the sovereign subject to the laws of the state would only "weaken the beneficial power of the tsar" and result in the monarchy turning into an aristocracy. Law is nothing if there is no power behind it. Thus, the Senate or the State Council would be given the role of preserving the inviolability of the laws to which the sovereign is subject. This would result in supreme power residing with these aristocratic bodies, or perhaps even worse, in dual power leading to a relentless struggle between this council and the sovereign. Karamzin is convinced that this would lead to legal uncertainty and the revival of despotic methods of government.

The correct path for Alexander's government, according to Karamzin, would be a return to Catherine's program and methods, which had cleansed the autocracy of the "contamination of despotism." The spirit of servitude had thus at least been eliminated from the highest social estates (ibid., p. 494). Returning to Catherine's system should by no means be carried out regardless. Karamzin is just as opposed to a violent lurch backward as to going forward violently. He is against reaction just as much as revolution. "The old system," he writes, "would now seem to us to be a dangerous innovation; we have become unaccustomed to it. . . . Means must be found that better meet today's needs" (ibid., p. 527). Karamzin develops these ideas in his 1811 memorandum. He considers a wholesale return to the system and methods of government of Catherine's reign to be impossible at this juncture. Yet he is still a resolute supporter of that regime's program of liberal absolutism, which is set out in the empress's Instruction and which he himself had expounded in line with the Instruction in 1802, in other words, at the beginning of Alexander's reign, in his "Eulogy" to Catherine.

There can be no doubt that the main point of the eulogy was not to praise Catherine, but to set out a government program for Alexander I. For our purposes, it matters little whether Catherine actually accomplished everything for which she was praised by Karamzin. What is important for us here is what Karamzin considered to be praiseworthy, that is, what program he recommended to the young emperor Alexander. However, it has to be said that Karamzin's testimony regarding Catherine is of great historical value, as Karamzin was anything but a courtier and, as a contemporary, knew much through firsthand experience.

In fact, every important liberal demand compatible with autocracy is found in this program.[5] Karamzin stresses above all "that in the person of the subject, Catherine respected the dignity of man, the moral being made for happiness in civil life" (*Historical Eulogy*, p. 29). In his view, fully in accordance with liberal principles, she put the emphasis on the human personality. He describes this as "the most important benefit, and quite new for Russia" (ibid., p. 29). Karamzin goes on to praise Catherine for her efforts to temper penal law, to make punishments more humane, and to ban torture. (He refers to Arts. 81–91 and 193–198 of the Instruction; ibid., pp. 44f.) He recalls that she allowed the so-called Secret Chancellery to sink into oblivion (ibid., pp. 30f). The chancellery had been set up by Tsar Alexei Mikhailovich and had served Peter the Great as an instrument during his reign of terror. It was officially abolished by Alexander I. Elsewhere Karamzin wrote of this chancellery: "I appreciate all the grandeur of Peter's great achievements and think, fortunate were our forebears who witnessed those deeds!—But I do not envy them their good fortune! It is much merrier to live at a time when the ground at the Preobrazhenskoe (the location of the Secret Chancellery) is not doused in blood but with water to cultivate vegetables and lettuce!"[6]

Karamzin also stresses the liberating effects of the 1785 charters, as well as the decree of February 19, 1786, which forbade citizens from calling themselves slaves (*Historical Eulogy*, p. 76). Karamzin welcomes the separation of judicial and administrative powers in the regulation of provincial administration (ibid., pp. 63f). Karamzin thought the proposal to give the Senate powers to scrutinize new legislation to ascertain whether it conformed to fundamental law, and to make representations to the monarch about it, contained in Articles 21, 23, and 24 of the Instruction, was very useful. Catherine was absolutely correct, Karamzin continues, when she pointed out that the fall of empires is primarily caused by "rulers thinking they should exercise their power more through changing the existing order than complying with it, and attaching more importance to their imagination than to laws" (ibid., p. 55).[7] Karamzin highlights the attention Catherine paid to developing trade in Russia and writes, "She gave trade all the means to flourish and expand; she gave it freedom" (ibid., p. 34). Thus, for example, she revoked all the privileges of the port of St. Petersburg.

In Karamzin's opinion, it would be very desirable, in line with Articles 295, 296, and 261, to grant peasants the right to own land. "In the empress's own words," writes Karamzin, "on the land, property rights provide the main motivation to be industrious" (ibid., p. 49). Thus, Karamzin is in favor of peasants becoming owners of land, but he is against the emancipation of the serfs. He argues against it most notably in the "Letter from a Country Dweller" in 1802[8] and in the "Memorandum on Ancient and Modern Russia" in 1811.

Karamzin expressed his views on the question of the emancipation of serfs most extensively in the first of these writings, which is manifestly autobiographical. Here Karamzin writes that, living at a great distance from the country because of service and travel and inspired by the spirit of philanthropic authors, as well as the hatred of any abuse of power, he decided to do something from afar for the benefit of his serfs. Although he did not grant them freedom, he left them all his land on payment of only a very modest rent [obrok] ("Letter," p. 240). He did not appoint a steward—stewards were often worse than the worst masters—and proposed that the peasants themselves should choose an elder to ensure that things were well managed. He gave the peasants assurance that he wanted to protect them from every kind of oppression.

When he returned to the village after a long absence, he found, contrary to all his expectations, extreme impoverishment everywhere. To obtain an explanation for this state of affairs, so inexplicable at first sight, he summoned some peasant elders so they could tell him what, in their opinion, had caused this poverty. They told him that his father had always lived on the land and supervised not only his own fields but also those of the peasants. By contrast, the freedom he had granted the peasants had turned into their ruin, that is, into the freedom to be idle and get drunk. The lazy peasants started to lease their allotments very cheaply to others. The vice of drunkenness started to spread. This vice had recently been on the increase in Russia in general. In many villages there were taverns, although to the credit of some of the gentry, one has to say that they did not permit "the building of temples to the rough Russian Bacchus" on their estates, despite the loss of the income that a tavern brought in (ibid., p. 242).

This news from the peasants moved the landowner to change everything again. Karamzin writes: "I reestablished the landowner's fields (*gospodskuiu pash-niu*) and became a hardworking farmer. I began to take an interest in every detail and provided the poor with everything they needed for cultivation. I declared war, albeit a bloodless one, on the lazy. I spent the whole day from sunrise to sunset in the fields with them. I went to great lengths to ensure they too worked just as hard on their own fields" (ibid., p. 243). Karamzin also says that he saw to the sanitation in the village. In this way, the peasants became prosperous with cereals, horses, and livestock and were grateful to him for this turn in their fortunes. He could speak with pride about it to the friends of agriculture, as well as the friends of mankind.

Foreign travelers, he adds, maintained that the peasants would not work very hard because the masters could always appropriate the fruits of their labor (ibid., p. 244). This was, however, merely a theoretical observation. What sort of master would take cereal, horses, and other belongings from their peasants? (ibid., p. 245). On the contrary, says Karamzin, the progress in agriculture and the recent prosperity of the peasants connected with it were due to the efforts of landowners. Good masters, those who really cared for their peasants, in particular for their education (i.e., acting according to the decree on the establishment of village schools), were a prerequisite for peasant prosperity. Being aware of this must be a source of the greatest satisfaction for masters. "How pleasing," he goes on to say, "is the knowledge that I live for the real benefit of five hundred people whom fate has entrusted to me" (ibid., p. 251). Moreover, Karamzin concludes: "The most important right of the Russian gentry (*dvorianin*) is to be a landowner (*pome-shchik*); his main duty is to be a good landowner. Whoever fulfills this duty, serves his fatherland as a true son, serves the monarch as a true subject, for Alexander wishes farming people to prosper" (ibid., pp. 251f).

If Karamzin opposed emancipation, then he was opposed, to an even greater extent, to the gentry being relieved of their many duties as landowners. This is also confirmed by his comments on this question in his *Memorandum on Ancient and Modern Russia*. Here Karamzin articulates his conviction that the condition of emancipated peasants would be worse than that of the serfs because upon emancipation the landowner's duty of care toward the poor among his peasants would disappear.[9] In addition, all emancipated peasants would become landless tenants (the land without doubt being the property of the landowner) to whom the master had no moral duties. He was therefore permitted to consider them as an object of exploitation. In place of the landowner, responsible for administration in the country, there would be a coarse, uneducated, and generally corrupt *ispravnik* (district police chief). Finally, the paternalistic court of the often cultured and tolerant lord would be replaced by a court of equally uneducated and corrupt provincial magistrates. Overall, removing the gentry's duties would entail the bureaucratization of the entire local administration.[10] This, however, would not just disadvantage the landowners and the peasants but also represent a great danger to the state itself. Karamzin writes: "By removing their (the landowners') administrative powers, he (the tsar) would, like Atlas, lift Russia on his shoulders. . . . Would he be able to support it? Letting it fall would be terrible" (*Memorandum*, p. 513). Besides, emancipation would conflict with national tradition: "I do not know whether Gudonov did the right thing when he deprived the peasants of their freedom. (We do not know the circumstances at the time), but I do know that it is not feasible to give it back to them. At that time, they behaved like free men; now they are servile" (ibid., p. 513).

From a historical perspective, Karamzin's advice cannot just be dismissed out of hand. In fact, neither the peasants' education nor their way of life prepared them for an existence as free, independent citizens from either an economic or an administrative perspective. As much as they were often good, loyal, and religious, of necessity they had to exhibit features in their psychological makeup, engrained in them through decades, or rather centuries, of living as serfs.

In particular, the emancipated peasant would have had no right to own land, and even his moveable possessions did not amount to much. The process by which a human being is refined by the things he owns, which Hauriou calls *dégrossissement*, had thus not yet begun for the peasants.

When Karamzin therefore, following Catherine, recommended that the peasants should be allowed, in particular, to acquire property, he certainly pointed the way for the peasants to become free men and independent subjects in economic life not just in name but also in reality.[11] Nevertheless, Karamzin was convinced that, for the moment, it was not possible to abandon the gentry's paternalism vis-à-vis the peasants. However, this form of tutelage over peasants, who would have owned land and indeed become proprietors, would of course have taken on a different character from having landless serfs at one's disposal, itself a form of property. It would inevitably have become a form of official supervision. This would have led to a combination of the better parts of the old and new systems, as Karamzin had proposed. On the one hand, what would have been retained from serfdom, for the time being, was the official supervision of the peasants and the administration on behalf of the state, undertaken by persons who were largely independent, although subject to state inspection. On the other hand, it would have led to spontaneous, progressive growth in peasant ownership, that is, to the gradual creation of the conditions required to turn the peasants into free citizens in the context of a free civil society. It is therefore incorrect to believe that Karamzin was simply in favor of retaining serfdom in perpetuity or that he regarded serfdom as something positive.

Karamzin's traditionalism and the ideas related to it, which have so much in common with Savigny's, have been regarded as a pretext for not putting him in the liberal camp. In my view, on the contrary, Karamzin's traditionalist ideas contributed to the progress of liberalism in Russia. Karamzin's significance in this regard lies in the fact, as mentioned above, that he called on the absolutist monarchy to adopt and go on to implement the liberal program, at least insofar as it envisaged civil liberty and not political freedom. He championed the view, and contributed considerably to its dissemination, that putting liberal principles into practice did not require a break with historical tradition, with the traditional forms of government created by Russia's historical development. In so doing, he showed how the highest historical power—the monarch—could cooperate with the advocates of liberalism, indeed with critically minded opposition circles, in order to fashion and consolidate a liberal system in Russia. In short, he pointed to the only way at the time for liberal ideas to be realized.

The essence of true liberalism—as I have tried to show in my introduction—includes the conservation of what is in place, especially existing rights, which only permits an evolutionary reform of the existing order in order to promote greater freedom, greater tolerance, and more genuine compassion. Rationalistic planning, abstract constructions, and logical deduction from theoretical principles conflict with the essence of liberalism. To champion the implementation of liberal reforms in the context of the existing order, to endeavor to apply liberal principles in the framework of the state as determined by history, therefore means to take a realistic path, in particular one that is compatible with the essential principles of liberalism. In Karamzin's case, it would be more correct to say that he pointed the way.

Alternatively, attempts might be made to impose liberalism as a rationalistic program, as a series of principles derived from a theoretical concept. In this field of rationalistic planning, liberalism would not be able to compete with socialist doctrines, to which such planning is central. This was shown—and I would like to highlight this in anticipation—at the end of the nineteenth century when wide circles of liberal supporters broke with historical traditionalism and began to profess political radicalism. They adopted a program to implement individual liberal demands without taking into account the given historical context where they would be put into practice or the natural and practical sequence required for their implementation, merely because these demands were considered theoretically correct. At the same time, they demanded immediate and complete implementation. It soon became apparent that this political radicalism was not in a position to compete with socialist and revolutionary doctrines and in fact was forced to adopt demands in its program that were contrary to the principle of private property in order more or less to hold its own in its rivalry with revolutionary doctrines.

This was actually where the real trouble lay with Alexander III's antiliberal measures. The retreat from the implementation of the liberal agenda that they represented was not that significant. If these laws had been repealed quickly, or indeed simply not been brought into force or just applied with a light touch (the Italian expression "the law has been passed; a way round it will also be found" comes to mind),[12] the damage that the implementation of these provisions was bound to cause could easily have been avoided. The real reason these laws were detrimental was that they destroyed the faith of many liberal supporters in the possibility of working with the monarchy and the imperial government in implementing liberal reforms. This contributed significantly to the victory of radicalism over genuine, that is, conservative, liberalism.

Karamzin set out his political ideals once more in the poem "Osvobozhdenie Evropy" [The Liberation of Europe], written in 1814[13] and prefaced by Sallust's saying "Men's achievements in agriculture, navigation, and construction all depend on intellectual excellence."[14] Karamzin's rejection of all nationalism and imperialism in the relations between nations, and all tyranny in internal affairs, is here very clearly stated. His ideal of traditionalism is given a precise and subtle expression. All this seems to complement in such a remarkable fashion what has gone before that I believe it is worthwhile to set out the main ideas contained in this poem.

Here Karamzin urges the peoples of Europe to be virtuous, as their rulers would not then violate the sacred laws. The one evil would be conjured up by the other. As long as the people remained virtuous, the rulers could not become evil. God, who was above the rulers, would not allow it ("Liberation," pp. 259f). If, on the other hand, the people succumbed to the temptation of bogus freedom, and rose up against their legitimate rulers and against the commandments of faith, punishment would be unavoidable. This had once again been shown by the example of the French, who received their retribution in the form of first anarchy and then tyranny (ibid., p. 259).

The tyrant, driven by boundless ambition and the desire to rule the world, had oppressed not just his own people but also other nations. In so doing, he had violated God's commandments and consequently the limits imposed on rulers by these commandments. No ruler on earth is appointed to rule the world. "Rulers," exclaims Karamzin, "let God rule the whole world!"[15] Rulers must render unto God what they have been entrusted with and honor him through the "peaceful happiness of the people" and not through territorial conquest, which cannot be achieved without shedding the blood of the weak (ibid., p. 258). Karamzin, however, is against not just the oppression of weaker neighbors but also the oppression of the weak within the nation. Generally, Karamzin is moved to deep outrage by the oppression of the weak, wherever he encounters it. For example, in 1788 he was pained by the situation of the Jews without rights in the Frankfurt ghetto and a year later by the persecution of aristocrats by the revolutionary mob in France.[16] At the height of the Terror in 1793, he writes to his friend the poet Dmitriev: "Dear friend, I am living in the country with nice people, with books, with nature, but often . . . the terrible events in Europe move my whole soul. . . . Thinking about the destruction of cities, the loss of people, oppresses my heart. Call me a Don Quixote if you wish, but this famous knight could not have loved his Dulcinea as passionately as I love humanity."[17]

Of course, the ruler had to bear arms, the poem continues, in order to protect what God has entrusted to him from internal and external enemies ("Liberation," p. 259). He must never desire, however, to rule over foreign territory, "for the ruler does not live for war," but "he must preserve peace" (ibid., p. 258). "Of course, among primitive peoples, the warrior is ranked highest. Nevertheless, the age of reason is a civic age (*grazhdanskii vek*)" (ibid., p. 259). In this age, the first duties of the ruler are passing laws, promoting justice, and spreading education: "There will be no Napoleon, if you love the still light of knowledge" (ibid., p. 259). Indeed, after the fall of Napoleon—so Karamzin believes—there would never be another who would dare, in the footsteps of the Tyrant of Gaul, to achieve immortality by violence and deceit through the "hell of joyous victories" (ibid., p. 258). Should one such emerge, he would be defeated even more quickly than Napoleon, who ruled not with the scepter but with the sword, like a crowned executioner. Under the rule of his triumphant violence, hearts and feelings became coarsened (ibid., p. 256), although he was defeated in the struggle against the altars, freedom, and true rulers (ibid., p. 262). The second Napoleon would fall even faster, as the nations would know what they were dealing with. It was not for nothing that people now welcomed the return of peace (*tishina*) after many years of exile, bringing with it the revival of science and commerce (ibid., p. 257). It was only possible for this peaceful existence to flourish if the existing order, equally liberal and conservative, were retained. Here Karamzin returns to his favorite idea: "In government, novelty is dangerous; think how difficult it is to create a society that takes hundreds of years to establish. Destruction is much easier. So do not invent some new calamity in the hunt for perfection, which is impossible in this world!" (ibid., p. 260).

It is therefore not surprising that Karamzin was opposed to the plans of the members of the various secret societies that proliferated in Russia at the time to bring down the existing order and replace it with a new rationally constructed order based on logically deduced progressive principles. Karamzin was quite consistent in being hostile to the revolt organized by these societies—the Decembrist revolt. In his letter to Dmitriev containing an account of those days, he calls it "the senseless tragedy of our insane liberalists."[18] He urged Nicholas I (he was in the palace at the time) to put the revolt down with guns. He wrote to Dmitriev: "I, a peaceful historiographer, longed for the sound of cannon, as I was convinced that there was no other way of dealing with this revolt. Neither raising the cross nor the Metropolitan making an appearance had any effect."[19]

Karamzin himself calls the rebels liberals (*liberalists*); by contrast, no one in Russia at the time took him for a liberal. This should not mislead us. Nevertheless, we must consider Karamzin as a precursor of liberalism in Russia (in the true sense of the word, as defined in our introduction). On the other hand, we must deny the Decembrists a positive role in the development of Russia toward liberalism. Incidentally, Karamzin was already regarded abroad as a liberal. For example, Karamzin reported to Dmitriev that the journal *Constitutionel* (no. 13, October 1820) praised his liberalism in discussions of his "History of the Russian State." He writes, "They even praise my liberal outlook (*liberal'nost'*) in contrast to our liberalists."[20]

Having just brought up the subject of the Decembrists, in my view, this milieu and the revolt it spawned deserve detailed examination. There has not been a shortage of research on this topic, but a fresh study would not be superfluous. As far as the history of liberalism in Russia is concerned, however, they do not merit much attention, for the following reasons: (A) Although there were genuine liberals among the Decembrists, there were even more supporters of political radicalism, even representatives of socialist thinking. That all these different elements came together in the revolt is surely just a matter of historical chance. The extremists, not the liberals, undoubtedly took the lead in planning and carrying out the revolt, as has often been the case in Russia, where there is a tendency to see extremists as the "real thing." In this respect the words of one of the Decembrists, A. A. Bestuzhev, are revealing: "As far as I was concerned, I described myself as an ultraliberal, *in order to gain the trust of my comrades,* but inwardly I was closer to the monarchy and a moderate aristocracy."[21]

These words clearly show that the moderate elements felt compelled to fall into line with the extremists and to air views that were more radical than their own personal convictions. (B) Although liberal ideas and opinions were represented among the Decembrists, the revolt nevertheless had an extremely negative, indeed fateful significance for the development of liberalism in Russia. Certainly, in this respect it is only comparable to the murder of Alexander II. In the first place, the revolt had a devastating effect on the young Nicholas. It was undoubtedly a shock from which he never completely recovered and had an impact that determined the antiliberal character of the whole of his long reign—especially as the revolt, formally speaking, took place under the banner of liberalism.[22] Second, this revolt, as a violent revolutionary act, contributed to establishing a revolutionary tradition in Russia and not a liberal one. It must be regarded, therefore, as the starting point of the revolutionary movement, which flared up from time to time during the nineteenth century. This always aroused and reinforced the reactionary spirit in Russian ruling circles, thus hindering Russia's progress toward liberalism. Ultimately, through its victory all traces of liberalism were swept away, culminating in the triumph of socialist totalitarianism. (C) The Decembrist revolt led to the demise of circles where liberal ideas were studied and discussed. With them, the ground disappeared on which liberal ideology might have at least taken root and developed.

Even before December 14, 1825, however, insofar as the secret societies were not interested in formulating liberal demands or spelling out a liberal program, but rather dedicated themselves to making plans for a revolutionary uprising, they impeded rather than advanced Russia's progress toward liberalism. There can be no doubt that the revolutionary outlook of these societies was a significant factor in pushing Alexander I to give way to pressure from antiliberal circles and in fact to rely on their support. Fateev, in an interesting work on the subject of Alexander I, cites a speech given by the tsar to the Warsaw House of Representatives, in which he ascribed the cause of the revolutionary upheavals that had broken out in a number of countries to the fact that the sacred principles of legality and freedom were often confused with subversive doctrines.[23] Alexander I had always viewed revolutionary attitudes and action as an impediment to achieving liberal reforms. For him, revolution was the negation, not the realization, of liberal principles. It is incidentally self-evident that Alexander I, as head of state, would have considered it his duty to oppose those who preferred revolutionary theory and plans for an uprising and who chose the road of violence rather than the road of reform. It is thus quite understandable that for Alexander, turning to antirevolutionary elements became a necessity for the defense of the principles of genuine liberty, of liberty in the context of the legal order.

Sadly, it was not just on the left but on the right too that it proved impossible to distinguish between the principles of legality and freedom on the one hand and subversive ideas on the other. As long as the revolutionary actions of the left compelled Alexander I to rely on the support of right-wing circles, he was prevented from implementing liberal reforms, as these circles rejected not just revolutionary ideas but liberal reforms as well.

Alexander was thus forced to abandon the path of liberal reform.[24] Inwardly, however, he remained a supporter of liberal ideas to the last. One of the most knowledgeable experts on Russian history, Vernadsky, has contested the view that the last years of Alexander's reign saw the triumph of reaction and that Alexander was won over to a reactionary position.[25] Fateev shares this view. Closing down the Bible Society and the Freemasons' lodges and tightening censorship were, in Fateev's opinion, all measures that Alexander had to take to shore up his authority, threatened as it was from all sides. Despite all this, Fateev stresses, Alexander I never renounced his liberal plans.

There is in fact evidence that Alexander I wanted to continue on the path of liberal reform right up to the end of his life. In the first session of the new Polish Sejm, from March 15 through March 25, 1818, Alexander said in a speech spoken in French: "The system in place in your country has allowed the immediate establishment of what I have granted you, by putting into practice the principles of these liberal institutions about which I have never ceased to care and whose influence I hope, with God's help, to extend to all the countries that providence has placed in my care."[26]

Just a few weeks before his death, on August 28, 1825, Alexander I told Karamzin that it was his firm intention to proclaim a "Basic Law"—that is, a constitution—in Russia.[27] Indeed, the fact that Novosil'tsev drafted a constitution (Gosud. Ustavnaia Gramota) on his orders in the years 1818–20 is further proof that Alexander retained his liberal ideas.[28] It is possible, therefore, to agree with the following from Fateev: "All of which demonstrates that this period of Alexander's reign too cannot be called reactionary. This period could only be called reactionary if one compared it with the promises Alexander made at the time of his accession."[29]

Yet which statesman or period has ever really fulfilled all their hopes and promises? It has to be said in Alexander's defense that, as stated above, he was essentially unable to fulfill them because those who were meant to support him in implementing liberal reform succumbed to the dream of a revolutionary up-heaval. In the political circles of Russia at the time, liberalism turned into radical-ism and in so doing forsook the path of the historically possible, its only chance of success. This is the first occasion on which radicalism triumphed over liberal-ism, a victory we shall encounter again later, a victory that, in my opinion, was calamitous for Russia's progress toward liberalism and ultimately prevented lib-eralism from taking hold in Russia. One can therefore say that the Decembrists, indeed even before that the secret societies, set in motion Russia's fateful swings between reaction and revolution. After that point the path of Russian liberalism between these two elemental forces became very narrow.

Under Nicholas I, therefore, liberalism continued to be advocated by those who supported it under Alexander I—Speransky and Mordvinov. Yet during the trial of the Decembrists, these two men did not sit among the accused, but with the judges. Mordvinov continued his work on the State Council; Speransky de-voted himself to the codification of the law. Finance Minister Kankrin must also be included in the ranks of influential advocates of liberalism at the time, albeit of a purely economic variety.

The question of whether one can speak of liberalism during the reign of Nicholas I will be addressed in a later chapter. In the meantime, something must be said about the history of the codification of the law under Alexander I and Nicholas I, and essentially therefore about Speransky's work on codification.

Chapter 5

The Codification of the Law

Speransky's first attempts at codification—
Karamzin's criticism of Speransky's plans for
codification—Karamzin's and Savigny's ideas—
Continuation of the work of codification under
Alexander I—Codification under Nicholas I

Speransky, as mentioned in the previous chapter, had already discussed the problem of codifying Russian law in his early writings. Moreover, he intended not only systematizing the old laws but also updating and improving existing law. In his opinion, it was possible to start adopting Western law or at least to take advantage of the achievements in the field of jurisprudence in Western countries. Karamzin too had already expressed a view on the problem of codification in 1802: "What a crowning achievement it would be for Alexander's reign, if his sovereign will (*monarshaia*) were fulfilled, if we were to have a complete, systematic collection of clearly and wisely drafted civil laws."[1] And further: "All one needs for that is a philosophical method for categorizing the subject matter (*predmetov*), and then we shall envy neither Frederick the Great's recently improved codex nor the clever draft of the French one and shall pity the English, whose courts constantly lose themselves in a labyrinth of contradictory writs."[2]

It was quite natural, incidentally, for political writers of the time to take a position on the question of codification. The codification, or at any rate the systematization of law, had been on the agenda since Peter the Great. During the whole of the eighteenth century a number of commissions, up to nine in total, had worked on producing a new *ulozhenie* (law code).

In the early years of Alexander's reign, Senator Count Zavadovsky had already been given the task of presenting a report to sum up what had been achieved before regarding civil legislation and to draw up a plan to continue this work. The whole matter, however, was soon passed on to the Ministry of Justice. A special commission—the Commission on Laws—was set up within the Ministry of Justice under the direction of the deputy minister of justice, Novosil'tsev. Baron Rosenkampf, a Balt who had studied for a time at the University of Leipzig, was appointed as the secretary and senior civil servant of this commission. Korf writes: "One can't take away from Rosenkampf that he had a sharp intellect or an extensive theoretical knowledge. However, his knowledge of Russian was limited and his knowledge of Russia even more so."[3] It is not surprising, therefore, that the commission achieved nothing under his direction.[4]

On August 8, 1808, Speransky was appointed to the council of the commission. Up to then, this council had only consisted of the minister Lopukhin and the deputy minister Novosil'tsev. Speransky, however, only started to restructure the commission after his return from Erfurt, where he had accompanied Alexander and had an opportunity to talk with Napoleon. The commission was divided into a number of departments. Rosenkampf remained on the commission as head of the section entrusted with the completion of the civil code. However, all the work done by his department was nearly always ruthlessly revised by Speransky. A special committee or council of high dignitaries was set up to whom the drafts of the commission were presented. As Speransky himself observed, the point of this council was to familiarize the public with the work of the commission and thus increase trust in its work. After the establishment of the State Council in 1810, the Commission on Laws was incorporated into it. Consequently, the above-mentioned special committee was discontinued. Its place was now taken by the State Council's Department for Laws. Speransky was appointed director of the commission, which considerably strengthened his position.

The State Council, which was opened on January 1, 1810, completed the scrutiny of the first two parts of the Civil Code (laws regarding persons, and property law) in forty-three sessions from January 18 to December 14 of the same year, with the tsar acting as chairman and Speransky as director of the commission presenting the drafts. These parts were then printed so that they could be revised a second time. Soon after that, Speransky was disgraced and exiled, first to Nizhni-Novgorod and then to Perm. Alexander, under pressure from influential circles, felt he had to sacrifice Speransky. Speransky's fall cannot be discussed here in detail, nor can the criticism that his reform plans attracted from various quarters. We have to focus on the role that he played in the history of the codification of Russian law, and thus the criticism of his draft statute book is of interest. The arguments aimed at this draft were put forward primarily by Karamzin in his paper *Memorandum on Ancient and Modern Russia,* which has already been cited a number of times above. These arguments are very instructive. This is the voice of Historicism,[5] which reacted against the mentality of the eighteenth century—a mentality from which Speransky, in part at least, could not free himself during his long life, although his thinking was much wider than people usually assume, bringing together various shades and tendencies. Karamzin writes:

> The manifesto already stated that the first part of the law code was ready and that the remainder would be ready without delay. In fact, two volumes have been published under the title of the *Draft Ulozhenie*. However, what do we find? Nothing less than a translation of the Napoleonic Code! What a surprise for the Russians! What a travesty! Thank God that we have not yet come under the iron scepter of this conqueror; we have not yet become a Westphalia, or a Kingdom of Italy, or a Duchy of Warsaw, where, to the dismay of the people, the translated Napoleonic Code counts as the civil code. Has Russia existed for about one thousand years as a powerful state, and have we been working for one hundred years on a law code just to bow our grayed heads before a book written in Paris by six or seven ex-lawyers and ex-Jacobins? Peter the Great loved everything foreign, but he did not give the order, for example, to adopt Swedish laws and to pass them off as Russian.[6] In fact, he knew that the laws of a people must stem from their own ideas, customs, traditions, and the particular circumstances of that country. We could have had nine *ulozhenie* (law codes) if all one had to do was to translate.[7] (Karamzin, *Memorandum,* p. 523)

Here Karamzin is expressing an idea that essentially corresponds to the following idea from Savigny: "This view, in summary, means that all law . . . is created by custom and traditional beliefs and subsequently through jurisprudence" (*Vocation of Our Times,* pp. 13f). In general, one can find several places in Karamzin's paper corresponding to statements in Savigny's book. This is particularly interesting, as the direct influence of the one work on the other must be ruled out. Savigny's book appeared in 1814 and thus three years after Karamzin's paper. Savigny could not have been aware of Karamzin's paper, as it was only intended for Alexander and was only known at the time (and for a long time afterward) by quite a small number of people besides the emperor. I will attempt here to set out the most important passages where they are consistent. It would be an interesting piece of research to ascertain the sources that are common to these two works. One of these sources was Bacon, the other Montesquieu. Savigny refers directly to Bacon, and although Bacon is not mentioned in Karamzin's paper, one cannot mistake his influence. Both Savigny and Karamzin refer to the same chapter of Montesquieu's *De l'esprit des lois.* I suspect that one could establish other such sources.

Furthermore, Karamzin points out that just from a political and patriotic point of view, adopting the Napoleonic Code was unacceptable. He writes:

> Leaving all else to one side, one has to ask whether now is the time to offer Russia French laws, even if they could easily be applied in the circumstances of our society. All of us who love Russia, its reputation, its well-

being, and the tsar, and who are so filled with hatred for this people stained with the blood of Europe and covered in the dust of so many shattered countries, how can we lay the Napoleonic Code on the altar of the fatherland, if the name alone makes our hearts tremble? (*Memorandum*, p. 524)

Savigny's words sound very similar: "The law code served him (Napoleon) as a means to bind nations, which is why it would have been damaging and repulsive for us, even if it had any intrinsic value, which it does not. We have been spared this humiliation" (*Vocation of Our Times*, pp. 57f).

For Karamzin, however, the political arguments are not decisive. This can be gathered from the fact that he also rejected the work of Speransky's predecessor, Rosenkampf, because the latter had a translation made of the Prussian statute book and certainly considered copying a number of laws from Frederick the Great's Law Code in the new *ulozhenie*. Karamzin writes, "Russia is not Prussia. What purpose can be served by translating the Law Code of Frederick the Great?" (*Memorandum*, p. 522). "It is certainly useful to know this statute book, but it is no less useful to know the Justinian or the Danish law codes. These should not be seen as the model for our own legislation, but rather as the subject for general reflection" (ibid., p. 522). Karamzin mentions a further volume containing various preliminary studies and comments: "We look at this and rub our eyes. . . . A mass of learned words and phrases taken from books! Not a single idea drawn from an examination of the particular character of Russian civil society! Our good compatriots will think that the authors were not on Russian soil but on the moon, and they will wish that these theoreticians would either come back down to earth or give up drawing up laws for us" (ibid., pp. 522f).

In drawing up the new law code, says Karamzin, one must start by examining the real conditions in Russia, by examining the "unique civil society of Russia." Anyway, he adds, adopting foreign laws would be misplaced, because "an old nation does not need new laws" (ibid., p. 524). The job of the commission must be to put Russian laws systematically in order (ibid., p. 524).

Improving or repealing existing laws would be permitted, if shortcomings or contradictions became apparent when they were applied in practice in the courts (ibid., p. 525). Only then could laws, which had been systematically ordered, be subject to "general criticism" as to "whether they were the best for us in the current situation of Russian civil society." "That would show the necessity," Karamzin continues, "of improving some laws, especially some of the horrible, barbaric parts of the criminal law. They have fallen out of use long ago; why do they survive as a disgrace to our legislation?" (ibid., p. 525).

Putting laws into systematic order, Karamzin writes, should not be restricted to a case-by-case description, but should also lead to the formulation of general rules, based on which other possible cases, that is, those that had not been foreseen in the statute book, could be decided. Without such general norms, laws would not be complete, as only the former could ensure the highest degree of completeness. Neither should these general principles be drawn from for-eign statute books, as Russian law, just like Roman law, had its own principles. Karamzin writes, "If you establish these, you will give us a system of law" (ibid., p. 525). Reading Karamzin's words here, it is hard not to recall some parts of Savi-gny's *Beruf*. For example:

> Considering the subject matter, the hardest and most important task is to make the statute book as comprehensive as possible, and this is just a mat-ter of understanding this task properly, which everyone agrees is necessary. As it has been decided to make the statute book the only legal source book, it is also supposed to contain in advance the decision for each potential case. People have often thought like this, as if it were possible and desirable to gain a comprehensive knowledge of all individual cases as such through experience and then to decide each one by referring to the corresponding place in the statute book. Anyone who has only observed legal cases at-tentively will easily understand that such an effort has to be in vain, because there is virtually no limit to the number of variations in real-life cases. Furthermore, the latest statute books have given up any attempt to cover the field exhaustively, without at the same time putting anything in its place. There is, however, another way of being exhaustive. . . . Each part of our law has elements that determine the rest: we could call these the guiding principles. (Savigny, *Vocation of Our Times*, pp. 21f)

At another point Savigny highlights the advantage enjoyed by Roman jurists, which consisted in "having for each principle an example of its application in a particular case, and for each case . . . at the same time a principle that determined it" (ibid., pp. 30f).

Even if the basic principles and subject matter for the Russian statute book had to be taken from Russian law, according to Karamzin, it was permissible to copy existing examples from other countries when arranging the material and grouping legal provisions together. Karamzin, however, does not recommend the Napoleonic Code or the code of Frederick the Great for this purpose, but rather the Justinian code (*Memorandum*, p. 525), especially because Tsar Alexei Mikhailovich's law code had largely already followed the subject categorization of this law code.

When Karamzin talks about the codification of law, he is thinking about pro-ducing a statute book for Greater Russia alone. He is strongly opposed to forcing the new statute book on other nations:

> Let me add another thought to what I have already said about Russian law. Our state comprises several nations, each of which has its own particular civil law (*grazhdanskie ustavy*), such as, for example, Latvia, Finland, Poland, even Little Russia. So is it really necessary to introduce a unified system of law? Certainly it is, but only on condition that this change does not entail

any real lasting harm for these regions. Otherwise, definitely not. The best way would be to bring about this change gradually through a series of gentle preparatory steps. . . . First, however, there should be a thorough investigation as to why, for example, Latvia and Finland have this or that law, whether the conditions that produced it still exist, . . . whether the new law would not ruin their customs, whether the bonds between the different classes of the country concerned would not be weakened.

Karamzin concludes with a quotation from Montesquieu—"Is it so important for all citizens to follow the same laws, if they follow them faithfully?"—and adds yet another thought: "Beware of following the foolish advice of people who believe that it is enough to give an order and everything will fall into place" (ibid., p. 526). On this point too Karamzin's ideas are remarkably close to those of Savigny, who developed them with regard to the differences in the laws of the German states (*Vocation of Our Times,* pp. 41f). Savigny is critical of the idea that national unity requires the same law for the entire nation. He points out that it is an error "to believe that the universal would be revitalized by the obliteration of all local differences." On the contrary, "if a special self-confidence could be produced in each social estate, in each town, indeed in each village, then national life would be invigorated by this heightened and diversified local life" (ibid., p. 42). The assertion too that the administration of justice itself and legal business would be hampered by these differences is not borne out, according to Savigny, by any experience. Even if this were the case, the uniformity of law could still not be recommended. Savigny writes: "Harm would result from facile and arbitrary modifications to civil law, and even if they made things easier and simpler, this gain could not outweigh these political disadvantages" (ibid., p. 43). He says, however, that the demand to introduce the same law for all the German states was not based in the end on reasons of national unity or on the requirements of the administration of justice. The real reason for this demand—according to Savigny—"consists in the incredible power that the mere idea of uniformity in all areas has exercised for so long in Europe; a power about whose abuse Montesquieu already gave a warning." Savigny, like Karamzin, is referring here to chapter 18 of book 29 of *De l'esprit des lois,* with the title "Des idées d'uniformité" [Ideas of Uniformity]. Here is the original French of the words quoted by Karamzin: "Lorsque les citoyens suivent les lois, qu'importe qu'ils suivent la même?" [When citizens obey the law, does it matter if they obey the same one?]

Karamzin is skeptical as to whether there were people in Russia capable of writing such a "pragmatic law code," that is, of producing a systematic statute book, in which amendments to existing laws could be made, based on the experience gained from judicial practice and even in part in accordance with the humanitarian requirements and principles of justice. He therefore recommends "moderating these demands" and, instead of publishing a pragmatic law code, restricting oneself to issuing an ordered and complete collection (*svodnuiu knigu*) of Russian laws. Karamzin is certainly indebted to Bacon (if not exclusively) in his conviction that producing a systematic law code was an extremely complicated and difficult undertaking, which demanded the utmost care. Bacon wrote, "Atque opus ejusmodi opus heroicum esto,"[8] and warned, "Ut hujusmodi legum instauratio illis temporibus suscipiatur, quae antiquioribus, quorum acta et opera retractant, litteris et rerum cognitione praestiterint."[9] This view is also Savigny's starting point in his book (he refers directly to Bacon; see ibid., pp. 20f), and he concludes that the codification of law is essentially a matter of "not changing but retaining existing law, which must be correctly understood and rigorously expounded." I think it is highly likely that Bacon was at least one of the sources from which Savigny drew the idea that existing law was superior to newly enacted law. Law should not be amended unless there is a genuine need to do so and without full consideration of all aspects. This is an idea that Karamzin expresses in his own words, already cited above: "An old nation does not need new laws" (Karamzin, *Memorandum*, p. 524).

Let us now return to how the codification progressed. The Great Patriotic War broke out just a few months after Speransky's fall, and yet, notwithstanding the war and Speransky's removal, the work on codification was not halted. During 1812, a draft of the third part of the Civil Code, which had essentially been prepared by Speransky himself, was revised by the State Council. The Commission on Laws was once again restructured in the course of the same year. The office of director, which had become vacant after Speransky's exile, was abolished, and a three-man council was appointed to lead the commission, which once more came under the Ministry of Justice. The new council asked the ministry whether the draft Civil Code should stay as it was after the commission had received the revised version back from the State Council, or whether it should again be redrafted. The council opted for the latter and at the same time again raised the question as to which method should be chosen for the new draft, that is, whether it should follow the path of adopting foreign laws or keep firmly to existing Russian law, restricting itself to plugging the most important gaps and correcting the most obvious shortcomings. In its request for clarification, the council emphasized that laws had become enshrined over time and through their long survival:

> Civil law directly concerns social relationships that have been developed
> in the course of hundreds of years, and one cannot assume, therefore, that
> these can be transformed by issuing a new statute book without throwing
> the existing order into confusion. We are mistaken if we believe that by
> amending the printed word of the Civil Code, existing law will change just
> as easily and quickly and that the laws of another country will lead to the
> same effects here, as where people are used to them. It is not just people
> but time itself that determines the principles of legislation. . . . Experienced
> people can certainly produce a well-written statute book in a couple of years,
> but if they substitute foreign principles for those that are really accepted,

then this statute book will be nothing more than a systematic exposition of law that does not exist.[10]

These observations, however, had no real influence on the working methods of the commission, where Rosenkampf once again played the leading role. The commission continued working on further drafts, extensively making use of foreign models. The draft of a new Criminal Law Code was published in 1813, the Commercial Law Code in 1814, and later the first part of the Code of Civil Procedure. None of these drafts, however, was finally ratified.

After returning from exile, or, more accurately, from his post as governor general of Siberia, Speransky was appointed to the State Council in 1821 and entrusted again with the task of leading the Commission on Laws, without, however, holding any office in the commission. Speransky suggested to the tsar the idea of putting the Civil Code once again (for the third time) to the State Council.[11] This third revision again took up thirty-eight sessions of the State Council. This time, Speransky himself emerged as the chief critic of the draft. In the end, the State Council decided to amend 721 articles.

Speransky, who in Korf's view "was aware of the weakness of the whole undertaking"[12] (thus probably including the parts that he himself had also prepared), used this opportunity to convince Alexander it would be better to begin the whole project again and postpone the revision until a new Code of Civil Procedure had been drafted. After that nothing much happened in the field of law codification up to the death of Alexander I. In March 1823, the draft of the Commercial Law Code was put to the State Council at the suggestion of the minister of finance. The State Council was not at all satisfied with this draft, which had been prepared under the leadership of Rosenkampf in 1814, and sent it back to the commission. On August 18, 1824, the draft of the Criminal Law Code was put to the State Council, but this was not ratified either.[13]

The question as to why Speransky did not insist on the final revision and ratification of the Law Code, but rather grasped the first pretext to bury the draft, certainly merits closer examination. Is it a sign that he fundamentally changed his attitude to the question of the codification of the law, indeed his views on the theory of law in general, over the years? This can certainly not be ruled out. As I pointed out in chapter 3, one should not overstate Speransky's radicalism before 1812. Conservative ideas increasingly influenced him between 1812 and 1821, and a certain conservative outlook took root in his thinking. We know that Speransky had read Hume and Stuart in his youth and studied Bentham and Adam Smith, who were regarded at the time as very modern, but surely none of these thinkers, not even Bentham, could be regarded as radical. Then he spent a lot of time studying French legal literature, not so much the representatives of the school of natural law, but Tronchet and related authors, who had left behind their enthusiasm for rationalism and based their work of codification extensively on old French law. It remains doubtful whether Speransky was influenced later by the German historical school. Speransky only learned German at the age of fifty, and Korku-nov, the Russian constitutional law expert, is of the opinion that the ideas of the historical school remained foreign to Speransky, although he had read Savigny. Korkunov maintains that Speransky did not really understand Savigny's *Beruf.*[14] It is, however, difficult to come to a judgment on this. Speransky certainly notes with satisfaction that Savigny had to acknowledge in his "System of Contempo-rary Roman Law" that in countries where a codification had been undertaken, jurisprudence had made good progress. This, however, is not sufficient proof that he had not absorbed any of the ideas of the historical school. Korf also notes that, while in Irkurtsk, Speransky read Klopstock, Schlegel, and Müller, most probably Adam Müller, one of the most important conservative figures.[15]

Speransky often met Karamzin after his return from Siberia, and they even visited each other.[16] It can be assumed that the intellectual world of this man, who was so full of ideas, did not fail to exert an influence on him. Speransky too made a positive impression on Karamzin. Korf writes:

> After Karamzin was better acquainted with Speransky, he became con-vinced that Speransky was not prejudiced in his ideas, that he was not in the least unbending or sectarian, that, on the contrary, he was extremely flexible, versatile, and understood everything. What other impression could Karamzin, with his intellect and powers of observation, have gained? . . . From then on he tried by all possible means to support Speransky in his dealings with Emperor Alexander.[17]

Codification was one of the first problems that occupied Nicholas I. He turned the Commission on Laws into the second department of "His Imperial Majesty's Chancellery" and put Professor Balugiansky at the head of this depart-ment. Speransky, still a member of the State Council, was charged with carrying out the practical work, without at the same time holding a particular post. Spe-ransky's first act was to write two papers. The first was a history of the work of the Commission on Laws; the second was a plan for a continuation of the work. Speransky here offered the emperor two options: either to write systematic stat-ute books, as had been attempted under Alexander, or to go down the road of incorporation, in other words, to produce a clearly organized edition of existing laws. The emperor was firmly in favor of the latter approach. In drafting the Svod [the *Svod zakonov,* or "Law Code"], Balugianksy, Speransky, and others had on the one hand to follow the model of the Justinian Code and, on the other, to base their work on the principles set out by Bacon.[18] These principles were the ideas, as we have seen above, that formed the basis of Karamzin's paper *Memorandum on An-cient and Modern Russia.* Therefore, it is not surprising that the plan now adopted for the work of producing the Svod was essentially close to Karamzin's views.

There has been much debate as to whether Speransky always kept strictly to Russian law or whether sometimes provisions from various foreign statute books were after all "smuggled" into the Svod—that is, whether the Svod contains certain elements based on borrowings from foreign law. Vinaver, who dedicated an article to this question, succeeded in proving foreign sources in some cases, although these were only isolated exceptions.[19] Overall, Speransky carried out the work in line with the agreed plan.

In Korf's opinion, Speransky was well aware of the significance that the Svod would have for Russia:

> Insofar as we knew Speransky, we could be sure that he was aiming for a distant goal, namely to make our laws more accessible. Rescuing law from its chaotic state, and thereby reeducating the people and introducing them to the world of law, would extend their ideas of law and justice and thus make them more receptive to nobler ideas and develop their readiness to take part in measures undertaken for their benefit. In any event, the Svod served as an important antecedent for the development of the self-assurance and autonomous activity that occurred . . . much later on in our country, but for which, without doubt, Speransky's work laid the foundation.[20]

It would be hard to better these words of Korf to express the significance of the codification of law as accomplished by Speransky for Russia's progress in a liberal direction.

Chapter 6

Nicholas I

Consolidation of the principle of private
property—Question of the emancipation of the
serfs—Legislation to protect the peasants—
Approach to the peasant question in government
committees in the reign of Nicholas I—Comments
on the nature of the emancipation of the serfs

The question as to how significant Nicholas I's reign was in the context of
Russia's development toward liberalism is certainly not easy to answer. Intellectual freedom was restricted, and censorship was rigorous in all areas. After
1848, these measures were further intensified. On the other hand, it should be
acknowledged that some of the gains made under Catherine II and Alexander I,
which eventually had to pave the way for the establishment of a liberal order in
Russia, were preserved and even consolidated under Nicholas I. It is also hard to
deny that this consolidation was a prerequisite for Alexander II's liberal reforms.

In the previous chapter, we pointed out the significance of the codification of
the law for the development of a general legal consciousness in Russia and consequently the emergence of the conditions for a liberal order.

Some material aspects of liberal legal consciousness, however, were also able
to take hold under Nicholas I. Recognition of the gentry's land as their private
property, which had been affirmed in Catherine's Charter to the Nobility, became
deeply rooted in the legal consciousness of the entire gentry class, as well as the
dynasty itself. This legal awareness is shown in the very precise example of a
decision made by the Committee of December 6 (1826). In its session on September 28, 1827, this committee discussed measures that were meant to ban the
sale of serfs without land and, when enacting legislation on this matter, stressed
the necessity "of making clear that as far as the government and the law were

concerned, the property rights of landowners were sacred and inviolable, in order to preempt misleading talk and unfounded speculation about the future relations between peasants and landowners. At the same time, it was observed that this should be mentioned cautiously—positively, but briefly and in passing, like a right about which there could be no doubt whatsoever."[1]

Nicholas I was convinced that this principle was sacred. In a speech to the State Council, which he gave on the reading of the draft law on so-called contracted peasants, he stressed that, besides anything else, this law was useful, because it unambiguously "expressed the government's will and conviction that land belonged not to the peasants settled on it, but to the landowner."[2] He pointed out that this clarification was of great importance for maintaining order in the future, in the conviction, no doubt, that, in his own words, "I doubt that any of my subjects would dare act against me, as soon as he knew what my precise will was."[3]

It is precisely Nicholas I's conviction that land was the private property of the gentry that has to be seen as the main obstacle to the emancipation of the serfs during his reign. That he was personally a supporter of emancipation—in fact, that emancipation was one of his dearest wishes—is shown by a series of statements he made to a variety of people. On the other hand, Nicholas I saw himself as bound strictly by existing law, even if such law was not personally to his liking and stood in conflict with his own ideas. According to the Russian historian Kizevetter:

> Neither Nicholai Pavlovich nor his brother Constantine harbored any
> sympathy for constitutional forms of government. Tsar Nicholai Pavlovich
> always recognized that a constitutional regime was completely alien to
> his whole outlook and his nature. He took the earliest opportunity, at the
> Polish uprising, to dispense formally with the constitution that Alexander
> I had proclaimed in Poland. It is all the more important therefore to note
> that Nicholai Pavlovich . . . considered it his duty to respect constitutional
> proprieties strictly, as long as this constitution was still in force.[4]

It is also known that Nicholas I was sharply critical of the French king because the latter violated the constitution that he himself had recognized. He considered that breaking the law was incompatible with a monarch's honor.

The experience in the Baltic provinces had shown that emancipating the serfs without leaving them any land would severely damage their economic situation. There was therefore no question of emancipation on those lines. It was only possible to emancipate the serfs if they were granted a part of the landowner's estates. For that, however, it would have been necessary to break with the principle that land was the private property of the gentry, as recognized and confirmed in law. The government was thus not empowered to take land away from the gentry. Nicholas I was not flexible enough to resolve this dilemma.

He may also have been reluctant to move toward the emancipation of the serfs for lack of support for such plans among the gentry, his collaborators, or the top ranks of the bureaucracy. In 1834, he told his future minister of state domains, Kiselev: "I have read your report. . . . One part in particular interested me: where you talk about the emancipation of the serfs. Both of us share the same feelings about this important question, which my ministers don't understand and which scares them." The emperor continued, pointing to a box on a shelf of his office: "Look, since coming to the throne, I have been collecting all the evidence I need to proceed with the case against serfdom, to liberate the serfs throughout the empire, when the time is right."[5]

The awareness that the emancipation of the serfs was a necessity had eventually to gain ground among the gentry.[6] If not their understanding, then their social and legal instincts must have told the gentry that the survival of serfdom was not compatible in the end with their own new status, with its civil rights, with the liberty that had become a reality for the gentry and townspeople since Catherine. Civil liberty as a privilege for the aristocracy might have been compatible with slavery, but not with serfdom as it had developed in the context of the Russian system. There was, moreover, no historical basis for slavery in Russia. Representatives of the gentry were clear about this, as well as the fact that from a legal perspective, serfdom was quite different from slavery. D. Miliutin stressed this point in a lecture to the Société d'Economie Politique [Association for Political Economy] in Paris on May 5, 1863.[7] According to Miliutin, it was unthinkable for serfdom in Russia to be turned into real slavery. What was perhaps possible was a return to an older form of serfdom, that is, to the seventeenth-century system. The peasantry would have understood such a development and possibly even welcomed it. This would have entailed, however, a considerable increase in the state supervision of the gentry, who would also have become much more dependent on the state, which would ultimately have been incompatible with the principles of the 1785 Charter.

Interestingly enough, there was in fact a subtle shift in precisely this direction under Nicholas I, although this was not in any way the government's intention. It was simply the inevitable consequence of the fact that nothing can last forever, especially not a transitional state of affairs. As long as the government was unable, or did not dare, to grant the serfs free citizenship and civil rights, thereby finally consolidating civil society in Russia, there was no alternative but to take measures that belonged rather to the old system of serfdom. Nicholas I, speaking to the State Council, officially described serfdom as a manifest evil, but at the same time he declared that "to touch it (*prikasat'sia*) would be an even greater evil." As long as it was deemed impossible for the time being to grant the serfs their liberty, there was no other solution—if one wanted to do anything at all to help the serfs—than to limit the power of the landowners over the serfs and to subject this power to state control.

Gradovsky writes that under Nicholas I more decrees were issued for the protection of the serfs vis-à-vis the landowners than under any of his predecessors—

about 108 in total between 1826 and 1855.[8] The Ministry of the Interior issued two rescripts, on June 19 and September 6, 1826, that protected the interests of the peasants. The first instructed landowners to treat the peasants "in a Christian and legal fashion." The duty of watching over the landowners in this respect was imposed on the marshals of the nobility, and disciplinary action was threatened if they neglected to perform it. The September 6 rescript dealt with the detailed regulation of this supervisory role. More decrees and laws followed later, all with the aim of restricting the powers of the landowners over the serfs. In 1827, landowners were banned from transferring their serfs to mining companies. In 1827 and 1828, landowners were forbidden from banishing their serfs to Siberia; in 1833, from buying or selling serfs without the land to which they were bound; in 1841, from selling individual family members, if that would separate them from their families. An attempt was made in 1845–46 to regulate the rights of landowners to punish the serfs; in 1853, leasing land on which there were serfs was forbidden; in 1854, there followed a ban on delegating certain landowners' rights to stewards. All these laws were aimed at limiting the power of landowners over serfs, but they all had one thing in common—namely, that although they limited the rights of landowners, they did nothing to grant new rights to the serfs. A legal order was established to which the landowners were subject—that is, they were bound by this order. This order benefited the serfs (or at any rate it was supposed to), although these laws did not grant the serfs any new rights that would give them redress against landowners. That the serfs had absolutely no right to file a complaint against a landowner was completely in keeping with this situation. A serf had no recourse against a landowner who contravened any of these laws. Only the marshal of the nobility or the local police could take action against a landowner who treated his serfs in an "unchristian and illegal manner." One can get a clear idea of the way things were from an Interior Ministry circular from August 1849:

> According to the law, marshals of the nobility must be informed about the conduct, way of life, and wealth of the gentry, as well as the condition of their estates; they must see to the needs of the gentry and concern themselves with the welfare and order of this class. After the Senate investigated the case of two regional marshals of the nobility, who had been brought to trial and relieved of their office on the orders of the highest authority on account of their toleration of the extremely cruel treatment of serfs on the part of a landowner and his wife; after the cruel behavior of this landowner, as well as the ruination of the serfs who were forced to live off charitable donations, had been established by the court; and taking into consideration that this abuse had lasted several years and the very fact that the regional marshals of the nobility and the members of the local police did not know about the aforementioned facts, it was demonstrated that they had been negligent in the fulfillment of their duties. The Senate decided, in addition to dismissing the aforementioned marshals of the nobility from office,

according to Articles 43 and 442 of the Penal Code, to issue them with the severest reprimand in open court and to enter this on their service records. (The same punishment was also meted out to the police officers.) . . . The Senate instructed the Ministry of the Interior . . . to inform all marshals of the nobility about this punishment.[9]

There is no mention in this Senate decision of a possible attempt by the serfs to file a complaint against the illegal behavior of the landowner or in any way to assert their rights. The serfs are merely mentioned as objects in the care of the state authorities. The idea that serfs could be entitled to claims of their own is completely absent here. Another aspect of this case is also typical. The marshals of the nobility, who were elected by the gentry to represent the interests and protect the traditions of this estate, were used by the government to watch over other members of the gentry like police officers and were punished in the same way. This picture of how extensively bureaucratized the relationships within the gentry had become is quite depressing.

Nicholas I did not intend to stop at the individual measures mentioned above, which were aimed at limiting the power of the serf-owners. He had in mind to put the relations between serfs and landowners on a new footing with general and specific regulations. During the reign of Nicholas I, there were six secret committees dealing with the peasant question, although three of these were only concerned with specific questions of peasant life. The overall peasant question was dealt with by the Committee of December 6 (1826), the Committee of 1839, and the Committee of 1846. These committees were seeking not to abolish serfdom, but rather to regulate the relations between the peasants and the landowners within the existing structure of serfdom. This was a necessary consequence of the fact that the regime rejected both of the following solutions as unacceptable: on the one hand, the personal emancipation of the serfs without giving them land;[10] on the other, the expropriation of land belonging to the gentry in order to provide the peasants with land.

Speransky presented a review of the peasant question to the Committee of December 6.[11] In Speransky's opinion, one had to try to restore the original form of serfdom, that is, that the serf should be bound not to the landowner in person, but rather to the soil, and also that a contract should set out the duties of the serfs to the landowners.[12]

Count Kiselev was asked to prepare these proposals by the Committee of 1839. His proposals also tried to find a way that avoided either emancipating the serfs without land or expropriating the landowners. Kiselev's view was that one had to continue to regard the land as the property of the landowners, but that one should also provide (obezpechit') the peasants with this land. A duty would be imposed on the landowners to leave certain parcels of land (nadely) to the peasants, while the peasants would cultivate this land and pay a certain amount of compensation to the landowners in return for its use. Under this system, there would be limits, on the one hand, to the individual liberty of the serfs, as they remained bound to the soil (and thus no longer to the landowner in person), and, on the other, to the property rights of landowners, as they had the duty, mentioned above, of providing land for the peasants. Both the size of the plots to be allocated to the peasants and the amount they had to pay for them as compensation were to be laid down in law.

The arguments that Kiselev deployed against giving land to the peasants not just for their own use but also as their property are extremely interesting. First, he considered the property rights of landowners to be sacrosanct and inviolable. Even irrespective of this, however, he was against turning the serfs into free proprietors from a purely political point of view. It was clear to him that civil rights and civil liberty are the basis of political freedom. Making the serfs property owners would have of necessity entailed broad masses of society participating in government, "because of property rights (*po pravu votchinnoi sobstvennosti*)," which in turn "would have destroyed the equilibrium between the different organs of the state through the power of the unfettered majority."[13]

The proposal was diluted significantly in the decree enacted in 1842 based on Kiselev's draft. It was left to the peasants and the landowners to come to their own agreement as to the area of land and the amount of compensation to be paid by the peasants. Any attempt to lay down legal guidelines for either was abandoned. Even more important, however, was that it totally jettisoned any requirement that the landowners give land to the peasants, that is, effectively impose this duty. Such a provision, which was quite practicable under the old system of serfdom, now appeared inconceivable. Catherine's charter had been in force for over fifty years, and the right to dispose freely of their property was taken for granted by the gentry. This right had only a short time before been enshrined in the *Svod zakonov* (Law Code) and thus confirmed once again. It was not just the gentry, however, who regarded their unrestricted property rights as not up for discussion. The tsar also took account of these views and admitted that the right of landowners to dispose freely of their property should not be curtailed. When Prince Golitsyn pointed out in the State Council that the entire arrangement would remain a dead letter if the law did not impose on landowners the direct obligation to hand over land to the peasants, Nicholas I gave the following typical response: "Although I am an absolute autocrat, I would never dare to resort to such a measure. Equally, I would not dare to order the landowners to draw up a contract with the peasants. I repeat, this has to be a matter they must decide freely between themselves."[14] The law on "contracted peasants" was then enacted on April 2, 1842, on this voluntary basis. It thus remained merely an imperial recommendation and only had, as Prince Golitsyn had predicted, very limited practical significance.[15] The emperor was forced to accept that his subjects did not always act according to his wishes, even if they knew exactly what he willed.

Even after 1842, Nicholas I and his government did not lose interest in the peasant question. Another committee was set up in 1846 to advise on measures that were considered a necessary preparation for the eventual emancipation of the serfs. This committee only met once, when the minister of the interior, Count Perovsky, proposed a significant plan.[16] According to this plan, the peasants were to remain bound to the soil, thus remaining as dependents. They could, however, no longer be described as serfs, as the landowners would only retain powers over the serfs described by Perovsky as "political." Members of the gentry would retain their role as administrators, magistrates, and tax collectors, but they would no longer be described as owners of serfs. The peasants were to remain bound to the soil, so that they could pay the landowners and their state taxes on time, which would safeguard the revenue of the state and the income of the landowners. The amount the peasants paid in contributions was to be laid down in law, as were the peasants' rights in respect to their moveable and immovable property. This draft law represented a return to the principles of the old system of serfdom. It was the law that would control the disposal of land belonging to the gentry. Although in principle the land remained the property of the landowner, it had to be left to the dependent peasants for cultivation. How much was paid would also be laid down by law or through agreements that were binding on both parties and sanctioned by the state, that is, whose content was probably also determined by it. The landowner thus became a state official and tax collector, who received a part of this revenue at the time of collection. The relationship between the peasant and the noble again became of matter of public law.

Insofar as the state claimed to have rights over a landowner's property, the owner's right of free disposal was unavoidably restricted. Limiting this right is then only a step away from asserting that there are conditions to owning property. Furthermore, this step would be quite logical from a legal perspective. If the state prescribes particular ways of managing property, it follows that it can impose sanctions if such requirements or regulations are not obeyed. Certainly one possible sanction can—quite naturally—be expropriation. This is the justification for making property ownership conditional. Fulfilling a certain duty to the state (a duty to manage one's property according to regulations) becomes a prerequisite, a condition of ownership. Once ownership has become conditional in this respect, there is nothing to prevent the state from adding further duties to be carried out as prerequisites or compulsory conditions of ownership. One example of such a duty can be the duty to work in the service of the state for a specific number of years. This would restore the binding duty to serve the state, (i.e., the compulsory nature of state service) and in this respect revoke the decrees of 1762 and 1785. It could be countered that this limitation of the property rights of landowners never got beyond the planning stage. This, however, is only true up to a point. In 1853, a law was enacted forbidding landowners from leasing out land if there were serfs on it, which represented a direct legal restriction on the rights of landowners. Furthermore, for years, even decades, there was a succession of draft laws in which limitations on landowners' rights were considered. If the government shied away from enacting this legislation, it was only because the tsar, as he himself said, did not dare to ignore the gentry's view of its rights. Nevertheless, the government apparently did consider, at least in principle, that it was possible to limit landowners' rights, although this would have been incompatible with the principle of the inviolability of private property. There was thus no guarantee that it would not implement these plans, at some point, admissible as they were from the perspective of the all-powerful autocracy. One can even imagine that without the subsequent emancipation of the serfs, such a course of action would have been inevitable.

Because it was unthinkable in Russia, as mentioned above, to change the status of serfs to that of actual slaves, who would thus become the private property of landowners, only two options remained: either restore the old system of serfdom and with it the state-controlled nature of the relations between master and serf or implement the so-called emancipation of the serfs—that is, sever the existing ties between serf and master. The former would have entailed the loss of the unconditional nature of the gentry's ownership of land and eventually the restoration of compulsory state service. This course of action would have led automatically to the annulment of Catherine's charter. In this case, the gentry would have lost the civil liberty granted in the Charter of 1785, the legal status that was the basis for property and other civil rights. The second option would allow them to keep their civil liberty and all their property. The gentry would retain the legal status that had led them from the old system of serfdom to a civil society. In exchange, however, they had to abandon their rights over their "baptized property," that is, their rights over the serfs.

Whether the gentry in mid-nineteenth-century Russia were genuinely aware of these options is most unlikely. One can suppose, however, that the supporters of emancipation among the gentry adopted this position because of the survival instinct of their class, which enabled them to anticipate the consequences for the gentry of not abolishing serfdom.

Initially, people naturally expressed quite different motives. Mostly it was a question of an emotional response, which was certainly not at all hypocritical. For many of the gentry—for people brought up in the European spirit of freedom— it was actually an unbearable psychological burden to own serfs and to control them. Furthermore, the more a nobleman became an owner of private property, a private individual, the more burdensome the administration of the serf communities must have seemed.[17] Nevertheless, the abovementioned survival instinct could go hand in hand with these more conscious motives. One can certainly assume this, especially as the second of the abovementioned motives can be seen as stemming directly from this instinct. My hypothesis is supported by the fact that in emancipating the serfs there was hardly any thought—as we shall see later— of granting the peasant the status of the truly free citizen, of the free property owner, but rather above all a haste to sweep away all the ties that bound serfs and masters.

It is nearly a hundred years since the emancipation of the serfs, and one is left with the impression that it was not so much a matter of liberating the serfs from the landowners as of liberating the landowners from the serfs, that is, from all the duties that came with ownership of an estate with serfs. Although this sounds paradoxical, I am really inclined to describe the act of emancipation of February 19, 1861, not in the first place as the liberation of the serfs, but as the second liberation of the gentry. (The first came in 1762 and 1785.) The gentry were freed on February 18, 1762, from doing obligatory state service (from their duty to enter into state service), while on February 19, 1861, they were freed from official duties in respect to their estates. I do not wish to imply that Alexander II's peasant reform did not also greatly benefit the peasants. It represents, however, a step toward the abolition of the old system of serfdom, because it was above all an important contribution to definitively changing the status of the gentry into that of private citizens, private landowners. It is precisely for this reason that the emancipation of the serfs marked a stage on the road to liberalism. It can also, however, be described as a liberal measure, in that it swept away the dependency of the peasants on the masters, a dependency that had been such an obstacle, if not an insurmountable one, to peasants becoming proprietors. This will be examined in more detail below.

Gradovsky maintains that under Nicholas I certain restrictions were imposed on serfdom. These restrictions, however, or the easing of serfdom, were achieved not through an attempt to consolidate a civil society in principle and to extend it to the peasants, but rather, on the contrary, through a certain if limited return to the pre-Catherine forms of serfdom. The creation of a class of free citizens, of independent proprietors and farmers from the mass of serfs, would have actually amounted to a profound revolution. The conservative Emperor Nicholas I was in no way capable of doing this, still less inclined to do so. He had made the principle of preserving the existing order the cornerstone of his rule. Even when he had reforms in mind, he wanted to carry them out in such a way as to make any innovation invisible to outsiders, that is, the entire population, with the exception of those who belonged to the narrow initiated circle of officials who were entrusted with the matter. The drafting of reforms, even sometimes of unimportant administrative measures, had therefore to proceed behind closed doors in secret committees, about whose aims and work the members of other committees and officials from other departments were not allowed to be informed. Nicholas I had no alternative, insofar as he was unable, or perhaps unwilling, to make the peasants into genuinely free citizens, but to look for legal measures in the very context of serfdom itself against the evils that were created by this system, or perhaps rather by its degeneration. As Speransky had already pointed out, such means could now only be found by taking the route back to the authentic system of serfdom.

Conservative in inclination, Nicholas I did not wish, however, to infringe on the gentry's privileges, their civil rights, their status as free proprietors, granted by Catherine. Therefore, the many laws and decrees that he enacted to the benefit of the serfs, which restricted the powers of the landowners over them, were extremely limited in scope. Nicholas I's measures in respect to the peasantry did not in any way amount to a consistent reform program. The government only felt its way tentatively from one measure of limited significance and equally limited effect to the next, without having any clear idea as to the point of these measures, and was above all extremely concerned not to make any significant changes to the status quo. It is not surprising either that among all the laws enacted by Nicholas I, which in general tended to restore the pre-Catherine system of serfdom, there is also one law regarding the peasantry that exemplifies moves to extend civil society. This is the law of March 3, 1848, by which serfs were allowed—albeit with the permission of the landowner—to acquire land as private property. In the opinion of the highest-ranking officials of the time, continuing to withhold this right from the peasants would have been a great injustice, because, as was stated in one of the official reports of the time, "next to life, property is the most important earthly good."[18]

Chapter 7

Nicholas I (continued)

The reign of Nicholas I as a transitional epoch—
The law on state serfs—The deepening gulf
between the peasants and other classes—Cultural
life under Nicholas I

The reign of Nicholas I represents a transitional epoch in the true sense of the term. This has often been overlooked because Nicholas I—and more precisely the figure of the tsar, rather than his personality—overshadowed everything. The autocrat dominated every sphere of life. Everything was represented in him and by him. Everything became the business of an inflexible bureaucratic hierarchy, to then be filed away in official archives. Hence, an impression was created of uniformity, order, stability, and firmness. In reality, however, this was an era when one system imperceptibly began to take the place of another and when civil society began to supersede the old regime of serfdom. Sometimes the government seemed to adhere to the principles of the one, then of the other, without grasping the contradiction between the two, without noticing that they were incompatible. Certainly very little of this incessant, one could almost say enormous, effort ever went further than the work of secret committees and the preparation of countless drafts, precisely because the government was unable to declare its unambiguous support for either of these systems, for either of these conflicting principles.

Nicholas accepted the principle of private property.[1] He certainly had no thought of fundamentally restricting the sphere of civil law. He definitely had no conscious intention of replacing relationships based on civil law with those under administrative law through the continuous extension of regulation and control, that is, of transforming them into relationships under public law. On the contrary, many of those close to him in government had what one must describe as liberal views in respect to freedom of trade and economic policy in general.[2]

Nicholas I, however, felt that it was his duty to look after the moral and material well-being of his subjects. This sense of duty had its roots in the principles of the police state and in the traditions of the Orthodox empire. Because of this tradition, he could not imagine that there were any barriers to prevent him from exercising his will benevolently or that there were rights or legal regulations that could not be changed or violated even when implementing measures he was convinced would promote the well-being of his subjects. Yet Nicholas I was quite sensitive to issues of legality. Kizevetter, as we have seen, pointed out that Nicholas felt bound by the provisions of positive law and regarded it as his duty to obey the law to the letter, apart from anything to set a good example to his subjects. There was no obvious solution for the tsar, however, if a conflict arose between his duty to respect the law and his duty to care for the welfare of his subjects, a duty that in an absolutist police state or an Orthodox empire symbolizes *la superlégalité constitutionelle*.[3] There were no norms, and neither could there be any, of course, for such an eventuality. Ultimately, it had to come down to the emperor's judgment. Sometimes, as when regulating the relationship between the serfs and their masters, he could not bring himself to violate the acknowledged rights of the landowners in the interests of the peasants. At other times, in contrast, he was not so concerned about the well-established rights of his subjects. The supreme order of November 29, 1848, represents an extreme example of this.

The Ministry of the Interior issued the following circular for the information of provincial governors on December 16, 1848, containing the following:

> The Emperor, whose attention had been drawn to the extraordinary increase in the use of matches, has noted that for fires occurring in 1848 arsonists used matches to commit their crimes, which in towns alone destroyed property to the value of over 12 million silver roubles. The Emperor, therefore, on November 29 deigned to issue this supreme order:
>
> 1. That match factories will only be permitted in the capital cities (Moscow and St. Petersburg)
>
> 2. That the street sale of matches is to be completely banned
>
> 3. That all match factories in the provinces are to be closed within a month of the owner receiving notice.[4]

The well-established rights of the match-factory owners were not respected; after all, the emperor had to take steps to protect his subjects from the danger of fire.

There was in fact a prevailing attitude on the part of the sovereign and his government that it was their role to take care of everything and everyone and that, by contrast, to look after one's own interests was to show a lack of respect for the state and was therefore dangerous politically. This attitude was generally characteristic of Nicholas I's legislation, or at any rate the actions of his government. Deviations from this predominant tendency were rare.

The laws on state peasants are a typical example of legislation based on paternalism and the providence of the state. The significance of these laws is apparent from the fact that at the time virtually half of the entire population of Russia were state peasants. No figures are available for the time when these laws were enacted. However, the figures for the time around 1860, which D. Miliutin used in his abovementioned lecture in Paris, will suffice. The total population certainly grew between 1840 and 1860, although the proportions among the different social groups—which is the only significant point here—hardly seem to have changed. Before the emancipation of the serfs, there were in Russia (not counting Poland, Finland, and the Caucasus):

23 million serfs

26 million state peasants

4 million townspeople

1 million gentry

650,000 clergy[5]

These 26 million state peasants were peasants on state domains covering an enormous area. If one excludes Siberia, Transcaucasia, the Cossack regions in European Russia, the military colonies, and the land belonging to mining enterprises, in the 1830s the state owned 87 million *desiatin* in arable land and pasture,[6] as well as 119 million *desiatin* in forests in European Russia.[7] To understand Nicholas I's legislation, one has first to look at the situation of state peasants in the preceding centuries.

In the seventeenth century, state-owned land was made up of the following categories:

Uninhabited areas

Land settled by state peasants[8]—state domains

Crown land and the tsar's estates

Estates linked to service, that is, estates given to gentry in the service
of the state

Landed estates linked to service were given parity with hereditary estates by the law of 1731, by which both categories were described as "immovable property." In Zablosky-Desiatovsky's opinion, this resulted in the estates linked to service ceasing to be owned by the state and becoming private property.[9] There is, however, a different view, according to which the estates belonging to the gentry only really became their private property in 1785. In any case, the amount of state-owned property declined further in the eighteenth century (thus in either 1731 or 1785) through the transformation into private property of the estates linked to service. It was also not possible to compensate for this reduction through the secularization of church property implemented in Catherine's time—still less through the confiscation of the estates of statesmen who had fallen out of favor under her predecessors. This decline in the quantity of state-owned property did not mean, however, any reduction in the numbers of state peasants, because in the seventeenth century, peasants on estates linked to service were already also regarded as serfs. Incidentally, certainly since the reign of Peter I, it is correct to describe peasants on crown estates as the tsar's serfs.

There had always been a rural population on state domains. These peasants were freemen. They were only under an obligation to the state to pay a variety of taxes, make payments in kind, and undertake certain services. All these obligations were called *tiaglo,* and that is why the *volostnye zemli* (state domains) were also called *tiaglye.* The state peasants' freedom of movement was restricted at approximately the same time as the emergence of serfdom on hereditary estates (at the turn of the sixteenth to the seventeenth century) and estates linked to state service. Every state peasant was bound to his commune, especially because the system of mutual liability for all communal taxes and services was vague and applied extremely inconsistently. Although freedom of movement was not abolished in principle, when a peasant left a commune he was under an obligation to find a replacement who could take on his duties in the commune. Understandably enough, this made any real possibility of moving away legally extremely unlikely.

The complicated question as to whether state peasants should be described as serfs—that is, as the property of the state—has been answered in different ways by historians. In Zablotsky-Desiatovsky's view, the fact that the state was able to give estates including state peasants to members of the gentry seems to indicate a positive answer.[10]

State peasants had always formed communes that were administered by elected *starosty* (elders) or *sotskie* [literally *centurions*]. The commune had not just the right but also—perhaps above all—the duty to hold these elections. The main duty of these elected elders was in fact to apportion taxes and payments in kind between the members of the community and to ensure their collection. In this connection, they had the responsibility of ensuring that the commune meet all its obligations promptly. An edict of May 19, 1769, laid down the following: "In the case of peasants not paying their poll tax for a whole year, the eldest and elected peasants will be brought to the town, where they will be held under guard. They will be used to undertake hard labor for the town without pay until the whole tax debt has been met."

Zablotsky-Desiatovsky writes, "It is remarkable that this edict appeared in the early years of Catherine's reign, while she was still completely influenced by the liberal ideas of the eighteenth century."[11] In fact, Catherine's other measures in relation to state peasants also have a markedly illiberal character. They rest on the no doubt correct assumption that, according to the law as it stood, it was not the state-peasant communes but the state that was the landowner and that consequently these measures were based primarily on fiscal considerations.[12] To declare that these estates should belong to the peasant communities would have certainly amounted to a move toward liberalism, but that would have required first drawing up a new legal status for state peasants. Again, this was only conceivable following the Charter to the Nobility and the Charter to the Towns, which had created a precedent. Catherine had also considered a charter for peasants who were not serfs, but this plan belonged to those projects that never became law.[13]

Before Kiselev's reform, the supervision of the state-peasant communes was entrusted to *zemskie ispravniki* (rural commissioners) in the districts and to the fiscal authority in the provinces. The situation of the state peasants was in no sense enviable, although in contrast to serfs, they were not subject to the power of landlords. Speransky had already maintained in 1827 that the first step toward an overall solution of the peasant question, that is, toward the reform of serfdom, had to be a change in the situation (*ustroistvo*) of the state peasants. He described their situation as quite bleak in his report on the condition of state peasants. Speransky writes: "This part of the population (*etot rod liudei*) is no less impoverished and insolvent than the serfs belonging to private estates." Speransky pointed out that the allocation of burdens and duties was vague and extremely inconsistent. He continued: "The *zemskie ispravniki* are nothing other than landlords, the only exception being that (after a certain time) they can be replaced and made accountable. Thus, they have no reason, for a period of three years, to spare the peasants, whom they neither keep for themselves nor pass on to their heirs."[14]

Nicholas I, who trusted Speransky more than anyone when it came to the peasant question (and possibly other areas as well), adopted these ideas. On his initiative, the reform of the legal status of state peasants was separated from the general solution to the peasant question and given particular emphasis. It was, however, not easy to find anyone who could be entrusted with this task. Initially it was thought that Kankrin, the minister of finance, would be suitable. However, the minister, who had submitted his own draft regarding this matter to the State Council, withdrew it as unsatisfactory. Nicholas I then turned to Count Kiselev and appointed him as chair of the committee that had been tasked with finding a solution to the problems relating to the class of state peasants. Incidentally, an earlier commission, headed by Kurakin, had been set up to deal with the same complex issues.[15]

According to Kiselev, state peasants were impoverished because of two factors: a lack of safeguards and a lack of supervision. Because of the lack of safeguards, state peasants were unlawfully overburdened with taxes and labor, while drunkenness and other vices spread among them because of the lack of supervision.[16] He went on to argue that village administration was in the hands of the most corrupt elements of society and was itself the main cause of all oppression and disorder. Village officials took bribes from the better-off peasants and helped them exploit village affairs to their own advantage and oppress the poor. Naturally, he went on, these better-off peasants were against any reform, as the existing administrative disorder was in their interest. "On the other hand," writes

Kiselev, "the poorest and most numerous class of peasants, having full confidence in the government, expects its lot to be improved through the measures it will take."[17]

Kiselev's optimism, however, soon proved to be misplaced. On the contrary, rumors about the government's reform plans had greatly unsettled the state peasants. They were especially alarmed by rumors that the government wanted to turn peasant villages into a sort of military colony and introduce collective tillage. Rich peasants started transferring to the townspeople's estate.[18] What is particularly interesting here is the reference to the fact that the peasants feared the introduction of collective cultivation. This certainly contradicts the presumption that "Great Russians" were instinctively predisposed to collectivism. Kiselev also reported to the tsar in 1842 that opposition to the introduction of the potato was mainly "because in the opinion of the peasants the planting of potatoes was tantamount to introducing collective tillage."[19]

Count Kiselev himself thus had to concede just a few months after the report of May 17, 1837, that nowhere near all peasants were looking forward "with total confidence" to the "reorganization" that he had planned. In a report of November 26, 1837, he writes: "Each new administrative authority . . . naturally causes many to feel dissatisfied. . . . The peasants themselves will form an unfavorable first impression. . . . These people will see all measures of public welfare undertaken by the authorities as coercive."[20]

Nevertheless, Kiselev thought that his draft legislation did not fundamentally break any new ground and did not go further than existing laws.[21] He believed that the only purpose of his reform was to ensure the proper application of these laws and to deal with any obvious flaws. He thought that dissatisfaction could only arise from efforts to maintain the existing disorder, as this encouraged unrestrained license, the peasants often "preferring the comfort of their pernicious habits to all the promises of better conditions."[22] He therefore considered that it would be a great mistake to abandon the reforms. In his opinion, if the government did not act, there was a danger that measures to make up for any failings "would be undertaken not on the initiative of the government, but rather because of pressure from below."[23] In general, Kiselev was profoundly convinced that paternalism bestowed benefits on the people. He went on a journey through Russia in the summer of 1838, during which he noted in his diary that the peasants would be happy "if they were under the direction of an unoppressive, paternal authority providing welfare support."[24]

Such power was to be exercised by the Ministry of State Domains and its subordinate institutions in the provinces and districts, in the *volosti* (small rural districts) and villages. At the provincial level, these were the state-domain chambers (*palaty gos. imushchestv*); in the districts, these were the heads of district (*okruzhnye nachal'niki*); in the *volosti* and villages, these were the administrative officials and courts elected by the peasants themselves. A clerk, however, was appointed to the village administration by these authorities. The district heads appointed clerks to the village administration, and the state-domain chambers appointed the clerks to the *volost'* administration.

It was the job of all these administrators to care for the welfare of the state peasants. Above all, it was their job to ensure that the land owned by the state was shared as fairly as possible among the communes and among the individual farms within each commune. In addition, they had to ensure that the burden imposed on individual farms was in proportion to the area of each farm's allotted land. In practice, this left much to be desired. There were instances of communes, for example, where each farm only received half a *desiatin* for its "souls" (i.e., members of the farm), whereas in other communes farms were allocated twenty or even more *desiatin* for each "soul." Six hundred thousand "souls" received no land at all.

Many peasants were forced to settle on land belonging to a landowner or to move in large numbers to another province. There were even cases where state-owned property was leased by speculators who then in turn sublet it to state peasants. Taxes and other burdens were not shared equally among the individual communes. Earlier attempts by the government to make the sharing of land among the communes fairer often only served to make things worse for the peasants, while the implementation of these measures was often accompanied by repressive measures against the peasants.[25] In addition, the distribution of land within individual communes was often inequitable: "The kulaks (*miroedy*—a term often used for kulaks in the nineteenth century) often managed to cheat the other peasants."[26] Furthermore, even in these cases government intervention was only rarely successful.

The new order was supposed to do away with all these ills. The newly established institutions were meant to supervise the village administrators and indeed the village communes in general. They were, of course, not allowed to force the village assemblies or administrators to adopt specific decisions, if these fell within the latter's area of responsibility. It was, however, their duty to ensure that these decisions did not conflict with existing law. Provisionally, however, as long as village administration was insufficiently developed, the powers of the district leaders had to include not just the roles of supervision and welfare provision but also the authority to take positive measures.[27] Incidentally, it is doubtful whether this power was based solely on the fact that peasant administration was underdeveloped and over time would thus become redundant. This authority had in fact another more deep-seated legal basis. Elsewhere Zablotsky-Desiatovsky writes: "One of the reasons the bureaucracy was unable to restrict itself to purely negative action with regard to the peasants, that is, to their supervision, was that the land on which these peasants were settled was the property of the state, and this property had nothing to do with welfare, but was rather an administrative matter."[28]

The point of this decision-making power, however, was not supposed to be the economic exploitation of the peasants, but rather improvement to their welfare. This is what mainly distinguishes the Ministry of State Domains from the *udel'noe upravlenie* [the administration of crown land]. According to Zablotsky-Desiatovsky: "This *udel'noe upravlenie* is not a form of state administration; it is a type of landed estate management (*upravlenie pomeshchich'e*) that is not primarily concerned with the peasants themselves, but rather with extracting as much income as possible from property."[29]

Interestingly enough, the *udel'noe upravlenie*, of all things, did not cause much dissatisfaction. Tsar Nicholas once remarked that this *upravlenie* was one of the few areas about which one did not hear any complaints. By contrast, complaints from all sides piled up regarding the Ministry of State Domains. In particular, the peasants complained that the reform brought with it a significant increase in the number of administrative offices, which had to be maintained by the communes themselves. Furthermore, the fact that senior officials from the district and the province appeared more often also entailed not inconsiderable extra expenses for the communes. Last, the peasants pointed out that if there was a poor harvest—precisely when welfare relief was required—the new officials could be accused of indifference.[30] However, criticism of the new system came from other quarters besides the peasants. There were many who were fundamentally opposed to the idea of paternalistic state welfare and who put forward the view that it would be preferable to "leave the peasants to their own devices."[31] Poltoratsky, the military governor of Yaroslavl', remarked ironically to Baron Korf: "The landowners are going to put up a monument to Count Kiselev. Since the introduction of the new administrative system, the situation of the state peasants has become so desperate and unbearable that many serfs now prefer their own situation and dread the possibility of becoming state peasants."[32]

The fact that the peasants preferred a situation in which they were subject to exploitation rather than one in which they were under paternalistic supervision was certainly an interesting phenomenon. This is perhaps understandable because exploitation demands an approach to the exploited that, even if hard, is nevertheless rational. By contrast, if someone is a ward, there is a danger that he can fall victim to the inhumanity of sentimental idealism.

The idea of paternalism, in particular the idea that the state should provide land for the peasants and also ensure that the peasants divided this land up among themselves, more or less equitably, sprang from the fear that a section of the people would become proletarian. Because of this fear, which arose from certain political prejudices, the government was prepared to accept all the economic and other disadvantages of this backward agricultural collectivism just to be able to arrest the natural process by which the population was becoming more diverse.[33]

State peasants were better off under the law than serfs. They had had the right to buy land for themselves since 1801. Legal redress was available to the communes to defend their interests concerning the state land that had been allocated to them for their use.[34] State peasants were permitted to enter into contracts. They had a relatively free choice of occupation; they could turn either to arable farming or to craft trades, could set up smaller factories, and were allowed to transfer to the estate of the townspeople. One problem was that the legal status of the state peasant was not sufficiently secure. State-peasant communes could be converted into military colonies. State peasants could come under the control of the *udel'noe vedomstvo* (the administration of the appanages—crown estates). They could even be given to individual landowners as a gift and thus made into serfs. (This, however, no longer occurred in the nineteenth century.) Transferring state peasants by means of an order into the estate of the serfs, at least before 1848, resulted in their losing all potential property rights, as well as a considerable curtailment of their rights to contract debt.[35]

It would, however, be doing an injustice to Kiselev and the Ministry of State Domains, which he founded and led, to ignore the positive achievements of this ministry, which were in fact not inconsiderable. In 1838, the first year after the ministry was established, there were still hardly any elementary schools in Russia. In 1838, there were only 60 schools, with 1,880 pupils, on the state domains. In 1866—that is, when the state peasants ceased to be the responsibility of the Ministry of State Domains and were put under the General Department for Peasant Affairs—there were 7,869 schools with 280,000 pupils. In addition, in 1838 there were still not nearly enough churches. By 1866, one could count 12,795 churches; 5,987 chapels; and 166 houses of prayer. Of course, the majority were Orthodox churches, but there were also churches of other Christian denominations; in addition, there were 1,818 mosques in state-peasant villages. In 1838, there were hardly any doctors or hospitals (a total of 3 hospitals and 5 doctors) on the state domains, and young peasants who were unfit for military service were selected by village assemblies to carry out vaccinations against smallpox. In 1851, a health administration was set up within the framework of the ministry. By 1866, there were 269 hospitals and 170 doctors in the state-peasant villages. The Ministry of State Domains made an effort to combat the consumption of alcohol. In this area, too, ministry officials had a measure of success. In 1850, there were 15,700 taverns selling spirits in the state-peasant villages, or one per thousand inhabitants. By 1854, this number had fallen to 10,726, or one tavern per 1,600 inhabitants. In 1850, the state peasants spent six million roubles on alcohol, whereas in 1854 they spent only three million rubles. In this period, criminality also decreased among the state peasants. Whereas in the three years from 1834 to 1836, 5,614 state peasants were sentenced to imprisonment, from 1852 to 1854, there were only 2,035 such offenders. To raise the morale of the state peasants and to motivate them to work harder, the ministry started awarding various prizes and rewards, which took the form of money, agricultural tools, and honors such as medals and certificates of merit.[36]

The big drawback of this experiment was, of course, the sheer bureaucratic nature of the whole system. In spite of the fact that the peasants themselves could elect the village and *volost'* administrations, an independence of spirit and the ability to manage by themselves did not emerge. In addition, these elected representatives in reality only continued to follow the instructions of officials. This fit in with the general attitude that all decisions and orders had to come from above. Any initiative on the part of the people was rejected as inadmissible and considered a sign of mistrust of the government. During Nicholas's reign, individuals were elected to fill various administrative posts in the districts and provinces. Even here, however, these elected individuals were not the representatives of free social forces (*obshchestvennost'* in Russian), but rather merely officials who were selected by means of an election in certain social estates on behalf of the government. It is only with some reservations that one can accept Kizevetter's view that some features of the later *zemstvos* (the form of local self-government introduced in 1864) had already emerged with these services—in particular the services for health, transport, poor relief, and education.[37] Certainly, the experience of the elections held during the reign of Nicholas I provided at least a partial basis for *zemstvo* elections. Nevertheless, there was a fundamental difference. At the *zemstvo* elections, various social groups elected a genuine, common form of self-government. This local self-government was not an arm of the government, but represented society. There were elections under Nicholas I, but those who were chosen were elected officials.

According to Kizevetter, what distinguished the reign of Nicholas "was not the lack of reforming effort, but rather, on the contrary, the self-assurance with which the ruling bureaucracy dealt with the basic problems of government."[38] Kizevetter's view is only partly correct. It is true insofar as the bureaucracy was not in fact lacking in self-assurance, but it is wrong inasmuch as Kizevetter evidently draws no distinction between self-assurance and decisiveness. Nicholas I's government had no doubt that it alone was qualified to solve the problems of the state, put everything in order, and master everything, and that it could in fact succeed. The idea that it might have to depend on the help of other elements in society, which were not included in its ranks, was fundamentally alien to its way of thinking. By contrast, it is hardly possible to describe this government as decisive. There was no sphere where it had the courage to carry out far-reaching consistent reforms. It was only bold when preparing its draft projects.

At the time of Nicholas's accession, the legal status of the peasants (both serfs and state peasants) was based on legal principles that belonged in essence to serfdom, whereas that of the gentry and the townspeople rested on the principles of law, on which civil society was founded. Remaining true to his beliefs, Nicholas I did not change this. Thus, what had been achieved under Catherine and Alexander I in the development of liberalism was saved from destruction. In accordance with his character and despotic tendencies, Nicholas I could easily have reversed all the liberal progress made by his predecessors and could have restored the system of serfdom for those classes of society for which it had been abolished. Nicholas's rigid conservatism, however, saved Russia from such a deeply reactionary policy. Whatsoever survives for decades is usually secured through the mere fact of its survival. That is to say, under Nicholas I some of what had been achieved under Catherine and Alexander I, which had to lead ultimately to the establishment of a liberal order, was not only retained but also consolidated.

Far be it from me to justify the attitude of Nicholas I and his government. On the contrary, I feel I can assert that the reign of Nicholas I was extremely disastrous for the future development of Russia. Nicholas I was convinced that the monarch's will could decide everything, that the monarch could order the various estates of his empire to live under different legal systems—to breathe different legal atmospheres, so to speak. The idea that the monarch's will was not the only power, but that legal principles were also a power that could shape a person's character, even their mind, was completely alien to Nicholas. He was probably not in a position to notice over the years of his long reign that the gulf that separated the upper and lower classes in their legal consciousness was growing ever wider. If he had been able to notice this phenomenon, would he have also been able to understand its real significance? I doubt it. The only thing that mattered to him was that his subjects obey the monarch's will to the letter. If they really did so, they probably acted according to different legal principles, but always according to the tsar's wishes—that is, in the final analysis everything was in order. Unfortunately, this view is naive, as it is quite unsatisfactory, of course, if different social classes have conflicting views of the law, and it remains unsatisfactory despite this being the government's intention in the first place. In addition, this can ultimately result in a social catastrophe. One should not underestimate the danger that arose from the fact that for decades Nicholas's government did nothing to allow the peasantry to follow the same evolution as the gentry and the townspeople, after his predecessors had switched these upper classes from the track of serfdom to the track of civil society.

The statistics cited above show that even the bureaucratic machinery of the Ministry of State Domains was able to achieve some positive results. The benefits it brought in some areas were even quite considerable. It is interesting to note that the reign of Nicholas I up to 1848 was a period during which university education in Russia made considerable progress. Moscow University in particular flourished during this period. This was thanks above all to Count Uvarov, who was minister of education for fifteen years under Nicholas I, until 1849, and Count Stroganov, the curator of the Moscow Education District. Stroganov made the greatest efforts to find bright and talented people and attract them to Moscow University. During his time as curator, Redkin, Krylov, Kriukov, Chivilev, Inozemtsev, Kavelin, Solov'ev, Kudriavtsev, and Buslaev, among others, were appointed. Korsh was appointed as the university librarian. Stroganov, who was personally neither very talented nor highly educated, was nevertheless inspired by the deep love of education typical of the age of Alexander I. He devoted all his attention to the university. Chicherin writes that several generations of students felt deeply indebted to him. Uvarov was a much more significant figure. Even Cicherin, who was in general very critical of his contemporaries, stressed that Uvarov was a man of wide intellectual horizons and all-around learning: "He was an enlightened man, in the true sense of the word, as only magnates in the reign of Alexander I could sometimes be."[39] Uvarov tirelessly protected the interests of university education, whose nature and purpose he understood well, even from the despotic policies of Nicholas I. He did everything possible at the time to promote genuine education.

Contemporaries had already noted this favorable development. The magazine *Moskovskii Nabliudatel* (Moscow Observer) noted, "Moscow University is rapidly starting to acquire distinction and importance." In the magazine's opinion, the factors that lay behind this were, first, making the entrance examinations more demanding and then sending young academics to Berlin for further training: "The appointment of young lecturers who have trained for a teaching career in Germany represents an important milestone in the annals of Moscow University."[40] Chicherin tells us what Moscow University was able to offer the talented and truly motivated student: "The university gave me all it possibly could. It widened my intellectual horizons; it introduced me to new fields of knowledge of which I had been ignorant up to then; it fostered in me a burning love of science and taught me to take a serious attitude to it; it even revealed to me the moral value of science for the human soul."[41]

Admittedly, not all of this was achieved solely through the program of official lectures, but doubtless above all thanks to personal contact with the professors, which was intense. Chicherin writes: "The contact between the professors and the students was very cordial. . . . On certain days large numbers of students always gathered at Granovsky's, at Kavelin's, at Redkin's; there were lively discussions, and not only about academic matters but also about current affairs and literary publications."[42] In general, this was a time when intellectual life was mainly found in private houses, and ideological debates took place in private salons—a clear example, incidentally, of how the autonomy of private property favored intellectual freedom. Such salons or circles were especially numerous in Moscow. Chicherin recalls in his memoirs: "I once said to I. S. Turgenev that he railed in vain against the Moscow intellectual circles in his *Hamlet from the Shchigrov District*. They were the lungs that at the time allowed Russian thought, oppressed as it was from all sides, to breathe. . . . Turgenev agreed with my comment."[43]

In fact the most educated and brilliant representatives of the intellectual circles met in some of these salons (e.g., at the house of N. F. Pavlov, where Chicherin lived as a student). There was an exchange of ideas among people with a great depth of knowledge who often possessed a true gift for eloquence. One can imagine how brilliant these salons must have been just by recalling the names of those who attended. There were the most significant figures among the Slavophiles: Khomiakov, the Aksakov brothers, the Kireevsky brothers, the young Yuri Samarin; and from among the Westernizers: Granovsky, Chaadaev, and Herzen. Chicherin writes that it was in these circles "that I was gripped for the first time by one of the highest and noblest endeavors of the human soul, the enthusiasm for knowledge."⁴⁴ "I wanted to become an active participant of this intellectual ferment." "It was here that my ideal of intellectual and moral dignity was formed."⁴⁵

Especially after 1849, these circles remained the only centers of intellectual and spiritual life. In fact, in 1849, the government started to eradicate everything in the universities that seemed suspicious (and what could it not regard as suspicious after the events around Europe of 1848?). In that year, Uvarov was forced to resign, and Stroganov was replaced by Nazimov. Philosophy, a dangerous and suspect discipline, was cut from the curriculum, and the professor of philosophy dismissed (it was Katkov at the time). A clergyman (the priest Tarnovsky, as Chicherin noted disdainfully) was entrusted with giving lectures on logic and psychology. Nazimov's task was to impose military discipline on the students, while the number of students (with the exception of the faculty of medicine) was restricted to three hundred.

Despite the eminence of the participants in the abovementioned salons, the discussions that took place there bore little fruit. The dispute between Slavophiles and Westernizers (the main topic of discussion at the time) was purely theoretical and remained at the level of abstraction. The history of this dispute does not belong directly to the history of liberalism. I would like, however, to quote the view of Chicherin, Russian liberalism's most important thinker, on this subject, as it is symptomatic of his general outlook:

> All this Slavophile preaching seemed strange and irrational. . . . I loved
> my fatherland dearly and was a sincere son of the Orthodox Church. From
> this standpoint, it seems the Slavophile doctrine could appeal to me.
> They wanted, however, to make me believe that the entire Russian elite,
> after coming under the influence of Peter the Great's reforms, despised
> everything Russian and blindly idolized everything foreign. This might
> be true of a few St. Petersburg salons, but having grown up in the Russian
> heartlands, I never in my life encountered this. They wanted to convince
> me that the peasants, among whom I had lived and whom had known since
> childhood, represented the highest ideal of mankind, and this seemed
> totally absurd to me. They wanted to instill in me a loathing of everything
> that I was proud of in Russian history: that is, the genius of Peter the Great,
> the glorious reign of Catherine, the great deeds of Alexander. The man
> who brought enlightenment to Russia (Peter) was presented as someone
> who had corrupted the nation's ideals, and by contrast the feeble-minded
> Feodor Ivanovich (Tsar Feodor I) was portrayed in Khomiakov's *Educational
> Library* as the ideal tsar because he never missed a church service and rang
> the church bells himself. It was maintained that we had no need of lectures
> from the West on the subject of liberty, taking as evidence pre-Petrine
> Russia, which, however, was marked by complete servitude from top to
> bottom. The education that I had come to respect since childhood and the
> science after which I thirsted . . . were presented as dangerous lies of which

one had to beware as if they were poison. In its place, there was the promise of a Russian science, of which no one had heard, which still does not exist to this day, and which was supposed to develop one day from principles preserved intact in the peasant world. All this was so far removed from the real needs and situation of Russian society, and in such contrast to what plain, sound common sense told one, that to us outsiders the Slavophile party must have seemed like a strange sect, coming as we did from the provinces and not completely confused by the debates in the Moscow salons. In the world beyond the Moscow salons, Russian life and Western education were able to get along splendidly, and there was no conflict between them. On the contrary, the progress of the one was to the complete advantage of the other. All my parents' efforts were aimed at providing me with a European education, which they considered the best possible accomplishment for a Russian and the surest means of serving the nation.[46]

Chicherin, as a genuine scientist, was particularly critical of the Slavophile doctrine that the national psyche was the fundamental source of knowledge: "According to (Yuri) Samarin's theory, the scientist must immerse himself in the life of the people before embarking on scientific research. One's research method, instead of emerging naturally from studying a specific object, is predetermined by principles rooted in the national psyche. Evidently, no one familiar with genuine scientific inquiry could accept this notion."[47] Moreover, Chicherin pointed out that although the Slavophiles rejected Western culture and education, their own doctrine was essentially rooted in Western Europe. In fact, their own critique of the West was based largely on a critique of the development of modern Europe that was expounded in Munich in particular: "Even the utmost philosophical importance of the Orthodox Church," writes Chicherin, "that is, the principle on which the Slavophiles based all their intellectual sensibility, was preached at that time by Baader, one of Schelling's most eminent followers."[48]

According to Chicherin, not only the theoretical content of the Slavophile doctrines but also their influence was harmful: "They did not awaken any self-confidence in Russian society, but on the contrary, they ended up discouraging the patriotic feelings of those who were incensed by their efforts to value the backwardness of Russian culture above European education."[49]

The tone of the discussions also left Chicherin feeling dissatisfied. The debates were full of wit and conducted with brilliance and flair. Yet what predominated was not the effort to analyze and elucidate problems more deeply, but rather the eagerness to claim an ideological victory. On his long trips abroad, or more accurately during his stay abroad from 1858 to 1861, Chicherin often bitterly recalled the Moscow debating soirées and regretted that they lacked the spirit of genuine scientific inquiry that he had encountered in the West. The figure of Lorenz Stein, the Viennese professor of constitutional law and the philosophy of law, made a great impression on him. Chicherin relates: "Here for the first time

I encountered what it was to live in a genuine atmosphere of scientific inquiry, which leads one to tackle problems calmly and simply, as the subject of objective research, and not as a party matter and the cause of bitter dispute." In addition, he continues: "Instead of the vehement arguments of these barren intellectual gymnastics, there was the opportunity for a calm exchange of ideas, which left one feeling completely satisfied intellectually. After a conversation with Stein, I felt all the emptiness of our latest polemic with the Slavophiles."[50]

Chicherin felt the same after his contact with the French scientific world in Paris, observing the calm exchange of ideas between dedicated men of science when he attended a dinner for economists: "This was what I could only dream of in my fatherland. How lofty all this was compared to the complacent philistines at home with their arrogant intolerance, who, instead of learning with humility, got the idea into their heads that one had to despise Western science."[51]

Chicherin's critical remarks are certainly, at least for the most part, correct, and yet one cannot deny the high intellectual and spiritual level of the circles where the most significant representatives of the Slavophiles and Westernizers met. One has to pay tribute to the moral and intellectual atmosphere that prevailed in these circles. There were also other circles, however, sometimes merely insignificant and sometimes downright obscure. Here primitive ideas and narrow, rigid views predominated, accompanied by personal resentment and class hatred—real depositories of negativity and destructive willpower. Here nihilism was the dominant ideology and served as the political program for revolutionary socialism. These circles, however, only emerged during the reign of Alexander II —after the government had begun seriously to implement liberal reforms.

PART 2

THE DEVELOPMENT OF CIVIL LIBERTY, 1856–1914

Chapter 8

The Emancipation of the Serfs

Preparation of legislation for the emancipation
of the serfs—Psychological impact of the
emancipation—General intellectual atmosphere of
the 1860s—Katkov's and Chicherin's views

Alexander II's reign has justifiably been called the Era of Great Reforms. From the outset, Alexander II considered the emancipation of the serfs as the most important and urgent of tasks. This can perhaps be explained by the fact that, as he himself relates, his father, Nicholas I, on his deathbed extracted his promise to find a solution to this problem. Thus, Alexander tried right from the start of his reign to convince the gentry that emancipation was necessary. When he returned from Paris after concluding the peace treaty to end the Crimean War, he turned to the marshals of the nobility for the Moscow province and explained that they had to think about liberating the serfs. He said, "Better to abolish serfdom from above than wait for it to be abolished by force from below."[1]

Soon after this Moscow address, Alexander asked the deputy minister of the interior, Levshin, to draft a memorandum setting out the historical development of serfdom and measures to restrict it. The Committee for Peasant Affairs was formed on January 3, 1857, followed almost exactly a year later, on January 8, 1858, with a new committee that in fact directed all the preparations for the emancipation of the serfs. On February 18 of that year, this committee was given the title of the "Main Committee for Peasant Affairs." During the course of the same year, special committees were set up in all the provinces. Each one consisted of the provincial marshal of the nobility, a representative of the gentry from each district, and two further members of the gentry appointed by the provincial governor. Each committee also had a secretary or an administrator. These committees were initially given the task of preparing drafts of a law emancipating the serfs; later they were meant to be given the task of implementing the reform. On April 2, 1858, these committees were handed a program of work approved by the Main Committee. It was pointed out in this program that the new law was to be called "the law on improving the condition of peasants on private estates." This was to avoid using the term *emancipation*. The problems, which the new legislation was to deal with, were summarized in ten chapters.[2] In fact, these committees concluded their work so that they could be wound up after eighteen months, the last being disbanded on September 4, 1859. Other institutions were set up, however, to implement the reform.[3]

The drafts that emerged from the individual provinces diverged considerably, as they were based on differing principles. It was then decided to set up a commission to harmonize these diverse drafts. This commission consisted of members of the Main Committee and a further five individuals, including General Rostovtsev, who has been described as the soul of the emancipation. In addition, two editing commissions were set up, which Rostovtsev also chaired. He was able to attract people whom he personally trusted to sit on these committees, and it was thanks to this circumstance that, for example, Nicolas Miliutin, Yuri Samarin, and Prince Cherkassky were recruited to join the commissions. The first of these commissions consisted of two sections: one covering law and administration and the other focused on economic affairs.[4]

The legal section in the first commission was given the task of defining the peasants' personal and financial rights, as well as the property rights of the gentry. The section for administrative affairs had to deal with the organization of the peasant communes and determine the relations of the peasants to the landowners, on the one hand, and to the administrative authorities, on the other. The commission for economic affairs had to find a solution to economic issues, in particular the problem of the redemption payments that the peasants had to pay for their allocation of land.

Later a third commission, the financial commission, was set up to deal with the question of which measures were required to help the peasants with their buyout of land.

Rostovtsev died shortly before this work was completed and was replaced by Panin, the minister of justice. Panin was no supporter of the reforms and was in fact one of the greatest skeptics in the government. He was, however, a disciplined official who carried out all instructions from the tsar to the letter. Panin's appointment, therefore, did not adversely affect the emancipation of the serfs.

The groundwork undertaken by the commissions was completed in September 1860, and it was then possible to move to drafting the final text of the emancipation proclamation and the legislation. An expert, Popov, was assigned to the

Main Committee to carry this out.[5] The editing commissions were wound up on October 10, and on the same day, the Main Committee began reviewing the results of these preparations.

Alexander II recognized like no other the dangers of the situation. He knew that the frustration of people's hopes and the continuous tension would become intolerable over time. He therefore made efforts to drive the emancipation process forward as rapidly as possible. In this connection, he replaced the ailing chairman of the Main Committee, Orlov, with Grand Duke Constantine Niko-layevich, who had always supported him vigorously in his reforming efforts. With a new chairman, the Main Committee met almost daily. The reports of the Main Committee were signed off as early as January 14, 1861. The original copy was presented to the State Council, where the draft statutes were again revised. Even here the work proceeded quickly and was completed in the short space of time between January 28 and February 16. Alexander signed the proclamation that was the preamble to the statutes emancipating the serfs on February 19, 1861.

A short time before, he had given the text of the proclamation for a final check to the metropolitan of Moscow, Filaret, who suggested one significant alteration. The draft read, "On this day of great joy for the Russian people . . ." It was this phrase that Filaret deleted. He told the tsar that the proclamation should not contain any phrase that did not reflect, or could offend, the feelings of the Russian people. He certainly had in mind that the reform was a solution demanding great sacrifices of the gentry without completely satisfying the wishes of the peasants. With his typical acumen, the metropolitan had put his finger on the conventional insincerity of this phrase and advocated its deletion. The metropolitan considered it unacceptable that the imperial proclamation should contain any words that the Russian people would think untrue. This is in complete contrast to modern totalitarian regimes, which demand that people accept government propaganda and assertions as the truth, regardless of whether or not such statements are true.

It is interesting that people with differing points of view remarked that the emancipation of the serfs was for many a disappointment. The radical left-wing poet Nekrasov wrote, "A great chain snapped. One end struck the gentry, the other the peasants."

In fact, neither the expectation of the imminent emancipation nor the announcement of the emancipation manifesto calmed the situation down or created a feeling of trust and optimism. On the contrary, tension grew everywhere. This tension resulted less from the conflict over specific demands or the always unavoidable friction from the implementation of individual measures. Rather, the disappointment, it should be stressed, had much deeper roots than the injury to special interests or the failure to satisfy them. The tension was produced by the general atmosphere resulting from the spread of a revolutionary mentality. In his *History of the Russian Revolution,* Kulczycki writes:

The intellectual climate in Russia between 1857 and 1870 in many ways resembled that which prevailed in France before the outbreak of the great revolution, even if it had its own particular characteristics. Looked at more closely, the most striking features were realism, rationalism, and utilitarianism, a glorification of life and freedom. . . . A feature of realist philosophy was the rejection of all metaphysical ideas. . . .

Idealist philosophy, of which Hegel's system was the foremost example, slowly lost its foothold. It was replaced by Feuerbach's monistic materialism, which in turn was itself superseded by the vulgar materialism of Vogt and Moleschott and various positivist schools of thought. . . . This realist movement was closely linked to an extreme rationalism. The followers of this rationalism did not shrink from the most radical conclusions of their philosophy; they were not in the least inhibited by tradition; they had only one wish, which was to live, in public and private, according to utilitarian principles in the widest sense. The generation of that period had boundless faith in progress and human happiness; after all, had not they themselves just climbed out of the swamp of reaction and ignorance, witnessed for themselves the triumphant march of science, and participated in the destruction of centuries-old institutions (the abolition of serfdom)? At the time, these people were convinced that Russia was a blank sheet of paper on which to write with ease whatever science and a social conscience dictated.[6]

It is apparent from this excellent characterization of the ideological trends dominating these intellectual circles that they were gripped by the belief that the end of Nicholas I's reign had ushered in a completely new era, that the time of reaction was over, and that the emancipation of the serfs was the first step on the road to continual progress.

If the atmosphere and mentality in these circles can be imagined, it becomes evident why the act of emancipation only met with disappointment. In fact, the emancipation raised hopes that were not fulfilled, indeed, were impossible to fulfill. From this point of view, freedom, consisting on the one hand merely of the recognition of specific rights by the state, and consequently by the individual on the other (i.e., rights based on positive law and guaranteed by the protection of the courts), did not match expectations. In the view of such circles, the emancipation of the serfs was meant to lead to a completely different sort of freedom or, at the very least, to be the first definite step toward it. This freedom had nothing to do with specific and necessarily limited rights, but, in line with their boundless expectations, it was going to sweep away, in a general and fundamental way, all obstacles on the path to the realization of unlimited potential. This freedom was meant to be, at the very least, something like a run-up to the celebrated leap from the realm of necessity to the realm of freedom.

Some sort of mystical faith, or at least a form of political mysticism, was inherent in such expectations of freedom. The term *political mysticism* is all the more justified as belief in liberty and progress, the free and rational construction of a world order, was combined with belief in values dormant in the people, precisely as the Slavophiles understood it. It was enough to liberate these values from the shackles of a repressive social order to allow them to attain complete fruition.

This also explains why the thinking in these circles was in a sense thoroughly nonpolitical. To ask who was going to inaugurate the age of liberty and progress, or who would lead Russia on the path of reform and emancipation, seemed beside the point. Would it be the autocrat himself or a people's revolution? Either would do. Herzen's attitude was typical in this respect. As long as he thought that Alexander II had implemented the emancipation of the serfs in the way he wanted, he considered it an advantage that Russia was governed by an absolute monarchy. A parliament consisting of representatives of the aristocracy would have trimmed and distorted the emperor's reform plans to the benefit of the upper classes; it was just as well that the autocrat's hands were not tied by such a representative chamber in his progress to reform. That Herzen really did place his hopes on Alexander II is shown in particular by the fact that he often addressed the tsar directly in his journal *Kolokol* (The Bell), which had appeared in London since 1857. This was certainly in the belief that Alexander II would listen to his ideas and advice. It is interesting to note that even such an extreme radical and socialist as Chernyshevsky initially welcomed Alexander's plans for reform. In the journal *Sovremennik* (The Contemporary), we read: "The blessings promised to peacemakers and all men of goodwill will also crown Alexander II with happiness, the like of which no other monarch in Europe ever received, for it is most fortunate to prepare the way for the liberation of one's own subjects and carry it out in person."[7]

As, however, this confidence in the monarch was not underpinned by any firm political principles, indeed did not have any political foundations whatsoever, but was really emotional in character, it melted away just as quickly as it had appeared. The true nature of political radicalism stood clearly revealed. The list of demands began to grow, and to those that had not been met were added those that were impossible to meet, at least given the circumstances at the time. The path of peaceful reform embarked on by the government was rejected, and revolutionary action was proclaimed the only effective means.

The intoxication associated with the idea of revolution and revolutionary struggle took hold in some intellectual circles. The Russian intelligentsia, totally lacking in any political experience, was unable to resist the temptation inherent in the idea that the desired goal could be reached directly through the violent destruction of an existing order that stood in its way. The tendency of absolutism, and in particular the autocratic rule of Nicholas I, to consider itself the guardian of its subjects would now reap dire consequences. Suddenly the ward felt the urge to act independently, for which it proved to be wholly unprepared. At the same time, the intelligentsia blocked its own participation in the preparation and implementation of the reforms through its revolutionary attitude; that is, it excluded itself from any practical work that alone could have provided it with some training in political thought and action.

Particularly regrettable was the way radicals and revolutionaries appealed to science and scientific progress and, what is more, stressed that they alone were entitled to speak in the name of science. They thus handed all the best arguments to the reactionaries. If science, and philosophy in particular, justified having to destroy the existing rule of law in its entirety, it was not enough to state that this did not demonstrate that philosophy was useful or that it might be destructive. One would positively have to say that the harm it caused was obvious and its usefulness extremely questionable. Even the Slavophiles could feel more confident in their assertion that the wisdom of the West was a spiritual poison.

Defending science and scientific freedom from, on the one hand, the monopolistic claims of the revolutionaries and, on the other hand, the suspicions of the reactionaries was a thankless task. This task was left to liberal Westernizers, conservative liberals such as Chicherin and Katkov, who were convinced that these revolutionary teachings had nothing in common with genuine science and that rather their dissemination was the result of the suppression of scientific thought, of scientific freedom. Katkov wrote in his newspaper *Moskovskie Vedomosti* [Moscow Gazette] (1866, no. 205):

> All these false doctrines, these pernicious trends, emerged and coalesced in a society in which respect for free and vigorous scientific inquiry was unknown and excluded from any official discussion of its most vital interests, in a society in which all aspects of life were submitted to censorship and put under police surveillance. These false doctrines and pernicious trends, about which so many complaints are heard today, were the product of repressed, underdeveloped thinking, in which everything instinctive became servile and, in the lower depths, brutalized.

Chicherin also believed that the spread of revolutionary ideas could be attributed to the repression of intellectual freedom under Nicholas I: "This senseless propaganda, whose aim was the destruction of the whole existing social order, coincided with the moment when the government emancipated twenty million peasants from their two-hundred-year-old serfdom." He continues: "Russia was showered with invaluable benefits from above (i.e., by the monarch). The dawn of a new age spreads out, and below, it is already crawling with reptiles who had bred in the darkness of the previous reign and who were ready to . . . overpower the burgeoning new forces."[8]

Chicherin's brother, Vasilii, provides an extremely interesting explanation for the sudden upsurge of radicalism and revolutionary ideas in Russia in the early years of Alexander II's reign: "People aiming God knows where with their demands . . . chatter, I believe, because they do not know what to do with the relative freedom they enjoy. They are liberals who yearn for an iron fist, who feel lost when they are no longer on the leash. . . . The whole of Russia longs for the rod, and not just the lower classes, but the upper classes too."[9] At first, this sounds paradoxical, and yet it is very likely that it gets to the heart of the matter. Most revolutionary programs proposed the formation of an extraordinary committee, a committee to unite and lead the revolutionary struggle, which of course would have to be given dictatorial powers. In the opinion of the revolutionary journal the *Great Russian,* for example, the movement had to be organized along these lines: "Clear-thinking people of strong character, given the power to punish, would have to take over the leadership. . . . No individual should undertake any important action without informing the committee in his town about it."[10]

Is it in fact surprising that the mentality that had developed under serfdom continued to survive and have an influence? This was probably obvious to an observer. To Chicherin's credit, he saw that the main obstacle and danger for Russia's progress toward liberalism lay not in the vestiges of the actual conditions of serfdom, but in the vestiges of the mentality produced by serfdom. This mentality was impervious to both the nature and the limits of true liberty and deadened the capacity for self-discipline. This mentality, a product of serfdom, produced a dark rebellious instinct, coupled at the same time with a tendency to blind obedience, to servility. Hence the yearning for the iron fist, which Vasilii Chicherin wrote about in a letter to his brother. If the tsarist iron fist was not hard enough, it had to be replaced by the newer harder fist of a committee of the revolutionary dictatorship. Chicherin was right when he detected an even greater danger in this future revolutionary power than that of the old absolute monarchy. He writes, "At the sight of this communist movement, a liberal who is honest has no option but to support the monarchy."[11] He comments that the absolute monarchy belonged to the past and would be transformed inevitably over time into a constitutional one, when the conditions allowed it. Since the reign of Catherine, he continues, the absolute monarchy had decided to recognize civil rights and civil liberty and to grant them to increasing sections of society. This development, according to Chicherin, would inevitably lead one day to the establishment of a parliament in Russia, that is, to the granting of political rights to Russian citizens. By contrast, the aim of the revolutionary movements was, in Chicherin's opinion, the creation and establishment of socialism, which brought with it the abolition of private property and hence of civil liberty in general. The loss of civil liberty would inevitably make it impossible for political freedom to survive. The socialist system, in his view, would have to end in dictatorship, which would be incapable of developing into a freer system. The very nature of the socialist system would inevitably perpetuate this dictatorship. Later, in the 1890s, Chicherin wrote in his magnum opus, *A Course on Political Science* [*Kurs gosudarstvennoi nauki*]:

> Today's social democracy, with its extensive organization, with its hatred
> of the upper classes, bent on the destruction of the entire current system,
> leads inevitably to dictatorship. Insofar as the ideal of suppressing all civil
> liberty is inherent to it, it must also threaten political freedom. Democracy

can only survive as long as this party remains weak and is not in a position to influence the running of the state. Its strength, however, is clearly growing, and that must inevitably lead to profound upheavals. If it succeeds somewhere or other in gaining the upper hand, it will only be able to hold on to power by means of awful terror. On the other hand, an all-out dictatorship would also be needed to defend society from the threat of destruction. Whatever the case, given the mutual hatred fueling both sides in this internal class war, only a power that is independent of society will be able to preserve social order and maintain the necessary unity of the state.[12]

Chapter 9

The Emancipation Laws and and Their Later Interpretation

The rights granted to the peasants immediately after emancipation—The problem of the land buy-out system—The peasants' definitive legal status in the wake of the emancipation laws—The tendency to accept the restrictions on peasant property stemming from the buy-out of land as customary

How far did the emancipation laws go in granting the serfs their liberty—that is, liberty understood as a body of civil rights based on positive law and protected by the courts? The question requires some analysis. The emancipation laws brought in a transitional period—a transition between serfdom and the status of free rural inhabitants that, according to the legislation, the peasants were to attain through emancipation. During this transition, the peasants were still obliged to provide certain services for their former masters. These included the *obrok* (rent) payments and even work in lieu of rent, which were open, however, to amendment following emancipation and whose extent was subject to state control. This transitional phase was necessary to protect the landowners from ruin and to allow them to move from an economy based on serf labor to one based on wage labor. Although in itself reasonable, this period did not need to be prolonged over twenty years. On the positive side, this period, although long, was fixed; that is, the services provided by the peasants were of a limited duration. At the end of this period, the peasants would finally no longer have to carry out duties for their masters. During the transitional period, the peasants were called *vremenno-obiazannye;* that is, they were subject to temporary obligations.

Thus, the question regarding what the peasants were granted immediately after the emancipation laws came into effect is quite distinct from the question regarding what rights the legislation intended them to have after the end of the transitional phase, or following complete emancipation.

The peasants were granted personal freedom; that is, there was a declaration that they were recognized as free individuals. At the same time, the landowners' police powers were transferred to the village communes. Similarly, the landowners' judicial powers were transferred partly to the elected *volost'* courts in the peasant communes and partly to magistrates. The landowners were required to set aside plots of land so that peasants could sustain themselves economically. These plots consisted of the *usad'ba,* on the one hand, and arable land, pasture, and meadow on the other.[1] With regard to the *usad'ba,* the peasants were given the legal right to purchase it. When a peasant had finished making the redemption payments, the peasant or the farmstead became the proprietor of the *usad'ba.* By contrast, peasants could only purchase the remaining land allocated to them if they came to a voluntary agreement with the landowner. The state was prepared to make the purchase easier for the peasants by means of substantial financial support, but it did not yet consider it possible to force landowners to sell the arable land, pastures, and meadows that they had to make available to the peasants. (This sale by the landowners was only made compulsory in the 1880s, a measure that was certainly passed because of the end of the transitional period.) Overall, the nature of the property relations of the emancipated peasants was based on Count Kiselev's ideas. Land was and would remain the property of the landowners, although they were required to make certain parts of it available to the peasants for twenty years.

At the time of the drafting of the emancipation laws, the significance of the question as to what would happen at the end of the twenty-year period was already clear. Provincial committees, individual members of them, and those on the editing commissions often made their opinions known on this issue. As was the case with all the problems discussed in connection with the emancipation, many varied and often conflicting views were expressed. It was of course clear to most people (in fact to nearly everyone) that it would be unthinkable for the landowners to take back this arable land and pasture after twenty years, which would have turned the peasants into day laborers or even simply vagabonds. This would have been totally against the spirit of the whole reform. Some demanded that the peasants' legal right to buy the *usad'ba* should be extended to cover all land that was made available to them. Others contended that peasants should be able to farm the land for an indefinite period, which would only end if they bought it, in other words, only when the plots of allotment land made available to the peasants became their property. This second view was a variation on the first, except that there was no set period laid down for the purchase. Last, according to a third view, this use of the land should be converted into a free leasehold.[2] The first of these views formed the basis of subsequent legislative regulation.

The arguments deployed by those who held this view are illuminating and quite in the spirit of liberalism. Skrebitsky informs us that in the opinion of Count Stroganov, governor general of New Russia and Bessarabia, the resolution of the Ekaterinoslav Committee, relating to the allocation (*nadelenie*) of arable land, pasture, and meadow land to the peasants, for the transition period only, would compromise the excellent aim of improving the condition of the peasants, as in this way the peasant will lose his motivation and not be interested in building up his farm. . . . Consequently, the numbers of beggars and homeless people would increase.[3]

Similarly, the majority on the Tver' Committee declared, "Individual liberty can never become a reality without property rights." They then posed a question:

If the peasants were granted their personal freedom and the right of free movement while the landowners were given unlimited rights over all land, would it not mean that the landowners were merely relieved of all their former duties to the peasants, thus making the latter vulnerable to even more arbitrary treatment from the landowners? A peasant would be forced to accept any conditions that the landowners wished to impose, which would mean that all his wealth, indeed his whole life, would depend on the whim of the landowner. This did not even exist under serfdom, as the landowners were under a solemn duty to provide the peasants with the necessary means of making a living.[4]

Thus, the point made by the majority on the Tver' Committee was that if the emancipation of the serfs was intended to be a true liberation, then the land, allocated to the peasants for their own use, had to become their permanent property. These words are also significant insofar as they provide direct evidence that at least some representatives of the gentry were aware that the 1861 reform was not only a matter of emancipating the serfs. It was also the last stage in the process of the liberation of the gentry begun in the eighteenth century, as previously mentioned in the chapter on the reign of Nicholas I.

It is understandable therefore that the gentry also found it desirable from the point of view of their own property rights to set a time limit on the compulsory right of the peasants to farm the gentry's land. It was Koshelev, precisely the representative of the gentry who could least of all be accused of class self-interest, who pointed this out.[5] Skrebitsky writes:

Koshelev cannot support the editing commissions, as their efforts at drafting are concerned less with the demands of justice than with the aim of improving the condition of the peasants at any price. They are taking the liberty of violating laws and rights to achieve this, without there being any compelling reason to justify measures above the law. The peasants have to be provided with land with the emancipation, so the compulsory purchase of land must be carried out according to the law. This is made all the easier as the Svod [civil code] offers the appropriate means—namely a buyout (*vykup*) of land. Instead the legal and economic affairs commissions are introducing an unprecedented form of limited land ownership, by which the members of one class are granted the complete right of disposal over the immovable property of another class, without a time limit, at that, and in exchange for services at a rate fixed once and for all.[6]

Shidlovsky also points out that the creation of a system of limited ownership amounted to an arbitrary violation or distortion of Article 432, volume 10, of the Svod, or the Russian civil code.[7] These comments by Koshelev and Shidlovsky show to what degree the provisions of volume 10 had become an active component in the Russian gentry's legal consciousness. Compulsory purchase in line with the provisions of civil law was regarded by the gentry as legitimate—as legal. By contrast, the limitations on the property rights of the landowner, which, taking a historical perspective, can be seen as springing from the legal tradition of serfdom, were described by the gentry as unjust and, what is more remarkable, as a radical innovation, a view, however, that is not borne out by history.

That this was not just the opinion of a few isolated individual members of the gentry can be seen from the fact that a declaration on similar lines was issued jointly by thirty-four members of the so-called Second Appeal Committees (*vtorogo priglasheniia*), as follows:

> The editing commissions believe it is just and necessary to recognize the land rights of the peasants, without overturning the rights of the landowners to the same land. They are not deterred by the incompatibility of two sets of rights (property rights) to the same land. It seems very simple to them to let the landowners keep this right in theory, while in practice transferring it to the peasant. "Communist principles" are adeptly applied in all the chapters proposed by the Economic Affairs Commission. Nevertheless, one can see straightaway that the whole system is based on the negation of property rights, that is, on the disruption and disintegration of society, whose very goals and existence are determined by the protection of individual and property rights.[8]

The antiliberal views within the editing commissions (as well as on the provincial committees) were not just evident from the way they deviated from the basic principles and provisions of Russian civil law—from the provisions of volume 10 of the Svod—in their approach to the landowners' property rights. This could also be seen even more clearly from their proposals regarding which sort of legal status the peasants would enjoy after emancipation. In general, this is the same approach that emerged so emphatically in the 1880s and 1890s, the "period of reaction," and that was reflected in a series of laws. The change in direction of the '80s and '90s no longer comes as a surprise to the historian, once he takes into account how strong antiliberal opinion already was in the 1860s, even among those who were directly involved in preparing the emancipation statutes. Up to a point, this approach was already able to prevail in 1861 and influence the text of the emancipation statutes.

Just as the 1861 Manifesto imposed a duty on landowners to transfer their immovable property, their land, to the peasants, so too were the peasants now required to accept their allotment land together with the obligations to the landowner that were imposed in return for the right to farm this land. Only after the peasant had finished paying for his *usad'ba* (farmstead) was he allowed to give up the plots that he had been allocated.[9] That meant, however, that his freedom of movement up to that point was merely theoretical and that until he had paid off his *usad'ba* the peasant remained bound to the soil, in other words, a serf. Some committees insisted that the peasants should be refused the right to give up their allotted plots, even after they had paid off the *usad'ba*. First, the landowners pointed out, they would be unable to farm or lease these plots, particularly in the sparsely populated northern provinces, if the peasants gave them up. This would result in land lying fallow.[10] Second, they objected that this right would make the peasants vulnerable to the ruinous path of proletarianization, especially because peasants were not motivated regarding agricultural work.[11] Moreover, this would consequently enable them, in those areas where industry had been developed, "to make a decent living and earn all their income not from agriculture but from trade."[12]

Several proposals were put forward, all of which were aimed at limiting the extent of the peasants' property rights to the *usad'ba* itself, which they had already purchased. Most of these proposals concerned the right to sell. According to one such proposal, the peasants would only be allowed to sell their *usad'ba* to their former master or to their village commune or finally to individual members of the commune. If none of these declared an interest in buying the property, it could be sold to an outsider—in the sense that he would be allowed to buy the buildings, dismantle them, and take them away, while the plot on which the *usad'ba* stood would go to the village commune.[13] Some committees proposed that the peasants should be forbidden from dividing the property among their heirs,[14] while others were against the sale of the *usad'ba* for settling debts. Typical was the opinion of Prince Vasil'chikov, who spoke in favor of restricting the rights of peasants to set up workshops in their *usad'ba* "as these were given to the peasants for agricultural purposes."[15]

It is interesting that these restrictions on the right of disposal, and the right to sell in particular, seemed so natural that Muraviev, the governor of Pskov at the time, actually said, "The condition that they (the *usad'ba*) were not to be sold to anyone but the member of the commune or the landowner does not belong among those limits on property rights that can properly be described as restrictive."[16]

In the end, liberal, or at least more liberal, thinking won the upper hand in the drafting of the emancipation statutes. After the end of the transitional period, the peasants were to have the same legal status as free landowners. The peasants were to be granted the same civil liberty, the same civil rights, as members of the other estates living in the country, just as Alexander II wished. In a marginal note to the Main Committee's resolution on these lines, he wrote, "God willing."[17]

The provisions of the 1861 emancipation statutes too are unequivocally of the same tenor. According to Article 22 of the so-called General Statute (general here in contrast to local—i.e., the main emancipation law), the obligations that the peasants were committed to, and the contracts they entered into, were based on the general provisions relating to debt in Russian civil law. Articles 33ff of the General Statute, as well as Articles 159 and 165 of the law on land buyouts, are of particular importance. All these articles indicate that the intention of the legislation was that the conditions under which peasants could own land would be governed by the general provisions of Russian civil law. If not directly at the end of the transitional period, this could happen when the peasant had finished paying for his land. To begin with, one should also bear in mind that the landowners' property transferred to the former serfs' communes in the context of the emancipation could be allocated in practice to individual farms as well as to the commune. In addition, a farmstead or a commune could buy this allotment land.

We can now examine the provisions of the emancipation statutes that deal with the property rights of the peasant. Article 33 states: "Each peasant can buy immovable and movable property, as well as sell, mortgage, and in general dispose of it in accordance with the broad legal provisions of the law as they apply to free rural inhabitants."

According to Article 34, village communes were also given the right to buy and dispose of immovable property. One thing that the commune could do was to divide among its members the property it had acquired, which then became the private property of these members. Article 36 goes even further and states: "Any member of the commune can ask to be given a plot as his own property from the land bought by the commune, in proportion to his contribution to the purchase of that land." In certain circumstances, however, the commune could choose to pay a sum of money to the peasant instead of allocating him a plot of land. Article 37 is not concerned with land purchased by peasants, but rather the plots that were allocated to them in the context of the emancipation, that is, their allocated plots (*nadely*). As far as these plots of land are concerned, it was decreed that during the first nine years after the general *polozhenie* became law, a peasant could not sell or mortgage them to anyone other than members of the same commune. (During this nine-year period, the commune too was not allowed to sell its allocated land—cf. the statute regarding the purchase of land.) Otherwise, the use and disposal of this land followed the same provisions as Articles 33ff, cited above.

Article 159 of the law, dealing with the purchase of land, is of particular significance. Its second part states: "On completion of the repayments for the loan (i.e., the loan that the peasants received from the state to make their redemption payments to the landowners), the provisions of the general statute applying to peasants released from serfdom and land acquired as property by these peasants will be extended to land they have bought (i.e., the allotment land bought through the redemption payments)." The intention of Article 159 is clear. The plots of allotment land should be regarded as the peasant's private property at the end of the buyout process. The peasant's property rights after the buyout should not differ in any way from those of other free rural inhabitants and should conform to the general norms of Russian civil law; that is, they should be governed by the provisions of volume 10 of the Svod.

Village communes were not to be privileged at the expense of the individual peasant. While there was no intention in the legislation of breaking up the commune forcibly, neither was it to receive any particular protection. Article 165 states:

> Up to the full repayment of the loan to buy land, the transfer (*vydel*) of land to individual farms from the total acquired by the commune (i.e., land allocated to the commune) can only take place with the agreement of the commune. However, if the head of the farmstead, who requests such a transfer, pays off the whole of the loan corresponding to his plot to the district fiscal authority, then the commune has a duty to transfer a corresponding plot of land, if possible in one piece, which it has itself chosen.

What was clearly intended by this legislation, as can be seen from all these provisions of the emancipation statutes, was that the completion of the redemption payments should present the peasant with the opportunity of owning land as his private property.

While the redemption payments were still ongoing, the peasant's right of disposal over his allotment land was subject to various restrictions. Article 169 of the law on buyouts allowed the peasant to sell his allocated plots only to members of the same commune during the first nine years after the law came into effect. (It was possible, however, for the buyer to join the commune for the purpose of this purchase.) The buyer then had to take on all the obligations in relation to any further redemption payments. After the said nine-year period, the peasant (the head of the farmstead) was also able to sell the land allocated to the farm to persons who were not members of the commune. Such a buyer had to pay off the remaining debt at the time of the purchase. According to Article 170, the land that was allocated to the commune or the individual farmstead could not be remortgaged as a matter of principle before the final repayment of the buyout loan. Article 167 forbade the subdivision of plots of land, if these had been allocated to individual farmsteads rather than the commune. This was also the case if the land was sold.

From the point of view of the legislation, the purpose of all these restrictions on the peasants' rights to dispose freely of the land allocated to them was to guarantee that the peasants paid back their buyout loans. These restrictions were therefore temporary and were to lapse with the final repayment of the loan. The original justification for these limitations, however, was soon forgotten, or at any rate overtaken by other considerations. The view that peasant land ownership was fundamentally different from land ownership of other social estates became widespread. This ownership, it was felt, was not of private property, as defined by Article 420, volume 10, of the Svod, but rather a distinct form of immovable property. A logical consequence of this view was that the abovementioned restrictions were regarded as a natural part of peasant property and therefore had to remain in force.

According to this view, land was allocated to the peasants to ensure they could make a living or, to be more exact, make a living as peasants. Securing the peasants' livelihood was regarded as being in the interest, or even the duty, of the state. The peasants' allotment land was thus a form of property whose purpose was to satisfy the interests of the state and to enable it to fulfill its duty in this respect. It therefore served as an arrangement of convenience. If this property existed to secure the interests of the state, then it had to be protected by special legal provisions. A ban on any form of disposal that might reduce the size of the property was quite naturally part of these protective measures. Accordingly, it was logical to prohibit the sale of this land to persons who did not belong to the social estate of the peasantry, or at any rate to put obstacles in its way, if possible, as well as to remortgage and divide the plots of land or the farmstead. After all, a peasant could not feed himself or his dependents from a plot that was too small and thus no longer suited to the aim of supporting the peasant family.

Once you take the view that peasant-allotment land is a form of property to secure peasants' livelihood in the interest of the state, the conditions are in place for a special legal regime not only governing the peasant's ownership of land but also extending to the other legal relations of members of the peasant social estate. Thus, even after the emancipation, the idea persisted that different social estates in the empire could live according to different strata of law, that their legal relations could be based on different legal systems. This created the conditions for the ever-widening gulf in the legal consciousness of the peasant estate and that of the other estates of the Russian empire.

Looked at more closely, the legal provisions concerning peasant land ownership provide a clearer idea of the outlines of the legal system to which the peasant estate was subject. As mentioned above, this special legislation did not just apply to the peasants' property rights. The regulation of other legal relations of the members of this estate was also based on this special regime. All the legal relations to which someone is subject are interdependent. It is not always possible to regulate one part of these relations through provisions that are based on the principles of one legal system, while regulating the other parts by norms that are rooted in another. At the time, moreover, there was a conscious effort to extend and develop peasant law as a self-contained legal system isolated from the law governing other social estates.

The practical outcome of these efforts can be seen in the many decisions of the Senate and in a series of laws that were enacted under Alexander III. Incidentally, it is noteworthy that in so doing, the Senate exhibited a tendency that was typical of the thinking of quite diverse circles and that generally became predominant. Zaitsev has drawn attention to this:

> Apart from a few isolated figures who did not directly exert any decisive influence, it is with some amazement that one observes how politicians with differing views, from the most reactionary to the most extremely revolutionary, as well as scientists and writers of various schools of thought, from different sometimes opposing motives, were all enthusiastic about the idea of a system of peasant law that was specific to the Russian nation. So-called *Narodnichestvo* (populism) should not be seen as narrow revolutionary party dogma; it was rather a very widespread and powerful spiritual movement, although taken to extremes by the revolutionaries. Usually people assume, with some justification, that one of the causes of the 1917 revolution can be found in the breach between the government, the intelligentsia, and the people. One should not ignore the fact, however, that *Narodnichestvo*, as understood in the broadest sense of the agrarian ideology of the Russian intelligentsia, was nothing other than a refinement of the peasant consciousness of law, which had been the result, to an extent, of government action and embedded in law. Government, high society, and people were thus united on the question whose ill-fated solution led to the fall of the Russian Empire.[18]

Chapter 10

Peasant Law

The farmstead—Other important aspects of
peasant law

At the time of the emancipation, land was not allocated to individual peasants, but rather to village communes. This seemed advisable not least because of the practicalities, thus making the process of land allocation much simpler. The land given to the communes could either be subdivided once and for all among the farmsteads belonging to the commune, or particular plots (arable land) could be given to certain farmsteads for a limited time. At the end of this time, the land had to be redistributed among the farmsteads, taking into account the changes that had occurred in the composition of the farms in the commune in the meantime. It is thus possible to identify two types of peasant land ownership—land could belong either to a commune as a whole (this could correspond to a single village, a part of a village, or even a group of smaller villages—called *obshchinnoe vladenie*) or, on the other hand, to an individual farmstead (*podvornoe vladenie*). This latter form of property was certainly just a variation on the former. First, the deeds issued when the land was allocated were not given to the individual farmsteads, but to the commune. Furthermore, the deeds only showed how much land a farmstead was to receive, but not where this land was located or the boundaries of the plots. Sometimes a statement was even added to the effect that the commune could exchange one plot for another. It was not allowed then, however, to alter the area of the plot, and this constitutes the real difference between communal ownership and farmstead ownership.[1] Communes had the right to move over to farmstead ownership, if a village assembly voted for it by a two-thirds majority. In principle, it was also not impossible to change from farmstead to communal ownership.

Neither communal nor farmstead ownership constituted individual private property. All the land allocated to the peasants (*nadel'naia zemlia*) was a resource that formed the material basis for the state to fulfill its obligation to ensure a livelihood for the peasantry. No one was granted any individual rights, any property rights, in relation either to this land or to a single part of it. Parts of the overall land bank were allocated either to the communes or to farmsteads. Each peasant had to belong to a commune and a farmstead, which meant that every peasant had to be provided with land on account of this membership. This entitlement to be allocated land was not at all the same as a right, as understood in civil law. It was an entitlement to a state benefit, similar in nature to ration cards, an allocation of coal, or the entitlement of the homeless to be housed. The profound, fundamental difference between this entitlement and a right can be seen clearly from some of its features.

First, a peasant only enjoyed this entitlement while he remained a member of the farmstead. If he definitively cut his ties to the farmstead, the entitlement lapsed without any compensation. This was the logical outcome of the fact that any individual farmstead member's share of land was not defined, indeed, fundamentally could not be determined.[2] Individuals were not granted a specific right over a particular part of the property. For example, it was not possible for a member of a fifteen-person household who wanted to leave the farmstead to have any claim on the equivalent of a fifteenth of the value of the farmstead and its land. On the other hand, a member of the farmstead did not lose his "right to land," even if he left the village for a longer period without definitively cutting his ties with the village, such as in the case of someone going to earn a living in a town, for example, as a worker or artisan. In this case, he was regarded as being on leave (*v otluchke*), and his entitlement was suspended. If he returned, he could renew his claim and had to be taken back by the farmstead to share again in its routine work and livelihood with the other members. It was not possible entirely to relinquish this entitlement, or "right to land"; in practice, it was only possible not to exercise it. If a peasant, earning his living as an artisan in the town, declared that he was permanently relinquishing his "right to land," this would not have registered anywhere and would have been of no consequence legally. On returning to the family, he could then reassert his entitlement to land, notwithstanding any previous statements to the contrary. This shows particularly clearly that it was not a matter of a right as understood in civil law, but rather an entitlement to a state benefit, which the beneficiary could not simply relinquish at his discretion. As we know, one of the principal characteristics of a right is that it constitutes a claim that a person can waive without authorization or without having to justify it.[3]

Accordingly, it is not possible to talk of inheritance law in relation to farmstead property. If the family—the farmstead community—died out, the farm and its land reverted to the village commune. As long as the family "lived," its remaining members on the farmstead would jointly farm the plots allocated to it. No one could receive an inheritance. The head of the farmstead was not the proprietor of the goods belonging to it. He was the head of the family and thus the head of the "agricultural concern" that the farmstead constituted. This was stressed repeatedly by the Senate and with unambiguous forcefulness in the "opinion" expressed on January 4, 1888, ratified by the tsar:

> The arable land and the *usad'ba* plots making up the allotment land are not considered purely as the property of the person in whose name the deed of sale was issued, but as belonging to all the members of the family. If, however, certain expressions such as "the purchase of land as the personal property of the head of the farmstead" or "the plots of land purchased by the head of the farmstead constitute a person's separate property" appear in some articles in the emancipation statutes (Articles 116 and 120 of the law on land buyouts, 1902 edition), this does not mean that the land purchased by the peasant is his own personal private property. In other words, as the head of the farmstead, he acts rather as its representative in purchasing the land as the property of the farmstead.[4]

In particular, the Senate denied the possibility of disposing of land through a will. Ruling no. 29 of its First and Second Courts and the Court of Appeals, of November 3, 1897, established that "it is not possible to dispose by will of a peasant's allotment land, nor the movable goods necessary for its exploitation." In this connection, the Senate pointed out that as owners of the allotment land "the village commune and the farmstead are recognized as legal entities. If, however, the land allocated to a peasant is the property of a legal entity, the disposal by will of this land is excluded by the very nature of such entities."[5]

The Senate need not have fallen back on the dubious assertion that the village communes and the farmsteads were legal entities in order to preclude the possibility of the peasants disposing over their land allocation through a will. In fact, in the same ruling, the Senate relied more than anything on another, certainly more convincing argument:

> As far as land allocations are concerned, the proprietors (the peasants) do not own this land according to property law as defined in Article 420 in part 1 of volume 10, by which the owner has complete control over his property. It is rather a form of property with a quite special basis arising from the general aim of the state to ensure as far as possible the livelihood of the peasant estate. In order to preserve this land bank, which is needed to provide for the peasant population and which is allocated to the peasants in the form of plots, the right of disposal regarding these plots has to be subject to considerable restrictions. As a result and taking into account the fact that the law is silent as to whether a peasant has the right to pass on his

land by will, one has to conclude that the intention of the legislation was not to grant the peasant such a right.[6]

This conclusion was quite correct. The denial of the freedom of testation in respect of allotment land was one of a series of limitations on the right of disposal over this land, all of which were aimed at preventing a reduction in the land bank, whose purpose was to secure the peasants' livelihood. In fact, this restriction was consistent with the general curtailment of the right of disposal of the peasant over his allocated land and the fact that the head of the farmstead could not be regarded as being subject to property law.[7] By contrast, the Senate's view that the village commune and the farmstead were legal entities can hardly be justified.

Zaitsev was right to be extremely skeptical about designating the village commune, and especially the farmstead, as legal entities. He states in his lectures on administrative law, "Even supposing that the farmstead could be a legal entity, it is nevertheless unlike any category of legal entity as recognized in civil law."[8] He makes the same point in a very interesting article written in German, "Die Rechtsideologie des russischen Agrarwesens und die russische Agrarrevolution" (The Ideology of Law in Russian Agricultural Life and the Russian Agrarian Revolution):[9] "The farmstead is not a legal person in civil law. . . . The farmstead . . . is no more the private owner of the farm property (than is the head of the farmstead). The farmstead exploits the plots of land that have been given to it out of the whole so-called land allocation, which has been taken out of private commerce for the use of its members."

It seems evident, in my opinion as well, that it is impossible to designate the farmstead or the village commune as a legal entity.[10] Both the farmstead and the commune were only recipient "subjects," that is, entities that were allocated land from the overall land bank that was set aside to ensure the livelihood of the peasants. They were entities that provided the means and the structure enabling the members of the peasant estate, and hence of the communes and farmsteads, to lay claim to their entitlement to be allocated land, to "their right to land." Actually, the only difference between the farmstead and the commune where land was periodically redistributed—in other words, the village commune or *mir*—is that the individual peasant could lay claim to his "right to land" in a direct way as part of the farmstead. On the other hand, as part of the commune, he was only able to do so indirectly through the farmstead.

One can see therefore that too much significance has often been attached to rural collective property in Russian agrarian life. What is significant is not the periodic repartition of land within the commune, but rather the singular nature of the peasant's "right to land," which is not a natural right, but represents a legal entitlement to an allocation of land from the state.

One should also bear in mind that however little the property of the farmstead belonged to a legal person, neither was it communal property, as understood in civil law. The Senate repeatedly drew attention to this:

The communal property of the farmstead is not a communal property right as defined in general by civil law, but is determined by the legislation on the peasantry.[11] . . . The provisions of the emancipation statutes give the head of the farmstead, as the eldest member of the family, who, as its (the family's) representative, is responsible for its taxes and services, and in charge of its production, the right to run the farm without the approval of the younger members of the family.[12]

According to a definition from another Senate ruling, the head of the farmstead, as "the representative of the farmstead and head of the farm's production[,] does not require the agreement of the younger family members in the way he chooses to farm their plot of land, provided he keeps within the limits of what is economically viable."[13] These rulings from the Senate show that in fact the farmstead was not communal property. It is well-known that under civil law the disposal of communal property requires the agreement of all those who share ownership.

Concerning the situation of the head of the farmstead, the Senate emphasized repeatedly that "the head of the farmstead is not the owner of the allotment land, although the deeds relating to the plot of land are made out in his name, but rather a representative of the farmstead in the eyes of the commune and the government."[14]

It can be seen from the regulations resulting from this and other Senate rulings that the powers of the head of the farmstead to manage the farm, to determine by himself the use to which the plots of land allocated to the farmstead were put, did not derive from his property rights. They were based on the fact that he was recognized as the representative of the farmstead by the commune and the government. He was thus held accountable to them for the performance of the farmstead. It is particularly important to note that the duties for which the head of the farmstead was responsible did not just include the prompt payment of taxes or the repayment of the buyout loan, but also the effective management of the land allocated to the farmstead. After all, the land had been allocated to the peasants to secure their livelihood—or rather to secure it in the interests of the state. Poor, inefficient farming of land allocated to a farmstead would not have served the interests of the state. Insofar as securing the livelihood of the peasants was seen as the job of the state, logically the state had to reserve the right to make the efficient exploitation of the land the duty of the head of the farmstead and consequently to lay claim to certain powers of supervision for itself.

The effective use of the allotment land did not just depend on the head of the farmstead managing it well, but also on whether the able-bodied members of the farmstead remained there to do their farm work properly. Thus, it was in the state's interest not only to allocate land to the peasants but also to ensure that they took it over, kept it, and remained on it to farm. Of necessity, this meant that the head of the farmstead had to be given certain patriarchal police powers over the members of the family of which he was the head. This was natural as far as the members of the family who remained on the farmstead were concerned. The head of the farmstead, however, also retained such powers over those family members who worked in the town after obtaining permission from the commune and a valid passport issued by the *volost'*. A member of the farmstead, in possession of a valid five-year passport (it was impossible for a peasant to obtain one for a longer period), could also be ordered back by the head of the farmstead with the help of the police. This naturally derived from the view that it was desirable or normal for household members to remain on the farmstead. Moving away, in particular working in a town, was by contrast an exceptional situation for which one had to be "granted leave" and in which one would always be regarded as "on leave" (*v otluchke*).

The nature of the legal provisions governing the situation of the head of the farmstead in general is derived from this concept. This situation was certainly not that of an independent person who enjoyed property rights, but rather of an "official" who was selected, who was supervised in the performance of his duties and, if necessary, removed from office. He was even entitled to a pension (of a rural sort), that is, to an appropriate proportion of the total production of the farmstead in order "to have enough to live on" (*na prozhitok*).[15]

Just as the head of the peasant family was responsible for all the farmstead's contributions, so all the heads of the various farmsteads within a commune (even in those communes where land was not periodically repartitioned, i.e., in village communes that were not field communes) were mutually responsible for the payment of taxes and any other contributions (*krugovaia poruka*).

The particular nature of the duties placed on the peasant, and the method of ensuring that they were carried out, required a special form of peasant administration (carried out by officials elected by peasants). In addition, special state agencies were needed that were responsible for supervising the peasant administration and had in fact to take a paternal interest in peasant affairs in general. Of these, the *zemskii nachal'nik* (the appointed "land captain") should be mentioned first. Article 39 of the law on the *zemskie nacha'lniki* of July 12, 1889, states: "The role of the *zemskie nachal'niki* is to look after the economic and moral well-being of the peasants in his district concerning the matters for which the village and *volost'* assemblies are responsible." How wide-ranging these powers were can be seen from the provisions of some of the articles of the general legislation; for example, according to Article 78, section 2, "The responsibilities of the *volost'* assembly include making decisions on all matters regarding the economic and social life of the *volost'* in general."

This attempt to give the *zemskie nachal'niki* paternalistic powers cannot be seen as particularly auspicious, as patriarchal power in the hands of an official appointed by the Ministry of the Interior is somewhat perverse. The attempt to reinstate the old patriarchal relations in a bureaucratic form (i.e., in the way of things, not as better or worse) also stood in direct contradiction to what was required at the time. Then, the need of the hour was to replace arbitrary and informal patriarchal power, wherever it had hung on, by legality, by relations that were set out precisely in law. Yet here we have an attempt to delay this natural development and to create a new office that retained the old patriarchal powers. Karamzin's worst fears were thus realized: the peasants were subjected to the arbitrary power of low-ranking provincial officials. For Karamzin, this was one of the main arguments in favor of retaining serfdom.

The maintenance of a special administration for peasant affairs was not the only consequence of the particular nature of the peasants' property rights. All the other special features of the legal status of the peasant were likewise derived from the view that the peasants' acknowledged "right to land" was fundamentally different from the property rights of those of other social estates. For example, the reason why most of the legal relations of the peasant class were not largely governed by the provisions of general civil law as applied to other social estates, but rather by local, unwritten peasant common law, was certainly because the norms of Russian general civil law were not permitted to cover the most important aspects of peasant property relations. This in turn led to the creation of special peasant courts. It was assumed that those elected from the peasantry to sit on them would be familiar with local peasant customs.

Overall, the legal status of the peasants had the following characteristics:

The peasants, whether they were former serfs or state peasants, formed communes to which all peasants had to belong. For the most part, the members of these communes were liable for taxes and other contributions (*krugovaia poruka*), for which they were mutually responsible. This system of mutual guarantees resulted in a high degree of dependency on the commune, a dependency that implied, in the end, a clear-cut restriction on peasants' freedom of movement. Obtaining a passport of long duration, without which a peasant could not leave his village, depended on the consent of the village assembly. Furthermore, the assembly's approval or refusal often depended on economic considerations. Those peasants who were not themselves independent heads of family also had to get permission from their head of household. How much the individual peasant was dependent on the farmstead has already been analyzed and does not need further elucidation.

The functions of the courts and the village administrations were exercised by members of the commune elected by the village assembly. Naturally, these bodies were only competent to deal with members of the peasant class. Peasant courts (*volost'* courts) and peasant administration were under the control, indeed the management, of special supervisory bodies, not the offices of the general administration.

The peasant courts were first allowed, but in fact later forced, to base their decisions regarding civil matters not on the provisions of written civil law as it applied to other social estates, but on local common law.

The sentencing regulations by which peasants were punished were not the same as general sentencing policy. For some crimes, peasants received milder sentences than did members of other social estates. By contrast, peasants could be sentenced for some offenses for which there was no punishment laid down for other social estates. This would involve some forms of improper conduct, such as drunkenness or dissipation, that were not normally considered criminal. Peasants could be given punishments that had long been abolished for other estates. Until 1904, peasant courts, for example, could impose sentences of corporal punishment on males from their social estate under the age of sixty. In 1898, Witte wrote to the tsar pointing out the necessity of abolishing the right of peasant courts to impose corporal punishment, as "birching . . . hurts God in man."[16] He went on to stress that the special powers of the peasant courts stood in flagrant contradiction of a sense of justice and of law in general: "It is interesting that if a provincial governor were to hand out beatings to peasants, . . . the Senate would take up proceedings against him, but where this occurs thanks to the malevolence (*kaverza*) of the *volost'* courts, it is regarded as normal."

These regulations covering the sentencing of peasants are symptomatic. The punishment of dissolute behaviour and the use of corporal punishment (particularly as this punishment could only be imposed by the *volost'* courts, whose members, it was assumed, stood for the good old values and customs) indicate that the peasants were seen as a special part of society, as a group needing instruction and paternalistic care, whose moral welfare especially required protection. It would be wrong to suppose, however, that this endeavor sprang from a conviction that peasants were particularly amoral. Quite the contrary: this paternalistic attitude was based on the idea that the peasant was a "simpler"—a more unspoiled and straightforward—person, that he embodied special moral and spiritual values (quite in the way the Slavophiles and Populists saw them). It was precisely for this reason that it was thought necessary to make a particular effort to protect this morality, to keep the peasant away from anything that might corrupt him. It seems peculiar and barely comprehensible today that punishment by the birch was retained in the *volost'* courts for so long, because there was a belief that imprisonment, especially in a town, would corrupt a peasant. This was because a peasant, even having been in jail just once for only a short time, would be regarded for his whole life as a thief, as a "bad person" or criminal, by the other peasants. He would also see himself in this light and thus ultimately become morally debauched. By contrast, it was believed that paternalistic punishment "at home" was effective in instilling morality. The power of the commune to exclude its dissolute members through a majority vote, a power that meant resettlement in Siberia, was also based on this propensity to reinforce the moral protection of the peasant estate.

The way peasant property rights were conceived also shows that the peasants were considered a class requiring paternalistic care and protection. The land that was allocated to the peasant (his *nadel*) could not become his private property. The peasant could not enjoy the same right of disposal over this land that the members of other social estates had over their property. If the peasant were granted the right of disposal, he could have sold his *nadel,* his land, and become a proletarian. This had to be avoided, and the peasant had to remain working the land. That was why the state had allocated him land, which the exchequer had taken and bought at great expense from the gentry. The peasant was to remain not simply an agricultural laborer, but a peasant. This was not purely to secure the material basis of his livelihood, but also to preserve the spiritual side of peasant life, as the peasantry embodied particular moral values. Consequently, turning the peasants into proletarians was considered the path to moral degeneration.

Chapter 11

The Peasant Question in the Reign of Alexander III

Alexander III's legislation—Limitation of the
peasants' property rights through this legislation
and Senate rulings—Consolidation of the view that
peasant land allocations were a state resource—
Reasons used by the government to justify the
protection of agricultural communes—Spread of
concepts of civil law among the peasants

The idea that it was the state's duty to secure the peasants' livelihood, and in general to care for them in the spirit of paternalism, became particularly entrenched during Alexander III's reign. Accordingly, the idea, apparent in the 1861 statutes, of allowing the peasants to enjoy rights under civil law and making their allotment land into genuine private property receded progressively. The land allocated to the peasants was regarded more and more consistently as a special land bank, whose purpose was to secure the livelihood of the peasants as farming people. The survival of this resource therefore had to be secured in law. The fair distribution of this land bank among the peasants had to be—at least up to a point—given legal force. This reinforced the special nature of the peasants' legal position concerning property, which inevitably deepened the peasants' isolation as a social estate from the rest of the empire's population. A series of important laws were enacted that embodied all these tendencies, while Senate interpretations of the law, as we have already seen, extensively and systematically further reinforced the special status of the peasant estate. Of these laws the following must by highlighted here:

The law of March 18, 1886, making the division of farmstead property among the members of the farmstead more difficult

The law of 1889, creating the office of *zemskie nachal'niki* and considerably increasing the powers of the *volost'* courts

The law of June 8, 1893, laying down regulations for the redistribution of land within the rural commune and, among other things, stipulating that the general repartition of land was meant to take place at intervals of no more than twelve years

The law of December 14, 1893, making the sale of any land (even by the commune) extremely difficult (because of the repeal of Article 165 of the law on land buyouts) and making severance from the commune virtually impossible

According to this last law, the restrictions on the peasant's right of disposal over his land were not even removed on completion of his buyout payments. This resulted in these restrictions becoming a quasi-inescapable feature of peasant land ownership.

As described above, the Senate often (but not always) defined peasant ownership of land as ownership by legal entities—the farmstead and the commune. This view was completely alien to the peasants, something that did not escape Witte's attention. Witte told the Extraordinary Committee (dealt with below): "Research shows that the right to own communal land is held by the commune as a legal entity, but in the view of the peasants (who after all do not understand what a legal entity is), the real landowner is the state, which allocates to the members of the commune the land to cultivate for a set period of time."[1]

This precisely reflected the views of the peasantry, except that Witte thought that the only reason the peasants had not themselves adopted the Senate's view that land was the private property of the commune as a legal entity was that they did not understand what a legal entity was. Witte's explanation is too superficial. There is no proof that the peasants were incapable of understanding a legal entity. The Russian peasant had never proved to be intellectually inferior, and the basic concepts of civil law are everywhere in accord with basic common sense. The foundations of civil law, law with over a thousand-year history, are like theological texts. They can be the subject of complex academic and theological debate, even though their fundamental content is accessible even to an uneducated person.

The peasant's view that the land allocated to him belonged to the state had much deeper roots than the inability to understand a legal entity. It derives from the legal ideology of serfdom and the legal consciousness, which was fostered in the peasantry under that system and which only slowly declined after the emancipation. This was, therefore, just at a time when the other social estates had developed a legal consciousness well beyond that of serfdom and that in general was governed by the legal concepts of a civil society. According to the legal ideology of serfdom, land had always been the tsar's land; that is, it belonged to the state. The tsar allocated the land to the peasants and then allocated the peasants together with this land to the gentry. The peasants had to feed the gentry, so these could serve the tsar. The gentry had to serve the tsar, which was their duty, which was the sole basis under serfdom for their right to be fed by the peasants settled on

the land, that is, to "own" the land. The peasants had never recognized the transformation of gentry land ownership brought about by the 1785 Charter, not least
because this meant the peasants themselves became the property of the gentry.

It is possible that the peasantry could even have accepted this legal revolution, but surely only if they were at least given a certain stake in the advantages
of a liberal system of law. It might also have been feasible if, as Karamzin had
hoped, the peasants' sense of economic initiative and entrepreneurial spirit had
been given free rein and if, as Catherine had already intended, the land handed
over to them by the gentry for farming had been declared their permanent property. Alongside such a transformation of the peasants' land into their permanent
property, the gentry could have retained only some specific sovereign rights in
relation to this land—somewhat on the lines of Montesquieu's doctrine of *pouvoirs intermédiaires* [intermediate powers; powers that exist outside or beside the
centralized state], as invoked by Karamzin, or possibly like the "political" rights
that are featured in the Perovsky Committee's project. It is possible that these
sovereign rights would quickly have evolved into powers under administrative
law delegated by the state. This development would have run in parallel to the
other, that is, the consolidation of permanent peasant land ownership into genuine private property. Yet hardly any aspects of these eighteenth-century liberal
ideas were brought to fruition in the nineteenth century. It is thus not surprising
that the peasants clung to their old ideas, that is, to the conviction that the plots
of land allocated to them were part of a huge state-owned land bank and that they
were entrusted with them now just as they had been for centuries. From the peasant's point of view, the emancipation meant no longer having to do compulsory
unpaid labor and paying *obrok* [quit rent] to their former masters. From their perspective, this was only fair and logical: after all, the gentry had been freed from
their compulsory state service long ago, in 1762 or 1785. If the gentry then voluntarily entered into state service, they received a salary for it, which was paid in
cash. Neither did they still need to be fed by the peasants. As far as the legal situation regarding land was concerned, however, nothing had changed. Everything
remained as it was. The land belonged to the tsar, the peasant farmed it, and so it
was natural that land was allocated to the peasants by the state.

It is only this legal consciousness that explains why the peasants still refused
to enter into contractual agreements with their former masters, as foreseen by
the emancipation statutes, even if such agreements resulted in a direct and manifest improvement in their situation. The peasants often obstinately refused such
an agreement, even if it protected the size of their plots, while reducing their *obrok* rent. Evidently, receiving what they already considered rightfully theirs from
the hands of their former masters offended their sense of justice.

It is quite natural, therefore, that the peasantry, whose outlook was deeply
rooted in serfdom, took the view that the land allocated to them was a state-
owned land bank. Much more curious is the fact that representatives of government tended to think in the same way. The Tver' provincial governor, for example,

took precisely this position. After the repeal of Article 165 of the law on land buyouts by the law of December 14, 1893, the question arose as to whether it was desirable to allow former serfs to buy their plots after all and to extend to them the provisions on land buyout of Article 15, section 2, of the law on state peasants.[2] This was put, along with other matters, to the government advisory committee reviewing the situation of the rural population. A majority of the committee was in favor, but the Tver' provincial governor expressed his disagreement with the majority decision.[3] He tabled the following minority opinion:

> I cannot agree with the opinion of the committee on the matter of the buyout of allotment land belonging to rural communes. While the committee argues in favor of replacing Article 165 of the law on land buyouts with Article 15, section 2, of the law on state peasants, it does not go far enough—it may wish to introduce restrictions on buyouts, but it still allows them in principle. I am totally convinced that the interests and aims of our rural commune are best served by the complete abolition of the right to buy allotment land. I believe that the right to buy land, without doubt, stands in contradiction to communal farming and leads to a form of individual ownership. . . . If the committee considers the communal ownership of land to be the only thing that can save our peasants from proletarianization, it is inconsistent not to remove the factor that could lead to the breakup of the rural commune. Furthermore, if you consider the question taking into account the role of the state, it is only possible to reach one conclusion: there can be no individual peasant ownership of allotment land. We know that the state has allocated land, purchased from the landowners with state money, to the peasants emancipated from serfdom. Even if the state initially took on the role of creditor and lender from whom the peasants more or less bought their land, this relationship long ago underwent a change. Nowadays the redemption payments are nothing other than a land tax. Thus, one would be justified in considering the land allocated to the peasants as state property, which has been left to the rural communes for farming for an unlimited time. For this reason, the government has indicated through a series of measures that the state does not relinquish its right of ownership and has decided to maintain this right in the interests of future generations of peasants.[4]

Along with the view that land allocated to the peasants was a state resource, there was an effort to protect the rural commune as an institution that was meant to ensure the equal distribution of land among the peasants. In doing so, the government was convinced that by taking this approach, it had drawn closer to the standpoint of the peasants. Apparently, officials were of the opinion that the abovementioned laws, enacted during the reign of Alexander III, conformed to the peasants' wishes. The Office for Peasant Affairs in the province of Archangel declared: "The peasants welcomed with particular enthusiasm the law of Decem-

ber 14, 1893, which only allows the buyout of communal land by individual commune members with the agreement of the commune."[5]

This was, of course, a significant measure for the protection of the commune, and many were convinced that the peasantry was very attached to the commune. In 1894, the Ekaterinoslav Advisory Committee stated: "The majority of
the peasant population has a positive attitude to communal land ownership, as
it well understands that the commune does not just ensure that they prosper as
individuals but also provides for their descendents as well as orphans, the elderly,
and the handicapped."[6]

Even Witte, who had by the 1890s already become convinced that peasant
land ownership had to be reformed along liberal principles,[7] attempted in his
memoirs, written toward the end of his life, to justify Alexander III's antiliberal
legislation with the claim that these laws were inspired by a mission to protect the
vulnerable. They were entirely consistent with the ideology of the Orthodox empire and stemmed from an idea deeply rooted in the consciousness of the people.
Witte writes:

> Alexander III has often been reproached for creating the *zemskie nachal'niki*
> and, in general, for establishing the principle of the paternalistic treatment
> of the peasantry, almost as if he assumed that the peasants would remain
> forever stuck in their herdlike mentality and morality. . . . This was an error
> on the part of the Emperor Alexander III. However, I have to bear witness
> that this mistake was not only made in good faith but also sprang in large
> measure from his spiritual warmth. Emperor Alexander III took to heart
> the plight of the Russian peasantry, as he did all the weakest in Russian
> society in general. He really was the epitome of the autocratic monarch, and
> the concept of the autocratic Russian tsar is inextricably linked with that of
> the protector of the Russian people, the protector of the weak, because the
> esteem in which the Russian tsar is held comes from Christian principles.
> This is linked to the concept of Christianity, to the concept of Orthodoxy,
> which consists in protecting all who are weak, who are in need, and all who
> are suffering, but not in supporting us, that is, the Russian gentry, even less
> the Russian bourgeoisie, who do not even have the goodness and nobility
> that are still found in Russian gentry.[8]

It is possible, even probable, that Witte gave a true account of Alexander III's
motives. There is, however, no compelling reason to suppose that Alexander III's
legislation represents the only course of action consistent with the idea of the
Orthodox empire. On the contrary, a succession of thinkers from the eighteenth
and nineteenth centuries had maintained that putting the ideals of the Orthodox
empire into practice required applying liberal principles. The most significant
representatives of this point of view include Catherine II, Karamzin, Speransky,
Alexander II, Katkov, and Miliutin. If Alexander III took the view that the only
way for a ruler to treat his subjects, consistent with the ideal of the Orthodox em-

pire, was paternalistically, then that was his personal opinion, or rather an error on his part.

These idealized concepts did not bear the slightest relation to real life. On the contrary, the plight of the weak in the rural communes was especially dire. There was to all intents and purposes no social provision in the villages. The Kursk Advisory Committee was compelled to observe that "those in need of social care almost always have to depend on charity."[9]

What was achieved was not provision for the weak, but the oppression of the strong, who found obstacles in their way at every turn. When land was repartitioned, it was often taken from the most hardworking. Because of the system of mutual responsibility for taxes and redemption payments, the richer peasants had to pay for the poorer ones, and that did not always mean those suffering from misfortune, but the lazy, the drunken, and the profligate.

The positions of the state and the peasantry began to diverge over time. Whereas the state now supported the concept of state property with respect to the peasant class, liberal ideas began to take hold in the minds of the peasants themselves. This provides a particularly interesting example of how positive law can take effect as customary law in a sphere where the former was not meant to apply, without the support of the state and even in the face of opposition from it.

The whole evolution in the condition of the peasantry assisted this process. The peasantry, of course, was not completely cut off from the life of the other social estates, which would have been the only way this development could have been held back. On the contrary, the peasants were continuously and everywhere in contact with the members of other estates, and this included legal matters. To some extent, they themselves were a party to legal transactions.

A peasant was able to buy other land besides his allotment land and then become a proprietor, as understood in Article 420, part 1, volume 10, of the Svod. If a peasant was "given leave" to work in industry or trade in the city, his legal situation was governed by the provisions of general civil law (or commercial law). Furthermore, if a peasant entered into a contract with the member of another social estate, in other words with a person who did not come under the jurisdiction of the *volost'* courts, his contractual relations were based on the provisions of volume 10 of the Svod. In general, he could see the legal situation of the other estates and was constantly able to observe and easily appreciate the advantages they enjoyed. The restrictions on an owner's right of disposal always seem more just and necessary because of social conditions to those who impose them on others, than they do to those whose civil liberty is curtailed as a result. It is hardly surprising, therefore, that the peasants, or at any rate a great number of them, also wanted to have the same civil liberty as the members of other estates. The peasants became aware of the advantages that would result from turning their property, in particular their land, into private property, as understood in volume 10 of the Svod. They could also appreciate the benefits of being able to base their contractual relations on the provisions of Russian commercial law and bringing their lawsuits before educated crown judges and magistrates, rather than the dubious members of the *volost'* court. In a memorandum, Witte cites evidence from local committees to the effect that before 1889, when more important lawsuits were still dealt with by magistrates, and not by the *volost'* courts, the peasants tried all they could to twist things in such a way that even more minor matters of litigation also came before the magistrates.[10]

The *volost'* courts, however, also frequently based their judgments on the provisions of volume 10 of the Svod, or on Senate rulings, and not on local customary law. Witte was not the only one to comment on this, which he saw as a healthy development,[11] while the editing commission of the Ministry of the Interior, set up to revise the legislation regarding the peasants, condemned it. Moreover, the same editing commission pointed out that *volost'* courts avoided basing their decisions on legal custom not only when the existence of a legal custom was in doubt or there was difficulty establishing its true meaning but also when a legal custom did in fact exist.[12] In the view of the editing commission, two factors accounted for this undesirable development: first, the influence of the clerks of the *volost'* courts, who often came from outside the area where they were appointed, and second, the fact that district tribunals (*uezdnye s'ezdy*) were set up to act as courts of appeal for the *volost'* courts. These district tribunals often lacked any members who were familiar with local customary law. It was only natural, therefore, that these tribunals also applied the provisions of written law when dealing with peasant cases.

Admittedly, the Ministry of the Interior's editing commission was aware that the tendency of *volost'* courts to rely not on customary law, but on the provisions of written law, was caused by the fact that peasant customary law in Russia was underdeveloped and imprecise. It was thus incapable of providing a sufficient basis for the desired level of legal certainty, whereas referring to a specific article of volume 10 of the Svod offered a clear basis for most legal situations. Moreover, the Ministry of the Interior's editing commission, which usually took a position diametrically opposed to Witte, agreed with him that the development of peasant customary law had been greatly hampered by the dependence of the peasants on their masters under serfdom, insofar as the peasants' property relations were entirely dependent on the will of their masters.[13] Witte went on to point out that such customary law could not be developed among the state peasants either, as according to Article 921, volume 10, of the Svod, part 2 (1857 edition), they came under the general state courts, and their legal affairs were governed by general civil law.[14]

As a consequence of the rudimentary and uncertain nature of customary peasant law, the decisions of the *volost'* courts, even if based on custom, could often mask the interests of an influential group of peasants within the commune or the fiscal and bureaucratic demands of administrators dealing with peasant affairs. "Customary peasant law" was a very useful smoke screen for the government's tendency to limit the peasants' right of disposal over their land and to consolidate the land allocated to them as a state-owned resource. This may explain why the *volost'* courts were pressured so persistently, and in a way that would otherwise have been incomprehensible, into keeping to customary law when arriving at their legal judgments. The authorities for peasant affairs particularly tended to overturn *volost'* court decisions if these contained a reference to articles in volume 10 or to civil law rulings of the Senate.[15]

Witte pointed out in his memorandum that there was no reason to doubt the assertions of most local committees (see next chapter) that "during the time since emancipation, the peasants were increasingly influenced by the principles of general civil law, while customary law, even if it existed, had been forgotten."[16] Witte even noted that legal custom, everywhere customary law was still encountered, gradually began to follow the principles of general civil law, principles that had taken root in the consciousness of the people.[17] Witte's observation is also based on statements from the overwhelming majority of local committees. Witte was thus in complete agreement with the opinion of the local committees that the peasantry was increasingly adopting general Russian civil law and the provisions of volume 10 of the Svod as if they were customary law. He concurred that the principles of civil law increasingly dominated and shaped the legal awareness of the peasants. At the same time, elements of the old legal consciousness suited to serfdom were being superseded.

This trend to adopt the principles of civil law was also based on the "tendency to individualize the law," as Witte observed with great clarity. It is noteworthy that this trend did not date from the 1890s or the turn of the century, but from the end of the 1860s and the beginning of the 1870s, as had been ascertained by Senator Liuboshchinsky's commission.

This move on the part of the peasants to individualize their rights, especially to turn their allotment land into private property, grew stronger over time as the peasants' interest in this property increased. Immediately after the emancipation, taxes and redemption repayments were higher than the income that could be derived from the allotment land. One could even rent land for less than these payments. So the peasants tended to leave their allotment land and rent another plot or to go and work in the towns. As the peasants in the commune were bound by the system of mutual guarantees (*krugovaia poruka*), as indeed were the tax authorities, those who remained in the commune had an interest in making it more difficult to leave the commune. The commune would thus only let one of its members leave if he was prepared to leave his property to the commune without compensation (and not always then, in the case of a member who was a reliable taxpayer). A member whose land was a source not of profit, but rather of liabilities, was often prepared to dispose of it as quickly as possible, even if he did not receive anything for it. When, however, the value of land and the income that could be derived from it grew significantly thanks to a general increase in prices, and income thus began to outstrip taxes and redemption payments, the peasants began to regard their allotment land as a valuable asset. They started to reject the possibility of abandoning this property without compensation on leaving the commune. Witte thought this was quite natural: "Anyone who has debts will be happy to agree to collective responsibility; he will be glad to accept guarantors and fellow debtors. . . . On the other hand, anyone who has property rights will strive to secure the full exercise of this right without sharing it with other parties. . . . That is all too human."[18]

As long as land ownership was a burden, a *tiaglo,* and the peasants' freedom of movement was restricted by the *krugovaia poruka,* that is, the collective liability of the commune and farmstead members for taxes, as well as the restrictive conditions on the issue of passports, land ownership had to be based on the principles of collectivism and service.[19] These principles are in fact completely in accord with the nature of public duty, which initially formed the fundamental element or the real basis of the exploitation of land allocated to the peasants, for so-called peasant land ownership. After, however, the burdens placed on the peasants in connection with the allocation of land had become only a partial factor in their land ownership, because of the economic developments mentioned above, the public-law aspect of the regulation of peasant landownership had to be seen by the peasants as a restraint.

The need arose to leave one's land to one's nearest blood relatives, even when they lived in a town, "on leave of absence," to divide the farmstead property among the members of a growing family, and above all to dispose of one's land, that is, sell it, if one left the commune for good. The peasant, however, had no lawful way of undertaking any of these legal transactions. Witte writes, "On quitting the commune, the peasant was deprived of the possibility of selling his property in such a way as to ensure that the contract would be legally binding."[20] As a result, unofficial ways of completing these legal transactions were developed, which Witte ironically describes as "legal custom" (*obychnye*).[21] Incidentally, irony was misplaced in this case. It was a genuine customary right, which owed its content to codified law, that is, a customary right that, in Witte's own words, was "permeated by the principles of general civil law." It was only because the government rejected the possibility of basing the peasants' legal affairs on the provisions of general civil law that this legal custom was not recognized by the government. This in turn resulted in there being no legal protection for transactions under this customary law. Thus, for example, a contract concluded under this customary law could only remain valid if both parties kept to it, and no legal dispute at all arose between them. After all, the higher courts had forbidden the *volost'* courts to recognize as legal those transactions undertaken by a peasant in accordance with the provisions of volume 10 of the Svod.

Another point is just as important: this legal custom had become essential not only because of the lack of legal avenues recognized by the government for dealing with the transactions mentioned above but also because there was no possibility of it evolving even gradually out of existing, recognized, special peasant law. A private-law framework could not take root in the soil of public law regulation. Witte poses the question: "Is it possible to have the regulation of the burden of the *tiaglo* and the methods to ensure the punctual fulfillment of these duties as one's starting point and to construct on these principles a framework of property law, including endowment, division, sale, disposal by will, inheritance, and so on?"[22] This tendency to individualize law, to turn peasant land allocations into private property as understood in civil law—in other words, the replacement of public law by private law in the area of peasant land ownership—was a move toward greater freedom. Russian peasants therefore strove quite instinctively to achieve more civil liberty for themselves, which would have resulted from applying the principles of civil law to their legal affairs.

Witte quite clearly understood this aspect of the problem as well:

> One cannot consider the latter (general civil law) as a system of norms that forces the citizen to make his arrangements (*opredeliat'*) under private law in one way or another. On the contrary, an ideal system of civil law offers a very broad framework in which there is room for all relations in accordance with the freedom of will and the nature of the individual case.
>
> Civil law has many so-called permissive (*dozvolitel'nye*) norms, whose application is not required in law.
>
> The law only offers a certain rule and assumes that if the citizen has not made any special declaration of intent concerning their legal affairs, they will want to follow what the law lays down in respect of their case.
>
> By contrast, peasant law, insofar as it is based on the legal principles of serfdom (*na nachalakh tiaglovogo perioda*), is embodied in numerous norms of a regulatory and interdictory nature (*povelitel'nogo i zapretitel'nogo kharaktera*). Such is the nature of these principles, that all of them are concerned not with rights but with public duties, which, in common with all duties in general, are regulated through binding imperatives.
>
> Given the current economic situation of the peasantry, norms of such a binding nature have an extremely restrictive effect on the field of autonomous economic activity and initiative. On the other hand, general civil law will offer the necessary leeway for it. Many of the actually existing legal customs can comfortably (*svobodno*) be accommodated within this framework.[23]

Chapter 12

The Peasant Question in the Reign of Nicholas II before 1905

The peasant question in the early years of Nicholas II's reign—Establishment in 1902 of the "Special Advisory Committee" to investigate the needs of the agricultural sector under the chairmanship of Witte and the editing commission of the Ministry of the Interior—The editing commission's perspective—Witte and the peasant question

Such then was the situation of the peasantry at the start of Nicholas II's reign. The draft of the abovementioned law of December 14, 1893, which was enacted shortly before the death of Alexander III, was extensively criticized in the State Council, especially by the former finance minister, Bunge. The entire State Council expressed the view that a far-reaching, comprehensive review of all the legislation on the peasantry had to be undertaken.

Spurred on by this, the minister of the interior at the time, I. N. Durnovo (not to be confused with Peter Durnovo, who was also minister of the interior in the Witte administration in 1905), approached the tsar as early as November 27, 1893, that is, even before the law was enacted, with a report insisting that the entire review should be left in the hands of the Ministry of the Interior.[1]

The Ministry of the Interior had drawn up a program that was essentially a list of all the problems needing attention. This program, consisting of sixty-six issues, was presented to the specially created provincial advisory committees (*soveshchaniia*). These had to respond to the questions presented to them in light of their local experience. These committees and the Ministry of the Interior were in no hurry. It was only in 1897 that four volumes, containing the resolutions of the advisory committees, were published. The committees took a quite conservative position, in line with the views of the Ministry of the Interior. In fact, Durnovo thought that the approach to the task set by the State Council hardly needed new ideas, but rather that the regulations set out in any new laws only needed to accommodate the practical needs of daily life, needs that were fully reflected in administrative practice relating to peasant affairs.

Witte must have found the outcome—the collection of resolutions from the provincial advisory committees—disappointing. In any case, as he pointed out in his report for the year 1897, which he presented as finance minister to the State Council, steps had to be taken to normalize the peasantry's economic and legal situation. Tsar Nicholas II did not respond, however, and neither did he the following year when Witte tried to remind him of it in a private letter. There the matter rested until the end of 1901. Witte probably had to admit that he could not make any further progress, unless he first found support for his plans among conservatives.

Witte was only able to raise the peasant question again at the beginning of 1902, after Sipiagin, a conservative but also a personal friend, had been appointed minister of the interior. Witte was able to persuade Sipiagin to begin making the necessary approach to the tsar to this effect. The outcome was the supreme order (*povelenie*) of January 14, 1902, announced by the minister of the interior, to start the revision of legislation concerning the peasantry. This initial order was followed by a second one on January 22 by which the "Special Advisory Committee" (*osoboe soveshchanie*) to investigate the needs of the agricultural sector was appointed. This advisory committee was empowered to set up regional committees at the provincial and district levels and to gather their views on a wide range of issues concerning the peasant question. The material that the local committees sent in was published at the beginning of 1904. It was very extensive, comprising fifty-eight volumes. It formed the basis for Witte's well-known memorandum, which has been cited several times above. The work of the Special Advisory Committee did not proceed smoothly. After Sipiagin fell victim to a terrorist attack on April 2, 1902, Pleve, one of the most extreme antiliberals, was appointed minister of the interior, and he, unlike Sipiagin, was not prepared to compromise. In contrast to the more moderate Sipiagin, who was the archetypal aristocrat, or "grand seigneur," Pleve was combative, possessed enormous willpower and energy, and was in a way similar to Witte. Witte and Pleve represented two conflicting approaches, two opposing principles, and were personally antagonistic. That the two of them could not remain ministers at the same time is understandable. Pleve won the day, and Witte had to go, resigning from his post as finance minister on August 16, 1903. It was, however, an honorable withdrawal, as Witte was appointed chairman of the Committee of Ministers. The post of chairman of the Committee of Ministers, which could be seen as the most senior in the empire, nevertheless did not possess any direct scope for independent action. As a result, it offered no opportunity to determine the course of events, which must have been a bitter pill to swallow for such a proactive personality as Witte.

This appointment, which felt more like disgrace to Witte, made it even more difficult for him to lead the preparatory work for the revision of the legislation on the peasantry, all the more so because Pleve had already been trying to oust Witte from this area. As early as June 1902, that is, long before the work of the Special Advisory Committee chaired by Witte was discontinued, Pleve, on the tsar's authorization, had an editing commission set up in the Ministry of the Interior, chaired by the conservative Stishinsky, the deputy minister of the interior with responsibility for peasant affairs. Its job was to finalize the revised draft legislation on the peasantry.[2] It is interesting to note, and typical of Nicholas II's approach, that the Special Advisory Committee led by Witte was not closed down at the time of the creation of the editing commission of the Ministry of the Interior.[3] Witte, however, understood that he had to play a waiting game. He allowed the regional committees to continue their work and took care of preparations for the publication of the material they collected and for its processing in St. Petersburg, but the *osoboe soveshchanie*, whose membership included the minister of the interior at the time, remained inactive.[4] Certainly it was not only the formation of the Ministry of the Interior's editing commission that motivated Witte to bide his time, but also the Manifesto of February 26, 1903, whose content conflicted with his own views on the peasant question.

The Ministry of the Interior's editing commission worked very energetically until October 1903, and a series of draft laws were published as early as the end of 1903, that is, even before the Witte committee's collected material was published. These draft laws were even preceded by a summary of the work of the editing commission. The beginning of this report contained an outline history of the way the peasant question had been handled since 1893. Significantly, there was no mention here of the Special Advisory Committee, led by Witte, and its work. No one reading this report would have suspected that such a committee had ever existed.

This summary or report is very interesting. It sets out the conservative circles' program for a solution to the peasant question, including a rationale for the principles that underlay it. As Witte's 1904 memorandum sets out the liberal agenda for a solution of the peasant question, it is possible to form a clear picture of both points of view.

The draft laws prepared by the Ministry of the Interior under Pleve were never enacted. On the other hand, Witte's agrarian program formed the basis of the Stolypin government's famous agrarian laws that were passed after the 1905 revolution. It would seem, therefore, that it would be important to study Witte's program in particular, and up to a point, this is correct. It is, however, important to understand the conservative point of view. Only then does it become clear what resistance liberal legislation had to overcome.[5]

The aim of the antiliberal forces was to maintain and strengthen the extraordinary position of the peasantry. In their view, the peasantry and its special mentality were the best guarantee for autocracy in Russia. The abovementioned report of the Interior Ministry's editing commission states the following:

The peasants have been schooled through constant hard work and have been accustomed from time immemorial to a monotonous pattern of life. The insecurity of farming has instilled in them an awareness of their dependency on the external forces of nature and hence of the concept of a higher order (i.e., put simply, of God). As a result, the peasants stand, and have always stood, on the side of the positive and creative ideas of society and the state (i.e., the autocracy). Thus, by the very nature of things, they are the pillar of the unbroken historical traditions in the life of the people and their protection against all the forces of disintegration and destruction. Thus, the rural population forms an estate, not only according to the formal letter of the law but also because of its intrinsic steadfastness and solidarity.[6]

On January 14, 1902, as previously mentioned, the tsar had ordered that the revision of the legislation concerning the peasantry should be based on the principles of the emancipation statutes. Naturally, the conservatives were also well aware of the basis of the so-called inalienability of allotment land. This was the ban on turning this communally owned land into private property by means of redemption payments, as well as on the tightening of restrictions on the peasant's right of disposal of his allotment land outside the commune. Both were based on the law of December 14, 1893, that annulled the famous Article 165 of the law on land buyouts. The intention of Article 165 had been precisely to enable peasants to leave the commune with their allotment land, to own it as private property, and to dispose freely of it in accordance with the principles of Russian civil law. The Interior Ministry's editing commission had no alternative but to assert that the 1893 law, while diverging from the letter of the 1861 legislation, was nevertheless consistent with the principles of the emancipation statutes and was its logical extension (M.V.D., *Trudy redaktsionnoi kommissii*, vol. 1, p. 11).

The thinking in Pleve's Ministry of the Interior was in line with the outlook of the antiliberal forces, which was embodied not only in the laws of 1886–93 but also in Senate rulings. Accordingly, land taken by the state from the landowners and allocated to the peasants was a resource to secure the peasants' livelihood. This aim was considered a state duty, and as a result, "supervision by the state and its involvement in the future of the allotment land was totally justified" (ibid., p. 17). Therefore the allotment land "could not be equated with privately owned land" (ibid., p. 17). And, the document goes on to state, "the land allocated to the peasants, insofar as it is determined by the state, cannot thus be the subject of free legal transactions and therefore is not subject to general civil law" (ibid., p. 19). Special regulations, it was declared, would have to be enacted to regulate the disposal and use of this land and to guarantee that this land retained its original purpose (ibid., pp. 17ff). These regulations, in particular, would have to prevent not only the excessive fragmentation of allotment land but also its concentration in fewer hands, as this would lead to the creation of a class of landless peasants, which would be directly opposed to the government's aim when it embarked on the allocation of land to the peasants (ibid., p. 18). The editing commission explained:

> The government should take care that this land bank actually satisfies the needs for which it was conceived, namely securing the livelihood of the peasantry as an estate, that is, not just its individual members, but the great mass of peasants. Naturally, neither the law nor the government would want to restrict the entrepreneurial activities of individual peasants or to curtail their capacity to earn a living. Both the law and the government, however, must ensure that neither this entrepreneurial activity nor this capacity is developed at the expense of the land bank, which has a particular, wider significance in the public interest, namely, as the basis for the livelihood of the mass of the people. The latter has a number of weaker elements, without sufficient strength or stability to withstand pressure from those with greater energy and who in the pursuit of their ends are sometimes not fastidious in their choice of means. (Ibid., p. 14)

In the view of the Ministry of the Interior's commission, this restriction of the economic freedom of those belonging to the peasant estate could not be that disadvantageous, as the law conferred on all strong individuals, on those who were intellectually above the level of the peasantry, the possibility of transferring into other social estates (ibid., p. 16). According to Pleve's (and Stishinsky's) ideas, there was no place in the peasantry for those who no longer required paternalistic support. This was not the destruction of kulaks as a class, but these were preventative measures to guard against the formation of a kulak class, that is, to stop the growth in the numbers of peasants who no longer belonged to the rural communes, but who were economically independent and free owners of land.

It was not merely allotment land, however, that was supposed to be put beyond the reach of general civil law. In general, it was considered undesirable to introduce civil law into the peasant world or to regulate the property affairs of the peasants through the provisions of volume 10 of the Svod (ibid., p. 13). Elsewhere, the editing commission stresses that "the legal affairs of the peasants have been shaped according to the principles of family and communal life . . . at the expense of the principles of individualism and capitalism. However, the whole of civil law is based precisely on these two" (ibid., p. 67).

The editing commission therefore considered it right on principle that the legal affairs of the peasants should be regulated according to special customary law. It is very symptomatic that the commission insisted on this demand, despite—as noted above—being aware of the shortcomings of such customary law and despite itself pointing out that it was often very difficult to establish what a legal custom might be. Furthermore, in reality, appealing to legal custom often masked "the intrusion into the field of civil law of considerations arising from the interests of the commune or the tax authorities" (ibid., p. 64). Finally, it noted that the economic life of the peasants since emancipation had become increasingly varied and that many new legal matters, for which there was no provision in legal custom, had become part of peasant life (ibid., p. 63). Civil society is one of the most important forms of liberty. That is why those reactionaries who were hostile to it were prepared to accept all the disadvantages of so-called customary law and perpetuate the shortcomings of the legal system to which the peasants were subject, to prevent the advance of the principles of civil society (or, as they said, capitalism, in which they were totally at one with the socialists).[7]

From this general position, the editing commission came out in support not just of the *volost'* courts as the specific jurisdiction for the peasant estate, but also of the special administrative authorities (*zemskie nachal'niki*) charged with the paternalist care of the peasantry. It was also in favor of giving preference to rural communes over individual ownership and measures to protect them.

The commission set out the general case for the government's special powers, which allowed it to supervise and oversee the peasantry. It pointed out that for the state to put aside a land bank to secure the livelihood of the peasant estate amounted to an act of welfare and paternalistic care on its part. It went on to explain that the state was even at that moment continuing to expand the amount of land available to the peasants at the expense of state domains, as well as taking further measures to the same end. The editing commission then declared, "Whoever acts as another's guardian also has the right to oversee those who benefit from his paternalistic care" (ibid., p. 15). This statement is symptomatic. Does it not reveal the ultimate true reason for opposing the transformation of peasant land into private property? The Ministry of the Interior insisted on restricting the property rights of the peasants, because these restrictions served as the best basis for its paternalist surveillance of the peasantry.

The particular legal nature of peasant land ownership in fact resulted in having to give preference to communal over individual ownership, at least for the time being. If the land allocated to the peasants was a resource to secure the livelihood of a social estate in the interests of the state, it was only natural that land should be distributed from time to time to the members of this estate (at least in the context of the commune). Furthermore, even in cases where the land was not owned or used by the commune but by individual farmsteads, care had to be taken to distribute the land evenhandedly among the peasants. The commission favored establishing a maximum area for land ownership, which no individual farmstead was allowed to exceed.

The editing commission took issue with the view that the rural commune was one of the principal reasons for the fact that the peasants had an "underdeveloped sense of legality and respect for the rights of others," as land in general was seen here as collectively owned (ibid., p. 21). The commission thought that the conditions in which the peasants had lived at the time of emancipation, and that continued to exert an influence, had prevented the peasants from developing a respect for the rights of others. As serfs, the peasants had been provided with all necessities by the landowners, such as, for example, timber, wood for fuel, and animal fodder. The legal separation between landowners and peasants in terms of property rights that came with emancipation had not prevented the peasants from continuing to graze their cattle on the former master's pasture, to take wood for fuel from his forests, or even to cultivate his adjacent land for themselves. As people largely turned a blind eye to such practices, the peasants started to do the same not just on the land belonging to their former master but also on land belonging to other neighboring landowners (ibid., pp. 37ff). Overall, "the conditions in which the peasants found themselves prior to emancipation could not prepare them for a free, independent existence as owners of the land that was allocated to them and that they were granted the right to buy" (ibid., pp. 35ff).[8] Moreover, according to the commission, "the extent to which the rights of others are respected depends mainly on the general cultural level and standard of living of the people" (ibid., p. 23). The commission continued: "In particular, this or that attitude of the people regarding land does not spring from the greater or lesser extent of its right to its land, but on whether its land secures its livelihood" (ibid., p. 23).

This materialist reflection has, without doubt, a striking similarity to the socialist approach. Accordingly, the heart of the matter, in the opinion of the editing commission, lay not in "changing the legal nature of ownership" (ibid., p. 23), but rather in the transition to *khutorskoe khoziaistvo* (independent farms), which was seen here as a purely agrarian technicality. Nevertheless, the Interior Ministry's editing commission did therefore admit the possibility of a peasant leaving the rural commune, while keeping his allocation of land in a single block.

This departure of the stronger peasants was not to happen against the wishes of the majority of the commune, for such a departure could arouse hostility. To guard against this, measures had to be taken to encourage the remaining majority to see such departures in a positive light, such as granting tax breaks to those remaining in the commune (ibid., p. 95). In this way, the majority in a rural commune would be compensated for the loss of its individual members, exactly as the landowners had been in 1861. The landowners, though, had received compensation, at least in principle, not for the personal liberation of the peasants, but for the land transferred to the peasants, land that had been legally recognized as the former's private property. At most, it was only possible to talk about indirect compensation for the personal liberation of the peasants insofar as, in some cases, the amount of compensation (the redemption payments) for the land exceeded market prices. According to the commission's proposals, on the other hand, the commune apparently had to be compensated through tax relief for the personal liberation of its members. This was because the peasants, were they actually to leave the commune, would receive no more land as a separate block than they had received earlier as members of the commune in the form of disparate fragments.

Thus, the conservative position amounted to this: the peasantry formed an estate whose legal status differed fundamentally from that of all the other estates. The most important aspect of this legal position can be summarized as follows: the peasant's right to his land was not a right as understood in civil law, but it constituted an entitlement under public law to be allocated or provided land by the state.

As minister of finance, Witte was compelled to study the peasant question in detail:

> I knew little about the Russian heartlands, particularly the peasantry. I was born in the Caucasus and then worked in the South and the West. Since I became the mechanic of that complicated machine that constitutes the finances of the Russian Empire, I would have been quite foolish if I had not understood that this machine would not work without fuel. . . . This fuel constitutes the given reality of the Russian economy. As the majority of the population was made up of peasants, I had to get things clear in my mind about this sphere. (*Memoirs*, vol. 1, p. 446)

Witte's statement should not be understood in a basic fiscal sense. Peasant prosperity meant the expansion of the internal market and represented a necessary condition for Russia's industrialization, which Witte was energetically pursuing.[9] It was only natural, therefore, that Witte give his full attention to the problem of raising the living standards of the rural population. Witte's autobiographical comment is also significant insofar as it shows that Witte was one of the few who approached the solution to the peasant question solely from the point of view of economic progress, rather than ideological preconceptions.

After Witte had analyzed the nature of the peasant question from an economic perspective, he concluded that the main problem lay not in the field of economics, but in law. In his opinion, what stood in the way of economic progress were neither the generally unfavorable economic conditions nor even the economic and overall cultural backwardness of the rural population. Progress was hindered, indeed made nigh on impossible, by the particular legal status that was peculiar to the peasantry. Witte found support for this view in the statements made by members of the local committees, the majority of whom were of the view that "achievements in agriculture depend directly on so improving the legal situation of our peasantry that it would encourage the spirit of enterprise and initiative in the peasants; without this and without spreading education among the peasants, all sorts of measures in the field of agricultural economy and technology will only have a limited effect."[10]

In his memorandum, Witte proposed a program that was diametrically opposed to all the demands of the conservative one. Witte advocated that all the judicial and administrative bodies peculiar to the peasant estate be abolished (*Memorandum*, p. 10), as should the special penal provisions applying to the peasants (p. 31). General civil law should govern the peasants' relations under private law (ibid., pp. 22ff). The peasant should once more have the right to leave the commune and to acquire as his private property the land allocated to him as part of the commune (ibid., p. 33). Farmsteads should be made the private property of the heads of household (ibid., pp. 37ff). Finally, all restrictions on the freedom of movement should be lifted.

Witte was convinced that all the points of this program were intrinsically linked. In his opinion, it was extremely important to lift the restrictions on the peasant's freedom of movement that arose, in particular, from a concern to safeguard tax revenues. Accordingly, it was necessary to abolish the formal conditions that made it difficult to obtain a passport for a longer period of residence away from the commune, as well as those that formed an obstacle to withdrawing from the commune. Witte, however, saw quite clearly that this in itself would be insufficient. In his opinion, the main thing that bound the peasant to the commune was the absence of the right to demand that the commune give him ownership of his share of the allotment land. Witte maintained that withdrawing from the commune was made impossible for the peasant by the fact that the legal means to sell his share of land were denied him (ibid., pp. 42, 44). He continued that allowing such a possibility should not, however, be linked to the abolition of all legal regulations for the protection of smallholdings. Like many members of the local committees, whose opinions he refers to, Witte held the view that such protective measures should be maintained. These included a ban on the purchase of peasant land by members of other estates, the establishment of a maximum area of allotment land that could be owned, and a ban on the sale of allotment land for the discharge of debt and the organization of discounted agricultural credit (ibid., p. 86). Witte, however, thought that "the sale of land from one peasant to another had to be regulated by the conventions of general civil law" (ibid., p. 55), which necessitated replacing family ownership by individual property. As long as there was no shift to private property, the identity of those who enjoyed rights over the property would not be clear (ibid., p. 55), which was often the cause of intractable disputes between the head of the household and other members of the family farm (ibid., p. 95). He went on to state that only private property could ensure "the clarity and certainty of relations under private law" that were required for ordinary legal transactions (ibid., p. 93). It was necessary, therefore, according to Witte, to regulate the legal relations of the peasants through the provisions of general civil law and thus to give practical effect to the right to withdraw from the commune, that is, to recognize the freedom of movement.

Over time, Witte continued, the freedom to withdraw from the commune could lead to the complete disappearance of communal ownership, and in fact, it was very likely that this would be the result. Witte, however, did not consider this development regrettable. None of the advantages that people liked to claim for the institution of the *mir* existed in reality.

It was often said that the rural commune stopped the peasants becoming proletarians. The facts did not bear this out. In those areas where communal ownership predominated, the proletariat was a quite normal feature (ibid., p. 83). In general, communal ownership did not prevent the process of differentiation in the peasant class. There were many communes where the majority continually became poorer and only a small minority became wealthier through the ruthless exploitation of the land and their fellow peasants in the commune (ibid., p. 86). Witte pointed out that by contrast, there was no concentration of property in the hands of the few in Western Russia, where private ownership predominated and "capitalist energy" was much more intensive than elsewhere in the empire. Here peasant land ownership had proved to be quite stable (ibid., p. 86). Furthermore, it was incorrect to say that the rural commune could form the basis for the development of cooperatives. The rural commune was a form of collectivism, while on the other hand, "cooperative unions could only be set up on the basis of a rigorous personal property law" (ibid., p. 84).

In Witte's view, therefore, the rural communes offered none of the advantages that people expected, but rather their existence had to be regarded as quite detrimental. The fact that the composition of a peasant's property depended on majority decisions of the communal assembly (ibid., p. 87) had largely prevented the development of an awareness of civil law. However, Witte saw this awareness as the necessary basis for any sound economic and, indeed, general cultural progress (ibid., p. 93). In particular, he went on to say, as communal ownership hindered the development among the peasants of respect for the rights of others, it had the effect of encouraging the spread of revolutionary, socialist tendencies. Witte declared in a session of the Special Advisory Committee: "I believe that if the policy of educating the peasants on land use that accompanies the periodic equalizing repartition of land, and generally under conditions that alienate the peasants from the general legal order, is pursued with the same determination as before, then Russia will experience massive historical turmoil."[11]

Witte was even more convinced of this view after the revolution of 1905. He writes in his memoirs: "Perhaps the chief cause of our revolution was the backwardness in the development of the principle of individualism and thus the consciousness of property, as well as in the demand for a civil society (*potrebnosti grazhdanstvennosti*) and in particular for civil liberty."[12] This explains Witte's surprise that most ministers of the interior thought it right, particularly on grounds of public order, to protect the *obshchina* (rural communes) and that these ministers really thought that the institution of the *mir* was a protective barrier against the revolution. The higher the tide of revolution, the more obstinately the Interior Ministry clung to this view. Witte writes: "After the fateful day of March 1 (in 1881, the day on which Alexander II was assassinated), reaction finally got the upper hand. The *obshchina* became the darling of the Ministry of the Interior for political considerations, which were embellished by Slavophile and socialist literature."[13]

Witte concedes: "It (the rural commune) certainly offers advantages from the organizational side of policing—it is easier to watch over a herd, than each member of the herd on their own."[14] However, how did these advantages relating to the technicalities of policing compare with the fact that, as Chicherin emphatically points out, the village commune "was the most fertile ground for the spread of socialist ideas"?[15]

The survival of the rural communes was all the more dangerous because, in Witte's view, the emancipation of the peasants had already been implemented under conditions that were extremely unfavorable for the development and consolidation of a consciousness of civil law in Russia, taking a similarly unfavorable form. Witte stressed that the extensive expropriation of land, which had belonged to the gentry and been transferred to the peasants, conflicted with the awareness of civil rights "such as had taken root since the time of the Roman Empire." No doubt, sacrificing the principle of private property out of political necessity may have been unavoidable then, as Witte says in his memoirs, but at the same time the adverse effects of this step, that is, shattering the principle of private property, became inevitable.[16] However, the expropriation of the landowners was not the only factor to have an adverse effect on the principle of private property. The way in which this land was transferred to the peasants (state provision) and the general attitude toward the peasantry (paternalism) had prevented the latter from developing a consciousness of civil society. Rather, Witte continues, this path had encouraged the growth of a mentality among the peasants that was alien to a consciousness of civil law and the principles of a civil society:

> If the government takes on the role of paternalist policeman, which is out of place in the workings of government in a modern state, sooner or later it has to discover all the joys of this approach. . . .
> —If you are my custodian (as one day the peasants will surely ask it), and I am hungry, feed me. . . . If you have kept me in harness, and not given me the freedom to work as I will, and taken away any incentive to work, cut taxes, as I don't have the means to pay. If you regulate the ownership and use of land so that we cannot farm more intensively, give us enough land for the growing population.
> —There is no land.
> —How come? Just look at how much land the tsar's family, the government (state domains), and private landowners have!
> —But that is land belonging to others.
> —What does that mean, others? The tsar is an absolute ruler, and it looks as if he wants to protect the gentry, or they have him in their pocket.
> —That would violate the principle of private property. Property is sacred.
> —And it wasn't under Alexander II? And yet, he decided to take it from the gentry and give it to us. So Nicholas II simply doesn't want to do it.
> That is how the peasants think.[17]

Witte thought that such reasoning on the part of the peasants, arising from obtuse government policy on the one hand and unscrupulous revolutionary agitation on the other, was extremely dangerous. He was preoccupied by the mentality of the peasants underlying such reasoning for the following reasons:

1. It formed a barrier to abolishing the remaining vestiges of serfdom on the land and the establishment of a civil society in peasant life, which he regarded as the only real solution to the peasant question.

2. It encouraged plans for a fresh expropriation of privately owned land and its redistribution to the peasants, which he thought was an illusory solution.

3. It made the peasants receptive to revolutionary propaganda.

Witte was depressed by the fact that reactionary opinion had refused to recognize this danger but had on the contrary accused Witte's Special Advisory Committee of revolutionary leanings merely because it had spoken out against the rural commune and for private property.[18] These circles were profoundly convinced that the peasantry, which had retained its outmoded patriarchal way of life, was unconditionally loyal to the tsar.[19] Accordingly, they persisted in continuing the old patriarchal policies, hanging on to the idea of paternalist relief, and preserving the old peasant forms of collectivism—the rural commune and the farmstead—and were determined to cling to everything that, as Witte saw it, inevitably encouraged this pernicious mentality.

Chapter 13

The Agrarian Program of the Left-Wing Parties

Rural collectivism and socialist ideas—Agrarian program of the Kadets (Constitutional Democratic Party)

As Chicherin pointed out so clearly and forcefully, there was a close affinity between the old forms of peasant collectivism and the ideal of the socialist collective. Chicherin highlighted that, on the one hand, as we have already noted, the rural commune influenced the outlook of the peasants, so that they became especially susceptible to socialist ideas, while on the other hand many socialists viewed the commune with particular enthusiasm, because they perceived it as an embryonic cell from which a socialist society could develop. The Socialist Revolutionary Party, which saw itself above all as the defender of peasant interests and which enjoyed, at least for a time, considerable support among the peasants, wrote the following in its program:

> As far as agrarian policy . . . is concerned, the Socialist Revolutionary Party aims, in the interest of socialism and the struggle against bourgeois ideas and property, to harness those views, traditions, and way of life of the Russian peasants that are rooted in the rural commune, in particular the view by which land is the common property of all working people. To this end, the party will strive for the socialization of all privately owned land and bring it under social ownership. The right of disposal over this property will be left to the democratically organized communes and associations in their area, on condition that the principle of equitable use is respected.[1]

Members and supporters of the Socialist Revolutionary Party developed and commented in numerous publications on these ideas in the party's program. For example, the leader of the party, Chernov, wrote, "Implementing the socialization of land means, if I can put it like this, turning rural Russia into a single enormous commune."[2] The implementation of this program would have entailed the end of legal dualism not by extending civil society to include the peasants, which was the aim of the liberals, but rather by eliminating civil law and fully implementing rural collectivism. All rights to land ownership would have been changed into the "right to land," understood as an entitlement under public law to be provided with land by the state, that is, would have taken the form that the antiliberals defended so adamantly against the liberals. It is astonishing that the tsar and his circle did not notice sooner, or worry about, the possibility that the socialist parties would embrace their reactionary agrarian program rooted in the traditions of serfdom and purge it of the half-hearted approval of private property that coexisted beside the collective ownership of the commune. The Left could thus win the sympathy of the peasantry through the determined pursuit of this coherently designed program.[3] It was only with the 1905 revolution that the scales fell from their eyes. These elite circles finally grasped that there were only two outcomes: either to be swept aside by a socialist dictatorship or to eliminate the vestiges of serfdom with determination and transform tsarist Russia into a constitutional monarchy.

The first modest steps in this direction were indeed already under way before the outbreak of the revolutionary upheavals of 1905.

Besides government representatives and the socialist parties, the Union of Liberation, and the Party of Constitutional Democrats (Kadets) that emerged from it, saw themselves as the true representatives of efforts to achieve greater freedom and produced their own agrarian program.[4] This program, just like the overall approach of the Kadets at the time, had all the hallmarks of a compromise, in which tactical considerations played a major part. As Maklakov's memoirs show, the tactics of this party were linked to the demands of their program, whereas the program was largely determined by tactical considerations. On the one hand, judging from their agrarian program, the Kadets did not envisage campaigning against private property as such or making collective ownership the only desirable type of property in general. On the other hand, their program contained nothing to accelerate the decline of the rural commune or any demand to declare the farmstead the private property of the head of the household. Doubtless, there were many among the Kadets who shared the views expressed by the committees set up by Witte and who thus agreed with Witte's agrarian program. This is apparent from articles that were published in a collected edition called *Nuzhdy Derevni* [The Needs of the Countryside] in 1904 by a number of future members of the Kadets, which were based on material collected by these committees. V. M. Gessen, for example, in an article entitled "Foundations of Law," highlighted that the most important point was to "to ensure the liberty of the individual (i.e., the inviolability of the rights of the individual)." This was the only way to develop "the initiative, the enterprise, and the economic independence" of the population.[5] In support, he cites Montesquieu's words, which had already been invoked by Prince Ukhtomsky in one of the committees: "Countries are not cultivated because they are fertile but because they are free."[6]

Gessen, however, was principally concerned with the arbitrary nature of administrative paternalism, with the restrictive rules for the issue of passports and similar matters, and not with the legal capacity of the peasants in the field of civil law. In this respect, Gessen's article lags far behind Witte's sharp, penetrating analysis. Later, with the outbreak of the 1905 revolution, and the spread of socialist ideas and sentiments connected with it, which the Kadets treated with the greatest respect, this aspect of the peasant question was even further neglected.[7] In order to compete with their political rivals on the Left, the Kadets in fact adopted as the first point of their agrarian program (Art. 36 of the party program) an additional allocation of land to the rural working population, which was suffering from a shortage of land. A land bank was to be set up for this purpose from land owned by the extended imperial family (*appanages*) and the state, from monastic land holdings, and from land obtained through the expropriation of large landed estates.

The principles by which land was to be transferred from this land bank to the needy population were to be consistent with local forms of land ownership and use. Land could therefore be given to the peasants as their own property or communally owned (Art. 37 of the party program). It is apparent from the wording of this article that the Kadets carefully avoided taking a position against rural communes and for private property and that they saw all forms of land ownership as being of equal value or at least saw all owners having the same rights.

The Kadet Party's program, incidentally, displays great similarity with the position that had always been held by antiliberal elements in government circles. It is hardly possible to mistake the fact that allocations from a state land bank, based on the principle of paternalist relief, was the old position of antiliberal opinion. (This was also something that had already been put to the test in 1861.) The only real difference between the Kadets' agrarian program and that drafted by the editing commission in Pleve's Interior Ministry was that Pleve and his supporters thought that the 1861 expropriation of gentry-owned land and its allocation to the peasants from the resulting land bank, in accordance with the wording of Article 8 of the general *polozhenie* (statute), was a one-off exercise, whereas the Kadets wanted to repeat it.

Since the Kadets adopted socialist ideas solely for tactical reasons, and then only to a limited extent, their program was inconsistent and hence remained fruitless. Because of this inconsistency, and because of the attempt to combine individualistic and anti-individualistic elements, it displayed a striking resemblance to the agrarian program of reactionary circles, which was also based, as we have seen, on the same internal contradiction. It was just that in the case of the

reactionaries, in contrast to the Kadets, this inconsistency was obscured or justified by the concept of social hierarchy. It is clear, however, that in other respects,
the positions held by the Kadets and Pleve were fundamentally opposed. It is all
the more important to stress, therefore, that these opponents had arrived at the
same position concerning the basis for a solution to the peasant question. How
shocked both sides would have been if only they had realized this! It is also interesting that the weakness of both programs had the same root cause: the desire to
avoid making a real choice.

The problem was unequivocally clear: in the area of land ownership, either
collectivism or the principle of private property ultimately had to triumph. It was
only possible in an absolutist regime bordering on despotism to divide the population into two parts, each under a different legal system. Faced, however, with
the pressure of the general cultural and economic development of the people, the
absolutist regime now began to crumble. It was time to choose between individualism and collectivism, and yet the Kadets tried to avoid making this decision.
Those who wish to avoid making choices in tempestuous times are condemned
to follow the decisions of others. As the revolutionary upsurge increasingly lost its
liberal tinge and took on a more socialist hue, the Kadets agreed to adopt as part
of their program the allocation of land to the peasants from a state land bank, a
position totally at odds with liberal individualism, and took a neutral position on
the rural commune and farmstead ownership.

The proposed expropriation of large private estates (which, incidentally, were
continuously shrinking—a process that accelerated over time through the sale
of land) to expand the land bank was certainly not a liberal measure, even if the
expropriation was to be carried out with fair compensation for the landowners.[8]
Maklakov was right to stress that Stolypin, in opposing this proposal of the Kadets and the Left in general, emerged as an exponent of liberalism, as a champion of the rights of the individual against the omnipotence of the state.[9] When
Stolypin criticized the Kadets' agrarian program and their legislative proposal in
the Second Duma, he pointed out that implementing this program would be the
first step toward the victory of collectivism:

> On the one hand, this draft law rejects the nationalization of land; on the
> other, it only recognizes the inviolability of property rights for the peas-
> ants. But as far as large landowners are concerned, it applies the principle
> of quantitative expropriation. If, however, the principle of expropriation is
> accepted in relation to large landed estates, if the first step on this road will
> have been taken, . . . then, given the growth in population, the principle of
> quantitative expropriation will also apply to the peasants, thus ultimately
> arriving at the very same nationalization. That is why the Left's (Socialist)
> proposal is more honest and sincere.[10]

This interesting line of argument recalls what Reutern had said earlier about
the restrictive anti-Jewish laws, namely, that one cannot violate the civil rights of

one part of the population without undermining the whole framework of civil society and finally ending up with socialism. It is in the nature of civil society that
it applies universally. It is true that civil society was introduced under Catherine
as privileges for the gentry and townspeople, but this could only be a transitional
state of affairs. In fact, it also spread to other groups in society over time. It was
only in respect to the peasantry that anyone endeavored to obstruct this process,
without realizing that civil society had either to extend to it or to founder. Equally,
the Kadets' neutral attitude toward the rural commune was not a position that
could be described as liberal. However, what really set apart the Kadets' agrarian
program from a genuinely liberal one was the insistence on the idea of provision
from a state land bank. In taking this approach, the Kadets did not envisage the
creation of this land bank as an interim measure or as a form of temporary state
intervention to carry out as smoothly as possible the transfer of land from the
large landowners to the rural population in need of land, but rather as a permanent solution. This meant, however, that the land bank, to be created from state-
owned land and the large estates, would not be transferred to the peasants in the
form of private property. It would remain a permanent state asset, from which
land would only be made available for the peasants to farm, only to lease (for
twelve years, as Manuilov proposed). We have already encountered this view in
the quotation of the Tver' provincial governor's minority opinion.

Certainly not all members of the Kadet Party shared this view. Some of them
were in favor of transferring land to the peasants as private property. Miliukov,
for example, the leader of this party, seems to have been more inclined to private property than to state ownership, without committing himself clearly at the
time—surely for tactical reasons.[11] Such an extensive and permanent involvement of the state in regulating agrarian affairs seemed dangerous to some members of the party. Rodichev's comment that, in his opinion, the state would need
dictatorial powers is interesting.[12] Manuilov, however, gave an unambiguous response: "If the interests of the state demand it, private law must give way."[13] It is
this more radical position that prevailed in the party. At the conference on the
agrarian question (Moscow, April 28–29, 1905), the question was still unresolved
as to "whether land expropriated for distribution to the peasants should be given
to them as private property or added to the state land bank, not to be sold, but
transferred solely for cultivation to the peasants, who were short of land."[14] It was
anticipated that it would be on the agenda at the next conference. Miliukov, however, found that by the third party conference, which took place only a few months
later, the idea had prevailed of a "sacrosanct land bank" from which plots of land
were to be transferred to the peasants, not in the form of private property but for
"long-term use."[15] It is interesting to note that this idea too was almost only ever
attacked from the left, only by supporters of nationalization, that is, state ownership of all land and the abolition of the private ownership of land in general.[16]
Only the eternal maverick Struve pointed out that circumstances could force the
party to move to the right in finding a solution to the agrarian question; that it

should not go any further to the left, at least if it wanted to stick to the path of leg-islation, not of revolution.[17]

Miliukov was aware that his party defended a position that has to be seen as the most cautious at the time. Not only the socialist parties' support (namely, that of the S-Rs) of collectivism but also the government's support of individualism was much more radical than the Kadets' program. According to Miliukov: "The draft agrarian legislation put to the First Duma would not destroy the forms of peasant ownership of allotment land; neither would it abolish private land owner-ship if kept within certain limits."[18]

The reform proposed by the Kadets was thus much more modest than the government measure making the private ownership of land universally applica-ble.[19] Miliukov also rejected the government's charge that the Kadets' agrarian program was based on abstractions. On the contrary, Miliukov believed that the government with its draft legislation was itself being doctrinaire:

> By contrasting their (the government representatives') individualism with the collectivist tendencies of the (Kadets') draft legislation, they forget that Russian reality is much closer in many respects to the audacious utopia (in the opinion of the government) of the (Kadets') draft legislation than their own (government representatives') dreams of making Russian agriculture more European. Where did such features as the "inviolability" of the farmer's private property, the efforts to raise the needs of the rural popula-tion above the hungry level of "the norm of consumption," the need to raise the cultural level and to intensify farming, come from: from European or from Russian reality? . . . These features were missing in the past, . . . and this past weighs heavily on today's Russia.[20]

By contrast, in Miliukov's view, the endeavors of the socialists were rooted in the past. Elsewhere Miliukov wrote: "In this country, the concept of private prop-erty has developed with the greatest difficulty. . . . The concept of the nationaliza-tion of land is by no means a novelty in Russia. The principle of the 'nationaliza-tion of land,' by which is meant that it is accepted that the state has the ultimate ownership of land, is an old Muscovite principle."[21] Nevertheless, Miliukov did not believe that implementing the Kadets' agrarian program would necessarily lead to the ultimate victory of this principle, as the Kadets' program left the door open to all possibilities. It was certainly possible, in his opinion, that allocating land from a state land bank could in fact lead to the ultimate triumph of the old Muscovite principle of ultimate state ownership of land. It was equally possible, however (and this was probably Miliukov's secret wish), that the cultivation of al-lotment land, insofar as it was on a long-term, individual basis, would take on a form related to private property ownership.[22]

In general, Miliukov was at pains to show that his party's agrarian program did not conflict with the principle of private property. In the context of the agrar-ian reform proposed by the Kadets, neither expropriation nor the establishment of a state land bank constituted, in Miliukov's opinion, a negation of the principle of private property. Miliukov maintained that the creation of a state land bank from expropriated land sprang precisely from the Kadets' respect for the principle of private property. In an article in which he commented on a speech by the government spokesperson, Gurko, Miliukov wrote:

> Mr. Gurko will probably be surprised to learn that one of the motives that compelled the authors of the draft law to create a land bank that could not be sold was precisely respect for the principle of private property. This principle does allow for expropriation as an exceptional measure. . . . Following the expropriation of land in the interests of the state, it would (however) be inconsistent to allow the same legal rights of disposal to others as were enjoyed by the old owner. Full ownership can be expropriated in the interests of the state, but can only be passed on in a conditional form. Otherwise, one would just be robbing Peter to pay Paul.[23]

These remarks really show how unsure the Kadets were of the legal basis of their expropriation plans. Gurko was possibly not the only one to be surprised by them.

Miliukov had even more arguments to demonstrate that expropriation, as planned by the Kadets, was compatible with the principle of private property. According to Miliukov, the Kadets, in contrast to the socialists, did not derive their expropriation plan from the right to land, which the latter saw as a universal natural right, but rather from the idea of state interest. The Kadets therefore "implicitly recognize and in practice retain the private ownership of land."[24] Accordingly, the Kadets did not regard expropriation as a procedure that would also be repeated periodically in the future, but rather as a one-off measure, rather like the expropriation of land at the time of emancipation during the reign of Alexander II.[25]

Miliukov's arguments are certainly not convincing. More realistic were his colleagues on the left of the party, such as Manuilov, who saw the implementation of the party's agrarian program as the first step to the eventual nationalization of land and to socialism in general.

Even if Miliukov had been right, and the expropriation that he favored had amounted to nothing more than a repeat of the expropriation procedure under Alexander II, this would still not have proved that it would not undermine the principle of private property. Even the expropriation in the reign of Alexander II was highly detrimental to the principle of private property, and as we have seen, Witte pointed this out in his memoirs. Certainly, a repeat of this measure had to shake respect for the principle of private property even more. It is quite difficult to understand why a party that saw itself as the defender of liberalism could so easily decide to advocate measures that would undermine private property, one of the fundamental principles of liberalism. This is all the more astonishing as Miliukov, as a historian, knew that the principle of the ultimate state ownership of land was not merely an old Muscovite concept. In the immediate past, the government had tried to apply this concept to the land allocated to the peasants just to perpetuate the old order, which Miliukov was striving to defeat:

> If only the government at the time had thought to sweep away all aspects of the legal distinction between the peasants and their former masters . . . then perhaps . . . the property of all owners of land would enjoy the same legal title. However . . . class antagonism was maintained artificially by the government itself, and now, forty years after emancipation, it is just as strong as ever. . . . In Russia, there is no single category of landowner as is generally understood in law, but rather old traditional categories persist: peasant and estate owner, allotment land and private land. The public-law nature of our land ownership has been retained and accentuated by the whole of agrarian policy of the last fifty years.[26]

It is surprising to compare this brilliant analysis of the situation, made by Miliukov the historian, with the weakness of the conclusions that he drew as a politician. Miliukov did not want to accept that, insofar as the antiliberal principle of state ownership of land still had living roots in Russian soil, accommodating it had to be extremely dangerous for the destiny of liberalism in Russia. Neither did Miliukov want to admit that his program in particular contained nothing to overcome the source of the dangerous antagonisms that he himself so clearly describes. Just at a time when the government had finally decided to abolish the traditional special antiliberal and anti-individualistic institutions of peasant law, Miliukov wanted to deny it his support, because the government's draft agrarian legislation was "revolutionary" and would undermine "relationships in the real world."[27] He would not acknowledge that his position was a capitulation both to the old Muscovite principle and to a socialism that represented a consistent return to that same principle.

Miliukov went on to maintain that it did not matter whether peasants were given land from a state land bank purely to farm or as their own property. He thought this was a legal nicety of only secondary importance even in countries where the private ownership of land had been established over centuries. It would be even less important in Russia, "where, because of a rural order with its communes and traditional farming, as well as the legal uncertainties of the land buy-out system, . . . the concept of private property to this day remains unclear for a large part of the population."[28]

Yet the exact opposite was certainly true. It was precisely the weakness of the principle of the private ownership of land that should have compelled a liberal party to do everything to strengthen the institution of private property, by clearly interpreting legal relations in line with liberal principles, and to break with the dangerous tradition of welfare through land allocation. Furthermore, Miliukov in particular could not have believed that measures to consolidate private property would have been an assault on the legal consciousness of the broad masses. Whenever he argued against the socialists, and against the project of nationalization, he highlighted how strong the peasantry's property instinct was. He certainly knew that a liberal program would have met the wishes, if not of all of the peasantry, certainly of a majority, as was shown when the Stolypin reforms were implemented.

Because of Miliukov's position, it was left to the government to implement a liberal agrarian policy. Here was another example of paradox in Russian history: it was the bureaucracy, and not society, that would implement the liberal program.

Chapter 14

The Peasant Question after 1905

Liberal legislation in the field of peasant law,
especially the Stolypin decrees of October 5 and
November 9, 1906—Conversion of the decree of
November 9 into the law of June 14, 1910; the law
of May 29, 1911—Debates on the Stolypin agrarian
reforms in the Third Duma

Even before the outbreak of the 1905 revolution, the government had taken several measures that have to be seen as making some progress in a liberal direction. At the end of 1902, Witte had raised the issue of the abolition of the *krugovaia poruka*, the system of mutual guarantees, as well as reductions in direct taxes and redemption payments that weighed heavily on the peasants. In an understanding with the minister of the interior, Pleve, Witte laid draft legislation regarding these matters before the State Council.[1] It is an open question as to whether Pleve himself was convinced of the necessity of ending this demoralizing arrangement or whether he had to give way to Witte. What seems to confirm the former possibility is probably the fact that the intention to abolish the *krugovaia poruka* first appeared in the Manifesto of February 26, 1903 (P.S.Z. 22581), that is, in a manifesto that Witte did not help draft and that bears all the hallmarks of Pobedonostsev's and Pleve's thinking.[2]

In fact, shortly afterward, on March 12, 1903, the "Opinion" of the State Council recommending the abolition of the *krugovaia poruka* was ratified (P.S.Z. 22629) and a decree (P.S.Z. 22627) issued abolishing the *krugovaia poruka*. One of the first measures of Prince Sviatopolk-Mirsky, the liberal successor to Pleve who was assassinated on July 15, 1904, was the abolition of corporal punishment in the *volost'* courts, following the Manifesto of August 11, 1904, proclaimed on the baptism of the heir to the throne.

On the other hand, other measures that are also evidence of a liberal course fall into the period after October 17, 1905. On November 3, 1905, that is, when Witte was chairman of the Council of Ministers, came the abolition of redemption payments, effective from January 1, 1907 (P.S.Z. 26872). On the very same day, another decree was issued giving the agricultural bank new powers, making it easier to increase the amount of land available to the peasants, who were suffering from a shortage of land (P.S.Z. 26873). Both decrees were preceded by a manifesto announcing these measures (P.S.Z. 26871). The decree of March 4, 1906 (P.S.Z. 27478), established the Committee for Rural Affairs in St. Petersburg and similar bodies at provincial and district levels that were later the main agencies implementing Stolypin's agrarian reforms. On August 27, 1906, by which time Stolypin was already chairman of the Council of Ministers, an order was issued to transfer part of the state-owned domains to peasant ownership (P.S.Z. 28315). In essence, this decree aimed at improving the economic situation of the peasants. Insofar as this measure was about transferring state property to private ownership, it has moreover to be seen as a liberal measure. At the end of 1906, the ban on the use of allotment land as collateral was relaxed, although not the ban on pledging such assets to private individuals or enterprises. On the other hand, peasants were permitted to borrow money from the agricultural bank by taking out a mortgage on their plots (P.S.Z. 28547). This decree was preceded by two other important decrees: the decree of November 9, 1906, that set in motion the Stolypin agrarian reform as narrowly defined and the decree of October 5, 1906, closely linked to it. This largely did away with the special situation of the peasantry as an estate set apart from the rest of the population.

The Stolypin agrarian reforms envisaged the implementation of an extremely wide-ranging program. A series of measures was meant to improve the economic situation of the peasantry and to transform existing farmsteads into viable agricultural concerns. We can pass over this aspect, especially as the economic problems of the Stolypin reforms have been brilliantly elucidated in a German-language study.[3] The reforms were intended to solve the peasant question in line with liberal ideas and marked a significant step forward in Russia's progress toward liberalism. We must therefore highlight here those provisions of Stolypin's agrarian legislation that reflect the liberal characteristics of the reform. These are few in number.

The decree of October 5, 1906 (P.S.Z. 28392), began by pointing out that it aimed to develop further the principles of the 1861 emancipation reform, which started to put the peasants on an equal footing from a legal point of view with the members of other estates, thus bringing this process to a conclusion. The decree went on to stress that the continued existence of some restrictive provisions applying to the peasantry and those belonging to other tax-paying estates was incompatible with the principles of the manifestos of August 6 and October 17, 1905 (P.S.Z. 26656 and 26803). It thus ordered the immediate lifting of these restrictions, especially as their retention was virtually pointless following the abolition of the *krugovaia poruka* and the redemption payments. The decree also announced that the Duma would be presented with draft legislation to reform fundamentally local administration and the rural judicial system.

Article I declared that all subjects of the Russian empire, with the exception of non-Russians, would be granted the same rights as members of the gentry estate regarding access to the civil service. This was certainly real progress toward extending the privileges of the gentry to all, as discussed above, which ultimately had to transform these privileges into recognized rights for all Russian citizens. According to Article II, the agreement of the commune was no longer required if a peasant wanted to enter the civil service, a secondary school, or university. It was further no longer necessary for a peasant to leave his village commune if he entered the civil service or obtained an administrative grade, a school certificate, a university diploma, or a degree (Art. 3). Peasants were now allowed to leave or join a village commune. At the same time, there was no requirement for a peasant to quit his former village commune before joining a new one. A peasant who had cut his ties to his village commune would simply be counted among the inhabitants of the *volost'* (Art. 4). Article 5 allowed peasants to be issued passports valid for an unlimited time, like members of other estates, and in general, they were granted unrestricted freedom of movement. Article 7 abolished the special penal provisions that had previously applied to peasants. Furthermore, the power of the *zemskie nachal'niki* to impose minor punishments without due legal process through an administrative procedure was removed (Art. 11). According to Article 12, decisions taken by village communes could only be overturned by district assemblies (*uezdnyi s'ezd*), where they were unlawful, but not simply because they were impractical. Of great importance is Article 8, which rescinded the provisions introduced by the law of March 18, 1886, making it more difficult to divide farmstead property between family members. Furthermore, peasants would be permitted to sign bills of exchange, even if they did not own any immovable property. Finally, some of the restrictions on peasant entrepreneurial activity were lifted.

One must also mention here that Article 4 appears to set out a peasant's right to sell his share of allotment land, even if he was a member of the peasant commune. The article is not clearly written, but it is manifestly not about the sale to the commune of allotment plots, acquired by individuals as their own property or belonging to the farmstead. Such transactions had already been permitted by the law of December 14, 1893, and, consequently, provided for by Article 19 of the General Statute (*Ob. Polozhenie*), 1902 edition. Evidently, Article 4 is concerned with plots of land in the peasant commune that were redistributed. In fact according to Article 4:

> Members of the rural population are free . . . to leave the village commune unimpeded, after having relinquished their participation in farming communal land or having sold the plots belonging to them, without meeting the conditions set out in Article 208 of the General Statute.

If this interpretation is correct, then the obstacles to a peasant leaving his village, which Witte had highlighted so emphatically and which he had identified as particularly disastrous, were removed.

This measure led to the decree of November 9, which set out the fundamental principles of the Stolypin reform. This decree consisted of a preamble and four sections. The reform's principles were embodied above all in the following articles of the decree: According to Article 1 of the first section, any head of a farmstead would be free to leave the peasant commune and to demand that it hand over to him as his own private property his share of allocated land. As such, this did nothing more than confirm Article 36 of the 1861 General Statute.[4] According to this article, members of the peasant commune had the right to demand a plot of land corresponding to the size of their contributions to the redemption payments, after these had been completed, that is, when the land finally became the property of the commune. At that point, these plots became their private property. After redemption payments were abolished through the Manifesto of November 3, 1905, it was quite natural and necessary to confirm the universal implementation of Article 36 of the General Statute. Plots belonging to a farmstead were made the private property of the head of household in Article 1 of the third section. According to Article 2 of the same section, if others besides the direct descendants of the head of the family belonged to the household, a household's property had to be owned jointly, as per volume 10 of the civil code (Svod), by all the members of the farmstead. Thus, farmstead property belonging to a collective was to disappear, to be replaced by private property. In the same way, household (usad'ba) plots, even within the rural communes, were converted into private property.

Article 1 of the second section decreed that the sale of farmstead land, now converted to private property, would be governed by the provisions of general civil law that apply to all sales of immovable property. Furthermore, Articles 12 to 14 of the first section dealt with the right of householders to demand that the commune provide them with a single unit of land in exchange for the diverse plots they had received. This was designed to combat farm parcelization and was thus a technical measure in the area of agriculture, which we do not need to dwell on here. Suffice it to say that inasmuch as the formation of consolidated property reinforced the independence of the owner and hence individualism, its implementation had to serve to underpin the psychological foundations of liberalism. The same is true for the law on land development of May 29, 1911, which was equally concerned with the technicalities of agriculture and was especially aimed at eliminating farm fragmentation. As such, this law was even welcomed as constructive by the Kadets, who were hostile to the Stolypin agrarian reforms.[5]

Stolypin's decree of November 9, 1906, was accepted by the State Duma and the State Council after some revisions and additions and then passed into law on June 14, 1910. This law bears the following title: "On the Modification and Development of Some of the Measures Concerning Peasant Land Ownership." In general, the 1910 law retained all the key features of the decree of November 9, 1906. It even surpassed it in combating the peasant commune. The law declared that in all peasant communes where no general repartition of land had taken place since the allocation of land, collective ownership was to be superseded by hereditary ownership, that is, private property (Art. 1). Initially, the Duma wanted to go further and extend this measure to those communes where no general repartition had been undertaken in the last twenty-four years. Here, however, the Duma encountered resistance from both the State Council and the government. The State Council and the government wanted to avoid anything that smacked of the compulsory breakup of the peasant communes. Furthermore, the government turned down this proposal as undesirable from a practical point of view.

Overall, it is not so much the individual amendments and additions submitted by the legislative bodies concerning the decree of November 9, 1906, and the draft legislation proposed by the government that are of interest.[6] It is rather the debates in the Duma and the arguments put forward by government representatives and the majority parties, on the one hand, and by the opposition parties, on the other. The content and the spirit of Stolypin's reforms, as well as the principled positions of both its supporters and opponents, were made clear through this debate.

The debates in the Third Duma lose some of their interest, in part at least because the Right, although unsympathetic to the draft legislation, did not wish to reject decisively the draft law either. If it had done so, it would have had to join forces with the Left parties and, what is more, oppose the government, which relied on the support of the tsar to implement the agrarian legislation. Thus, the enemies of constitutionalism and the supporters of absolute monarchy would have ended up opposing, in parliament, the will of the emperor. Immediately after the draft law was put on the order of parliamentary business, the right-wing parliamentary group instructed Metropolitan Mitrofan to issue on behalf of the entire group a declaration that was not so much a statement agreeing with the draft legislation as desisting from opposition. That it was not one of the usual spokesmen for the parliamentary group, but the highest-ranking religious dignitary from their camp, who was charged with issuing this declaration, seems to indicate that the party wanted to highlight the formal nature of the declaration. In other words, it wanted to stress the fact that it was not so much a matter of taking a principled stand, but rather a tactical stance determined solely by reverence for the will of the tsar and autocrat. The real mood of the Right, however, was revealed not so much by this declaration, as by the applause that speakers from the Left were now and then able to earn from the most extreme right-wing members (something that otherwise hardly ever occurred in the Duma), as well as by some of the speeches from their own side.

The position of the Kadets, the most important of the left opposition groups, was diametrically opposed to that of the Right. They rejected the draft law, but certainly not, at least not primarily, on a matter of principle, but above all because of a firm, tactical determination to remain an opposition party. That explains the weakness of the Kadets' arguments against the draft law. Principled opposition to the draft law came from the Trudovik group ("Labor Group," non-Marxist socialists), which acted as an irreconcilable opposition. Their speeches, however, were heavy with revolutionary rhetoric, and their tone was aggressive and provocative. The Octobrists and other majority groups regarded these speeches with disdain, mainly reacting to them merely with interjections. Thus, such speeches did not contribute very much to the discussions on Stolypin's reforms in the Duma. Much more comprehensive were the debates in the State Council, although some of what was said in the Duma was extremely interesting and quite enlightening.

The true position of the Right was most clearly expressed by the Duma member Bakaleev:

> Apparently, the State Duma has not chosen to develop and amend the existing peasant legislation, but to destroy it. . . . The existing laws are based on the inviolable nature of property in general, and not just of private property. By replacing the former collective ownership of the communes with the individual as proprietor, it has embarked on a course of violating . . . the integrity of property. . . . For . . . as has been shown by both the Right and the Left, allotment land was given not to individuals, but to the communes and family households.[7]

This speech shows that the Right still rejected any departure from the legislation of the 1890s, and Senate rulings that sought to consolidate the transitional period created by the 1861 emancipation statute into a permanent state of affairs, and regarded as undesirable the peasantry's shift from agrarian collectivism to private property. That this speech was not just an expression of Bakaleev's personal opinion, but gave a true reflection of the prevailing views on the Right, is shown by the fact that at the end of the debate on the third reading, the Right presented a proposal for a transitional period. This stressed that the new law was in line with the principles of the Manifesto of February 23, 1903. This was patently an attempt to allow a more restrictive interpretation later, when the law was applied in practice. It was an assertion denounced by the left opposition (Miliukov) as contrary to the facts, while the majority parties also rejected this transitional proposal as unacceptable. In fact, the work on the agrarian program, defended by Witte and his Special Advisory Committee, was paralyzed at the time by the Manifesto of February 26, 1903, while this new law essentially embodied the ideas contained in Witte's memorandum.

The Kadets' criticisms were hampered, as we have noted, by the fact that in theory they were by no means against private property. Their spokesman, Shingarev, specifically pointed out that in principle his position on the institution of private property was no different from that of Shidlovsky, the representative of the majority and spokesman for the commission. He stressed that he only re-jected "the way this institution would be introduced in the life of the people" as proposed by the Duma majority. He added that he did not accept the intention of "mechanically and forcefully foisting this institution on the peasant family, to whom it had been totally foreign up to now," and that he rejected the attempt "to destroy the concept of family property with the help of revolutionary legislation" (3rd leg., 2nd sess., part 3, col. 2871). In fact, the Kadets were not just against the provisions of the law that were meant to accelerate the breakup of the peasant commune, but were even more opposed to declaring family property the private property of the head of household. Shingarev explained: "The commission is not content with declaring that peasant communes, where there had been no repar-tition of land for a long time, should be dissolved. *It goes further.* . . and wants to establish the principle of the private property of the head of household . . . that is, a principle that is quite alien to the population in these areas" (ibid., col. 2855; author's emphasis).

Prince Volkonsky, the majority spokesman, also noted that "no other part of the present legislation had aroused so many objections" (ibid., col. 2858). The Kadets, however, also thought that the provisions that aimed at accelerating the breakup of the peasant communes were too radical and contrary to the people's legal consciousness. As evidence for this, at least in those regions where the peas-ant communes had not fallen victim to the process of disintegration, Shingarev cited letters from peasants in which the provisions of the decree of November 9, 1906 (which had already passed into law), were described as "a foreign yoke." They wrote that they were thinking of reestablishing the commune that they had unthinkingly dissolved in haste, on first impression, when the decree was pub-lished (ibid., col. 2887).

It is noteworthy that during the debates, the Kadets tried hard to accuse the government and the majority parties of revolutionary legislation and extremism, whereas these had always seen combating revolution as their main duty. It is not difficult to explain this as a tactic on the part of the Kadets. These were supposed to show that they alone could be seen as defenders of the concept and rule of law. They were the ones who stood between, on the one hand, the socialist revolution-ary parties of the Left and, on the other, the parties of the moderate Right, which wanted to implant liberalism and private property in Russia by means of revolu-tionary laws. Shingarev repeatedly appealed to the majority parties "to adopt a calm, gradual solution to the agrarian question" (ibid., col. 2897), not to be se-duced by the concept of personal property, and to take account of the realities of life, that is, especially the level of consciousness of the people (ibid., col. 2752f). The Kadets, and even the socialists, were at one with supporters of the far Right in accusing the majority parties and the government (less in the case of the latter than with the majority parties) of being too radical and of breaking too abruptly with existing law and the traditional legal consciousness of peasant folk.[8] Shingarev also warned the majority parties not to ignore the people's legal awareness, as implementing the law would then only provoke hatred, bitterness, and resistance on the part of the people (ibid., col. 2752).

The spokesman for the commission, Shidlovsky, countered these objections with the following arguments: the law was not attempting anything that was alien to the people or that went against the way things naturally developed. On the contrary, the move to private property among the peasants had been observed long ago (something the Kadets did not dispute, cf. Shingarev, in ibid., col. 2871). He continued that the government was thus accommodating this spontaneous development (ibid., col. 2867) and generally exercising a function that was, and ought to have been, quite normal for governments. Shidlovsky argued that the assertion that the law introduced private property by force was a misrepresentation. The law would not stop a group of people who voluntarily wished to share ownership, on condition that this joint ownership was based on a voluntary contract, and not on the *mir* constitution, as the peasant commune naturally could not be described as a voluntary association. He added that it was generally well known that the peasant commune was a compulsory association protected by the old laws (ibid., col. 2760). It was precisely because of this characteristic that the peasant commune could not be abolished without intervention by the legislature. Tantsov pointed this out emphatically:

> It is said that the peasant commune should be left alone. It should be left to live or die according to its own internal laws. Any intervention on the part of parliament has to be seen as coercion. (Shingarev from his seat: "that's right.") One would think that the peasant commune in its present form was the product of the freely developing economic life of the people and owed nothing to the external force of the law. If that were the case, and only in that case, one might be permitted to believe that it would disappear as freely and painlessly as it developed. Yet that is not the reality. Everyone knows that the state wanted to retain the peasant commune as a paternalistic institution for its own ends, especially for fiscal ones, thus changing it into an association of a coercive nature.[9]

In my introduction, I already pointed out that liberalism's method is to abolish institutions that were created by the antiliberal regime that preceded it and that are coercive. It would be difficult to contest that abolishing such institutions would be impossible without special measures, precisely because of their status in public law, that is, without compulsion, although that is exactly what the Kadets attempted to assert in the Duma.

Furthermore, according to the majority's view, it would have been a mistake to seek to abolish the peasant community while retaining family household ownership of land. What was the point of liberating the peasant from the shackles of the larger collective only to keep him bound to the smaller collective? In this way, he would be denied civil liberty, the enjoyment of the civil rights granted to other citizens, and the legal status of a free proprietor.

More precisely, the Kadets proposed that leaving the peasant commune should only be allowed at the time of a general repartition of land in the commune and then only on condition that the peasant who was leaving was given his share of land in one piece. The majority did not accept either proposal. It pointed out that the first demand would force repartitions where they were not even being considered and that these final, as it were definitive, repartitions would needlessly provoke a particularly intense fight over land among the members of the commune (Shidlovsky, in ibid., part 3, col. 2763). The majority also rejected the second suggestion, as it would have been a retrograde step even in comparison with Article 165 of the emancipation statute, which was repealed at the time. Under this article, all the strips of land that a peasant farmed could become his property on the early completion of the redemption payments. The exchange of these parcels of land for a consolidated plot was sometimes a difficult process to complete and was not made a necessary condition by the emancipation laws for transforming the use of land into land ownership. The Kadets' proposal would have made this exchange into such a condition, which would naturally have made leaving the commune much more difficult.

The most significant argument leveled against the law was put forward by the spokesman for the Trudoviks, Kropotov. Kropotov pointed out that the new law denied all those who wished to do so of the opportunity of claiming an allocation of land if they had not done so by the time the law came into force. This would apply to any member of a commune or farmstead who had been unable to claim his "right to land" in full (e.g., if someone had been absent on leave and working in a town) or only partially (e.g., if someone had not received extra land at the last repartition for his growing family). Kropotov said: "Both local customary law as well as statute and Senate rulings refer to the right of any member of the commune to demand that the commune should provide him with part of the land that had been allocated to it. To deprive them (the members of the commune) of this right was thus the same as taking land from the landowners" (ibid., col. 2874).

As far as I am aware, the Duma majority simply ignored what Kropotov said. Government representatives did not react to it either. It is certain, however, that the government should have been obliged not to pass over this argument in silence. I do not mean Stolypin's government in particular, but this government as the successor to a series of His Imperial Majesty's governments, which for decades had done everything, or at least had allowed things to be done, to prevent the gradual evolution of the entitlement to be provided with land in public law into an individual property right. The government ought therefore to have positively justified the abolition of this entitlement to be provided with land.

Such a justification would even have been possible if the government had set out the liberal position, on which, after all, the agrarian reform was based. In fact, from a liberal point of view, the transformation of peasant land ownership into private property would have meant that a civil society would at last have applied universally throughout Russia. This would have put the peasantry on an equal footing with the other estates, as had already been intended in 1861, and thus all vestiges of serfdom in relation to the peasants would have been removed. If civil law applied universally, it would have meant that a clear distinction between the realms of private and public law would have been established, and a fundamental separation of powers, embodied by the division between economic and political power, would have been achieved in the Russian state. Rights established in an autonomous sphere of civil law recognized by the state would have become inviolable because of this fundamental separation of powers. The independence of civil law embedded within an autonomous sphere would have been characterized above all by the state's recognition of the principle of private property, the freedom of individual initiative, and the freedom to take on contractual obligations. These rights, particularly property rights, are seen as sacrosanct, that is, as inviolable even for the state. Thus, the fact that individual rights supersede entitlements under public law means a significant guarantee of the freedom of the individual and his independence from the state. It is not possible, however, to transform previously fulfilled entitlements into individual rights without invalidating future entitlements. The abolition of these entitlements in public law is nevertheless necessary to establish the division between economic and political power and thus to guarantee individual freedom and the independence of the individual from the state. By contrast, the suppression of private property and individual rights in general leads to the removal of this separation of powers and to the assertion of the omnipotence of the state.

The government, however, passed over Kropotov's words in silence, thus leaving its theoretical position in this regard without clarification or justification. It must have been obvious that this entitlement in public law, which by its very nature depends entirely on state guarantees, could have been abrogated by the state at any time.

The speech of one independent Duma deputy, Storchak (apparently representing the peasantry), was different from those of the other deputies. This speaker highlighted the importance of the right of those peasants leaving the commune to dispose freely of the land that had been declared their private property when they left the commune. It was especially important for anyone who left the commune with the intention of settling in Siberia to be able to sell their land in European Russia to acquire a modest amount of capital for their resettlement. Storchak appealed to the government to take the necessary measures as quickly as possible to remove all restrictions that remained in this respect. He pointed out that a landowner who was not a peasant could sell his land unhindered, even if he lived abroad. It was unfair to withhold this right from a peasant who wanted to move to Siberia (ibid., col. 2753f.).

Not just opposition representatives but also some members of the Octobrist Party criticized particular sections of the draft law. Prince Volkonsky I,[10] for example, pointed out that the provisions of the draft law concerning the method of ascertaining the size of plots of land to be transferred to a peasant leaving the commune were a retrograde step in comparison with Article 36 of the 1861 emancipation statute. The Duma's draft legislation envisaged that in communes where a general redistribution of land based on the decree of June 8, 1893, had taken place, the area of the plot to be transferred to a head of household leaving the commune should be calculated according to the number of allotment units belonging to his farmstead at the time of his departure. In all other communes, however, the head of the farmstead was simply given all the land that he was farming at the time of leaving. By contrast, as we know, Article 36 of the emancipation statute stipulated that the area of the plots had to correspond to the amount of the farmstead's contribution to the acquisition of land by the commune (i.e., in proportion to its contribution to paying off the redemption payments). It is evident from a civil-law perspective that neither the allocated plots, adopted at the periodic redistribution of land in individual communes, nor the actual area of land use, if distinct from that covered by contributions to the redemption payments, really amounted to an incontestable legal title to private property. Prince Volkonsky clearly states, "Article 36 of the emancipation statute stipulates that what you have paid for is yours, but we are saying that what you have taken is yours" (ibid., col. 2922). (In Russian, this sentence sounds like a play on words: *oplatil—zakhvatil*). Volkonsky's assertion was greeted by silence from the deputies of his own party, whereas it provoked stormy applause from both the right and the left opposition benches.

These reservations were taken seriously in both the Duma and the State Council. One of the two spokesmen for the State Council's commission, Stishinsky, explained why it was necessary to deviate from Article 36 in the draft legislation.[11] He highlighted a range of factors that made calculating the contribution of individual farmsteads to the redemption payments well nigh impossible: the reduction in redemption payments, the waiver of arrears, family division, repartitioning in the communes, and especially the chaotic state of the accounts for these payments in the *volost'* administrative offices, which mostly had no records of the payments made by the older age-groups.

Chapter 15

The Peasant Question after 1905 (continued)

Debates in the State Council on the Stolypin
agrarian reforms—Further draft legislation in the
field of peasant law—Conclusion

The Right on the State Council, just as in the Duma, did not want to reject the draft law—the decree of November 9, 1906—out of hand, although it did suggest some amendments with the aim of slowing down the transition from agrarian collectivism to private property as sought by the legislation. Through one of these amendments, communes were to be given the right of first refusal on the land of peasants who had left. On the one hand, this meant favoring the commune and on the other, more important, in practice considerably reducing the peasant's chances of selling his land. The second of these amendments would have restricted the peasant's right of disposal over his land, by the requirement that his wife and eldest adult son had to agree to the sale, which would have protected the institution of family property.

Representatives of the Right went much further in their speeches than merely justifying these proposed amendments. Overall, they voiced at length their fundamental misgivings about the decree of November 9, 1906. The Right's position was set out, in particular, in Count Olsufiev's speeches, whose clarity of form, moderate tone, and fervor of deep conviction, as far as the spoken word can be judged from the shorthand reports of the debates, cannot be denied. Just like the left and right opposition in the Duma, Count Olsufiev stressed that the draft law broke too suddenly and sharply with all previous legislation. After all, in his view, a series of nineteenth-century laws had protected the commune principle, while even the Manifesto of February 26, 1903, itself took this very position. This sudden departure from a decades-old policy was, in his opinion, not because of any inconsistency in the positions of particular individuals (meaning Stolypin, no doubt), but because of government (*pravitel'stva*) in general. People were perplexed and wondered what the right thing to do was. The impression was created that "suddenly some sort of New World had been discovered."[1] The draft law, in Olsufiev's words, did not run counter just to earlier legislation, but to the way people thought: "The peasants have trouble understanding this law. . . . From what I have observed in the country, there is no enthusiasm for this law. On the contrary, people everywhere are bewildered" (5th sess., col. 1184).

Olsufiev regarded the abolition of the commune, as well as family property, as dangerous, but considered the latter even more dangerous than the former: "For my part, I think that the main danger in this draft law lies not in the abolition of the rural commune but in the irreversible switch from the centuries-old concept of the working family unit to the principle by which individuals would be able to make a sale (*prodazha*) of land without any restrictions. This is because private property conflicts with the peasants' general legal consciousness" (ibid., cols. 1183, 1184). That is why Olsufiev thought it was a mistake to proceed so hastily and extend to the peasants the legal status of all other inhabitants of Russia merely "in the name of a pseudo-liberating doctrine aiming to make everyone equal" (ibid., col. 1184). He was in no doubt that the law was based not on real need, but on abstract theory: "Doubtless, this new principle is being applied in the name of the doctrine that personal property will save everything, that a well-fed, conservative, enlightened bourgeois must come into being to counterbalance our uneducated, dark, frequently anarchic peasants from the rural communes. This bourgeois is now supposed to be Russia's salvation" (ibid., col. 1182). Olsufiev saw key circles in government and public opinion as supporting this doctrine:

> Professor Kovalevsky described the prevailing trend (*napravlenie*) in those circles now in power as physiocratic, but it is simpler to call them bourgeois. After all, the party currently leading the Duma (the Octobrists) is a bourgeois (*burzhuaznaia*) party. What can be more in conflict, however, with the principles of bourgeois liberalism than the continued existence of our segregated peasantry bound to the land commune? I ask you to bear in mind that I am not arguing against individual representatives of the government (certainly meaning Stolypin again), but against a certain trend in public opinion. (Ibid., col. 1464)

Olsufiev went on to observe that the outlook of this bourgeois tendency, embodied in the draft law, did not just run counter to the peasantry's legal consciousness, but also to that of the entire Russian people, by departing from the principle of support for the weak and placing its hopes on those who were stronger. In a session of the State Council on March 22, 1910, Olsufiev said: "Thus, our opponents are suggesting making the principle of the victory of the strong and the defenselessness of the weak the basis for legislation on the peasant question." This principle, however, he continued, could not be applied in general: "It cannot be applied either with respect to some national questions (e.g., the Jewish question) or to labor legislation. Furthermore, I consider this principle profoundly antinational. The Russian people have up till now had an unshakable faith (*sviato*) in the autocracy as the protector of the weak, and should they become convinced that this is no longer the case, bitter disappointment will fill the hearts of many millions of ordinary people" (ibid., col. 1463).[2]

According to Olsufiev, however, the views of the dominant school of thought were not merely doctrinaire but also simplistic. All the speeches of this group were "based on a single but also really uncomplicated schema: everything in Russia is bad; therefore because Russia has the land commune, it must be abolished" (ibid., col. 1460). It was not surprising, therefore, he continued, that what was happening on the land had to be seen not as the emergence of private property, but rather as the destruction of the rural commune (ibid., col. 1185). It was surely a mistake, he said, to explain the process of the destruction of the commune through pressure from local administrative bodies. This process, in his view, was rather driven by propaganda, which one could only call unscrupulous and which gave the peasants reason to believe that their land would be taken away if they did not leave the commune (ibid., col. 1183). This development, marked by a tendency to switch to private property, led him to believe that a reaction against it on the land was to be expected, that the pendulum would soon swing the other way (ibid., col. 1465). Count Olsufiev concluded his first speech with these words: "Bearing in mind these considerations, we, the representatives of the Right, in that we believe in the strength of the foundations of national life, hold that we, in particular the Upper House, must show the utmost caution in respect of this legislation. . . . I would especially recommend what, after all, must be the hallmark of the Upper House, namely caution and reserve in the face of excessive enthusiasm" (ibid., col. 1185f).

The representatives of the Right denied, in particular, that the lack of respect among peasants for the property rights of others was caused by the legal consciousness fostered by the land commune. They maintained that the existence of the rural communes in no way led to the excesses of the peasants against the property of the landowners during the revolutionary years of 1905–6. Bakhteev, for example, said:

> When I read that the pogroms on the estates in Voronezh province were caused by the fact that land ownership took the form of land communes, I have to recall that these pogroms took place six to seven months after those in Chernigov province, where there are hardly any land communes. Therefore, if one also wants to link the Chernigov pogroms to the type of land ownership, one would have to maintain that farmstead ownership (*podvornoe vladenie*) led to the pogroms. (Ibid., col. 1170)

This argument certainly cannot be regarded as persuasive. Farmstead ownership, after all, was not a form of private property either, but rather a form of collective ownership similar to the land commune. Just like in the land communes, the members of the farmstead did not enjoy individual property rights, but had an entitlement in public law to be granted land, as I have tried to show in detail elsewhere. What was present in the farmstead also applied to the land commune, only to a higher degree. That is why I expressed this opinion above and now wish to repeat it here: what was fundamental in the old agrarian system was not the existence of the rural commune, but the nature of the "right to land" in public law, to which members of the peasant estate were entitled. In addition, representatives of both the right and the left opposition in the Duma and the State Council were correct in pointing out that the most radical and, from their perspective, the most dangerous aspects of the draft law were not the provisions that accelerated the breakup of the rural commune. They were rather the abolition of the institution of family property or farmstead ownership and its conversion into the private property of the head of household and, in some instances, other members of the household. The sociologist M. Kovalevsky, who was a member of the State Council at the time, even said that "the world has never seen a greater agrarian revolution" (ibid., col. 1211). It has to be conceded that Krasovsky's attempt to refute this assertion with the point that, in reality, nothing had changed—that each Ivan and every Piotr stayed on the same farm as before—was unconvincing. The conversion of farmstead ownership into private property, that is, the replacement of the entitlement in public law to be provided with land by personal property rights, signified a profound change, even if each peasant did remain on his farm. This inevitably had to have a strong influence on the legal awareness of the peasantry. By their very nature, personal property rights are always specific and thus limited. By contrast, the entitlement in public law to be provided with land is a general and thus open-ended demand. It is obvious that because of this characteristic, this entitlement could not but feed the revolutionary mood. If the state does not satisfy this demand, or in the opinion of those who are making it does not satisfy it sufficiently, it stands to reason that the claim has to be satisfied through direct, or revolutionary, action. One has to act on one's own account, or, as it says in the Russian translation of the *Internationale,* to enforce the claim "with our own hands." It is evident that converting peasants into proprietors would invalidate the legal and psychological basis of such claims on the state. In turn, this would eliminate the circumstances giving rise to a revolutionary mindset.

Nonetheless, some people took the view that no single legal feature of peasant landownership would either encourage or prevent the development of a revolutionary outlook and the revolutionary mood that underpinned it and that only economic conditions were significant in this respect. We have seen that the Ministry of the Interior's editing commission embraced this view, while it was also put forward in the State Council by Professor Manuilov, who was doubtless mainly sympathetic to the Left:

Personally, I believe that the form of landownership has nothing to do with the pogroms on the landowners' estates and think that those who assume that the land commune encourages the development of revolutionary socialist ideas, and those who reject this, are both wrong. This is because the people whose standard of living is poor will look favorably on revolutionary ideas, irrespective of whether they live in the context of communal land ownership or private property. (Ibid., col. 1378)

This is an example of how the views of the Left coincided with those of the extreme Right. Even if you concede that there is a grain of truth in this view, it is hardly possible to deny that the legal awareness of a class is even more significant in making the members of that class susceptible or not to revolutionary propaganda. This legal awareness is the source of respect for the rights of others, or conversely, it leads to a disregard for those rights.

This conviction was articulated by the commission's first spokesman, Krasovsky. Krasovsky stressed that there was an indissoluble link between the principle of the equal redistribution of land in the communes and the concepts of some social theories, according to which each should receive everything according to their needs (ibid., col. 1269). He was convinced that the peasant would only respect the rights of others if he were granted the same rights as enjoyed by other Russian citizens (ibid., col. 1265). For this reason, he welcomed the draft law and the decree of November 9, 1906, on which it was based,[3] which introduced "the beneficial (spasite'lnoe) idea of property" to the conceptual world of the peasant (ibid., col. 1264). He particularly welcomed the decree, however, because the peasant himself changed from "being a beneficiary without rights to a proprietor with full rights (polnopravnyi) over his plot" (ibid., col. 1264). In his words, this was a necessary precondition for peasant prosperity. If this did not always result in a peasant becoming rich, at least it meant he was free. His situation would be comparable to that of a person without means in Western Europe, where there were also poor people, but at least their hands were not tied. By contrast, he continued, not only were people in the rural communes often poor and insecure, but also, what was worse, their hands were shackled (ibid., col. 1271).

In general, the supporters of the draft law stressed that it signified a determination to move to greater freedom.

Moreover, implementation of the law, in their view, did not entail coercive measures. Above all, it would be a misunderstanding of the law to believe that it would in every case force peasants to leave the land communes and compel them to become private landowners. Stolypin said, "I have too much respect for the good sense of the people to concede that the Russian peasantry would transform its agrarian system by command and not through inner conviction" (ibid., col. 1144).[4] Both Krasovsky in the State Council and Shidlovsky in the Duma, however, pointed out that the rural commune was an institution in public not private law (ibid., col. 1281). Therefore, the ties that bound the peasant to it could not be dissolved without passing a law doing away with their compulsory nature. This resulted in the paradoxical impression that "habitual defenders of individual liberty turned into advocates of compulsion, while voices in defense of freedom are raised from that quarter that is usually in favor of coercion from above or the commune" (ibid., col. 1278).

In addition, the supporters of the draft law vehemently rejected the claim that it harbored an antisocial bias in favor of the strong at the expense of the weak. Pinning one's hopes on the stronger (*stavka na sil'nych*) did not mean simply abandoning the weak to their fate. Butlerov said: "I must also refer to what Olsufiev said yesterday. He accused the government of discarding the principle of protection (*prokovitel'stva*) of the weak for the benefit of the strong by enacting this law. . . . This criticism seems to be completely unfounded. Shackling personal initiative . . . does not at all imply that the weak should be denied protection. In any case, such safeguards for the strong do not disadvantage the weak" (ibid., col. 1249).

This is a very significant observation. The so-called abandonment of protection for the weak really means nothing more than refusing to see all peasants, all members of the peasant estate, as categorically weak and treating them as if they all needed paternalistic support. A peasant would only be treated as weak if it turned out that he was indeed weak. The state, however, would no longer automatically bestow its paternalistic benefits on each peasant, a process that bound and actually weakened him.[5] Stolypin himself said, as far as one can tell from the shorthand report with a note of irritation: "The government has never declared that it is no longer responsible for caring for the weak, . . . but these should not weigh down like heavy manacles on the peasant estate alone, purely on the agricultural classes, on their enterprise, on their efforts to improve their lot" (ibid., cols. 1601f). Stolypin was suggesting here that the government intended that the burden of state provision for the disadvantaged elements in society should fall equally on all classes and not weigh down on the peasantry alone, as was hitherto the case.

Stolypin went on to stress that the break with existing law, with previous legislation, was not as radical as some opponents of the law supposed. The provisions of earlier laws that sought to prevent the transfer of peasant allotment land to the members of other estates would be maintained in respect to peasants whose land had been converted into private property. A peasant would only be able to sell this land to another peasant, would only be able to remortgage it at the peasant bank, and could not sell it to settle personal debt (ibid., cols. 1602f). In fact, the government was so cautious in seeking a solution to this problem that it was even accused of "not putting enough energy into its constructive bureaucratic initiatives" (*burokraticheskogo tvorchestva*—in a reference of one of Witte's speeches). Nor was the Duma reckless in its approach. On the contrary, the Duma actually adopted the amendment to the draft law, by which a peasant was only able to buy up to six plots of land (according to the norms of a particular area) in the same district. Thus, he concluded, the draft law did not break definitively with the traditional idea of providing the peasants with land, something that had to be seen as a social measure.

The uncertainty as to whether there would be a majority in the State Council for the government's draft law led Stolypin to intervene repeatedly in the debate and to both defend individual provisions in the legislative proposal and explain and justify the general principle of the legislation. He gave a particularly detailed account of his approach in his speech of March 15, 1910, with which he opened the debate. Here, Stolypin reminded the members of the State Council that the decree of November 9, 1906, had initially been interpreted by many as "an act of political impotence," that is, as an attempt to do something no matter what in a desperate situation. Now, however, it had become clear to everyone that this measure to consolidate private property "was the result . . . of a well-thought-out principled position to deal with what was happening in Russia at the time" (ibid., col. 1137). Political turmoil (smuta), Stolypin continued, had in fact been fed by much more serious social turmoil, which meant that purely political measures would prove ineffective in dealing with the revolutionary unrest. "Political reforms can only take on life, force, and significance when accompanied by social agrarian reform" (ibid., col. 1138). In his view, the fundamental cause of the disorder had to be removed, by "giving the peasants the opportunity to escape poverty, illiteracy, and agrarian muddle [zemel'nogo nestroeniia]" (ibid., col. 1138). If, Stolypin added, one wanted to judge correctly the decree of November 9, 1906, which laid the foundations of a new social and economic order for the peasantry, one had to look at it from a social perspective, and from a political one (ibid., col. 1138). In his view, this law represented a move toward granting the peasants equality with all citizens of the empire. Its success could be explained mainly because "it is inseparably linked to the greatest achievement of the last century, the emancipation of the serfs, and is perhaps the last act in the task of liberating (raskreposhchenia) our agricultural class" (ibid., col. 1144). He also stated: "A lot is said in this country about freedom, but the prophets of freedom in the abstract do not even want the most rudimentary freedom, the freedom to create, the freedom of initiative for the peasants" (ibid., col. 1142).

It was necessary to grant the peasants this freedom, and such a step would without doubt match the people's expectations and the popular mood (ibid., col. 1144). What Stolypin meant here was that the people wanted the freedom, the opportunity, to fight to improve their lot within the framework of civil society; that they would only attempt to improve their situation by taking the path of collectivist revolution, if they continued to be denied civil liberty.

In this speech, and in his later speeches in the State Council, Stolypin went on to reject all proposed amendments that served to protect the land commune or household ownership. All these amendments would, he said, mean retaining the principle of dependency, in the form of the bond (prikreposhcheniia) to either the land commune or the smaller unit of the farmstead.[6] These amendments would also entail the retention of the paternalism that Stolypin equally rejected, as he was convinced that "special provision, special protection, special privileges for the peasant can only lead to him remaining chronically powerless and weak" (ibid., col. 1142). That is why, in Stolypin's opinion, the real solution to the peasant question, through which the peasants would become strong and free, was not just a social issue but also a task facing the nation. He said, "As long as work of the highest quality, that is, free work and not forced labor, is not put to use on the land, our land will never match the competition from our neighbors' land" (ibid., col. 1604).

It was, of course, possible to disagree. Like the parties of the Left, one could regard the additional redistribution of land taken from the landowners as the only solution, a solution that Stolypin, just like Witte, rejected. In the first place, just like Witte, he thought it unworkable; second, it was incompatible with freedom. The following comment by Stolypin is very significant in this respect: "The decree of November 9 . . . came about at a time of disorder . . . when freedom was seen as a license to commit acts of violence and when people thought it was possible to overcome this violence by further violence, namely the forced expropriation of landed property" (ibid., col. 1137).

Stolypin stressed that he too did not want to overstate the impact of the November 9 decree and that certainly many more measures were required to improve the condition of the peasantry. It was necessary, he added, to organize a system of agricultural credit for small farmers and support for peasant farming through agronomic methods, while the education system in rural areas had to be developed. One could anticipate that without all these measures there would be temporary setbacks and disappointments. "Nevertheless," declared Stolypin, "I am firmly convinced that the basic principle of this law is right" (ibid., col. 1144).

The amendments proposed by the historian of law Sergeevich had nothing to do with the opposition to the draft law from the Left or the Right. In the first place, Sergeevich believed that not just the head of household but also other members of the farmstead ought to be given rights to leave the land commune with a plot of land. Why should a peasant not be allowed to leave the commune, he asked, merely because his head of household was against it? (ibid., col. 1514). Sergeevich held that this change was all the more desirable because "head of household" was not at all a precise legal term. By adopting Sergeevich's proposal, the use of the term "head of household" could have been avoided in the text of the law. Furthermore, Sergeevich was opposed to calling the plots of land given to a peasant on leaving the commune his property. There was no justification for describing this land as private property, considering all the restrictions that remained in place on the peasant's right of disposal in respect of these plots" "Such a characterization would lead one to suppose that allotment land was genuine property, which is not the case" (ibid., col. 1517). Kovalevsky expressed a similar point of view, but this was vigorously contested by Krasovsky, who pointed out that it was not unheard of in the West for measures to be taken to consolidate the land belonging to small farmers. Krasovsky added that a certain level of restriction on the right of disposal resulting from this did not entail, by any means, the abolition of private property as such (ibid., col. 1237).

The criticism that Witte made of the draft law had a certain affinity with these critical observations made by academics. He too thought that the individual holdings, created by the new law, were not truly private property, that is, not property as understood in general civil law: "This is not about abolishing the rural commune . . . to replace it with a genuine form of personal property, but it is about abolishing the rural commune to turn the peasant into a proprietor, the like of which is unknown in either the history or the theory of civil law in other civilized countries" (ibid., col. 1147).

This conclusion was inescapable, Witte continued, taking into account all the restrictions placed by the new law on a peasant's property rights when he left the commune. All existing legal provisions regarding land allocated to peasants, with all their adverse effects, were in fact also retained in respect of the ownership rights of this category of peasant. First, the ban on selling this land to settle personal debt remained, which in Witte's view had to make it impossible to develop the use of credit and hence to achieve any progress in the agricultural use of this land. This was especially true as the peasant bank, the only one where the new landowners were allowed to mortgage their holdings, was not sufficiently organized to carry out such transactions (ibid., col. 1146). Second, he continued, the new landowners would, according to the provisions in question, only be able to sell their land to buyers from a specific district and hence mainly to people with limited resources. Finally, in Russian civil law, a proprietor owned not just land but the resources found on it. The new law, on the other hand, did not give the new owners any rights to its resources. Furthermore, as far as inheritance rights, family partition, and the distribution of income among members of the family were concerned, these were still not to come under general civil law, but were subject to special peasant customary law. Yet, in Witte's view, it was well known that it was very difficult in Russia to distinguish between customary law and arbitrary power (ibid., cols. 1145f). This would certainly continue, insofar as "quasi-administrative courts," set up to take special account of the institution of the peasant *mir* in the provinces of Great Russia, remained responsible for the peasants, these "quasi-landowners" (ibid., col. 1148).[7]

Witte stressed:

> I belong to those who would gladly welcome a draft law to grant our
> peasantry the same rights in relation to private property to which all other
> subjects of His Imperial Majesty are fully entitled. . . . However, the law
> under discussion does nothing of the sort. . . . I know all the doubts I have
> expressed will be answered by saying . . . that the draft law aims to secure
> the transition of the peasantry from communal landownership to private
> property and that everything else is being mapped out and will come "later."

> This response, however, does not hold water. Everything that concerns the peasantry makes up an organic whole and demands the same determined and clear safeguards as the property of other sections of society. . . . And so it seems to me that it is not enough to stick to the following formula, "you should call yourselves landowners," but rather it should be clearly defined what this property right consists of. (Ibid., cols. 1147f)

Witte's words certainly reflect the originality and realism of his thinking, and undoubtedly, his criticism was based on the entirely correct idea that all the problems concerning the peasantry were part of a unitary whole. It was evident to Witte that the peasantry had to be granted a legal status based on standard legal principles as soon as possible, that is, exclusively on those of civil society. After this first step, further laws toward this goal had to be enacted as quickly as possible. Yet if one considers only the draft law in question, which alone was being debated, one has to regard his criticism as unjust and resentful. Stishinsky was right to counter Witte, when he said that definitely no minister, not even Witte in his time as minister of finance, could have accepted a criticism that boiled down to saying that any draft law that he proposed did not fully deal with all the needs of the people. Even if it were theoretically justified, he continued, to delay the publication of the decree of November 9, 1906, and then to enact, all at once, a series of closely coordinated laws dealing with various aspects of the peasant question, it would have been impossible in practice. This was because the abolition of redemption payments on January 1, 1907, meant that Article 36 of the emancipation statute had to come into force, which would have then required either repealing this article, or suspending it for a limited period, or issuing a decree that would lay down at least the most essential procedural regulations (ibid., col. 1219). In this instance, Witte unquestionably let himself be carried away by his well-known hostility toward Stolypin, whom he could never forgive for having taken his place, which he himself could with some justice lay claim to and, without doubt, still felt entitled to in his heart of hearts. There was therefore a great deal in his criticism that was personal and partisan, just as there was in the polemics against the Octobrists in the Duma from the Kadets, who could equally never forgive the Octobrists for having assumed the place in the Third Duma that they themselves had previously failed to assume in the First Duma. At the same time, it ill became Witte in particular to advance such criticism. It was easy for Krasovsky to show by quoting directly that the guidelines for the revision of peasant legislation drafted by Witte in 1905 had the same content and the same provisions overall as Stolypin's decree of November 9, 1906. He closed his comments with the ironic question, "Why is what was called property in Count S. J. Witte's draft law only quasi-property in P. A. Stolypin's bill?" (ibid., col. 1457).

This induced Witte, in turn, to highlight that, in fact, neither Stolypin's decree nor his own draft law contained anything new: everything had already been drawn up and prepared during his own period in office. It is thanks to Witte's vanity that we know the story of how the decree of November 9, 1906, was drafted. Witte reported the following in the State Council: At the beginning of 1906, after the abolition of the redemption payments, a commission (*soveshchanie*) led by V. I. Gurko was set up in the Ministry of the Interior with the aim of bringing existing peasant legislation in line with the Manifesto of November 3 1905 (which had abolished redemption payments). The recommendations of the commission were then debated in the Council of Ministers and, together with a memorandum, put to the State Council in the form of a series of draft measures. These were more or less the same ones as were later somewhat expanded and adopted in the decree of November 9, 1906. The draft met with some opposition in the State Council, which decided by a vote of twenty-one to seventeen to defer it,[8] on the formal pretext of first sending it for consideration back to the Duma, which was to be opened shortly. Witte declared that he was prepared, albeit with a heavy heart, to withdraw the bill, which he called the "Gurko Commission bill." The Council of Ministers thereupon decided to set up a new commission made up of representatives of several ministries (*mezhduvedomstvennaia kommissiia*), chaired by the minister of rural development and agriculture, A. P. Nikol'sky, to draw up general guidelines for the agrarian reforms. The commission completed this task, largely taking the work of the Gurko Commission into account. After the resignation of the Witte government, however, the guidelines that it drafted were not used and were placed in the State Council archive, which is just where Krasovsky found them. After Stolypin became first minister, Gurko was appointed deputy minister of the interior. "Now," concludes Witte, "the former chair of the former commission has the satisfaction of seeing his bill become law. Thus, V. I. Gurko was the man who did most work on the decree of November 9, 1906" (ibid., col. 1452).

In passing, Witte's reaction to Stishinsky's remarks, also repeated in Deputy Interior Minister Lykoshkin's speech, is not without interest (ibid., col. 1242). What Stishinsky said was that while the bill and the decree of November 9 were being drafted, material from both the Special Advisory Committee on the Needs of Agriculture and the Ministry of the Interior's editing committee was consulted.[9] Witte replied that he was left speechless on hearing such a claim. It meant trying to mix completely incompatible things, like "fire and water" (ibid., col. 1230).

Hardly anyone besides Witte saw as clearly as he did that the peasant question represented an integrated whole and that all aspects of the problem were closely linked together. This is stressed by Maklakov,[10] whose judgment seems particularly significant, as he knew Witte personally and certainly understood him better than most. Stolypin and his fellow ministers, however, were undoubtedly equally convinced that things could not be left as they stood with the law of January 14, 1910. Further legislation was needed to bridge the legal gap between the peasants and the other social estates, to surmount all the vestiges of serfdom

in respect to the peasantry, and at last to bring the legal relations of the peasants within the sphere of civil society. The law of May 29, 1911, which served as
an extension of the law of June 14, 1910, has already been mentioned above. At
roughly the same time as the bill passing the decree of November 9, 1906, into
law, Stolypin laid another bill before the Duma with the same aim of changing
the decree of October 5, 1906, outlined above, into law. Unfortunately, the Duma
took until 1916 to deal with this bill. In its defense, it can be said that passing this
law could be seen as a mere formality. After all, as long as it was not rejected by
the Duma, the decree of October 5, 1906, remained in force, and therefore, in
fact, the most important steps were taken to put the peasants on an equal footing
legally with other citizens of the Russian state as far as their personal rights were
concerned. Nevertheless, on passing the decree into law, the opportunity could
have been taken to add many important additional provisions to it, which Maklakov, appointed as spokesman for the Duma Commission, endeavored to achieve.[11]
It is thus regrettable that the law was not passed before the revolution because the
Duma was so slow. Similarly, a law on property rights, the *votchinyi ustav,* which
was also going to apply to peasant property, was not passed.[12] However, the law
reforming the local courts was passed on June 28, 1912, although it had little
practical significance, as it only came into effect on January 1, 1914, and then only
in ten provinces in South Russia.[13]

So it was that the process of extending civil society to the peasantry was not
completed by the time the 1914 war and later the 1917 revolution broke out. The
First World War largely exhausted Russia's strength. Russia was unable to bear
the double burden of fast-moving progressive social change and an external war
effort, and this produced a deep psychological and spiritual reaction. Everything
that had been accomplished in the previous 150 years on Russia's hard road toward its transformation into a liberal constitutional state, with sometimes more
and sometimes less success, was then swept away by the revolution. Retrograde
forces, supported on the one hand by collectivist traditions and traditional attitudes to the law inherited from serfdom and on the other by the utopian notions
and promises of socialist collectivism, won the upper hand. After the all-too-
fragile stratum of the new liberal order had been swept away, the bedrock of old-
Muscovite serfdom reemerged. Lenin could then, with certain success, set about
building his new socialist serfdom on this foundation.

Liberalism is certainly not in the least a national ideology or limited to one
nation. Nevertheless, in each country liberalism has one main specific task. In
Russia, the priority was to overcome the old Muscovite principle that all land ultimately belonged to the state. That this was not accomplished in time is why liberalism failed in Russia.

PART 3

THE DEVELOPMENT OF POLITICAL LIBERTY, 1856–1914

Chapter 16

The History of Political Liberalism in the Reign of Alexander II

Definition of political liberty—Local self-government as a form of decentralized power—Ideas underlying the creation of local self-government in 1864 (*zemstvo*)—Trends in constitutional thought prior to 1864—Granovsky—General widespread condemnation of the bureaucratization of all spheres of life at the start of Alexander II's reign— Basic features of *zemstvo* organization following the 1864 law (the 1890 *zemstvo* law)—The *zemstvo* as the heart of liberal thought and first expressions of constitutionalism in *zemstvo* assemblies—Declarations on a constitution by the assemblies of the gentry— Chicherin's position on the constitutional question in the 1860s—Revival of interest in a constitution after the war of 1877–78—Spread of nihilism and revolutionary terrorism and how this led to disarray in the government—Efforts of the government to engage with moderate public opinion—Secretary of State Peretz's plan—The Loris-Melikov plan— Revision of this project at a meeting chaired by Alexander III on March 8, 1881: arguments for and against

In Hauriou's view, the questions of political liberty and the decentralization of power overlap.[1] Thus, political liberty is the liberty enjoyed by the citizen thanks to the separation of powers anchored in the constitution. It is important to recall the difference between political and civil freedom. Although political freedom is an extension (*prolongement*) of civil liberty, there is nevertheless a fundamental difference between these two forms of freedom. Hauriou writes:

> The difference between civil and political freedom is that there is no connection between the former and the decentralization of power. After all, a quite considerable degree of civil liberty can coexist with a strongly centralized administrative system; trade and industry can flourish; and the people can devote themselves to their family life and enjoy their property.

Civil liberty can suffice for the well-being of the people under a good tyrant, a least for a certain period, so long as the bureaucracy is not overdeveloped and does not threaten civil society itself. On the other hand, political freedom is inconceivable without decentralization or without the separation of powers; it is aimed against that dangerous tendency of centralization that accompanies a bureaucratic regime.[2]

Insofar as the crux of the question of political freedom lies in overcoming the concentration and centralization of the state that arises with the growth of bureaucracy by decentralizing power, it has to be recognized, according to Hauriou, that "decentralized power and administrative decentralisation are two sides of the same constitutional coin. . . . It is quite wrong to imagine that decentralization is a reform that the bureaucracy can carry out by itself. Such a reform is not administrative in origin, and the bureaucracy left to its own devices can only centralize. It stems from the constitution and is closely linked to the development of the constitution."[3] Administrative decentralization can precede or follow the constitutional decentralization of power. In nineteenth-century France, for example, administrative decentralization followed constitutional reform at one moment, but preceded it at another.[4]

In Russia, administrative decentralization, that is, the creation of institutions of local self-government or *zemstvos* in 1864, preceded the constitution by several decades. At the same time, those who initiated this reform had no idea it would sow the seeds of a constitutional system on Russian soil. (As will be outlined below, this only dawned on Pobedonostsev in the 1880s, while it was only at the turn of the century that Witte clearly asserted that local self-government and autocracy were incompatible.)

On the contrary, it was thought that the organizations being established with the sole purpose of satisfying local economic interests would belong to the private sphere rather than the state. Meshchersky commented in his memoirs: "Valuev's starting point was that by establishing a self-contained *zemstvo* sphere in the provinces, that is, a sphere of economic activity (*zaboty*), he was creating an outlet for people with ability that would occupy and stimulate them and divert them from political ambitions in what could be called the general sphere."[5] In other words, Valuev really thought establishing institutions of local self-government would act as a counterbalance to agitation for a constitution.

At that time, constitutional ideas played only a minor role. Overall, people professed a belief in liberal absolutism and thought the autocracy had to adopt the liberal agenda and implement it systematically. Nevertheless, the same Valuev in 1863—at the very moment that he was preparing the *zemstvo* statute, in Meshcherky's phrase, "together with the dogmatic ivory-tower liberals"[6]—drafted a plan by which elected representatives from the *zemstvo* assemblies would be consulted during the preparation of draft legislation.[7] (This plan thus goes further than the famous 1881 Loris-Melikov project dealt with below.)

Furthermore, at the time, the fact that representatives of the provincial committees, set up in connection with preparations for the emancipation of the serfs, were summoned to St. Petersburg to a certain extent doubtless conjured up the idea of a representative assembly. Even more, however, the constitutional cause must have been fostered by the general sentiment that an age of reform had dawned.

As to the origins of these constitutional ideas, and how far they were in circulation before 1864, that is, before the creation of the *zemstvo* institutions, it is hard to say whether they sprang from memories of the striving for a constitution in the reign of Alexander I or whether they were purely Western European in origin. In addition, the following should be noted here: Granovksy, who died in 1855, shortly after Nicholas I, and who must be regarded as the leading liberal figure during the reign of Nicholas I, did not directly address the question of a constitution (it was, after all, a time when talk of it was forbidden). It is therefore unlikely that the constitutionalists of the 1860s, even those who were among the closest of his students, such as Chicherin, for example, owed their constitutional ideas to Granovsky's influence.

Granovsky having been mentioned, it is appropriate to interrupt this account of the history of political liberty to evoke this historian and thinker, who, during the reign of Nicholas I, was one of the few to hold ideas that embodied the essence of liberalism.

Granovsky believed that the creation of the moral, cultivated human personality was the end goal of historical evolution, together with the formation of a society that would correspond to the needs of such a personality.[8] At the same time, he resolutely rejected sacrificing life for an abstract ideal. He said in his lectures, "Ideas are not like Hindu idols on chariots that run over their devotees, who through superstition throw themselves under their wheels during festival processions."[9] In his opinion, the Slavophiles sacrificed the real Russia for an abstract image of a Russia of their own creation. He accused the Slavophiles of not caring for a living Russia, but for an old figure, conjured up from the grave, and of worshipping this idol that had sprung from their futile fantasies.[10] He followed the events unfolding in the West in 1848 with a great deal of inward excitement. He was, however, concerned that "the victory of the masses would bring about the destruction of the best fruits of civilization . . . that the triumph of the proletariat would bring about the demise of modern civilization just as the barbarian invasions had done in the ancient world."[11]

Socialism only seemed acceptable to Granovsky as a generally humanitarian outlook. He considered socialism's specific plans to be deficient and found socialist fanaticism and the class hatred that it preached reprehensible. He resolutely rejected Herzen's prosocialist statements, which appeared in the latter's book *S togo berega* (From Another Shore).[12] Granovsky wrote to one of his friends that he was eager to reply to Herzen in the latter's own newspaper.[13] After 1848, he began to believe that his hopes would only be realized in the distant future. As for his own times, he was only sympathetic to England, which alone had remained untouched by the turmoil in Europe.

If one has to call Granovsky the foremost proponent of liberal ideas in the reign of Nicholas I, then other university teachers at the time also used the writings of representative Western European liberal thinkers in their lectures and recommended them to their students. Leshkov, for example, a professor of administrative law, drew his pupil Chicherin's attention to the works of Mohl, while Vernadsky, a professor of economics, recommended Bastiat's *Les Harmonies économiques* [Economic Harmonies] to him,[14] and Vernadsky's predecessor, Chevilev, was a strict adherent of Adam Smith.[15]

As mentioned above, the establishment of *zemstvo* local self-government was not based on the concept of the decentralization of state power or the separation of powers, but on the view that society and the state were diametrically opposed. This idea led to the conclusion that it was thoroughly detrimental for the state to be involved in the civic realm. It was thought natural that the challenges in civic life should be met by the resources found within society itself and not by the bureaucracy. As Katkov wrote in his newspaper, *Moskovskie Vedomosti,* which was influential at the time:

> Our life was filled with sterility and abuses. Naturally, this was not because of the excessive, independent development of various vital forces, but on the contrary, the repression of all by one. Science? There was no science; instead, there was bureaucracy. Property rights? They did not exist. Bureaucracy ruled instead. Law and justice? There was no justice; the bureaucracy was there in its place. Even the church was bureaucratized. Bureaucracy does have its place, where, no doubt, it can be very useful, but where it substitutes itself for other forces, it produces nothing but chimera and harmful phenomena.

"Thus, for example," Katkov continues, "science can only flourish where it is respected, and where it enjoys autonomy and independence." Furthermore, "it has emerged that our literature has been spreading dangerous (revolutionary) ideas. Naturally, this was also not the result of an excess of freedom and independence, but exclusively because of the bureaucracy's paternalism."

In Katkov's view, this paternalism hindered the development of autonomous beneficial forces and because of this indirectly encouraged revolutionary literature. It was natural for Katkov to welcome the introduction of local self-government, that is, "establishing institutions, independent of the administration, as well as empowering sound reliable forces with a calling to live and to act." Chicherin too thought it was necessary to develop an independent sphere of activity for civic forces. In his opinion, "the state only needs to be involved in situations where private and civic action proves inadequate."[16] Leading public figures, however, were not the only ones to regard bureaucratization as an evil. Typical members of the bureaucracy too, such as Valuev, clearly recognized the disadvantages of an overdeveloped bureaucracy. In his *Duma Russkovo* (Thoughts of a Russian),[17] he laments that "attempts to impose what is right by force predominate everywhere; everywhere there is disdain and contempt for ideas that emerge without special authorization."[18]

Katkov certainly sensed that a step, however modest, had been taken toward introducing the principle of the separation of powers in the state. This can be seen from the following observations in *Moskovskie Vedomosti* (no. 13, 1864), in which he writes: "The principle of the noninvolvement of the state is not alien to government; neither is it something that conflicts with, detracts from, or impedes it. On the contrary, this principle is the very essence of wise government. All progress in both government and society stems from the development of this principle." This was the only way, in his opinion, for Russia to achieve any progress again: "Since the reign of Peter the Great, progress here in Russia has been nonstop and . . . unproductive. . . . There has been one reform after another, and everything has been imported from outside. . . . We started everything, as if we had no past." This came about because "in Russia there had never been any equilibrium between the forces of action, of movement, and the conservative forces of resistance, which could have provided these developments with confidence and effectiveness."

This in turn was the result of the fact that in Russia the state always played the decisive role.[19] Katkov writes: "In fact, in Russia, people and social forces have always taken a conservative course. They recognized the danger that life would lose those foundations, without which any development is meaningless, and resisted it." By contrast, Katkov continues, "throughout Russian history, the state has been a force that dismantles, gets things moving, and breaks with tradition." In Katkov's view, this equilibrium, missing up to then, had to be established through the creation of local self-government: "Conservative forces in society must be able to have a moderating effect on the actions of government. The vital forces in society must be incorporated into the institutions of the state." Insofar as Katkov speaks of including social forces in the institutions of the state, he evidently considers that establishing local self-government constitutes a form of the separation of powers, that it confers the concept of equilibrium on the state itself.

Hopes for the autonomy of civic forces were embodied in the *zemstvos*, the organs of local self-government that were established in 1864. The *zemstvo* institutions were set up following free elections that did not have a standard set of electoral rules. The electorate was divided into three subdivisions. The peasant electoral college was based on the peasant social estate,[20] while the remaining rural population (landowners) and townspeople were grouped according to a property qualification. Although these electoral groups did not have to belong formally to a social estate, they were composed quite consistently of members of these estates. The landowners were largely gentry, while the members of the town electorate were shopkeepers and employers, and so on. The property qualification for landowners in the first electoral college was between two hundred and eight hundred *desiatin*, depending on the region, or otherwise having immovable property in the country with a value of fifteen thousand roubles. The members of the urban electoral college had to own immovable property at a value of one to three thousand roubles, depending on the population of the towns, or a business with a turnover of at least six thousand roubles.[21] The electoral colleges elected the *glasnye*, or the members of the district *zemstvo* assemblies. It was not intended that the number of representatives for any one electoral college should significantly outnumber the others. It was laid down by law that the number of representatives for one electoral college should not be greater than the number of the other two colleges combined. Thus, the most a single electoral college could contribute to the total number of *zemstvo* assembly members was less than 50 percent. The members were elected for three years and made up the *zemstvo* assembly (*zemskoe sobranie*) of the district representing all the social estates. The district assemblies elected the members of the provincial assembly. Thereafter the executive committees (*upravy*) were elected. These consisted of three representatives at the district level and eight people in each province. These elections were always held in the capital city of each province.

Local self-government bodies were given extensive powers, similar to taxation, to raise revenue from the local population. The level of payment depended on property values or income. Local self-government bodies had extensive autonomy from the state, which restricted itself to inspection. Only the provincial governor had the right to veto decisions made by the assembly, in which case the matter was referred back to the *zemstvo*. The *zemstvo*, however, was entitled to come to the same decision again, if it did not agree with the provincial governor's objections, in which case it then had to be implemented. It just had to be approved by the Senate, as the highest administrative court, whose decision was binding. The minister of the interior too was allowed a veto, but this was not ultimately binding. If the minister put down a veto, the Senate also made a final ruling, although the repeated decision of the *zemstvo* could not be implemented until the Senate made its final ruling. Some types of *zemstvo* decisions required the approval of the provincial governor or the minister of the interior. If this approval was not forthcoming, and the *zemstvo* persisted with its resolution, the same procedure that applied to vetoes was put in motion.

The *zemstvo* had no powers of enforcement. If it needed to enforce a decision, it had to ask the regular police force to carry this out. It was not possible for *zemstvos* to order the police to follow their instructions. This was because the idea was that *zemstvos* were private, that is, civic, and not state institutions, which were only supposed to deal with economic affairs. It was overlooked that these institutions of local self-government also had functions that were of a normal administrative nature, that they had been granted significant administrative powers, and that the lack of a power of enforcement caused considerable difficulties. At the time, incidentally, the economic concept of local self-government came in for criticism not just in Russia but also in Western Europe. Gneist in Germany, for example, developed a constitutional theory for local self-government, in which he demonstrated that local self-government fulfills the functions of the state and that it therefore has to be linked more closely to the whole apparatus of the state. This was the path taken in Germany, where the *Landrat* (district chief executive) was the representative of the government, whereas the district assembly members represented the people, or civic society. Fulfilling a local administrative function thus entailed the cooperation of both elements, which has to be seen as a successful solution to the problem of how people and bureaucracy can work together. The French model of local self-government was roughly similar to the German one, as the *conseil du départment* exercised a control function beside the *préfet* [prefect, or departmental executive officer], who represented central government.[22] In Great Britain, on the other hand, the police were subordinate to local government. In Russia, therefore, the choice was between going down one or the other of these roads: either the French/German road or the British one.

The reform of local self-government, undertaken in 1890, was not unconnected with these considerations, on the one hand, and Alexander III's wish to reinvigorate the system of social estates, on the other.[23] The influence of the gentry was increased considerably in the *zemstvos*, whereas elected peasant representatives were replaced by representatives who were, in reality, only semielected, while their number was reduced. The *volost'* representatives could now only elect candidates, from among whom the district *zemstvo* members were appointed. Furthermore, local self-government bodies ceased to be called economic institutions, which amounted to adopting an approach based on constitutional theory. The attempt was made to link local self-government with the general administration, which, as we have seen, was not in itself a bad thing. In order to give this link a concrete shape, a traditional Russian form was chosen, namely the *prisutstvie*. This was a committee chaired by the provincial governor consisting of the provincial marshal of the nobility, the deputy governor, the public prosecutor, the director of the finance department, the chairman of the provincial *zemstvo* committee, and an executive official dealing with ongoing business. *Prisutstvie* ratification was required in a number of cases for decisions passed by the *zemstvos*. These decisions, however, had a much greater authority as a result, and in a certain sense they were then seen as decisions made by the government. The *zemstvos* were also given the right to pass *obiazatel'nye postanovleniia*, or bylaws dealing with local matters.

Even before the 1890 reform, in fact, right from the beginning, *zemstvos* were centers where progressive forces could start organizing and working for the future liberal development of Russia. Such elements were not in the least revolutionary. On the contrary, they were conservative-minded liberals, supporters of the gradual evolution of Russia toward liberalism, and some of them were, in particular, very skeptical about the introduction of a constitution. The reform in the 1890s did not change the spirit of the *zemstvos*, and liberal progressive thinking continued to survive there, because liberal ideas had always been upheld by representatives of the gentry in the *zemstvos*. As the new law increased the gentry's representation in the *zemstvos*, it was therefore not able to overcome their progressive stance and sentiment and their independent spirit or to suppress the liberal thinking that predominated. At most, the government could now count on the dutiful support of the peasant representatives it had appointed in the *zemstvos*, although these were only a small minority, with no influence at all. It should be added that not just this liberal thinking but all the activity of the *zemstvos*, indeed their very existence, should be seen as a precursor of constitutional government.

It is not surprising that individual *zemstvo* assemblies in the first years of their existence started articulating views that could be interpreted as constitutional, given that local self-government, a form of decentralization, was based on the same principles and inspired by the same spirit as constitutional government. The St. Petersburg provincial *zemstvo* assembly was the first, as early as December 1865, unanimously voting to approach the government to set up a central *zemstvo*. One might think that this demand had hardly anything in common with constitutionalism. It should be obvious, however, that over time a central *zemstvo* could have developed into a central representative assembly of all the *zemstvos*; in other words, without doubt it could have become an embryonic parliament. In 1867, the same St. Petersburg *zemstvo* assembly argued for *zemstvo* participation in legislative activity.[24] The *zemstvos* could not pursue this line any further, as the government quickly decided to act against it and to dissolve the St. Petersburg *zemstvo* assembly. Some members of the government, however, apparently considered this a rather severe measure and hence regarded it with concern. Meshchersky reports that he went to find Valuev in connection with another matter on the very day that the *zemstvo* assembly was to have been dissolved. Valuev received him, saying, "How can you expect a minister of the interior to have the time to respond to you, when it's a matter of closing down the *zemskoe sobranie*?"[25]

Constitutionalism was not just in evidence in individual *zemstvo* assemblies; even some of the gentry assemblies, especially in St. Petersburg and Moscow, came out in favor of a constitution. According to Meshchersky: "In St. Petersburg and in Moscow a certain intellectual ferment started to emerge toward the end of the year (1864). In some gentry circles, the idea gained ground that in addition to the district and provincial *zemstvos*, there should also be a central *zemstvo*, . . . a *zemstvo* chamber or *zemstvo* duma, as some called it at the time."[26]

In Moscow, where this agitation was particularly marked,[27] a petition pointing out the necessity of creating a central *zemstvo* assembly and a special central assembly of the gentry was submitted to the tsar in January 1865. Alexander II reacted sternly to this petition. In response, he wrote to his interior minister that the gentry were not entitled to seize the initiative as far as the reforms were concerned. Meshchersky's explanation for these leanings toward constitutionalism is that the gentry wanted to have greater political influence in exchange for the loss of the serfs.[28] Chicherin was apparently inclined to share this view.[29] This does not seem very convincing. The interest in a constitution in those years sprang from the general atmosphere of renewal that had been generated by several far-reaching reforms.

This intervention from the tsar brought to an end the efforts to promote a constitution for rather a long time. Later, in the 1860s and 1870s, the idea of convening an all-Russian *zemstvo* conference, or creating a central association of *zemstvos,* reemerged from time to time, but was rejected each time by the government. Constitutionalism as such did not directly reemerge in the *zemstvos* for a considerable period. It would be wrong, however, to attribute this retreat from constitutional ideas solely to the pressure from above. At the time, there were very many in society in general who did not believe that a constitution was possible in Russia. Even such a consistent and convinced supporter of a constitution as Chicherin thought that the conditions were not right in Russia at that time for a change from absolutism to a constitution.

Chicherin was convinced that a constitutional monarchy was the best form of government and that every civilized nation inevitably strives for representative government.[30] He stressed that the great advantage of a constitutional system was that there was an opposition with an unrestricted right to criticize and assert an opposing point of view, thus contributing to the clarification of any problem. By contrast, public opinion is silent in an absolutist system. Indispensible negative feedback then has to be passed on to the monarch by those who are entrusted with government. Chicherin continues: "It follows that the government is composed of elements who have no unity and who secretly fight each other. At the same time, the supreme power itself has to promote such in-fighting, as this is the guarantee of its independence."[31]

In Chicherin's opinion, it is obvious that in this way government sacrifices its essential unity, wastes its energy, and creates a demoralizing atmosphere. Even if constitutional monarchy offers the best system of government, Chicherin continues, it is not possible to maintain that the switch to a constitutional system is possible or even desirable under all circumstances. Certain conditions must be in place to enable the change. Chicherin wrote a major work, *O Narodnom Predstavitel'stve* (On Democratic Representation), to study these conditions.[32]

As a result of this study, Chicherin reached the conclusion that the necessary conditions for a change to constitutional government were missing in Russia. He set out this conviction in a paper,[33] but held back from publishing it on the advice of N. Miliutin, who pointed out to Chicherin that even if everything in his paper were true, it was still extremely undesirable for anticonstitutional comments to emerge from liberal quarters. Chicherin concluded that, from a conservative-liberal point of view,[34] the Russia of that time, that is, of the 1860s, more than anything needed liberal measures and a strong government.[35] Insofar as he believed that the government had above all to concentrate on the emancipation of the serfs, he adopted the position of liberal absolutism as his own, despite his theoretical preference for constitutional government.[36] Chicherin thought the switch to constitutional government was not only inopportune but also virtually impossible, as long as the emancipation of the serfs had not been accomplished: "Nobody at the time contemplated changing the form of government. Everyone grasped that this was impossible with serfdom[37] and after the centuries-old subjugation of society. The only thing people yearned for . . . was intellectual and civil liberty."[38] It was only after the 1877–78 war that constitutional ideas gained ground once more. It seemed absurd to have fought for the liberation of the Bulgarian people and to have established a constitutional government in the newly created Bulgarian state, but, on the other hand, to deny the Russian people, the liberators, the same freedoms now granted to the Bulgarians by their constitution. This was explicitly highlighted by the Tver' *zemstvo* assembly's petition.[39]

After the war, which had demanded great sacrifices on the part of Russia, it seemed to the government that the general situation in the country was extremely worrying, given the spread of nihilism and terrorist activity. People naturally wondered why, after the implementation of liberal reforms, nihilism was spreading and revolutionary terror kept flaring up again. It was obvious that the government had no clear idea of what it ought to do. One wondered what political theory to follow, what policies to choose, what educational principles to base the school system on, in order to stem the emergence of the nihilists and the revolutionaries. Thus, government representatives began to consider questions of state and even cultural questions from a position that was wholly inadequate, that was altogether incapable of providing a solution to these questions. It follows that the government was no longer capable of consistently sticking to its liberal course and was hardly in a position to keep to any definite political line at all.[40] It can be seen from this that the revolutionary movement posed a greater threat to liberal reform than the influence of reactionary circles. Of course the revolutionaries and their ideas were not able to have a direct influence on members of the government, but their emergence, in particular acts of terrorism, produced real disarray in government circles and deterred them from implementing liberal reforms. It must be remembered that resistance on the part of the supporters of the old order could not be effective, as long as the emperor was determined to continue on the path of reform. These people were supporters of autocracy and believed first and foremost in total submission to the will of the monarch and unquestioning obedience in carrying out his orders. Justice Minister Panin expressed this attitude most clearly when he told Grand Duke Constantine Nicholaevich: "I have my convictions, firm convictions, although people often think the opposite. According to the oath of allegiance, I am bound especially to find out what the views of His Majesty are. If I can ascertain directly or indirectly that the emperor takes a different view of some matter from my own, I am duty bound to set aside my own convictions immediately and act contrary to them with the same, if not greater vigor."[41]

Admittedly, quite a few holders of high office were critical of this attitude. Admiral Greig, for example, commented that this was "the most candid defence of baseness" that he had ever heard.[42] I do not believe in the slightest that it is right to see Panin's position as a form of self-abasement. After all, one would have to accuse all members of parties of self-abasement who see it as their duty to vote against their personal convictions for the sake of party discipline.

It was possibly because of this feeling of insecurity that the government felt the need to seek a rapprochement with moderate forces in society. On November 20, 1878, Alexander II approached the representatives of the social estates, requesting their support in the struggle against the false doctrines that were at the root of such disorder among young people, as this was necessary for the further peaceful and legal development of Russia.[43] Government circles began considering whether the representatives of the *zemstvo* and urban local government should be consulted on legislative proposals, whether it was necessary to "take local needs into closer consideration."

With this aim in mind, Grand Duke Constantine Nicholaevich asked State Secretary Peretz to prepare a proposal by which an assembly, elected by the provincial *zemstvo* assemblies and the town dumas, was to be attached to the State Council. Naturally, this assembly was to be purely consultative.[44] This proposal formed the basis, some months later, for Loris-Melikov's proposal. Loris-Melikov's proposal envisaged the creation of so-called preparatory commissions, probably on the lines of the editing commissions that had done the groundwork for the emancipation of the serfs on February 19, 1861. These commissions were to consist of appointed members, but in addition, a general commission to review the legislative proposals put forward by these preparatory commissions was to be established. Along with the members appointed by the government from the ranks of the preparatory commissions, there would also be elected members drawn from the provincial *zemstvo* assemblies and the town dumas. This commission would only have been given a consultative role, and any legislative proposals that it dealt with had to be put to the State Council (which incidentally was also only consultative). It is obvious that the significance and power of the State Council would in no way have been diminished by the creation of this consultative commission.[45]

On February 17, 1881, Alexander II ordered his minister of the interior, Loris-Melikov, to prepare a government announcement along the lines of this proposal proclaiming the creation of these commissions. The draft announcement was prepared and authorized by the tsar at 12:30 on March 1, at which point Alexander II expressed the wish that the meeting of the Committee of Ministers should be told of the proposal before its publication at its next scheduled meeting, on March 4. Two hours later, Alexander II fell victim to a terrorist attack. After the assassination, Alexander III, influenced by Pobedonestsev, decided to review the whole question, and with this aim, a consultative meeting was convened for March 8, 1881, to be attended by grand dukes, ministers, and representatives of the State Council.

A detailed account of this meeting can be found in Peretz's diary,[46] which he ends with the comment that he flattered himself to have captured the course of the debate "with almost photographic accuracy." In fact, his version is substantiated by the brief notes found in the diary of another participant at the meeting, Valuev.[47]

Pobedonostsev, the procurator of the Holy Synod, the post office minister, Makov (the former interior minister), and the aging eighty-five-year-old Count Stroganov opposed Loris-Melikov's draft proposal at the meeting. They all made the point that accepting the proposal would mean moving over to a constitutional form of government in Russia or at least taking a first step toward a constitution. Count Stroganov highlighted the lack of moderation in the press and stated that implementing the proposal would hamper the government in its battle against the excesses of the press. Makov too thought that this reform would not serve to consolidate the power of the state. He said that it would only be possible to put an end to revolutionary disorder by strengthening the power of the government, which, in the current situation, was the most important priority. Pobedonostsev went the furthest in his criticism. He stressed that Loris-Melikov's proposal represented a first decisive step on the road to a constitution. As experience in the West had shown, he said, a constitution was nothing more than an instrument of injustice and all kinds of intrigue. Furthermore, Pobedonostsev in fact rejected in its entirety the system of liberal absolutism established under Alexander II. He dismissed as talking shops all the institutions set up by the reform laws, including the *zemstvos,* urban local self-government, the new courts, and the free press, which were superfluous and alien to the people. He particularly regarded the organization of local self-government as a wedge driven between the people and the tsar. He described the bond between people and tsar as having an inestimable value that had to be preserved by all necessary means. It was especially important, in his view, to protect the people from the influence of intellectuals, who had lost touch with the traditions of the people. On the other hand, he went on to say, the intelligentsia could learn a lot from the people, who were the true guardians of all traditional virtues and positive values. Pobedonostsev stressed that the government's first priority was to look after the people, to support the people in their difficult battle against severe poverty, as well as to care for their moral welfare. The entire ideology of paternalism, of *popechitel'stvo,* expounded here with great passion, thus reappears in an unadulterated form.

Sol'slky, D. Miliutin, and Valuev, who supported the proposal, stressed that it was not about a constitution, but only about including men of experience from the provinces, who would not be given legislative powers but merely a consultative voice. Their role would definitely be restricted simply to offering an expert opinion on the legislative proposals prepared by the governmental commissions. Miliutin pointed out that such contributions were nothing new and that the proposal aimed at tightening up the rules for this long-established practice. In Abaza's opinion, the difference from earlier practice was only that before, the chairmen of *zemstvo* executive boards, mayors, marshals of the nobility, and so on, were consulted, and that although they may well have been elected, it was not specifically for the purpose of helping to draw up draft legislation. On the other hand, according to the proposal, the *zemstvo* assemblies, the town dumas, or gentry conferences would elect particular individuals who would assist the government in an advisory capacity in legislative matters. He added that without doubt this had to be an advantage, as it was quite possible that an otherwise excellent marshal of the nobility or chairman of a *zemstvo* executive board might prove inept in advising on legislation. Grand Duke Constantine Nicholaevich added that the new system for co-opting representatives of the public, which would become a permanent institution, also offered further advantages of a general political nature. These representatives of the public, he stated, would become a link between the monarch and the people, which would enable the tsar to be informed about the real needs of the people. Sol'sky spoke of his conviction that these representatives could be very useful for the government, as they would be accountable together with the government for its measures, which was especially important when measures had to be taken that were unpopular, as, for example, with the introduction of new taxes. Even without that, he commented, the existence of such a consultative commission would be of great significance for the government.

Valuev strongly disagreed with Count Stroganov's view that the creation of this commission would make the task of combating the excesses of the press impossible. On the contrary, in his view, the existence of this commission had to have a restraining influence on the press, as these consultative advisors would be invested with the authority to represent the public and thus act as a valuable counterweight to the journalists, those self-appointed (*samozvannym*) representatives of public opinion. Valuev was absolutely convinced that large sections of the public thought and felt completely differently from the authors of newspaper articles. Overall, the supporters of Loris-Melikov's project, especially Sol'sky and Saburov, held the view that these officially elected representatives of the public would certainly turn out to be moderate, even conservative people. Saburov thought that at any rate they would be more conservative than representatives of the bureaucracy, who "only breathed the St. Petersburg air and easily adopted the views and convictions of the newspapers." It was precisely as the representatives of conservative forces in the country that they could offer, in his opinion, solid support for the government. "It should not be forgotten," he said, "that the crown cannot simply rely on the support of a million bayonets and an army of civil servants."

Abaza and Sol'sky responded to Pobedonostsev's speech in particular.[48] Sol'sky pointed out that Pobedonostsev's criticism was wholly negative, "that he criticized everything, but had no proposals of his own." Abaza, the finance minister, immediately understood that Pobedonostsev's criticism was aimed at much more than Loris-Melikov's proposal and stressed that it was to all intents and purposes a condemnation of the government of Alexander II in general. Furthermore, he pointed out, Pobedonostsev completely disregarded the fact that besides the common people, there were also educated sections of society and that the priority of caring for the poor, which was generally accepted to be of the highest importance, did not exclude the necessity of considering the interests of the educated class. It was only by calling on representatives of this class to participate in government that this challenge could be met.

Furthermore, Makov's comment that the most urgent priority was the battle against revolutionary disorder did not go unchallenged. Both Abaza and Sol'sky pointed out that it was entirely wrong to consider the proposal under discussion from the point of view of the fight against revolutionary forces. Abaza thought that the battle against the revolutionaries would not be made any easier by repressive measures against the entire population or by distrust of all public opinion. Sol'sky commented that although one could not expect that implementing the proposal would provide a guarantee against the "crimes of socialism," that was nevertheless no reason to reject the proposal. He said, "To fight socialism, more than anything you need a good police force, something we do not possess." Abaza supported this view and, as finance minister, added that the treasury would allocate not just hundreds of thousands but millions for the police. He stressed, however, that the two issues had to be regarded as completely separate.

Valuev, who spoke third, after Loris-Melikov and Stroganov, came out in favor of the proposals, like most of those present at the meeting. His speech is of particular interest here because the most important part of it was not his support for Loris-Melikov's proposal, but the fact that it showed that similar plans had been put to Alexander II, not just by him but also by Grand Duke Constantine Nicholaevich. In a note that he later added to the original text of his diary, on November 11, 1882,[49] Valuev wrote that he had made a reference to his earlier proposal especially to distance himself from the "clique" around Count Loris-Melikov. He spoke about it at the meeting, despite being aware that Alexander III could only have been even less sympathetic to his proposal, which was certainly more radical than Loris-Melikov's. He also knew that in persisting with his own earlier proposal, he was hurting his own prospects. In fact, Valuev writes in the same note in his diary, "From that day on, I only carried on in the role of chairman of the Committee of Ministers for the sake of appearances."

As is well known, Loris-Melikov's proposal was not implemented. Even after its rejection, experts were called in to advise on draft legislation on a case-by-case basis.[50] The rejection of Loris-Melikov's proposal, however, meant abandoning the creation of a permanent institution that might have become the seed from which a representative assembly could grow.

Chapter 17

The Period from 1881 to 1902

Alexander III and his belief in autocracy—The
Manifesto of April 29, 1881, and the resignation
of Loris-Melikov and Abaza—The nature of the
antiliberal trend in the 1880s and 1890s—The
1891 famine and attempts by the general public
to systematically support government efforts to
combat its effects—The early years of Nicholas
II's reign—The Tver' *zemstvo* assembly petition—
Nicholas II's speech at the reception held on January
17, 1895—The *zemstvos'* initiative on the occasion
of the coronation festivities and the government's
reaction—Attempts by *zemstvo* representatives to
obtain government permission to merge individual
zemstvos—Unofficial consultation of *zemstvo*
representatives—Beseda—Growing opposition
in *zemstvo* circles—Pleve's meeting with Shipov—
The significance of Pleve's policies for the political
evolution of the *zemstvos*

Alexander III issued his famous Manifesto of April 29, 1881, in which he asserted his belief in autocracy and his firm resolve to protect it from any assault. The leading liberals in the government, Loris-Melikov and Abaza, drew the obvious conclusion and asked to be relieved of their posts. The fact that these requests were a direct consequence of the manifesto's proclamation of belief in autocracy was considered ungracious. In Abaza's case, Alexander III wrote in person that he regretted that the former had been unable to find other grounds for his resignation. The absolutist approach to government was made evident not simply by the fact that the idea of a transition to constitutional government had been definitively rejected and that even broaching the subject of a "constitution" was strictly forbidden. It was also that one began to obstruct the normal development, indeed the continued normal functioning of the institutions established by the great reforms, in order to prevent any relaxation of absolutist rule that could ensue from the development and working of these institutions. As a result, the measures taken by the government during this period had a distorting effect on these institutions. A few new institutions were set up, but these had nothing in common with the spirit or principles that had been the foundation of the reforms of the 1860s. Besides the legislation, already described in detail in part 2, which prevented the inclusion of the peasants in civil society, and its consequent consolidation and universal application in Russia, these measures too delayed the process of turning Russia into a constitutional state.

There was hardly any resistance to this absolutist trend during the 1880s. The public was appalled by Alexander II's assassination and gripped by profound feelings of shame and pessimism. It seemed out of the question to expect, let alone demand, that the tsar should continue the reform process. What was the point of reform if it ended in the cowardly elimination of its author? It was not absolutely necessary to believe that liberal theory had encouraged the terrorists in order to turn one's back on thoughts of reform. Nor did it follow that this ideology and its champions shared responsibility for Alexander II's murder, as Meshchersky, for example, maintains.[1] The supporters of liberal ideas, too, and the institutions created by the reforms themselves, felt inhibited from continuing the reforms, as Shipov testifies in his memoirs.[2]

It would be wrong, however, to believe that true reaction had taken hold of society. Even those whom one would describe as reactionaries, those who were not sympathetic to the new order and institutions created by the reforms or even regarded them with suspicion, did not seriously consider turning the clock back to Nicholas I's regime. They no doubt wished to combat what was damaging in the new institutions, but they wanted to pursue this battle within the framework of these new institutions themselves. Maklakov writes with some justice, "I cannot conceive that anyone in the 1880s would have seriously wanted a return to the old courts and officialdom from the time of *The Government Inspector* and *Dead Souls,* and so on, least of all the restoration of serfdom."[3] Besides, it was quite clear in general that no one could have implemented such a backward step, even if they wanted to. They simply lacked the power to do it.

Furthermore, the enemies of liberalism were more or less only united in what they did not want. They all considered a constitution disastrous for Russia, but there was no agreement as far as any positive program was concerned. Pobedonostsev, for example, had little sympathy for the law on the *zemskie nachal'niki.* He supported Manasein in the State Council, not Tolstoy. He stubbornly refused to lobby the tsar in support of the Tolstoy-Pazuchin draft law. Meshchersky's view is that Pobedonostsev's reluctance was based on principle, as he felt almost an aversion to everything connected with the gentry.[4] Pobedonostsev also only reluctantly accepted the new statute for the universities. Naturally, in Pobedonostsev's case, it is possible that this sprang from his negative mentality, which depressed even his friends. Meshchersky writes in his memoirs: "During the twenty years I have been friends with Pobedonostsev, I have never heard him offer a single positive suggestion in any field, as to any alternative course of action to the one he had criticized, still less any simple, straightforward and positive judgment about anyone."[5]

At any rate, it is striking that the enemies of liberalism did not constitute an organized group with a clear cohesive program. As we have seen, they were not inclined to undo everything that had been achieved by the reforms of the 1860s and to put all the developments of the previous twenty-five years into reverse. In this way, what had been established in the 1860s put down ever deeper roots and became reality. The transformation of Russian life founded on the liberal ideas that had formed the basis of the reforms of the 1860s proceeded imperceptibly. According to Maklakov:

> Broad sections of society lost all interest in politics. They devoted them-
> selves to their private lives, strove for personal success . . . and gave no
> thought to the struggle against the state. . . . At the same time, life moved
> on. Russian society renewed itself even during this reactionary period. A
> generation emerged that no longer knew anything of the era of Nicholas
> I or the conventions of that time. The reforms of the 1860s, the liberation
> of the individual and labor (even if not fully realized), began to bear fruit.
> The process of differentiation within the peasantry continued; towns
> became more prosperous; industry developed; the struggle to make a living
> became harder. Genuine social development does not require dramatic
> events. . . . Neither the ideas of a Katkov nor those of a Pobedonostsev, nor
> Alexander III's autocratic rule, could prevent Russian society from pursuing
> its interests or dispose it to think that it was only there to allow autocracy,
> orthodoxy, and the national spirit to thrive. This society thought much more
> about its own interests, and what was to its advantage, and putting its own
> demands to the government. It was not the professional politician, but the
> average citizen who began to sense in everyday life the shortcomings of our
> system. . . . With cultural progress, population growth, accumulation of
> wealth, and greater differentiation in the way people lived, the old bureau-
> cratic apparatus had to reform itself and adapt to new challenges.[6]

Two factors should be mentioned here that illustrate particularly clearly this transformation resulting from Russia's rapid development in the 1890s: first, the enormous progress made in all fields at this time by Russian science and the high standard of Russian universities; and second, Russia's strong economic growth, accompanied by changes in society, as shown by the increasing social im-portance of the entrepreneurial classes. In this respect, it was characteristic that when Witte toured the provinces as minister of finance, he sought to avoid official receptions and ceremonies, preferring to meet influential representatives from industry and commerce.

The political chill did not therefore prevent the gradual displacement of the old order by a new one. On the contrary, with greater calm in society, the ten-dency to concentrate on mundane work helped to consolidate imperceptibly the new order, which was all the stronger for it. Nothing could better demonstrate the usefulness of the *zemstvo* organizations to the general public or the government than success in their work. Nothing could strengthen the position of local self-government more than its practical achievements.

In Maklakov's opinion, this calm in public life lasted until 1891. In that year, various regions in Russia were devastated by a terrible famine. The public felt that it had a duty to help the starving, and the government authorized the organization of private aid. This task naturally required various representatives of society to come together and cooperate. It is noteworthy that the representatives of society and their organizations were not interested in competing with government agencies, or outdoing them with their own efforts, as happened during the 1914–17 war. Public opinion simply wanted to help combat the famine, without gaining any political advantage from it, and to support the government in its endeavors. This is all the more plausible, as in general the representatives of public opinion, even those who had devoted their life to local government, did not have in mind any further political reform or especially a constitution. It was the case, rather, that even those who criticized the bureaucratic nature of the state and were in favor of consolidating and extending Alexander II's reforms frequently preferred autocracy to constitutional government. This was the basic Slavophile position. There were also many others, however, who, while being sympathetic to a constitution and thinking it was inevitable, believed that the time was not yet ripe and that the absolute monarchy still had more to give. They believed that this monarchy had yet to complete more of the liberal program and in this way to create more of the essential conditions that alone would allow a constitutional government to achieve positive results.

Despite society's total loyalty, the government was unable to regard public initiatives without suspicion, even when these were to combat the famine. It was thought necessary to scrutinize the aid committees from a political perspective and ultimately to put an end to this autonomous action as quickly as possible.[7] Once the famine was over, suppressing the aid campaign seemed quite natural. The government's response, however, sprang from its general propensity to repress any autonomous action whatsoever. In turn, this came, if perhaps not directly from a clear conviction, then from an apprehension, which was first apparent in Pobedonostsev's famous, and as Valuev put it "outrageous" speech at the meeting held on March 8, 1881—namely that the liberal concept of autonomy, on which Alexander II's reforms were based, was incompatible with autocracy.

It is therefore quite natural that in their defense of Alexander II's reforms, liberals were especially at pains to combat the idea that the institutions created by Alexander II's legislative action, such as local self-government, autonomous universities, and an independent judiciary, were incompatible with absolute monarchy. Above all, they stressed that these institutions had been created by the autocracy itself and for that very reason could not be in conflict with it. This approach may have been a clever tactic, but doubtless, it was too simplistic and shallow an approach to this question. This is an example of the impoverishment of political thought in general in an atmosphere of oppression. How far this went is clear when one considers that the only political issue that people were brave enough to discuss in the press was the question of whether the achievements of Alexander II's reforms could be preserved.[8] Although I said that this position could be described as clever from a tactical point of view, this does not mean that it was actually purely a matter of tactics. On the contrary, it is much more likely that it sprang from real conviction. Unfortunately, however sincere the conviction, there is no guarantee that it is correct.

Maklakov was right to point out that, despite the sincerity of the liberal press, on this issue the views of its opponents rang truer and deeper: "The ideas that formed the basis of the reforms of the 1860s had in the end to undermine the absolute monarchy. The freedom of the individual and labor, the inviolability of well-earned civil rights, the courts as guardians of the law and not as the expression of the government's discretionary powers, and local self-government were all ideas that stood in contradiction to the "unlimited" power of the monarchy.[9]

Thus, the actual awakening of interest in politics did not occur immediately after 1891, but only a few years later, during the reign of Nicholas II.[10] Only the smallest minority believed that there could once again be a turn to liberalism under Alexander III, and only such belief could have revived an interest in politics. Witte was one of these few. After the death of Alexander III, he claimed that it might have been perfectly possible for Alexander III to abandon his antiliberal policies and resume the course set in the 1860s. "This," comments Maklakov, "is certainly difficult to believe and impossible to verify."[11] Yet it seems Witte was genuinely convinced of this. By contrast, many believed that the young tsar, Nicholas II, would return to his grandfather's liberal policies. It had after all been the pattern for over a century that Russia was ruled alternately by liberal and antiliberal tsars. The liberal Catherine II had been succeeded by the reactionary Paul, who in turn was followed by the liberal Alexander I. Nicholas I came after Alexander I. Following the reign of Nicholas I came Alexander II's age of liberal reforms. Now it was possible to hope that the antiliberal tendencies of Alexander III would be followed by a new wave of liberalism under the new tsar.

Anything the new tsar said that could possibly be interpreted in this way was greeted enthusiastically. On the other hand, people failed to heed anything that might dash these hopes.[12] The liberal newspaper *Russkie Vedomosti* praised the tsar's marginal notes to a report on the question of public education. Rodichev, a convinced liberal, a political radical even, shouted out in the Tver' *zemstvo* assembly, "Gentlemen, at this moment we shall address Nicholas II with our hopes, our belief in the future, with our aspirations. Hurrah for Nicholas II." Maklakov, who quotes these words of Rodichev, comments, "Anyone who knew Rodichev will admit that he could not have spoken these words purely out of tactical considerations."[13] Neither this speech by Rodichev nor the petition put to the tsar by the Tver' *zemstvo* assembly in any way hinted that a constitution was desirable. On the contrary, it was plain from both of these that all that the *zemstvo* circles expected of the tsar was the abandonment of antiliberal policies and a resumption of the course taken in the 1860s. The hope was expressed that the institutions of local self-government would be granted the right to give an opinion on matters that fell within their field of competence, so that not just the views of the administrators but also those of the people would reach the tsar. This attempt by the *zemstvo* representatives to petition the tsar, however, provoked a sharp reaction on his part. At a reception on January 17, 1895, the young tsar used a phrase that became famous when he described as "senseless dreams" the aspirations of the *zemstvos* to participate in the internal affairs of the state. With a few exceptions, most understood this phrase to mean that any thought of a constitution had been rejected. In fact, as Maklakov writes, it was a question of choosing between the liberal absolutism of Alexander II and the antiliberal absolutism of Alexander III. And the choice fell unequivocally on the latter.[14] This was therefore not simply to abandon any further progress toward liberalism; it was to condemn what existed already, for within certain limits, the participation of the *zemstvo* institutions in the workings of the state was no "dream," but a reality.

From that moment on, a gulf between public opinion and the executive began to form and continued to widen, leading eventually to the revolutionary situation of 1905.

The suspicion with which the government regarded the *zemstvo* institutions and any initiatives that sprang from them grew ever more intense. The antiliberals in circles close to the tsar were particularly hostile to any attempt by the *zemstvos* to act in concert, however innocuous that common action may have been. The following example is typical: at the coronation, due to take place on May 14, 1896, according to a long-established tradition, the leaders of the provincial *zemstvo* executive committees were meant to offer bread and salt to the tsar. The *zemstvos* had to procure silver platters and saltcellars for this. On November 22, 1895, Shipov, the chairman of the Moscow province *zemstvo* committee, received a letter from his opposite number in Samara, Plemiannikov, informing him of his committee's intention to propose that all provincial *zemstvos* should dispense with buying the silverware and together use the money for some charitable purpose instead. The Moscow committee then resolved to make available three hundred thousand roubles, made up of the contributions expected from all thirty-four provinces with *zemstvo* institutions, to the welfare office of the workhouses under the patronage of the empress. Shipov wrote a letter along these lines to all the chairmen of provincial *zemstvo* committees.

Shipov, however, did not send the letter immediately, but considered it advisable first to inform Grand Duke Sergei Alexandrovich, governor general of Moscow, about the plan, given the mistrust with which the government regarded all attempts by the *zemstvos* to cooperate in any undertaking. The grand duke replied to the effect that he had no objections to the plan going ahead and gave his consent. The next day, however, the grand duke, acting on the advice of his secretary, Istomin, summoned Shipov again and advised him not to do anything more for the moment, but first of all to discuss the matter with Goremykin, who had recently been appointed minister of the interior and who was shortly expected in Moscow. Goremykin received Shipov amicably, but told him that he did not consider a donation from the *zemstvos* to the workhouses to be a good idea. When Shipov answered that there was nothing to prevent the money donated by the *zemstvos* being used for some other purpose, Goremykin explained in plain terms that he regarded any common initiative from the *zemstvos* for the coronation as ill advised. After all, he continued, it was well known how many people and circles with influence distrusted the *zemstvos* and especially any tendency on their part to act together.[15] Thus, any concerted action by the *zemstvos* could only strengthen this opposition. The representatives of the *zemstvos* thought it best to back down. Their aim was to find some form or other of legal association and cooperation. To achieve this, they thought it prudent to avoid a conflict with the new minister of the interior.

When the provincial *zemstvo* chairmen arrived in Moscow for the coronation, they met a number of times to discuss various questions relating to the *zemstvo*, including the importance of regular contacts and how the work of the individual provincial *zemstvos* could be coordinated. All the chairmen of the provincial *zemstvo* executive committees were invited to a reception given by the minister of the interior shortly before the end of the coronation. When the official reception was over, Shipov approached the minister and asked him for an appointment so he could give him a message. Goremykin asked him to stay behind and invited him into his office. On behalf of the *zemstvo* representatives, Shipov told the minister that they attached great value to the provincial *zemstvo* chairmen being authorized to meet on a regular basis to discuss a range of practical issues arising from *zemstvo* business.

As such, this was a legitimate request, which even Goremykin had to acknowledge. Besides, following the absurd ban on the joint *zemstvo* donation to a committee headed by the empress, he was now apparently inclined to make a friendly gesture to the *zemstvos*. He explained, however, that he was unable officially to authorize such meetings, as there was no provision in the legislation or the *zemstvo* institutions for them. Shipov replied that he understood, but that he merely wanted to secure the minister's unofficial approval for private meetings of chairmen of the provincial *zemstvo* executive committees, so as to avoid creating any unwelcome impression of "collusion" concerning the organization of these meetings. Goremykin answered that it was quite clear to him that he had no power to ban private meetings of the *zemstvo* committee chairmen, but for his part, however, he simply advised that no other *zemstvo* representatives be included, to ensure that the meetings did not get too large and that they remained businesslike. He was also concerned lest the meetings were reported in the press, and finally that, "given their private nature, they should be held in private houses and not on *zemstvo* premises." Shipov told the minister that he found these conditions perfectly acceptable, but as *zemstvo* representatives had no influence on the press, they would be unable to prevent news of these meetings being published.

The minister's statement that he could not prevent private meetings is certainly of interest, as is his advice that they should be held in private houses to protect their privacy. At that time, many representatives of the *zemstvos* and of society in general still had their own houses, built on their own land, and did not need accommodation made available to them by the state, where a spy could be placed at any time. The houses were places where private life could carry on, and the state, inasmuch as it recognized civil society, did not see it as its business to control it, apart from special exceptional cases. Thus, civil society provided a solid basis for the freedom of political opinion and discussion, at least within this private sphere. From there opinions that had been formed so imperceptibly gradually trickled out, sometimes even gushed out, to become public. In passing, one can also draw the following conclusion: even if one holds that socialism does not necessarily have to lead to dictatorship, by contrast one has to assume that a consistently dictatorial regime must be socialist. This is inevitable just because of security considerations, because otherwise it cannot achieve the requisite level of surveillance of the citizen's private life.[16]

After this conversation with the minister of the interior, it was decided that the chairmen of the *zemstvo* executive committees should meet at the beginning of August in Nizhni-Novgorod, where at any rate many of them intended to go for the trade fair. Two issues, completely unrelated to politics, were put on the agenda: how to harmonize the accounting methods of the *zemstvos* and whether it would be useful to allocate money from the provincial-level *zemstvos* to the districts to implement compulsory education for all. The main discussion here was about how further meetings could be organized. All the participants thought that continuing and developing these meetings was extremely valuable. It was also pointed out that such meetings offered the representatives of the individual provinces the opportunity to familiarize themselves with the methods used by the executive committees of other provinces. In addition, they could coordinate measures that required governmental approval, as this would increase the chances of obtaining it. To hold the meetings on a regular basis, it was decided to set up a secretariat consisting of five of the *zemstvo* executive committee chairmen, to be responsible for convening the meetings and preparing the agenda. The next meeting was scheduled for March 1897 in St. Petersburg.

This meeting in St. Petersburg could not take place, as shortly after the Nizhni-Novgorod meeting, Goremykin withdrew his pledge to tolerate such gatherings.

Shipov's view is that the minister had to give into pressure from influential reactionary circles, and especially from Pobedonostsev.[17] Through the provincial governor, Goremykin informed Shipov that he had concluded that neither a permanent secretariat to prepare the meetings nor the meetings themselves could be considered private gatherings, especially as the chairmen of the *zemstvo* executive committees as such were state officials. That was why such meetings could only be authorized with the official approval of the ministry, for which, however, there was no provision in law, as he had mentioned before.[18] After that, Shipov naturally put a stop to all the preparatory work to convene the next meeting.

This government resistance to any show of activity that had not been ordered from the top, but was of an autonomous nature, even if totally legal and unequivocally sensible, was a baleful symptom of the decay in the genuine will and capacity to govern among those who stood at the top of the bureaucratic hierarchy and who bore responsibility for Russia's fate. As Hauriou writes:

> To govern is to lead; governments are often called the leadership; on the other hand, it is really about dealing with events, that is, all that crops up unforeseen nationally and internationally, everything new; the essential role of government is continuously to resolve fresh difficulties that occur and interest the group; as for old problems, if they reappear, if it is a matter of going over old ground, then that is not for government but for the administration to deal with.[19]

At the turn of the century, however, anything new was regarded only with suspicion and aversion by the government. The government increasingly lost the ability to solve new problems, to deal with the unforeseen, or to exploit for the general good any activity for which there was no basis in law or that lay outside the competence of the various government departments.

There has been a great deal of discussion and severe criticism of the bureaucratization of the Russian state under the last tsar. It was often pointed out that this bureaucratization was extremely detrimental, because it prevented the unfettered energy of the people from being harnessed and rendered the government's own actions ineffective. Nonetheless, the most harmful aspect of this bureaucratization has been overlooked, namely, that it led to the degeneration of government itself. A government that is bureaucratized from top to bottom tends to hang desperately on to the established way of conducting business once this is in place; that is, it deals with new contingencies and unforeseen problems according to tried and tested formulas. In this way, governments become prisoners of their own administrative methods, or methods that are actually bureaucratic or administrative in nature. In so doing, however, government forfeits its true substance, that of a power that can guide the country through new situations by mastering the unexpected and not by always denying or rejecting it.

What led to the government's fundamental rejection of anything new? As already mentioned, its tendency to view all matters of state from the perspective of the struggle against nihilism and terrorism was certainly quite perverse. Over time, this tendency settled into the basic position that the main role of the state was to ensure tranquility and order. Insofar, however, as maintaining such a state of affairs and not finding a solution to the actual problems in the life of the country was the focus of the government, this resulted in the ascendency of policing when considering state business, in other words, an administrative, not a political perspective. Policing is above all an aspect of administration, not of government. This is the start of a process leading to a government becoming the top tier of administration. The preservation of tranquility and order is of course a prerequisite for the state to pursue any of its aims. If, however, this goal is set above all others—if, more than anything else, the justification for the autocracy is that it is a regime that can guarantee tranquility and order like no other—then this is a symptom of decay in political thinking. To the extent that this development was a consequence of the battle against nihilism, it offers an example of how subversive ideologies also affect those who are fighting them. It must also be acknowledged how right the statesmanlike instincts were of those who at the time glimpsed Russia's salvation in switching to a constitutional regime. Actually, the tsarist government only behaved again like a real government with Stolypin. This was not just because of Stolypin's personality, but also because of the circumstance that by then Russia had a constitution and Stolypin was faced with the Duma.

Despite Goremykin's statement that he was retracting his authorization, meetings of zemstvo representatives still took place. These, however, were not planned, quasi-official meetings of the chairmen of the zemstvo executive committees, but rather gatherings of representatives who met "by coincidence" whenever they happened to see each other because of some public function or other in Moscow or St. Petersburg.[20] Thus, for example, such a discussion took place in Moscow in August 1898, when the monument to Alexander II was unveiled. That honoring the memory of Alexander II would inevitably become an occasion to pay homage to his rule and the liberal principles it served to implement is quite understandable. Here is a spectacular example of how the refusal of the government to acknowledge and officially sanction a natural and necessary expression of civic life backfired on itself and its aims. The meetings now took on a semi-legal character. All those who studiously avoided anything that might smack of opposition steered clear of them. As these meetings reached no decisions, and were unable to decide anything, there was no longer any reason to allow only the chairmen of the zemstvo executive committees to participate. On the contrary, it seemed natural to include other, more active and prominent representatives from the zemstvos. In this way, a certain involuntary, even imperceptible selection of the participants took place. The zemstvo meetings then turned into the exact opposite of what the government wanted, that is to say, into a coalition of progressive elements from the zemstvos, who were, at least to a certain degree, inclined to opposition. As a result, they acquired a political overtone, which the government suspected was everywhere, even where it was absent. As a result, the official technical meetings of the *zemstvo* executive committee chairmen were also banned by the government.[21]

There was another group, with a similar composition and character, drawn from *zemstvo* representatives of liberal and progressive public opinion. This was Beseda (Symposium), founded in the 1890s and initially based on purely personal contacts.[22] Over time, it became an organized focal point for well-known representatives of public opinion. This circle only became known through the publication of a series of works on the agrarian question, the basic principles of local government, the constitutions of other countries, and so on—in other words, works that would disseminate liberal ideas. These works, however, could not appear as Beseda publications as such, but only as the personal publications of its individual members before 1904, that is, prior to Prince Sviatopolk-Mirsky's appointment as minister of the interior, following Pleve's assassination. Nevertheless, according to Maklakov, the most important thing was not the publication of these works, but that Beseda formed a rudimentary organization enabling many representatives of public opinion from nearly every province to make contacts.

Beseda was not a political party with a defined program and quite consciously did not wish to become one. Here was a coalition of representatives of progressive opinion, who might belong to very different political currents. Men like Kokoshkin and Shakhovskoi, for example, who were members of Russian liberalism's left wing and who have to be seen as nonsocialist radicals, could belong to Beseda. At the same time, however, Slavophiles who dreamed of restoring an autocracy cured of its bureaucratic degeneration, such as, for example, Khomiakov, Stakhovich, or Shipov, whom Maklakov described as "the last knights of the *samoderzhavie*" (autocracy), could belong as well. One thing was a necessary condition for membership in Beseda: loyalty to the idea of local self-government, and not just theoretical approval.

Beseda members had to demonstrate their commitment to these ideas through practical service in the *zemstvo* or the local town council. Maklakov writes, "Beseda wanted to remain on the terrain of practical activity and experience and not submit to the doctrinaire ideas of intellectuals." Naturally, it took a wholly negative view of the concept of revolution. Overall, there was no evidence of demagoguery or a craving for popularity in Beseda. According to Maklakov again, discussions centered on what would benefit the people, not on the will of the people. Beseda ceased to exist after 1905, when political parties were officially sanctioned in Russia.

In the meantime, measures continued to be taken, not with the aim of abolishing local self-government outright, but of reducing the *zemstvos'* range of powers and limiting their autonomy. The practical effects of these measures were not that significant, but they did arouse ill feeling in *zemstvo* circles. The gulf between government and society continued to widen, which particularly concerned conservative *zemstvo* representatives. Shipov writes: "It was felt that if nothing was done soon to bring in the necessary reforms from above, the supreme power would, in the course of events, be forced in the none too distant future to agree to a radical restructuring of our state under pressure from the rapidly growing current of opposition in the country."[23] Shipov reports that this problem was discussed with increasing anxiety in the private meetings of *zemstvo* representatives and in society in general.

It was then decided to submit a letter to the tsar, with the aim of highlighting the main shortcomings of the current system of government and presenting the main principles of the necessary reform. The paper was to be circulated to and signed by as large a number as possible of respected representatives of public opinion. The text was drafted by a small group, and it is noteworthy that most of the participants were not supporters of constitutional government, but considered nonbureaucratic autocracy, as conceived by Slavophiles, to be the ideal form of government.[24] In the group, this outlook was represented by N. A. Khomiakov, Stakhovich, F. D.Samarin, and Shipov himself. On the other hand, the following were moderate constitutionalists: S. N. Trubetskoy, Pavel Dolgorukov, and Pisarev. Interestingly, the historian Kliuchevsky, who was neither a *zemstvo* member nor in any other respect a representative of public opinion, also took part in the group's work. In spite of this, the other members entrusted him with the task of editing the text of the paper. Shipov was asked to produce the first draft.

Shipov had mapped out nine propositions, in which he particularly highlighted that the main weakness besetting the current order was the lack of mutual trust between government and society. In his view, the government made the false assumption that autonomy in society and its participation in the internal running of government were in conflict with the principles of autocratic rule. This was totally mistaken; on the contrary, *samoderzhavie* was only possible given close contact between the tsar and the people. As a result, he added, the bureaucracy, which separated the tsar from the people, represented a great danger for the *samoderzhavie*. It was therefore necessary to safeguard the freedom of public opinion and support the institutions of local self-government. In addition, Shipov recommended including elected representatives drawn from wider society, and from local self-government in particular, in discussions of draft legislation in the State Council, very much along the same lines as Loris-Melikov had previously suggested.

These propositions were discussed repeatedly, but the small group attempting to prepare the draft could not agree. Trubetskoy, supported by Dolgorukov, thought it was utopian to try to resurrect the *samoderzhavie* with the full panoply of ideas that came with it. His position was that the government's arbitrary rule could only be eliminated if the state was bound by the rule of law, which was impossible without changing over to constitutional government.[25] By contrast, F. Samarin distanced himself from Shipov's propositions, as he thought that they only contained a one-sided critique of the state without highlighting the shortcomings of society. In his view, the state's lack of trust vis-à-vis the people was in any case partly justified by the nature of Russian society, where negative ideas, and a dismissive attitude to the their forbears' beliefs and national history, were in the ascendant.[26] Because of this impasse, the group abandoned the idea of sending a letter to the tsar.

The next opportunity for representatives of local self-government to meet came with the conference on the problems of cottage industry organized in March 1902 in St. Petersburg by the Ministry of Agriculture.[27] The guidelines for the organization of local committees set up by the Special Advisory Committee on the needs of the rural economy were already public by that time. According to these guidelines, only the members of zemstvo executive committees, and not zemstvo assemblies, could sit on these committees, which provoked a lot of discontent in the zemstvos. Some even went so far as to call for a total boycott of the work of the committees. It was then decided to convene a conference on May 23 in Moscow in order to agree to a common position on the problem of zemstvo representatives participating in the work of the committees.

Shipov was elected to chair this conference, and it was thanks in part to his influence that it rejected the idea of the boycott. In addition, the conference went on to work out a program that zemstvo representatives on the committees should, or at least would be able to, follow in the discussions of the issues raised in the committees. The conference participants also highlighted in this program the general conditions that hampered the development of agriculture and rural industry. To overcome these adverse conditions, they advocated in particular giving the peasants the same civil rights as enjoyed by members of other social estates. They also favored promoting public education, reforming taxation policy, and finally allowing the press, and representatives of public opinion in general, to discuss economic issues without restriction.

Although the conference rejected the boycott idea, members of the government nevertheless saw the guidance to zemstvo representatives on the committees as amounting to the organization of passive resistance.[28] This was the interpretation that Pleve put on the conference in his report to the tsar, who then authorized him to convey to the participants the emperor's extreme displeasure (vysochaishee neudovol'stvie). It was typical of Pleve that the more conservative a particular participant might be, and the higher up he was on the social ladder, the sharper and more formal the tone he adopted in passing on the imperial disapproval. For example, Pleve, when passing on the emperor's reprimand, did not ask Stakhovich, the conservative Orel marshal of the nobility, to sit or give him the chance to speak in his own defense. It is noteworthy that, in Maklakov's opinion, it was not the revolutionaries but the liberals whom Pleve regarded as his archenemies, primarily those who absolutely rejected any association with revolution and who aimed at legal cooperation with the state. No doubt, in Pleve's view, these people could subvert the *samoderzhavie* from the inside and were therefore the more dangerous: he pursued them mercilessly. On the other hand, he apparently underestimated the chances of a revolution in Russia. He had succeeded in stamping out the revolutionary groups in the 1880s, while later on an agent of his secret police, Azef, was at the head of the Socialist Revolutionary Party's Combat Organization. It seems he was convinced that it was not difficult to bring revolutionary excesses under control. He even endeavored to add a new legal dimension to the fight against revolution. He appointed the Moscow state prosecutor, a lawyer, to the post of head of the police department, and in 1903 court hearings of political trials were again introduced.[29]

In contrast to the way he had treated Stakhovich, Pleve received Shipov in an unexpectedly cordial manner. After he had conveyed the official reprimand, they talked for a long time (over an hour and a half), evidently with the intention of clarifying the true position and the real intentions of those who attended the conference. Immediately after getting back from his meeting with the minister, Shipov wrote a record of the conversation with, in his words, "almost stenographic accuracy."

Shipov particularly drew Pleve's attention to the fact that such meetings of *zemstvo* representatives were not completely new, but had occasionally taken place since 1895. Although they were not regular, they met now and then on the occasion of officially convened conferences (e.g., the farmers' conference, the conferences on the problems of rural industry and the problems of public education) to which representatives from local self-government had also been invited. *Zemstvo* representatives had always used these occasions to sound each other out privately. Shipov went on to point out that at the last meeting "general adverse factors were exclusively examined in the light of the needs of rural industry and economic prosperity,"[30] in other words, from the position that the government itself took in setting up the special advisory committees. Finally, he continued, the view that one should refuse to cooperate with the local committees convened by the government had been rejected by a significant majority.

Pleve gave a very characteristic answer to Shipov's explanation:

> I shall report everything you have told me to His Majesty, but I am not sure whether His Majesty will change His mind. For my part, as minister of the interior, I must tell you that what you have told me cannot be regarded as completely satisfactory. The fact that meetings that were not sanctioned in law took place over a number of years does not justify your last conference. Moreover, it is just as well that in this case, a sensible majority carried the day, and the minority accepted it. It might have been, however, the other way round; in other words, the majority might have been unreasonable, and then the reasonable minority possibly might have felt honor-bound to comply. That is why such an organization cannot be legally recognized.[31]

There is something oppressive, something that reveals the government's pathological weakness, in the minister's line of argument that a conference could not be legally recognized because it could produce a majority that might prove to be unreasonable.

Nothing else that Shipov added could persuade Pleve, who, even after his meeting with Shipov, remained true to his position of combating conservative liberalism. It was thanks to his efforts that Witte had to resign as minister of finance. The work of the Special Advisory Committee on the needs of rural industry, which had advocated a liberal program, was paralyzed through his opposition. Shipov, who had been elected for the fifth time as the chair of the provincial *zemstvo* executive committee, was not confirmed in this office by Pleve, despite the former being against a constitution and much more of a romantic supporter of the *samoderzhavie;* he also held the title of chamberlain at the court.[32] Pleve reproached Shipov with "inciting an opposition group in public opinion constantly to resist the government."[33] Pleve was even more explicit in the course of his interview informing Shipov of his decision not to confirm the latter in office:

> I consider your activities to be harmful in political terms, because you are systematically trying to extend the areas of competence and powers of the social institutions and create an organization seeking to unify the activities of the *zemstvos* in the various provinces. Although I have to acknowledge that we are moving in this direction and that the solution to this problem will come in the near future, this issue can only be solved from above and not from below and only then if His Majesty clearly expresses it to be his will.[34]

This act on Pleve's part certainly backfired. Instead of Shipov, F. A. Golovin, a convinced supporter of a constitution, was elected as chair of the Moscow province *zemstvo* executive committee.[35] Finally, Pleve told A. A. Stakhovich, adjutant to Grand Duke Sergei Alexandrovich and brother of M. A. Stakhovich, to whom he was no doubt particularly unsympathetic, that he intended to dismiss the latter from his post as marshal of the nobility. Only death prevented Pleve from carrying out this intention. He fell victim to a terrorist attack on July 15, 1904, an attack that was carried out by the revolutionary combat organization led by his agent Azef.[36]

Zemstvo representatives were also in no mood to concede. They endeavored to reach an agreement through Witte that the regular *zemstvo* assemblies be given the opportunity to voice their opinion on the problems concerning "the needs of rural industry," and to this end Shipov wrote a letter to Witte on July 8, 1902.[37] In autumn of the same year, Shipov called on all the chairmen of the provincial *zemstvo* executive committees to campaign for the repeal of the law of June 12, 1902, regulating veterinary services, which had considerably reduced the powers of local government in this field.[38] Their efforts paid off, as the provincial *zemstvo* executive committees were informed in a circular from the Ministry of the Interior on March 23, 1903, that His Majesty deigned to order a revision of the law of June 12, 1902.

However, the combined efforts of the *zemstvo* representatives, as described above, were only in the pursuit of specific, limited aims. Discussions concerning more general issues only began in April 1903. A conference was convened by the insurance committee of the Ministry of the Interior on April 20 of that year, to which *zemstvo* representatives were also invited. This again offered them the opportunity to meet unofficially in private apartments to discuss current issues. In particular the issue under discussion was what position the *zemstvos* should take in relation to the legislation announced shortly beforehand in the Manifesto of February 26, 1903, which partly concerned local interests. The manifesto announced a series of reforms, but said nothing about consulting representatives of the *zemstvo* institutions on the relevant draft laws, rather speaking only in general terms about inviting the most worthy people from the provinces. Thus, it was suggested that they should insist openly on the need for elected representatives from the provincial *zemstvo* assemblies to participate in the drafting of legislation. This proposal, however, was rejected, albeit only by a slim majority. It would have been too reminiscent of Loris-Melikov's "constitution," which, as was well known, was anathema to the tsar and his advisers. It was thus decided to ask the government to submit draft legislation to the *zemstvo* assemblies for their opinion, insofar as it touched on conditions in the provinces and local needs.[39]

This resolution was therefore passed more for tactical reasons; in fact, the idea that *zemstvo* representatives should be consulted in the State Council during the drafting of legislation had increasingly become generally accepted in *zemstvo* circles. One should not think, however, that all supporters of this idea among *zemstvo* members, or at least the majority of them, believed that this would sow the seeds of constitutional government. On the other hand, government circles saw, not without reason, the moves to make the participation of *zemstvo* representatives in drafting legislation a legally binding rule, as an expression of aspirations for a constitution. Pleve was right when he commented that the view that progress was impossible until the state was reformed was increasingly prevalent throughout society. Pleve was certainly accurate in his characterization of this opinion, or this sentiment, when he commented ironically: "If we submit our plans for road building to the provinces for discussion, we can be certain in advance of the response we shall get. They will point out that no reform of road building is possible under the present system of government, but if the state is reformed, the roads will improve all by themselves."[40]

It would be wrong to think that this view was wholly predominant in *zemstvo* circles. Even Pleve himself did not make that mistake. In fact, he stated that this view was actually held not by the elected *zemstvo* deputies themselves, but rather by those who were recruited from the ranks of the intelligentsia to work as specialists, known throughout the country as the "third element" who distorted the true voice of the *zemstvo* world. On the other hand, however, it would also be incorrect to exaggerate the differences in this respect between the elected representatives of the people and the technical personnel. The conviction had taken hold in ever-wider circles in society that without a transition to a constitutional government, no progress at all was possible in Russia. Men like Shipov were now merely a minority, even among the representatives of *zemstvo* opinion. They regarded the need for a political struggle against the government of His Majesty as a great misfortune and felt it their duty "to resist with all their might and with all available means the endeavours to establish a constitution."[41] They, like Shipov, did not want to abandon hope "that the state would give up the ruinous policy of suspicion and the persecution of free manifestations of private and public life."[42] The majority in the *zemstvos* began to join the avant-garde of political radicalism, that is, the so-called Union of Liberation (Soiuz Osvobozhdeniia).

It was essentially Pleve, with the unfathomable rigidity of his policies and the needless severity of his political measures, whom Russia had to thank for this development, which, as we shall see below, had an extremely detrimental effect on the process of transforming Russia into a constitutional state.[43] Shipov has left vivid testimony to this:

> Many *zemstvo* members told me that they agreed with my tactical political program and had not lost hope that the government would at last recognize the need to satisfy the moderate and loyal wishes of society. When the minister refused to confirm me in office, they lost all hope of a peaceful solution to this problem. They became convinced that the struggle against the existing political system was unavoidable. Such facts led me to anxious thoughts and fears that the gulf between the state and society would only get deeper and wider. Broad spectrums of society resented the minister of the interior's policies. The dissatisfaction with the conditions (*poriadkami*) that existed in our society also came to be felt about the fundamental principle of our state, that is, the autocracy.[44]

Maklakov too thought that Pleve's policies played into the hands of the "Liberation Movement" or the "Union of Liberation."[45]

Chapter 18

The Liberation Movement

Program of the "Liberation Movement," its
radicalism—Tactics of the "Liberation Movement,"
its alliance with revolutionary circles

The main aim of the "Liberation Movement: (*osvoboditel'noe dvizhenie*) was to bring down the autocracy in Russia and force a change to constitutional government. Those who joined this movement did not seek, in contrast to those who represented *zemstvo* circles, to overcome the division between the state and society. They were not interested in establishing mutual trust and normal cooperation between the representatives of government and the public at large.

The Liberation Movement emerged into the open with the publication abroad of the journal *Osvobozhdenie* (Liberation). Soon afterward, the Union of Liberation, an organized group, was founded. Petrunkevich gives a quite detailed account in his memoirs of the founding of the journal and the Union of Liberation. The idea of establishing a free newspaper in a foreign country had its origins in a small Moscow intellectual circle, whose members included Petrunkevich, Vernadsky, Shakhovskoi, Kornilov, and Novgorodtsev, among others. The idea began to take shape when Petrunkevich went to Tver' in 1902 for a *zemstvo* assembly meeting and met Struve, who had been exiled there from St. Petersburg. Struve decided that, should he not be given permission to travel abroad, he would go to Germany illegally, in other words, emigrate, which, in fact, he did soon afterward. "In the circumstances, the question as to who should be the editor of the proposed publication resolved itself."[1] In principle, Miliukov should have become editor in chief, but his friends did not want him to share Herzen's fate—to con-

demn him, as was then believed, to lifelong emigration. This was not, incidentally, merely for his sake; they also believed that he had to stay in Russia because
"a leading role was reserved for him in the struggle against the government for
the freedom of Russia."[2] D. Shakhovskoi and N. L'vov then held further negotiations with Struve in Stuttgart, where it had been decided to publish the journal.
A sum of one hundred thousand roubles was also handed over to Struve. It was
collected from supporters, "each one of whom was inspired by the idea and the
necessity of fighting for a constitution."[3] The first issue of *Liberation* appeared on
July 1, 1902 (new style).

In the spring of 1903, Miliukov wrote an article to clarify "the tasks and the
direction not just of the journal *Liberation* but also of the group that was founded
with the aim of fighting the autocracy."[4] In the autumn of the same year, a meeting also took place of those who supported *Liberation* as contributors of articles
or money.[5] The participants at this meeting first met in Schaffhausen, but as
they did not wish to stay in the same place, they met on three successive days in
Singen, Radolfszell, and then Hohentwiel, near Constance. Twenty people from
Russia came to the meeting. It is curious that ten of them came from a *zemstvo*
background, and ten were intellectuals. This was where the Union of Liberation
was founded. It was a union and not a political party, where differences of opinion
were meant to be tolerated and indeed were.[6]

They were united, however, in the struggle against the autocracy. Maklakov
writes: "The movement's program can be summed up in two words: 'Doloi samoderzhavie!' (Down with autocracy!), which they euphemistically referred to as a
binomial formula and which, according to the simple-minded view of a provincial
police officer that had got into the newspapers, was 'a well-known Russian saying.'"[7] This was a conscious choice, as can be seen from an article in the first issue of *Liberation:* "There is no point now in raising all those legislative issues that
will be dealt with by a future Russian representative assembly: reforms in economics, finance, culture, education and administration, employment law and the
agrarian question, decentralization and the restructuring of local government.
These problems and similar ones posed by Russian life provide an inexhaustible
seam for the future legislative work of a representative assembly."[8] "Therefore,"
Maklakov remarks, "for the time being there is nothing in the program except
'down with autocracy.'"[9]

Nevertheless, it was not possible to leave it at "down with autocracy" as a
program. In number 17 of *Liberation*, which appeared about a year after the first
issue, Miliukov had fundamentally to revise this position. Here he said that the
agrarian question and the question of the workers had to be raised without delay.
In his view, the Union of Liberation's program had to contain pledges that could
win over the support of the peasants and workers, and if it failed to attract these
groups, the party of "political liberation" would be condemned to stagnate piti-
fully. Maklakov was right to stress the significance of this turn, which was based
on the recognition that the masses were not interested in political liberty.

The decision of the Liberation Movement to raise the agrarian question and the question of the workers in order to win the sympathy of the corresponding social classes means of course that they had decided to approach these issues demagogically. Maklakov notes: "We did not consider how to solve these problems for Russia's sake, but how these issues could be raised for the sake of the struggle against the autocracy, in order to attract the masses."[10] And he adds: "This way of approaching the agrarian question and the workers' question dispenses with the need to treat them as a program. These questions became a matter of tactics."[11] Opposition circles thus began to look at social issues from a perspective that was divorced from their real character and content. This way of looking at these issues was just as inadequate as that of government circles, whose starting point in dealing with the most varied problems was the necessity of combating nihilism and socialist terror.

Sadly, however, the Union of Liberation's proposed solutions to purely political problems were no more felicitous than their social policies. Although they avoided a demagogic approach in this area, they instead posed the question of establishing a constitutional system in a purely theoretical, even dogmatic manner. The following schema was proposed as a solution: "First, a commission of representatives from existing social organizations and institutions would be set up to draw up an electoral law for the election of a constituent assembly. Then, on the basis of this law, an assembly would be convened to draw up a Russian constitution, and only after that could a normal legislative assembly be convened to deal with the current needs of the country."[12] Maklakov continues, "This was the plan, no doubt theoretically flawless, that was supposed to complement the curt slogan 'Down with autocracy.'" In his view, this program epitomized the radicalism that predominated in intellectual circles at the time.

It is certainly characteristic that this program, while not calling for the monarchy to be removed and replaced by a republic, did not allow any role whatsoever for the monarch in the process of reforming the state. The representatives from *zemstvo* circles presupposed that any sound progress in Russia depended on trust and cooperation between society in general and the state, and this was something for which they strove. By contrast, the members of the Union of Liberation were not in the least interested in an understanding with the monarch or with the forces of the old system in general. They demanded nothing less than unconditional capitulation and complete submission to the demands of the theoretically flawless program they had put forward. Blinkered as they were by certain theoretical principles, they wished to impose the same on government representatives as well. Maklakov provides a telling description of the Russian intelligentsia's doctrinaire approach:

> Their ideal was so far removed from reality in Russia that they made no attempt at all to make any organic connection with it. Publicists were not interested in which Russian institutions might suitably be transformed on

the European model. Even those among our historians who had studied in depth the question of how political systems succeeded each other, insofar as they spoke of our future, avoided taking the past into account, as it, just like inherited defects, could only be a hindrance. Censorship too encouraged such an outlook, as one had to avoid drawing clear parallels and analogies because of it. . . . This schooling (through censorship) accustomed the intelligentsia to see Russia as a tabula rasa on which at a certain time, for whatever reason, someone would somehow construct the new Russia according to the latest theoretical recipe.[13]

Maklakov was certainly correct is saying in defense of Russian intellectuals that the conditions in which they had to work and the burden of censorship had forced them in this direction. In reality, it was forbidden to write about the shortcomings of the autocracy—whether it was desirable to replace it with another form of government, what form that should take, and what means were necessary. As a result, Russian publicists, and even academics, turned their attention to other countries. In particular, they read the works on political science and constitutional law written in Western European languages. At the same time, they studied the political life and systems of other countries, while, interestingly enough, Russian researchers and publicists also made the existing institutions, parties, and ideological currents in other countries the subject of theoretical observation. They also judged the political situation in other countries purely in the light of their most rigorous theoretical propositions, not deviating at all from their own ideological stance. This assessment was thus always more or less a way of disguising the formulation and circulation of their own political ideals. When they criticized the British conservatives and the French opportunists and held up intransigence as the only acceptable outlook, they preached that radicalism was fundamentally correct and thus a political and ideological orientation that was justifiable whatever the circumstances. In the process, this critique served to ease the bitter awareness that attacking the autocracy in Russia was impossible.

If you consider that for decades this literature was the only source of political education for Russian intellectuals, one can hardly be surprised that, as Maklakov comments, "they displayed all the shortcomings of an opposition without responsibility, whose sole criterion for judging life was whether it lived up to their ideals, without taking into account what was possible in reality."[14] Because of this abstract way of approaching political and constitutional issues, the ideology of political radicalism and the theoretical concept of the constitution became articles of faith for many intellectuals in Russia. According to Maklakov: "A sober analysis of the various aspects of the constitution was replaced by mystical belief. No one was able to discuss the positive and negative sides of the argument or to raise the question as to what was practical in Russia."[15]

The tactics vis-à-vis the government and the autocracy in general were determined by this fundamental attitude. Insofar as it was believed that the constitution was the only salvation, and that nothing positive could be achieved under an absolutist regime, logically there was no need to reform the autocracy. On the contrary, all means had to be used to provoke and compromise the state.[16] An article with the title "Kak Borot'sia s Samoderzhaviem" (How to Fight the Autocracy), in number 21 of *Liberation*, illustrates this: "Constitutionalists must not miss any opportunity that offers the chance of intensifying or provoking conflict between the organs of autonomous social action and the autocratic regime."[17] In addition, in number 22, representatives of society were called upon "to put all their efforts, all their energy, into creating an atmosphere of dissatisfaction and protest."[18] To this end, in issue number 13, *Liberation* recommends two methods in particular: noncooperation and strikes.[19]

Acts of terrorism or preparations for an armed uprising were not on the agenda. The title of one of Struve's lectures held in Paris, "Ne Shturm, a Blokada" (A Blockade, Not an Assault),[20] gives the flavor of the Union of Liberation's tactics.[21] The fact that what the Liberation Movement really had in mind, namely, the elimination of the autocracy, was a negative program led them, however, to go along with all those who were also fighting the existing state. This had the consequence that the Liberation Movement felt no need to draw any clear distinction between its own ranks and the groups that were further to the left. This was still the case later on, after some positive elements had been added to the Liberation Movement's program. As stated above, their political program was purely formalistic: convening a constituent assembly and ensuring that all avenues to it were kept open. The social program consisted of propaganda taken from those parts of the socialist parties' program that seemed relatively harmless or that they could attempt to render harmless. The editor of *Liberation*, Struve, declared, for example, in one of the earliest issues, "Liberalism must acknowledge (*priznavat'*) its solidarity with the so-called revolutionary movement."[22]

In consequence of this declaration of solidarity with the revolutionaries, the Liberation Movement thought it right to take part in a conference of opposition and revolutionary organizations in October 1904 (in other words, not long before the first *zemstvo* conference, about which more follows below).[23] The conclusion was then reached that it would be advantageous for these organizations to establish an alliance. At the same time, it was stressed that this did not mean in any way that the participating organizations would have to change their programs or tactics. The Liberation Movement certainly did not pledge to join in the Socialist Revolutionaries' terrorist acts, but it did commit itself to not condemning terror, that is, actually tacitly condoning it. This was a position that would have been unthinkable for nineteenth-century liberals.[24] Gradually, the Union of Liberation went even further. *Liberation* began to justify terrorism and to criticize those who condemned revolutionary terror. For example, for this reason it even attacked such prominent liberals as the brothers Evgenii and Sergei Trubetskoy.

Given that the Liberation Movement had gone so far as to justify revolutionary terrorism, it comes as no surprise that it was also prepared to support all other forms of political disorder and social turmoil, in particular political agitation among students, disturbances in the working class, peasant pogroms, and finally national separatist or at least autonomist movements.[25] There is no need here to analyze these individually. The Liberation Movement's attitude to strivings for national autonomy really belongs to the history of national movements in the Russian empire. Maklakov is right about the student movement when he states that it "produced more noise than destruction and had more effect on people's nerves than on the foundations of public order."[26] It was not so much the autocracy but normal academic life and the necessary conditions for productive academic work that were subverted. Thus, it was most damaging not to the bureaucracy, but to members of the faculty, many of whom were liberals. The position of the Kadet Party, and the Liberation Movement from which it emerged, regarding the agrarian question has already been described above, in part 2. At this point, one must just add that the Liberation Movement did not merely advocate, as we have seen, the extensive nationalization of large landed estates, but often attempted to justify or play down direct acts of violence by peasants against landowners. For example, one of the Kadet Party speakers in the First Duma, Herzenstein, described the burning of landowners' houses as an "illumination." Also typical of this attitude is an episode, about which Maklakov leaves us an account, during the *zemstvo* conference in November 1905, which thus occurred after the conference had submitted to the influence of the Liberation Movement:

> If some people naively believed, for example, that the conference, in wanting to hold to account administrative officials for having tolerated pogroms, had all types of pogrom in mind, they were soon disabused. At that time, it was not only intellectuals and Jews who were victims of pogroms, but landowners too. The *zemstvo* conference, however, did not support all victims by any means. E. V. de Roberti had suggested not extending the amnesty to crimes involving violence against women and children. Koliubakin, however, detected in this "the marked class nature" of the trend emerging at the conference. De Roberti hastened to reassure him, "I did not have the gentry estates in mind. They do not face any great danger. That fifteen to twenty properties were burned down has absolutely no significance. What I mean here is the mass of Jewish farms and houses burned and plundered by the Black Hundreds."[27]

What, in fact, distinguishes these statements made by those who considered themselves liberal from speeches made at the conference of the revolutionary Peasant Union? There, one of the delegates proudly declared, "There was not a single act of violence; only landowners and their agents were beaten, and then, only if they resisted."[28] Given this attitude, therefore, any injustice toward an enemy is justified. This attitude is the hallmark of revolutionary terrorism and civil war, and it first flared up at the trial of Vera Zasulich, when the jurors acquitted her. At the time, this led Katkov to say that the revolution had already started.

There can be no doubt that the delegates at the *zemstvo* conference abandoned liberalism when they adopted this position.

Finally, as far as working-class unrest is concerned, it is useful to stress two points. The Union of Liberation was prepared, so as not to sour relations with its allies in the fight against the autocracy and weaken the united front, to accept that the Social Democrats could consider the working class as their exclusive sphere of influence, in which they would not tolerate any interference. This means that the Union of Liberation abandoned any attempt to rival the Social Democratic Labor Party's ideals of the socialist revolution and the dictatorship of the proletariat with their own ideal of a constitutional state, at least when the Social Democrats addressed the workers. In this way, they allowed the Social Democrats, and especially Lenin, to condemn political liberty, not to mention civil liberty, as bourgeois prejudice. In the process, they forgot that, particularly in a country lacking any deeper tradition of freedom, such slogans had to be especially potent and thus especially dangerous.[29] Nowhere else could support for the purely economic demands of the working class take on a political dimension as easily as in the old Russia, and this can be blamed on the attitude of the government itself. The autocratic state did not allow workers the right of association and the creation of workers' organizations. Workers were not permitted to defend their own interests and to stand up for their rights. The state saw it as its duty to protect the workers paternalistically, much as it did the peasants, and to look after the interests of the working class. It imposed obligations on employers concerning their workers that were often more onerous than similar ones in the Western countries.[30] This was made possible because the power of the autocrat was independent of its subjects, including capitalists. The result was that the government was held responsible by the workers for their standard of living and satisfying their economic interests. Quite naturally, therefore, the workers' economic demands took on a political dimension.

Indeed, the stance of the Union of Liberation toward groups on the left and the revolutionary forces ultimately had to have a more profound effect on the nature of the Liberation Movement. The refusal to draw a clear line between those who truly stood for liberalism and those who stood to the left of liberalism, outside the ideological framework of liberalism, led those liberals who joined the Union of Liberation to sacrifice their liberal ideals and lose their liberal identity. Of course, some of them did return to their liberal beliefs, having been disabused by the revolutionary events of 1905. Nevertheless, this turnaround had not yet begun in 1904 and even later on only involved a minority.[31] This had an extremely adverse effect on the fate of liberalism in Russia, and as a result, liberal constitutional government in Russia was disadvantaged right from its inception.[32]

Chapter 19

Liberalism in 1904

The *zemstvo* as the basis for the constitution—
Sviatopolk-Mirsky as minister of the interior—The
so-called First *Zemstvo* Congress in November
1904—The history of the *ukaz* of December 12,
1904—Witte's attitude to a consultative assembly
and to constitutional government—Witte's
qualities

E ven if several *zemstvo* representatives were founding members of the Union
of Liberation, overall, *zemstvo* opinion was extremely unsympathetic to the direction that the union was prepared to pursue through an alliance with the revolutionaries. Most *zemstvo* members preferred the road of peaceful evolution. The
representatives of very different political camps saw it as the safest and soundest
way to achieve constitutional government. According to this view, a future Russian representative assembly was to develop out of the *zemstvo* institutions. Witte
recalls in his memoirs:

> As I showed in my memorandum, *zemstvo* institutions represented a
> constitution from below that, without doubt, would have led eventually to a
> constitution from above through the natural course of social development.
> This was also the most peaceful way. Once *zemstvo* and urban local govern-
> ment had been granted, they could have been developed gradually. Instead,
> we had a struggle against them for quarter of a century. We could thus have
> arrived at a constitution without the excesses of a revolutionary upheaval.[1]

Liberals too, who regarded the transition to a constitutional system as the
natural conclusion and culmination of Alexander II's reforms, thought the *zemstvo* institutions were the effective foundation on which a constitutional system
could be constructed. Maklakov writes:

In the past, liberals used to believe that a constitution could be achieved via the "evolution" of existing institutions. In Russia, a nucleus existed from which the constitution could grow "spontaneously." This was local self-government, in other words, the *zemstvo*. The same general needs as were met by the state came within its sphere of responsibility. Like the state, it was an organization with coercive powers of enforcement, but it also embodied the principle of "democracy." It was enough to extend this principle downward and upward, and the constitution would ensue by itself.[2]

Maklakov thought this hope was not unrealistic; in fact, he believed that such a development was inevitable, irrespective of the intentions and ideals of individual *zemstvo* representatives. In his view, it was even furthered by those who did not want a constitution and remained loyal supporters of the autocracy: "One '*zemstvo* man' who rejected constitutional government on principle, Shipov, became, despite himself, one of the founders of constitutional government in Russia, simply because he was a genuine '*zemstvo* man' and promoted its cause."[3] Not only was this approach possible, but it also offered distinct advantages. Maklakov stresses: "It would have been a long road, but along the way cadres could have been trained, who by undertaking practical tasks could have learned about the country's needs and problems as they encountered them. They would thus have been prepared to take over from the old representatives of the state."[4]

It is noteworthy that even Petrunkevich, who thought an alliance with revolutionary forces was necessary in the interests of the struggle against the autocracy, asked, directly following the proclamation of the constitution on October 17, 1905, whether Russia's failure to arrive at a constitution through peaceful means would not have a detrimental effect on the survival of constitutional government. According to his memoirs: "From now on, Russia would be a constitutional, that is, a free state under the rule of law. The reforms of the 1860s were concluded in 1905, not through the free resolve of the tsar, but thanks to the obdurate struggle of the people. Was this a struggle of all the people, and would such a birth guarantee the stability of the constitution?"[5]

After Pleve had fallen victim to a terrorist attack, Prince Sviatopolk-Mirsky was appointed as his successor. This appointment signified a change to a liberal course. Maklakov's view is that even people in the tsar's inner circle were beginning to harbor doubts about the policies followed by Pleve.[6] Sviatopolk-Mirsky belonged to the most select court society. He was no career civil servant, but a military man. He had received his training in the Corps des Pages, and as a general, he belonged to the General Staff. One rarely encounters anyone who was held in such high regard as Sviatopolk-Mirsky. Witte, who in his memoirs was otherwise always critical, if not downright disparaging, toward virtually everyone bar a few exceptions, described Sviatopolk-Mirsky as "an outstanding individual because of his untarnished moral character."[7] Maklakov concurs,[8] while Shipov, who knew Sviatopolk-Mirsky well, speaks of him with great respect.[9] Even Petrunkevich, who was otherwise critical of members of the bureaucracy and the court, is sympathetic to Sviatopolk-Mirsky, recalling his simplicity and affability. Despite his moral integrity and intelligence, it was impossible to be sanguine about the new minister of the interior's ability to master the situation. In Maklakov's opinion: "Such an appointment would have been excellent after Sipiagin's assassination, but the two years of the Pleve government had made the task so difficult that it was beyond the powers of the honest and good-natured Mirsky. Someone of the stature of Stolypin was needed to get on top of the situation."[10]

Sviatopolk-Mirsky already pointed out in his first official declaration on September 16, 1904, that the success of government measures depended essentially on the government having a benevolent attitude toward and placing its confidence in organizations representing society and the social estates as well as the people in general.[11] By virtue of this declaration, hopes were raised in *zemstvo* circles for a new spirit of trust and cooperation between the government and the social organizations. These hopes were reawakened right after Mirsky's appointment, for even before the declaration, it was decided to convene a *zemstvo* conference. In so doing, they were quite certain that the government would not create any difficulties.

This moment shows clearly how far the positions of the *zemstvo* people and the Liberation Movement diverged in 1904. It became apparent that, as we shall soon see, *zemstvo* members had still largely retained their independence at the time vis-à-vis the Liberation Movement.[12] In fact, the Liberation Movement was in no way prepared to reciprocate the new minister of the interior's conciliatory gesture toward public opinion. On October 2, an article by Miliukov with the title of "Novyi Kurs" (The New Course), appeared in *Liberation*:[13] "Pursue your new course, but do not count on our support. We shall not give you even one of our people. We shall not give you any credit nor allow for any delay, as long as you do not adopt our entire program. . . . Perhaps you will succeed in tempting one of ours to join you, but know this: at the very moment when they have become one of yours, they will cease to belong to us, and will thus be useless to you."[14]

The decision to convene a *zemstvo* congress was taken by the *zemstvo* conference secretariat on September 8, 1904. This secretariat had been set up by the chairman of the Moscow Province *zemstvo* board, Golovin, and now reemerged into the light after a lengthy hiatus. Following Sviatopolk-Mirsky's declaration on September 16, 1904, the secretariat decided to broaden the agenda adopted on September 8 and include in the congress program a debate on "the general conditions in public life and any reforms as may seem desirable."[15] Shipov attempted to caution the majority on the secretariat against acting rashly, because, as he said, the resolutions of the *zemstvo* congress, which might displease the tsar, could easily undermine the position of the minister of the interior, who had only just been recently appointed. He thought it would be better to wait until Sviatopolk-Mirsky was safer in his post and only then raise general political questions in concert with him. The majority of the secretariat, however, stuck to its original decision.

Most of the members of the secretariat pointed out that for the time being only one member of the government had declared that he wanted to base his program on the trust of society and the desire to work with it. This positive direction on the part of the government was entirely due, in their view, to the circumstance that at that moment a liberal-minded representative of the bureaucracy stood at the head of the Ministry of the Interior, in other words, a coincidence. In the opinion of this majority, it was high time to give this development a legal basis no longer dependent on the goodwill of whoever was minister of the interior.[16]

When Sviatopolk-Mirsky heard that the *zemstvo* representatives were planning a congress, he hastened to obtain the tsar's agreement to authorize it. As he was insufficiently informed about the situation in the *zemstvo* world, he thought that it was still a matter of a meeting of the chairmen of the provincial *zemstvo* executive committees for sharing experience and for joint consultation about day-to-day questions relating to the work of the *zemstvo*. In other words, he thought it was the kind of meeting that had once been authorized by Goremykin and then banned again. Once it emerged, however, that it was by no means just the chairmen of the provincial executive boards who were to participate in the *zemstvo* conference and that general questions of a political nature were on the agenda, Sviatopolk-Mirsky found himself in an embarrassing situation vis-à-vis the tsar. It looked as if he had extracted an authorization from the tsar by giving false information, not for a meeting of official *zemstvo* representatives, but for a political gathering of unofficial representatives of opposition elements in the *zemstvos*. Sviatopolk-Mirsky then asked Shipov to come to St. Petersburg to clarify the situation. He pointed out that presenting the program as drawn up by the secretariat for this officially sanctioned conference would result in his immediate resignation.[17] Government authorization for this program, Sviatopolk-Mirsky later told the secretariat's delegation, with which he continued the negotiations, would mean that the government thought it was right to entrust the examination of general issues relating to the state to a group of private individuals. After reporting to the tsar, the minister explained, on receiving the delegation for a second time, that the government was prepared to recognize the purely private nature of the assembly and as such would formally ignore it. At the same time, he stressed, in more or less the same terms as Goremykin when the latter was minister, that there was no legal basis for a ban on private discussions in private houses.[18] The delegation signaled its agreement with this and in fact was completely satisfied. They were convinced, quite justifiably, that irrespective of whether the congress was official or private, its resolutions would resonate powerfully throughout Russia and would even make the government take notice. The recognition of the private nature of the conference cannot then be regarded as a concession forced on the *zemstvo* people. It is probable, rather, that they even saw it as giving them a certain advantage. In any case, the conference participants, especially the most representative among them, repeatedly stressed that they were aware of the private nature of the conference. At the same time they highlighted that the private nature of their discussions did not release them from their responsibility nor diminish it, not least because of the anticipated powerful response in the country.[19]

The congress lasted four days, with only the last being dedicated to specific *zemstvo* issues. The first three days were completely taken up with discussions of the last item on the agenda, that is, the general conditions for normalizing society and institutions. The congress put forward eleven propositions. In the first three, there was an outline of how society and government had become completely alienated from one another since the 1880s, because the government did not tolerate the participation of society in the business of the state and had introduced a comprehensive system of bureaucratic centralization and paternalism in all areas of society. In so doing, this bureaucratic system created a deep gulf not just between government and society, but also between the supreme power and the people. It was now vital, however, according to the fourth proposition, to create unity and an active relationship between the state and society. The congress further demanded real guarantees for the inviolability of the person (the fifth proposition); safeguards for the freedom of worship and freedom of the press (the sixth); equality of all citizens regarding their civil and political rights (the seventh), in particular granting the peasants the same rights as other estates (the eighth); and the extension of the powers of local self-government (the ninth). Finally the tenth and eleventh propositions pointed to the necessity of establishing a representative assembly. The supreme power had to enlist the help of the freely elected representatives of the people in carrying out the task of renewal in Russia "in the spirit of the affirmation of the rule of law and active collaboration between the state and society."[20]

The congress was unable, however, to reach any agreement as regards the tenth proposition. Two parallel versions were then produced and published next to each other in the conference report. The majority text (seventy-one votes) recommended conferring legislative powers on a representative assembly, that is, moving to constitutional government. By contrast, the minority version (twenty-seven votes) spoke only of "the regular (*pravil'noe*) participation in the legislative process of the people's representatives, that is, of a special, elected institution." It thus advocated an elected, consultative chamber. Maklakov was right when he wrote that what was at stake was not "more or less," not the same institution with wider or narrower powers, but two institutions of a different constitutional character. Shipov too points out that it was a question here of a deep difference of principle that was not just political, but rather encompassed different worldviews. In Shipov's opinion: "Law must always be the expression of the consciousness of moral and religious responsibility, which applies to the individual as well as society as a whole."[21] And he continues: "Without denying that a specific legal order must absolutely provide a rationale and rules for the active reconciliation of state and people, I see this legal order not as some independent entity, but only as the practical embodiment of the moral concept of the solidarity between the two, which should form the genuine basis of the state."[22]

It is characteristic that according to Shipov, the system of government of the oldest constitutional monarchy, Great Britain, is based not on legal principles, but on this ethical concept, as there

> the power of the monarchy is not only limited by the legal norms of the constitution, but through the profound awareness of the moral solidarity with parliament that is shared by the holders of supreme office and members of the ministerial council. In England as in Russia, religious and ethical sentiment and movements prevail over legal interests. I think it is possible, indeed probable, that the concept of Russian *samoderzhavie*, if it remains true to its fundamental principles, could, in the more or less not too distant future, be embodied and realized in a similar form to that of the English constitution through gradual evolution in our political life. Such an orientation in our public life would guarantee that it would evolve without any particular upheaval and avoid awakening legal interests or the selfish instincts of the people.[23]

Thus, the representative assembly of the kind that the minority in the *zemstvo* congress had in mind was to be a body that would create the moral solidarity between tsar and people, not one that represented the citizens' demands and rights vis-à-vis the supreme power in the state. For Shipov and his supporters, it was precisely this that lay at the heart of the representative assembly and seemed important, not the limitation to a consultative role of the assembly's powers. Elsewhere he stresses that from his point of view, it was irrelevant whether the assembly had full legislative powers or only a consultative role in the legislative process:

> Our opponents apparently find it quite incomprehensible that the question as to whether the assembly makes decisions or offers opinions is quite superfluous and redundant from the position we have adopted. This is because this point of view excludes the possibility of retaining an autocracy that does not take note of the representation of popular opinion and thinking. The difference in attitude to these issues lies in the fact that the advocates of the constitution base their concept of the reform of our state on law. By contrast, we think it is necessary to adopt an ethical and social basis for the impending reform, that is, an awareness of the moral duty that applies equally to the holder of public office as to the assembly.[24]

This difference of opinion between the majority and minority at the *zemstvo* congress, however, did not lead to a split. It was decided, as mentioned above, to reflect both views in the propositions. There was something more significant, which made it possible for both factions in the congress to stay together. Both groups started out from the view that what was desirable was unity between state and people, between government and public opinion. Neither faction wanted to be disloyal. Both regarded the resolutions of the congress as an appeal to the supreme power to take the road of reform and thus of cooperation with society.[25] Even the majority, which advocated a change to constitutional government, only wanted a constitution proclaimed by the tsar. The idea of a national constituent assembly was rejected. Even Kokoshkin, who would soon afterward become an ardent advocate of such a constituent assembly, spoke at the congress along the same lines, as Shipov recalls: "Kokoshkin stressed that national constituent assemblies only occurred in times of anarchy, which was not the case in Russia, and expressed the wish that the new system of government should be established at once by the supreme power."[26]

N. N. L'vov was even more resolute in defending this position. In a powerful speech, he pointed out that the principles of liberty and law had to be made a reality through an agreement with the historical power and that reform initiatives, such as those of the 1860s, had to come from the government. "N. N. L'vov's speech," writes Shipov, "drew loud applause of all-around agreement, because it expressed the genuine feelings, wishes, and hopes of the whole congress."[27]

It was decided at the congress to send a delegation to the minister of the interior to inform him about the resolutions agreed upon.[28] The minister responded that he was unable to receive a deputation from the congress, as this would amount to recognizing the congress and thus contradict the agreement that had been reached on the private nature of the congress. However, he did offer Shipov the opportunity of meeting him in private, so the latter could explain the congress resolutions.[29] During this meeting, Sviatopolk-Mirsky endorsed the congress resolutions and expressed his willingness to present them to the tsar. He just asked for an additional paper to clarify the rationale behind the congress propositions.[30] S. Trubetskoy was asked to draft the paper, and when it was finished, it was again discussed by a group comprising several prominent participants in the congress. It can count, without doubt, as a true reflection of the atmosphere that prevailed at the congress. Trubetskoy and Shipov handed over the paper in person to the minister of the interior on November 28, 1904.[31]

Here we find the same view as was repeatedly expressed by speakers at the congress, but formulated more clearly and elegantly, in a way that was typical of Trubetskoy, this significant Russian thinker, namely the idea that reforms should be implemented from above. "The initiative for this great and sacred matter (the rationale for political liberty in Russia)," writes Trubetskoy, "should emanate from the supreme power, which alone can implement it peacefully."[32] Elsewhere Trubetskoy comments: "Never before has Russia needed a strong government enjoying real authority and an organized society[33] to such an extent as now. Only their joint action can implement these beneficial reforms peacefully and establish a stable order based on law."[34]

Trubetskoy expresses the conviction that all the best and healthy forces in the country would rally around the government if it decisively took the road of reform. On the other hand, a return to the policies of the 1880s would be disas-

trous. After all, this policy had led Russia to external pogroms and internal unrest. Life itself condemned this policy. "At this time," stresses Trubetskoy, "not
the love of freedom, but patriotism demands reforms."[35] Retaining the status quo
would only mean everything stagnating more and more. In his view, at this time
every single problem automatically took on a political significance and became
the object of political strife, which of necessity hindered the way it was dealt with
in practice. This was not just the consequence of irresponsible agitation, but necessarily arose because the general political question overshadowed everything.
The whole direction of Russian life confronted everyone with the agonizing question: "Law or lawlessness, the unfettered arbitrariness of the bureaucracy or a
properly organized representative assembly?"[36] No single problem, not even the
most urgent, namely the peasant question, could be resolved without an affirmation of political liberty. Any attempt to establish a stable law-based order in the
land was in fact doomed to failure, unless it also applied to the whole nation, and
this, in turn, was impossible without the extensive participation of representatives of the public in the legislative process.

Sadly, it is not known to what extent, if any, the minister made use of the paper in his report to the tsar.[37] In any case, Sviatopolk-Mirsky not only made clear
that he was sympathetic to the congress resolutions but also adopted the propositions put to him as the basis for his program of government. He had legislation
drawn up at the beginning of December that set out a program of liberal reforms
in line with the wishes of the *zemstvo* congress. This was to be followed up by a
series of individual, detailed laws. In the final article of this legislative draft, there
was even a provision for consulting elected representatives in the legislative process. This article, however, was not included in the *ukaz* of December 12, 1904,
when it was made public, whereupon Sviatopolk-Mirsky promptly handed in his
resignation.

The story of the progress of this draft law is not without interest, and a brief account is given here. There is no shortage of sources: Witte discusses it in his
memoirs; Shipov reports what he heard about the fate of the legislation from
Sviatopolk-Mirsky; finally, Maklakov, who probably discussed it with both Sviatopolk-
Mirsky and Witte, analyzes these events. As is well known, Article 9 of the draft
law, concerning the consultation of representatives of local self-government in
the legislative process, was removed by the tsar after consultations with Witte,
and in fact on his advice. At the time, Witte's position was not properly understood by anyone, neither by public opinion nor by Sviatopolk-Mirsky, although
Witte had discussed it with him on at least two occasions. There was a great deal
of public anger, and Sviatopolk-Mirsky was appalled and felt aggrieved. He felt
himself betrayed by Witte's advice to the tsar, as, in his opinion, he had been
assured of Witte's total support. Sviatopolk-Mirsky, however, had misjudged the
extent of Witte's support.

After Sviatopolk-Mirsky reported to Nicholas II on December 2, 1904, about the *zemstvo* congress and presented him with the propositions agreed to there, he asked the tsar to convene a meeting of the most senior state dignitaries and to chair the meeting himself.[38] At first, the tsar was skeptical, but then he came around, and the following day Sviatopolk-Mirsky arranged for the relevant personalities to be invited to the meeting.[39] As a result, that very evening Witte sought him out to have a chance of discussing it before the meeting. He said that if the state needed reform, it would be better to go directly over to constitutional government. In contrast to the Slavophiles and Shipov, he was, in fact, far from believing that a consultative assembly could provide an institutional framework in which the moral solidarity between tsar and people could be realized. On the contrary, he was convinced that such an assembly would inevitably have to embark on a hard struggle to extend its powers, to obtain real legislative power, in other words, to achieve the transition to constitutional government. The attempt to retain the unlimited nature of tsarist power, or absolutism, and at the same time create a consultative assembly was, in his eyes, an attempt to reconcile the irreconcilable, which could only mean legitimizing the struggle at the heart of the state. Witte saw a representative assembly whose powers were limited to consultation as misconceived. It would be unable to offer the advantages of constitutional government, while at the same time undermining the autocracy, that is, depriving it of its positive potential.[40]

As the draft law otherwise embodied the program of liberal absolutism that Witte had himself always advocated, he had no alternative but to support it, especially as it recommended the very solution to the peasant question that Witte himself envisaged. Thus, Witte promised the minister of the interior that he would not oppose the article concerning the consultative assembly, although he could not support it either. Sviatopolk-Mirsky, however, put too optimistic an interpretation on Witte's words; in other words, he understood the promise to remain silent as a promise to support his plans. He was appalled when Witte failed to do this.

Overall, Witte did not attach the same decisive importance to the question of the representative assembly as both the supporters and the opponents of constitutional government did. He did not share either Pobedonostsev's mystical fear of a constitution or the blind faith of its supporters. In particular, the idea that some special features of the Russian character could stand in the way of introducing constitutional government was quite foreign to him. In contrast to Shipov, the advocate of a consultative chamber and the enemy of a Western-style constitution, he expressed the following view in a discussion in 1902:

> The only ones who are against me (i.e., my assertion that the existence of local self-government makes the transition to constitutional government inevitable) are those who, like my friend Prince A. D. Obolensky, live in a theoretical fantasy world and believe that the Russian people are inspired by some special idea. I cannot agree with them. I think that all peoples,

English, French, Germans, Japanese, and even Russians, are equal. Why should what is good for one not be good for the others? Are things in countries with representative government so much worse?[41]

Nevertheless, Witte did not think that the transition to a constitutional government was the most urgent priority. He thought rather that the time was hardly ripe for it and was confident that oligarchic constitutions were also a possibility, although in Russia the time for that had passed. It was feasible for Mordvinov to consider this during Alexander I's reign, when serfdom remained in full force, but it became impossible in postemancipation Russia. One could thus only envisage a more or less democratic constitution or at least one that was based on democratic principles. In Witte's opinion, however, its time had not yet come. The switch to constitutional government ought not to be attempted as long as the peasantry, or the majority of the population, remained subject to special laws. Moreover, given the continued separation of the peasants under the estates system, the prerequisites for a constitution had to be lacking. Witte was convinced that concluding the emancipation of the peasants had to precede the creation of a representative assembly. If the autocracy, he said, finally fulfilled its historic mission, that is, achieved the task of liberating the peasants, Russia would spontaneously move over to constitutional government.[42]

It was all the easier for Witte to think that it was possible to delay the switch to constitutional government, as he did not share the feeling of opposition figures that nothing positive could be achieved in context of the absolute monarchy. His own experience contradicted these assertions from opposition groups. As one of the autocracy's ministers, he was able to achieve significant successes in the development of industry and the railways, as well as in the area of finance. Maklakov comments:

> Witte did not ask whether life was in line with particular principles, but judged the usefulness of principles on their practical results.[43] Thus, he valued the autocracy precisely because it was a system in which, in his view, it was easiest to achieve concrete results. His position on the autocracy was thus fundamentally different from that of liberal public opinion, as well as of its opponents. Most of the supporters of the autocracy regarded it as a bulwark against reforms and the embodiment of the ideological formula: Orthodoxy, Autocracy, and the People.

On the other hand, opposition groups rejected the autocracy as a barrier to reform and an entity that stood in the way of the demands of the ideology of liberty and democracy.[44] In contrast to these two groups, Witte was in favor of the autocracy, because in his opinion it gave the implementation of reforms a high degree of certainty. He was convinced that some useful reforms could only be carried out if backed up by the unlimited power of the absolute monarch, while on the other hand such reforms could not be implemented in the context of a demo-cratic system on account of their unpopularity.

Witte was also indifferent as to whether *samoderzhavie* was consistent or in-compatible with the specific demands of this or that ideology.

In his view, the value of any state system was, in general, only relative. He thought, for example, that Russia would certainly finish up with a constitutional system. He only presumed this, however, not because he believed that constitu-tional government was an absolute good but because he thought that Russia was following the same path as all other countries and that consequently the condi-tions for the survival of absolutism would soon have to disappear, to be replaced by the conditions for a change to constitutional government. Maklakov renders Witte's thinking in the following terms: "As wealth increases, society becomes accustomed to independent activity while the habit of subservience disappears. It begins not just to want power but also to acquire skill in exercising it. Thus, con-stitutional government is demanded by the whole way of life (*uklad*) of a people that have become used to freedom and social discipline."[45] From these comments alone, one can see that Witte perceived that the necessary conditions for a consti-tution would emerge from the development of a quite different momentum from that envisaged by those who spoke for opposition groups.

Public opinion above all saw local self-government, the *zemstvos,* as a precur-sor to the representative assembly, in other words, as a condition for the change to constitutional government.[46] Witte too recognized this, as we have seen, but with significant reservations. In contrast to public opinion, he regarded the fact that the *zemstvo* assemblies represented a kind of schooling in parliamentary ways as a wholly superficial condition for a constitution. Besides, in his view, this school-ing could only prove useful in specific circumstances. This skepticism regarding the significance of parliamentary methods in the context of the *zemstvos* did not just arise from a personal aversion to these methods,[47] but also from his convic-tion that allowing the exercise of popular sovereignty in homeopathic quantities could only be detrimental, as long as one was not determined to switch quickly to constitutional government.[48] Despite their undisputed practical usefulness, he considered the institutions of local self-government to be harmful in the context of the overall political system and the balance of political forces in the state. Their existence meant the incorporation of a foreign body in the fabric of the autocracy, that is, an institution based on a principle directly opposed to the principle of autocracy, on democracy. Local self-government is after all not based on liberal-ism—which gets along with autocracy, or at least in theory is able to get along with it, so long as it is just a question of personal civil liberty, and not political liberty—but on the principle of democracy. This stands in direct contradiction to autocracy and cannot in fact be reconciled with it, as autocracy of necessity results in friction and internal strife, as history has proved. This friction was all the more unavoidable as the *zemstvo* was not a voluntary body, but an obligatory one with powers of enforcement, having extensive powers and duties, such as are also held by state institutions. For this reason, Witte believed that the existence of local self-government institutions was only justifiable if it had been decided to move to a constitutional or democratic system, which alone was in a position to avoid a struggle that was harmful to the state.[49] However, as long as this was not the aim, one had to do without local self-government established on a democratic basis. This was quite feasible, as local needs, in Witte's view, could be met through other means than the help of democratically established *zemstvos*. Maklakov thought that Witte had in mind the extensive development of cooperatives, that is, purely private associations without the prerogative of official power.

Thus, according to Witte, the existence of local self-government did not primarily fulfill the conditions necessary for a change to constitutional government. Witte was convinced, rather, that the best preparation for constitutional government was the hard school of life, or the struggle for personal success, a school that the peasantry especially had not yet experienced sufficiently. Again, Maklakov gives us an account of Witte's view in the following terms: "It is necessary that Russian people and society get used to fighting for their own interests, to relying on their own resources and to stop imagining that someone else can take care of them. A constitution is impossible in the absence of such an outlook."[50]

In general, Witte did not believe that a constitutional regime was possible in a country where individual civil liberty had not yet sufficiently taken root and where the peasantry was still deprived of this liberty. He thought, as mentioned before, that it was time for reform to deal with the peasant question, rather than the constitution, and that it was achievable under the autocracy. Maklakov comments: "This explains why Witte could not understand that Russian society had now taken up the difficult struggle against the autocracy and why it did its utmost to accelerate its natural decline, instead of using it to achieve the conditions without which a constitution would not do any good."[51]

Insofar as Sviatopolk-Mirky's program contained what was most important in Witte's view[52]—measures to remove the peasantry's special legal status—he was prepared to accept a first step in the introduction of constitutional government, even if premature and moreover planned in a form that was, from his point of view, undesirable. In fact, Witte went beyond his promise to Sviatopolk-Mirsky. At the meeting, he did not just remain quiet during the discussion about convening a consultative chamber, but helped weaken the arguments ranged against the idea, without, however, directly defending Article 9 of the draft law. The work on the text of the draft law, which was the responsibility of the Committee of Ministers' chancellery, which in turn reported to Witte as chairman of the committee, followed exactly the program put forward by Sviatopolk-Mirsky and approved by the meeting chaired by the tsar. Yet on December 11, Nicholas II asked Witte to see him to discuss once more the latter's views on Article 9 and whether it was really necessary to include it in the decree, as the tsar still had his doubts even after listening to his advisers at the meeting.[53] Witte then thought it was his duty to give a frank account of his position. He told Nicholas II that "he was not against the proposal as such but did not expect that implementing it would achieve very much"[54] and added: "If your Imperial Majesty thinks a gradual transition to constitutional government is advantageous, then convening the representatives can be agreed to, as it is a significant step toward a constitution. If, however, your Imperial Majesty wishes to retain the autocracy, then convening the representatives would be undesirable."[55]

It was only natural therefore for the tsar to remove the article from the draft law, as it would create an institution whose existence could endanger the autocracy that many who were closest to him resolutely defended. They regarded it as a beneficial and even sacred concept, whereas not just the autocracy's ideologues but even a pragmatist like Witte did not expect a consultative chamber to produce any positive results.

The position that Witte articulated was, from his point of view, perfectly logical. The skepticism about a consultative assembly was probably also fundamentally justified. Yet Maklakov was certainly right in maintaining that Witte committed a huge political error in speaking out in this way to the tsar, as it must have made it more likely that the proposal would be rejected.[56] After all, what was important at the time was primarily finding common ground with the representatives of the loyal opposition and antirevolutionary liberalism. In 1902, this form of liberalism had not yet adopted the demand for a representative assembly as part of its program. Now, after two years of the Pleve regime, *zemstvo* representatives, even supporters of the autocracy and opponents of a constitution, thought that convening a representative assembly was unavoidable. If this point were not included in the government's program, its sincerity and the honesty of its determination to implement liberal reforms would have lost all credibility.[57] Insofar as Witte's opinion as expressed to the tsar led to the withdrawal of the project to convene elected representatives to take part in the legislative process, he must be identified as the one who undermined the basis for an understanding between the state and conservative *zemstvo* liberalism.

Petrunkevich writes in his memoirs that one should describe the *zemstvo* congress of November 1904 as the opening shot of the 1905 revolution. This is not justified in my opinion, as the congress came out against the idea of a constituent assembly and stressed firmly that reform initiatives should only come from the existing state. Possibly, however, the failure of attempts to reach an understanding between the state and the conservative liberalism that the congress represented can be seen as directly contributing to the development of the revolutionary situation. After the congress, after this experiment, as Maklakov says, "the role of the loyal *zemstvo* was finished."[58] Hopes for an understanding with the state were dealt a heavy blow and as such were shown to be a fanciful dream. The inevitable conclusion from all this was naturally to see the revolutionary point of view as politically realistic. Thus, the failure of Sviatopolk-Mirsky and the *zemstvo* liberals to reach an understanding in fact contributed to the escalation of the revolutionary mood in the country.

Witte would later suffer the consequences of his political error of judgment. When he was appointed chairman of the Council of Ministers on October 17, 1905, it became apparent to him that one of the most important conditions for a successful transition to constitutional government in Russia was an understanding between the government and moderate liberals from the *zemstvos*. Now, precisely because of the failure of the congress in November 1904, these very people had been overshadowed or pushed to one side by more active political radicals, so that they no longer represented public opinion. As a result, Witte was forced to negotiate with the more radical representatives of public opinion, who were less inclined to compromise, and this led to the failure of all his attempts to court public opinion and obtain its support.

Witte is an interesting example of a great statesman, who was also only a mediocre politician.[59] In defending measures he had planned, Witte was actually only capable of deploying matter-of-fact arguments. When engaged in an argument, Witte found it intolerable not to come straight to the point or to take account of the understanding, the character, and the ideological position of the person he was addressing. Witte managed to get on very well with Alexander III, as the latter was apparently to a high degree receptive to plain speaking. On the other hand, Witte was unable to have any influence on Nicholas II, while he was often inept with representatives of public opinion. Maklakov comments: "The unvarnished truth with which he was so often able to get his way with Alexander III was no use when it came to Nicholas II. One had to strike a different chord to get a response from the tsar. Witte was determined to try, and it was one of the great humiliations of his life. However, he did not possess the required deftness; he was not enough of a courtier."[60]

As far as society was concerned, Witte only really came to know its representatives in the negotiations that he held with them when he became chairman of the Council of Ministers. He found it just as difficult to understand the mentality of the representatives of public opinion as he did Nicholas II. However, he also did little to influence them, restricting himself to meeting individuals to convince them of his clinical arguments. As long as Witte was able to talk with one or another individual, this was often quite effective, but as soon as he met a group of several representatives of society to discuss matters together, they would reject his proposals in the name of public opinion. Maklakov relates:

> He later recounted that these negotiations did little to build his confidence in representatives of public opinion. He considered that those people, who essentially agreed with him, but who would not stand by him on the pretext of public opinion, lacked civic courage. That some who submitted to the views of society without reservation would not defend this position when

they met him made an even greater impression on him. "Who makes public opinion?" he asked, mystified. "I have never met anyone who in private thought right what he demanded of me in the name of society."[61]

This perhaps explains why Witte clung to the autocracy and could not summon up any enthusiasm for moving to constitutional government. It was certainly no easy task to convince the autocrat, or sometimes to change his mind, but it was no harder than trying to influence public opinion, which is what is required in a constitutional system when you want to carry your ideas but are not prepared simply to follow public opinion. This was not the case with Witte. In Maklakov's opinion: "Witte was a strong individual who made up his own mind and did not follow the decisions of the majority. He knew for himself what Russia needed and had self-belief. He was not enthusiastic about the sport of politics that develops in a constitutional system. He was not interested in either the impression he made on the public or the views of the press. He was interested in results. He loved getting things done, even if it brought little personal success."[62] It is therefore probable that Witte clung to the autocracy because he had no political vocation. Autocratic regimes are indeed much less "political" than constitutional ones.

Chapter 20

The *Zemstvo* Congresses

Legislative work to put into practice the principles
proclaimed in the *ukaz* of December 12, 1904, and
public reaction to it—Further *zemstvo* congresses:
the February and April congresses in 1905—The
split between the Shipov group and the majority—
The May 1905 "coalition congress"—The reception
of *zemstvo* deputies by the tsar at the Peterhof Palace
on June 6, 1905—Trubetskoy's speech

The *ukaz* of December 12, 1904, was based, as we have seen, on the liberal
program drawn up by the *zemstvo* congress. Through this *ukaz*, the Committee of Ministers was charged with preparing legislation to secure the freedom
of the press, free speech, and religious tolerance, as well as a guarantee of legality in administrative affairs. The powers of local self-government were also to be
extended, the recourse to emergency powers curtailed, and unnecessary restrictions on nonnationals abolished. In addition, the Committee of Ministers was
instructed to continue the work of the Special Advisory Committee on the needs
of the rural economy and to propose legislation for a liberal solution to the peasant question. The role of ministers, however, was limited to outlining the basic
principles of these laws. Special advisory boards, whose members and chairmen
were appointed by the tsar himself, were to be set up to do the detailed work on
individual issues.[1]

The special advisory committee set up to prepare the legislation to ensure
legality in administrative affairs was meant, in particular, to deal in depth with
the question of reform of the Senate as well as administrative law. In a relatively
short time, the committee, which included the most eminent lawyers in Russia,
such as Koni and Tagantsev, submitted some valuable material to the Committee
of Ministers. Yet until the Duma was convened, no legislation based on this work

was enacted. Nor did the Duma, to which the material was subsequently submitted, make very much use of it.[2]

The advisory committee (*soveshchnanie*) to revise the emergency-powers legislation proved less successful. Although some members of the bureaucracy who otherwise kept their distance from liberalism, such as P. N. Durnovo, supported the revision of these laws (in Durnovo's case, his experience as director of the Police Department led him to the view that these laws did more harm than good in Russia),[3] this committee produced no draft legislation before October 17, 1905. Later the material from this committee was handed over to the Ministry of the Interior and was probably used by Stolypin for his draft legislation on the same issue, which he submitted to the Duma.

Kobeko, a member of the State Council and director of the Public Library,[4] was appointed to chair the advisory committee on the press. The liberal Grand Duke Konstantin Konstantinovich, president of the Academy of Sciences, also participated in the work of this committee, to which the academy also made some material available. This committee drafted a law on the press that formed the basis for the press law passed in 1905, when Witte was chairman of the Council of Ministers.[5]

The question of religious toleration was initially handled by the Committee of Ministers itself, although the metropolitan of St. Petersburg, Anthony, and individual members of the State Council were also consulted. The committee prepared a decree on religious toleration that was ratified on April 17, 1905. This decree regulated the situation of non-Christians and non-Orthodox Christians, that is, members of other denominations and sects. Witte writes: "This decree is of the same genre as the Manifesto of October 17, 1905; that is, it constitutes an act that cannot be implemented at first, but that no one is able to quash. They (*both decrees*) are more or less engraved on the hearts and minds of the vast majority of the people making up Great Russia."[6]

As the decree, however, only set out general principles, the details remained to be worked out, and an advisory committee was set up for this purpose. It is interesting to note the approach taken by the metropolitan of St. Petersburg on this committee. He did not oppose granting freedom to non-Christian religious communities and to non-Orthodox Christians. He did stress, however, that it would be unfair to grant others a freedom that was denied to the Orthodox Church. At that point, Witte, who shared the metropolitan's views, argued in a report to Nicholas II that the principles that ought to govern the relations between the Orthodox Church and the state had to be clarified in the Committee of Ministers.[7] Implementing them would ensure that this church too enjoyed the required degree of freedom. The tsar approved Witte's report. Witte then wrote a comprehensive memorandum with one of his colleagues, whom unfortunately he does not name, which he then passed on to the members of the Committee of Ministers. In addition, the metropolitan provided a list, prepared by professors of the theological academy, of points to be dealt with by the Committee of Ministers. Pobedonostsev succeeded, however, in persuading the tsar to take the matter out of the hands of the Committee of Ministers and give it to the Holy Synod to deal with instead. Nevertheless, Pobedonostsev was unable to claim victory for his own views with this move. On the contrary, the Holy Synod adopted resolutions that were far more radical than any that could have been agreed by the Committee of Ministers. The members of the Holy Synod were unanimous in calling for an All-Russian Synod and for the restoration of the office of patriarch as necessary preconditions for the reform of church-state relations. This resolution was a bitter setback for Pobedonostsev, who was unable to persuade the tsar to reject it. The only thing he managed to do was stop the tsar from immediately ratifying the resolution. In the words of the resolution, "the question of the convocation of the synod will be considered at a later date."

In addition, following the decree of December 12, 1904, measures were introduced to promote the cultural life of national minorities.[8]

It is evident, therefore, that as chairman of the Committee of Ministers, Witte made every effort to accelerate the drafting of the legislation proposed in the decree of December 12, although these efforts were not always successful. He often encountered resistance from influential antiliberal members of the bureaucracy, who tried, not without success, to arouse in the tsar distrust of the planned reforms.[9] Due to this resistance, the results from implementing the program put forward in the *ukaz* of December 12 were relatively modest. Those who considered any concessions superfluous, indeed harmful, succeeded once again in obstructing the preparation of draft liberal legislation. Thus, they made it impossible to achieve any agreement with public opinion and in particular the representatives of the *zemstvos*.

It was, however, not just on the Right that such an understanding was considered undesirable and the thought of compromise rejected. The Liberation Movement became alarmed by the tenor of the November *zemstvo* congress. It regarded the attempt to come to an agreement with the state as abandoning the full realization of its own goals and, consequently, regarded those who were ready to compromise as traitors.[10] Its supporters refused to help the government. Just like later, after October 17, they were not at that moment prepared to support Witte in drafting legislation intended to implement the liberal principles of the December 12 *ukaz*. For example, one of the main contributors to the journal *Pravo* (Law), V. Nabokov, whose help Witte wanted to enlist, told him quite plainly that he was not prepared under any circumstances to assist the current regime in any way.[11] The Liberation Movement resolved to do everything to sabotage the understanding between the *zemstvo* representatives and the government. To this end, it organized a series of dinners at the beginning of 1905. This campaign, which came to be known as the "Banquet Campaign," was carried out in an organized fashion, and a special commission, called the "Culinary Commission," was put in charge. These banquets were by no means always serious affairs. Many took part just because a gathering with good food and witty speeches is always enticing; some came out of curiosity, others out of snobbery, as the banquets rapidly became fashionable. Those, however, who organized and directed the events, made speeches that were radical in content and strident in tone. They demanded the introduction of democracy, the convening of a constituent assembly, and more on these lines. This enabled the leaders of the Liberation Movement (made particularly easy, as participants at the November *zemstvo* congress also frequently made an appearance) to create the impression in government circles that the *zemstvo* congress was not an honest attempt at conciliation, but merely a tactical maneuver. It appeared as though the representatives of public opinion had tried to wrest concessions from the monarchy by means of a ruse, to sap its power and make the struggle against it easier, so that it could be toppled all the more rapidly and replaced by a republic.

The inability to distinguish between the conservative liberalism of the *zemstvo* congress and the political radicalism of the organizers of the banquets, an inability that the latter only welcomed, had the consequence that on December 12, besides the *ukaz,* the government issued a further declaration. According to Maklakov, this was far more damaging than removing Article 9 of the December 12 *ukaz.*[12] This government declaration condemned, together with the banquets and even street demonstrations, the *zemstvo* congress, on whose resolutions the government had just based its own program, as an attempt to cause unrest and divert Russia onto a path that was alien to the spirit of the people. Those responsible were threatened with reprisals. According to Maklakov: "It was clear that when the 'declaration' and the threat of reprisals that it contained became public knowledge, it came to be seen as a revelation of the government's true intentions and the *ukaz* regarded as yet another sham."[13]

In this way, trust on both sides was undermined even further. It confirmed Witte's warning to Sviatopolk-Mirsky, even before the authorization of the *zemstvo* congress, predicting that it would not lead to a genuine understanding between public opinion and the government. He cautioned that, on the contrary, failure to bring about this agreement could only widen the gulf between society and the state. The only problem was that Witte had not foreseen that his own position on convening a representative assembly was one of the principal causes of this negative outcome.

At the same time, the tide of revolution began to rise again. Teaching at the universities ceased, and the students went on strike. The working class was in ferment. The bloody confrontation of January 9, 1905, heightened tension among the workers even more. Peasant pogroms started to occur. On February 5, Grand Duke Sergei Alexandrovich fell victim to a terrorist attack. The revolutionary tide was greatly strengthened through a general feeling of insecurity and a lack of trust following ever more setbacks in the war against Japan. The fact that revolutionary voices increasingly drowned out the voices of the moderate opposition is particularly significant. In a revolutionary pamphlet one could read, "The *zemstvo* representatives' November Theses were pushed aside by the demands of the workers' petition of January 9,"[14] and Shipov too observed how the idea increasingly gained ground that overthrowing the regime was necessary before the people's just demands could be met.

The mood of opposition, on the other hand, spread further to the right of the political spectrum. There was an increasingly widespread conviction that things could not go on as they were.[15] More and more *zemstvo* assemblies addressed the tsar one after the other, pointing out the necessity of convening a representative assembly, despite the government's December 12 declaration stressing that it was illegal for *zemstvo* assemblies to discuss general political issues beyond their immediate areas of competence. Equally ineffectual was Nicholas II's response to the petition from the Chernigov *zemstvo* assembly that convening a representative assembly was essential: "I find the behavior of the chairman of the provincial *zemstvo* assembly impudent and tactless. *Zemstvo* assemblies have no business discussing the problems of government." The point was that no one held out much hope of drawing up a program that would be acceptable to the tsar. What was significant was that not only those who had always belonged to opposition circles, but also those who had until then not supported any opposition movement, not even the moderate opposition, for example, figures like Prince P. N. Trubetskoy, decided to adopt a position that they knew had been branded as impudent and tactless by the tsar.

Furthermore, the attitude of circles that had traditionally rejected liberalism became less intransigent. Typical in this regard was the January 1905 petition to the tsar from the Moscow Assembly of Nobles, in which the highest ranks of the bureaucracy and court society were particularly well represented. It highlighted that the difficulties of the war made the reforms seem untimely. This implicitly conceded the necessity of reform, even if, as always, the only conceivable basis for these reforms lay in the unity between the tsar and the country, while any idea of limiting the power of the autocracy remained off limits. "Everyone understood," writes Maklakov, "that this petition could not form the basis for an aggressive reactionary policy."[16] It is noteworthy that some representatives of the Right began to associate themselves with liberalism, because they perceived it as a new force with which to oppose the revolution.[17]

Further *zemstvo* congresses were convened in 1905. The second congress took place as early as February, only a few months after the November congress.[18] Delegates to this congress were even elected in the provincial *zemstvo* assemblies, although their election only had a slight effect on the composition of the congress. The initiative belonged with the participants of the November congress. It was not difficult for them to secure the election of their political allies. One important consequence of this election, however, was that the *zemstvo* congresses became more convinced that they were accepted as genuinely representative of the whole *zemstvo* system. This conviction allowed them to continue thinking of themselves as representing the *zemstvos*, even after the political climate in the provincial and district *zemstvos* began to diverge from the political position of the *zemstvo* congresses. In fact, leftist views increasingly began to get the upper hand at the *zemstvo* congresses, as we shall soon see. At the same time, *zemstvos* in the provinces began to move to the right, especially after the years of revolutionary excess.

According to Petrunkevich, the February congress was convened to discuss whether the December 12 *ukaz* could really be considered as the genuine starting point for the implementation of a liberal agenda. "None of us," writes Petrunkevich, "placed any hope in the December 12 *ukaz* or the reformist leanings and talents of the chairman of the Committee of Ministers, Witte."[19] It was decided to start immediately to again address the issues that arose in connection with the program adopted at the November congress, in other words, primarily the plans for convening a representative assembly. This task was given to the congress-organizing secretariat, which was supposed to present the results of its work at the next congress, planned for April. As it became clear that nearly all the members of the organizing secretariat shared the opinion held by the November congress majority, that they should begin drafting a constitution, Shipov, immediately seeing that no one listened to his views, decided not to participate in this work. With the help of his friends from the minority, he was able to articulate the wishes and opinions of this group. Among them were, for example, P. Trubetskoy, N. Khomiakov, and M. Stakhovich. Shipov published a pamphlet, coauthored with O. Gerasimov, that set out his group's position in twenty propositions.[20] In this way, the differences between the two wings became more and more accentuated.

That it came to a split at the third *zemstvo* congress (April 22–26, 1905) was not unexpected. This congress was altogether significant for the evolution of the views of *zemstvo* representatives.

If the majority at the November congress had still been quite conciliatory vis-à-vis the minority, they were now no longer inclined to compromise. The minority felt under pressure to withdraw from the congress. The formal pretext for the break was the old difference of opinion on the nature of the representative assembly. Shipov seems to have honestly believed that this difference was the real cause of the split and deals with it at length in his memoirs. Maklakov, however, is surely right in describing the differences over the nature of the representative assembly as just a pretext for the split at the third *zemstvo* congress and perceiving the true reason to be the fundamental divergence of both sides vis-à-vis the monarchy on the one hand and the revolutionary forces on the other:

> The difference of opinion, however, was not about any particular point of the program or tactics. It lay in the realm of ideology itself. . . . The minority of the *zemstvo* representatives kept to the traditions of the *zemstvo* and rejected any new regime not based on a compromise with the historical state. . . . On the other hand the congress majority expected nothing from the autocracy. It waged open warfare against it and was prepared to welcome any allies in this war. Whether the state would find its demands acceptable was a matter of indifference. It was ready, however, to make concessions in order to enable all the enemies of the autocracy to build a united front and was not deterred by the prospect of revolution. On the contrary, it regarded the revolution as a means to ensure the victory of "liberty and law" in Russia. The two camps were thus in an analogous position: the minority, by seeking an agreement with the state, had to make concessions to it, whereas the majority, which wanted to build a united front with the revolution, was forced to make concessions to the revolutionary forces. An abyss opened up between the two sides.[21]

Essentially the old argument about the nature of the representative assembly was nothing other than a difference about whether to accept the concessions held out by the government and to declare a readiness to cooperate with it or to reject the government's program and be compelled to continue the struggle against it.

The government had in fact enacted three laws simultaneously on February 18, 1905. If the *ukaz* of December 12, 1904, and the government declaration issued on the same day had been inconsistent, so were these three laws. On the one hand, the manifesto continued the line set out by the government declaration of December 12, stressing that the foundations of the Russian state, sanctified by the church and underpinned by law, were sacrosanct and sharply condemning any attacks on them. On the other hand, liberal measures were announced in the rescript to the new minister of the interior, Bulygin, as well as in the *ukaz* that accompanied it. The rescript announced, "It was the tsar's intention to call on the most worthy men, enjoying the confidence of the people and elected by them, to participate in the preparation and discussion of legislation." The *ukaz*, however, went further. The rescript only held out the prospect of including the most worthy representatives of the people in the legislative process. By contrast, the *ukaz* allowed anyone to express an opinion on issues concerning the reform of the state. The Council of Ministers was now charged with the duty of receiving and studying all the reform proposals submitted to it, from whatever quarter.

Maklakov is right in saying that the threatening tone of the manifesto was negated by the rescript, while on the other hand, the hopes possibly raised by the rescript were neutralized by the language of the manifesto.[22] Nevertheless, the rescript was greeted with enthusiasm. Even if there was only the slightest cause for optimism, liberals were prepared to cooperate with the state in implementing liberal reforms. At the time when the rescript was promulgated, the Moscow provincial *zemstvo* assembly was meeting. Immediately after the rescript reached Moscow, the participants at the meeting organized a private session to define what position the *zemstvo* assembly should take vis-à-vis the tsar's decision to convene a representative assembly. Shipov recalls: "*Zemstvo* representatives were prepared to forget the oppressive and offensive impression created by the government declaration of December 12, 1904. They were ready to accept in a spirit of satisfaction and complete trust the announcement of the reform that was to create the basis for the active unity between the state authorities and the people."[23] This mood was also reflected in a telegram sent by the *zemstvo* assembly to the tsar. The telegram stated that the Moscow *zemstvo* was filled with gratitude and joy.

The Moscow provincial *zemstvo* assembly's enthusiasm was not dampened by the fact that the rescript only called for a consultative chamber. The rescript also explicitly stated that a necessary condition for implementing the reform was the sacrosanct nature of the Fundamental Laws; in other words, the absolutist nature of the monarchy had to be preserved. It also made clear that the reform was not meant as a break "with the firm historical links with the past."[24] One should certainly not attribute the Moscow *zemstvo*'s position entirely to Shipov's personal influence. The tsar's decision to convene an assembly was certainly welcomed not merely by the Slavophiles, who because of their general ideology considered the consultative nature of the assembly to be fundamentally desirable. It was also hailed by those constitutionalists who, whatever the circumstances, preferred a step, however modest, toward constitutional government in Russia by legal means, over the revolutionary overthrow of the old regime.

A certain disappointment crept in a little later because representatives of the *zemstvos*, and public opinion in general, were not invited to take part in the work of the consultative committee, which was set up by order of the rescript to draft the legislation for the planned assembly.[25] In the view of *zemstvo* opinion (even the minority), this went against the spirit of the whole reform. This allowed the members of the Union of Liberation who were present at the third *zemstvo* congress to exploit this disappointment and create a negative mood. The majority was more than ever determined to stick to its position not to agree to the establishment of a mere consultative chamber and to refuse to support the government in implementing this project in any way. As mentioned above, this decision was based on the fundamental rejection of any idea of cooperating with the government. Thus the split between the majority and the minority at the congress, which seems only natural, finally occurred. It appeared that there was a limit to their cooperation, when their fundamental differences could no longer be ignored.[26]

After the split, the minority intended to carry on even more energetically its work of formulating proposals and views concerning the impending preparations for the law on democratic representation and to submit them as quickly as possible to the government. A meeting of *zemstvo* representatives who supported the minority position was called for May 22, 1905. As these representatives gathered in Moscow, the news arrived of the destruction of the Russian fleet by the Japanese in the Tsushima Strait. The *zemstvo* congress-organizing secretariat, that is, the *zemstvo* majority, decided to convene a general *zemstvo* congress on May 24 because of this heavy setback for the fatherland. This congress is known as the "Coalition Congress." Maklakov relates: "How the situation had changed! Hitherto, there had just been *zemstvo* congresses. As in all bodies, you could have a majority and a minority, a right wing and a left wing. Yet here was the same Russian *zemstvo* as had unanimously demanded democratic representation in November 1904. After the April split, the two sides were so far apart that their joint discussions were already being described as a 'coalition.'"[27]

Maklakov also bears witness to the fact that neither side attended the congress with any enthusiasm and only came because neither dared to stay away at such a tragic moment; that is, they needed to demonstrate their patriotic unity.[28] At the congress, both sides stressed the need to avoid contentious issues. "If we start debating our internal political differences," said Petrunkevich, "there will immediately be a split. Therefore, it is better not to begin at all." The representatives of the Right echoed these views. Thus, the following issues were carefully avoided: constitutional government or a consultative chamber, universal suffrage or a property-based franchise, a constituent assembly or a constitution by proclamation. There were nevertheless some long, passionate debates. Whatever subject was touched upon, they kept coming up against the fundamental issue that no one addressed openly, but that was bound up in everything. Here at the fourth congress, just as at the third, this question overshadowed everything else, namely: "Whether the *zemstvo* representatives still wanted to cooperate with the historical state; whether they still held reforms from above as desirable; or whether they had become so disillusioned with the regime that they had resigned themselves to the revolution and wished that the regime would yield to it."[29]

The *zemstvo* "Coalition Congress" decided to turn to the tsar. Shipov writes that he was convinced at the time that the majority at the fourth congress wanted to address the state authorities just to demand an immediate change of regime in line with the principles adopted by the majority at the November congress, that is, demand a change to constitutional government. They were not interested, however, in reaching an agreement with the regime to enhance the prestige of the Russian state at this tragic moment. Shipov and his supporters, concerned at the majority's position, tried their utmost to prevent the majority from addressing the tsar in the form of an ultimatum or demonstration. They succeeded at first, after "heated debate,"[30] in staving off the proposal that the whole body of the congress (two hundred delegates) should go to St. Petersburg and demand that the tsar should receive them all together: "We decisively rejected the possibility of addressing the supreme authority in such an inadmissible way and endeavored to show that such a step could only severely damage public life and have a harmful effect on the situation of the country."[31]

After rejecting the proposal to take themselves en masse to the tsar, the *zem-*

stvo representatives decided instead to send a deputation to the palace to submit a petition. The text of this petition was drafted in such a harsh tone by the majority that the minority felt unable to support it. The minority insisted on the petition being extensively revised, the deputation limited to five or six, or anyone being included against whom the tsar could be biased in any way. This time the minority was only partially successful. Although the draft version of the petition was amended at some points, even after these changes, its aggressive tone was preserved. It was also decided that the deputation should consist of twelve members. Eleven members of the delegation were chosen from the majority, while Shipov was the only one from the minority. Furthermore, the deputation included Petrunkevich and Rodichev, two public figures who were particularly and personally unsympathetic to the tsar. Because of all this, Shipov felt he had to give up his elected place on the deputation.[32]

Nevertheless, the minority's resistance proved more effective than Shipov thought, which, incidentally, is not surprising, as the old *zemstvo* traditions lingered and continued to be influential even among those who belonged to the majority. Despite its harsh tone, the petition did not contain any ultimate demands and included references to cooperation between the state and local self-government; in other words, it was an example of traditional *zemstvo* ideology, which the minority at the congress advocated and which retained its influence on the thinking of members of the majority.[33] Although the deputation only consisted of members of the majority group, it did not act as if presenting an ultimatum, nor did it contemplate a demonstration. The deputation elected S. Trubetskoy, one of the foremost liberals in Russia, as its spokesman. Perhaps, however, the deputation's attitude, insofar as it was reflected in Trubetskoy's speech, was also influenced, at least in part, by the profound difference between the atmosphere at the congress and the reception in the imperial palace. In addition, this difference was certainly not felt just by the deputation at the reception itself, but already at the moment when it became certain that the reception really would take place.

A description of the tsar's reception of the *zemstvo* deputation at the Peterhof Palace on June 6, 1905, can be found in Petrunkevich's memoirs. Although this description is not lacking in interest, even as regards the formal setting, it lies outside the scope of this study. Of particular interest here are Trubetskoy's speech and the tsar's reply.[34] Trubetskoy began by pointing out that the deputation was motivated by a sense of duty and was conscious of a great collective danger. It was only because of this sense of duty and this awareness that they turned to the tsar in this manner. In reality, he continued, the danger was great. Some parts of the population were being stirred up against others, the common people against the "masters," Russians against non-Russians, and this was happening under the cover of patriotism. (This is no doubt an allusion to anti-Jewish pogroms.) In his view, such agitation and revolutionary excesses were not dangerous under normal circumstances. The most dangerous aspect of these disturbances, he said, which had spread through the entire country, was the general level of disruption, against which the state was powerless to act. The tsar himself had indicated the only possible way out of this chaotic situation, namely, convening representatives of the people, and the deputation was firmly of the view that this was the right step. They were also convinced, he continued, that not every representative assembly would be able to solve the problems it faced. "We do not consider ourselves empowered," he stated, "to express an opinion as to the definitive form of either the representative assembly or the electoral system." It is important, however, to stress, he went on, that the representative assembly had to bring about peace in the country and implement "reform of the state." That is why the representative assembly should not be based on the social estates. It was also important to find a proper place for the bureaucracy, which naturally plays and must play a role in every state. "It must not be allowed to usurp," he stressed, "the rights of the tsar as sovereign ruler, and it must be made accountable." Finally, Turbetskoy pointed out that it was imperative not to delay in allowing open discussion of all these issues in the various assemblies and the press.

The tsar's response was short but friendly. First, Nicholas II stressed that he did not entertain any doubt that the deputation was motivated by patriotic feelings: "Cast aside all doubt that I remain fully determined as tsar to convene a representative assembly. I am following the progress of this matter every day. Let the unity between the tsar and the whole of Russia be reborn, just as in the old times. I hope you will assist me in this task."

Petrunkevich was not at all satisfied by the tsar's reply. To start with, he maintained that the tsar had learned his speech by heart beforehand, which seems unlikely, as it was a reply to Trubetskoy's speech, which he certainly could not have known in advance. In addition, he accused the tsar of sidestepping everything that needed "clarity and certainty" and not explaining what role he foresaw for the representative assembly.[35] Petrunkevich's comments are in fact the epitome of partisan criticism. As we have just seen, Trubetskoy had also said that he thought it impossible to say anything definitive about the shape of the representative assembly. How could this have been expected of the tsar at a time when the planned conference to deal with the question had not even started work? In addition, the tsar was soon going to receive other deputations, and it was known that they certainly represented views that differed from those of the *zemstvo* congress deputation.[36]

By contrast, Petrunkevich speaks of Trubetskoy's speech with great enthusiasm. Trubetskoy had read his speech to the other members of the deputation on the evening before the reception. "It was approved," writes Petrunkevich, "and, with its power and the subtlety of its tone, it met everyone's expectations."[37] It is important to register this, as it means that this speech was not just an expression of Trubetskoy's personal opinions and convictions, but reflected the views of all the members of the deputation. It also shows that even the deputation's most radical members, such as Petrunkevich, approved of its moderate ideas and conciliatory tone.

On the other hand, the Liberation Movement reacted quite differently to this speech. An open letter to the editorial board of *Liberation,* signed by "an old *zemstvo* man" (*staryi zemets*), reads as follows: "A huge abyss lies between the feelings underlying the Moscow petition and the oratorical tricks that litter Trubetskoy's speech at Peterhof."[38] In the opinion of the open letter's author, the tone of the entire speech was one of "flattery." He accuses the speech of "violating the truth." The author cannot hide his disappointment, as he had expected an ultimatum, even if in a most deferential tone. In his view, the speech was nothing less than a collection of empty "Byzantine" phrases. The letter writer is particularly indignant that Trubetskoy had distanced himself in his speech from the forces of revolution, from the *kramola.*[39] At the same time, the letter continues, he should have been aware that things had only reached the point where the *zemstvo* deputation had been received at all by the tsar because of the struggle of the revolutionaries. The editorial board of *Liberation* too stressed that they were unable to declare their solidarity with Trubetskoy's speech, even though they thought some of the open letter's assertions were exaggerated.

Chapter 21

Further *Zemstvo* Congresses and the Aggravation of the Revolutionary Situation

The *zemstvo* congress of July 6–8, 1905—
Differences between Trubetskoy and Petrunkevich
—The conference of the radical group of
zemstvo representatives on July 9–10, 1905—The
government project for a consultative chamber, the
so-called Bulygin Duma—The August 6 laws—The
fundamental laws drafted by Liberation and *zemstvo*
representatives—The further escalation of the
revolutionary situation and the *ukaz* of
February 18, 1905—The revolutionary situation
leads to the constitution

The *zemstvo* deputation decided to present a report on the Peterhof reception of June 6 to the congress, and for this reason the next congress was arranged for July 6.[1] If hopes had been rekindled at the reception that agreement could be reached between the state and society as represented by the *zemstvo* circles, this was quite clearly shown to be an illusion only four weeks later, at the July 6 congress.

The Ministry of the Interior resolved to ban this congress and, to prevent it, sent a police inspector on its opening day to Prince Dolgorukov's house, where the participants had gathered. It was quite incomprehensible that a congress whose deputation had been received by the tsar should be treated in this way. It was also contrary to the February 18 *ukaz*, which had permitted meetings to be held to discuss issues to do with the forthcoming reform of the state. Apparently, however, the Ministry of the Interior had attached credence to some absurd rumors that the *zemstvo* congress intended to turn itself into a constituent assembly and set up a revolutionary provisional government.[2] This attempt to prevent the congress from meeting failed, as the police officers dispatched there were very hesitant when faced with men who only a few weeks before had leave to speak to the tsar in person; they restricted their activities to taking notes. The congress could thus proceed unhindered. Thus, the police did just enough to make the situation of those congress participants who were prepared to compromise difficult in the extreme.

The majority at the congress, however, were not interested in reconciliation with the state or in cooperating with it to implement reforms. This is unequivocally confirmed both by reports that were published in *Liberation* immediately after the congress and by Petrunkevich's memoirs, which he wrote many years later, as an émigré in Prague. This uncompromising attitude was not so much reflected in the decision to approve the draft constitution published a short time before by a group of constitutionalists, mainly *zemstvo* representatives, and to contrast it with the government's draft,[3] nor even in the fact that some toyed with the idea of boycotting the consultative chamber (the Bulygin Duma). This intransigence was mainly reflected in the decision to make an appeal to the people, as well as the resolution that was intended to call for passive resistance from the *zemstvo* institutions in particular but also the people in general. The congress delegates were themselves aware of this. A "Letter from a Congress Delegate" appearing in *Liberation* reads: "What characterized the whole congress was the recognition that it was impossible to obtain satisfactory reform from above without the moral pressure of the broad mass of the people. That we are now turning to these masses and that we are no longer placing our hopes on the state or our own strength, but on the masses, marks a significant change in the history of the Russian opposition's development."[4] This correspondent was of the opinion that, compared to earlier congresses, the mood of opposition had not just hardened, but could even be described as revolutionary. This mood, however, was not shared by all.

A minority found this revolutionary sentiment completely alien, did not wish to abandon the previous approach, and was sharply critical of the resolution calling for an appeal to the people. Even among those who declared their agreement in principle with an appeal to the people, there were many for whom Petrunkevich's plan was not feasible because of the harshness of its tone and its radicalism. After stormy debates, which lasted until two in the morning, two lawyers, Muromtsev and Nabokov, were asked to work on a new version of the proposal. They were able to complete the task by half past four that morning. They were, however, not the only ones who stayed up. Petrunkevich and Trubetskoy spent the whole night debating the resolution for an appeal to the people. Trubetskoy used all his powers of argument and authority to convince Petrunkevich of the harm the resolution could cause and to persuade him to withdraw his proposal in the next session, but in vain. Only many years later did Petrunkevich, wiser through bitter experience, concede in his memoirs that his erstwhile adversary had been right: "I have to admit that I was in favor of this step (the appeal to the people) and argued late into the night with Trubetskoy, who tried to explain to me how risky such an initiative was, not least because it was impossible to foresee its eventual consequences with any certainty. In the end he was proved right; the Moscow uprising in December 1905 proved it."[5]

At the time, however, he did not back down. What separated the two friends that night was the dividing line that runs between liberalism and radicalism. The radicalism as personified by Petrunkevich won the day, and not just at the *zemstvo* congress in July 1905. The first Russian State Duma, which met in 1906, was no liberal assembly but a radical one, which ultimately probably sealed its fate. The fact that Trubetskoy died just a few weeks after that night,[6] while Petrunkevich triumphantly made the opening speech in the first Russian parliament, can be seen to epitomize, as it were, the entire situation at the time.

Muromtsev and Nabokov significantly cut the text proposed by Petrunkevich. They moderated its tone and twice highlighted (once by way of a conclusion) that the *zemstvo* congress had no aims other than peaceful renewal in Russia and the calm introduction of reforms. Liberals could, indeed had to, agree with the main two criticisms leveled at the government in the appeal. It states, "The government does not permit people to act in their own interests, as is the case in other civilized countries." Further, "The peasants, although no longer bound as serfs, still do not have the same rights as other citizens."[7] There were several points in the appeal, however, that would have taken on a quite different meaning in the mind of the uneducated reader from that intended by the authors. The people were called on to unite in strength to fight for "life and property and, indeed, to defend the right to free assembly without fearing that someone would prevent it." How else could this last sentence be understood by the broad masses, to whom the appeal was addressed, other than as a direct incitement to fight the police, if they attempted to break up meetings? This sentence is unequivocal, especially in light of another resolution that was adopted (not without the fierce opposition of a considerable number of delegates). It was pointed out in this resolution that the struggle for natural rights sometimes justified violating formal law.[8] In particular, in the first draft of the resolution, local self-government bodies were recommended to resist all the bureaucracy's measures that were unjust, as well those that were unlawful.[9]

What the appeal said about the elections to the future representative assembly is also interesting. It pointed out rather demagogically that if the elections were not organized on the basis of universal suffrage, but more or less like the elections to local self-government bodies, the peasants would not be adequately represented in the Duma, and the "powerful" would have the upper hand.[10] The congress resolution clarifies this part of the appeal as well. The idea that universal suffrage must in all circumstances form the only basis for a genuine democratic assembly had become so firmly entrenched in Russian public opinion, even in *zemstvo* circles, that the congress thought it necessary to stress the following in the resolution: "Given the current form of local self-government, the people cannot view it as truly representing their interests."[11] In so doing, however, the congress put in doubt the powers of its own delegates. These words revealed an insecurity regarding its own position, which had to have extremely serious political consequences. With these words, it was tacitly admitted that the true representatives of the people were not the legally elected local self-government institutions, but the revolutionary left-wing groups. This was how forming a united front with these groups was justified.

Petrunkevich, in fact, stressed at the congress that such a step was essential. *Liberation's* correspondent wrote: "Petrunkevich made a speech that was meant as an introduction to the 'appeal to the people.' He asserted that Russia was in the grip of a revolutionary movement and suggested that the *zemstvo* should take its appointed place in this movement."[12] In practice, this meant that the *zemstvo* should join the Soyuz-Soyuzov (Union of Unions: a federation of professional associations). The few extreme right-wing delegates, who showed up at the *zemstvo* congress for the first and last time, understood Petrunkevich's speech as a direct call to revolution and walked out. In his memoirs, Petrunkevich reflects on his speech and his erstwhile position in general. Petrunkevich underscores that joining the Union of Unions (which he labeled "Group A"), as well as creating the Union of Unions itself, was influenced by the determination "to unify the efforts of all opposition elements and impose the Union of Union's discipline on the impatient."[13] Consequently, the *zemstvo* group was to ally itself with the revolutionary groups to exercise a moderating influence. It seems that Petrunkevich at the time sincerely believed in this aim. In his congress speech he said, "We can bring sense and enlightenment to the movement of the masses."[14] Although therefore the *zemstvo* delegates' decision to join the Union of Unions was at least in part really influenced by such considerations, virtually nothing came of Petrunkevich's plan to exercise a moderating influence on the revolutionary movement, despite his election as president of the Union of Unions. In his memoirs, he himself readily concedes that the *zemstvo* group among the organizations affiliated with the Union of Unions was powerless in the face of the rapidly growing revolutionary mood in society.[15]

The inability of the *zemstvo* representatives to have a moderating influence on their left-wing allies can be explained by the fact that they themselves were not critical enough of the revolution. At the time, revolution was surely preferable to the old regime even for Petrunkevich, one of the most moderate of the radicals. He must certainly have had only a very vague idea of the dangers of revolution. In this respect, the following comment made by *Liberation's* correspondent is very characteristic: "During the debates, some delegates were shocked by the use of some expressions such as 'acting in a revolutionary manner.' They confused the word 'revolution' with the concept of violence and terror."[16] The phenomenon of the French revolution had not produced an understanding of revolution in terms of its reality in the political consciousness of Russian opposition circles during the nineteenth century, in fact since the time of the Decembrists. The myth of the French revolution completely dominated this consciousness, which explains why most Russian intellectuals could only conceive of revolution as something beautiful, powerful, and salutary. In general, therefore, people were enthusiastic about the revolution. Maklakov, for example, writes about Mandelstamm, one of the most radical members of the Kadet Party, "Mandlestamm found intolerable the idea that the revolution could or had to be combated. He might doubt its inevitable victory . . . , but never that the revolution was just."[17] This outlook, as we have said, was nothing new at the beginning of the twentieth century. Maklakov relates that in the 1880s and 1890s the Moscow-based lawyer Dobrokhotov was firmly convinced that Chernyshevsky was the greatest genius in the history of mankind and Robespierre the greatest statesman.[18] Dobrokhotov was certainly not the only member of his generation to hold this view. This myth of the revolution—the French revolution—was what really made it possible to build a united front, even if only a temporary one, from Petrunkevich to Lenin.

Nevertheless, there were still sufficient numbers of delegates at the congress who spoke out resolutely against an alignment with the revolutionary movement and even opposed the toned-down version of the appeal to the people.[19] All the delegates from Kazan province took this line, as did Lizogub, the chairman of the Poltava provincial *zemstvo* executive committee, as well as Stakhovich. Lizogub firmly rejected adopting the extremists' tactics and stressed, "June 6 (the tsar's reception of the *zemstvo* deputation) was only a short time ago; there is still hope."[20] It is evident that these hopes, about which he speaks here, were hopes for unity between the state and society, in other words, the traditional hopes of the world of the *zemstvo*. Stakhovich voiced the fear that by taking this step, the congress would break with the very *zemstvo* institutions it was supposed to be representing. "It is essential, however," he continued, "that the congress should always speak in the name of these institutions. After all, that is its strength."[21] Of course, these critical voices went unheeded. The radical element triumphed, and its representatives simply ignored this criticism. The congress, however, did not actually decide that the *zemstvo* should affiliate with the Union of Unions. It merely adopted a resolution recommending that the *zemstvo* congress-organizing secretariat reach agreements with other organizations or opposition groups. Each of these agreements would be confirmed retrospectively by the next congress. It is interesting that the minority even resisted this resolution energetically. It proposed substituting "make contact" for "reach agreement" in the resolution.

On July 9–10, a conference of the radical and democratic group of *zemstvo* delegates took place directly after the end of the *zemstvo* congress. Of the 220 participants at the main congress, more than half, 120 in fact, took part in this conference. The conferences held by radical *zemstvo* delegates are called *zemstvo* constitutional conferences, no doubt because at the first *zemstvo* congress, just as in the beginning in general, the differences between the radical group and the conservatives were mainly reflected in the arguments about the question of moving to a constitutional system of government. Previously, *zemstvo* constitutional conferences had preceded the general congress. The aim of these conferences was to draft the resolutions that they wanted adopted by the main congress and work out the methods of influencing the congress.[22] The July 9–10 zemstvo constitutional conference, however, took place after the main congress. According to *Liberation,* this change was possible because the general congress in April had definitively adopted the constitutional position and no longer took account of the minority view from the November congress. This allowed the zemstvo constitutional conference, on the one hand, to focus on working out in further detail the program of the constitutional—or radical—group of the general congress and, on the other, to attempt to establish links between the zemstvo congresses and other opposition forces. The constitutional zemstvo conference thus decided to be represented in the Union of Unions. The radical wing was in no doubt it could act and negotiate in the name of the whole zemstvo movement, as it had a majority in the general zemstvo congress. Accordingly, it unhesitatingly regarded its delegation to the Union of Unions as representing all zemstvos. In doing so, however, the majority went beyond the resolution passed at the general congress, which was the only basis on which it could or indeed had to act. This resolution, in fact, only authorized the secretariat and not the majority, and then only to reach agreement with other organizations, not to join them.

It is typical of the situation at the time that the zemstvo constitutional conference thought it necessary to distance itself from the deputation to the tsar and S. Trubetskoy's speech, as these had made an unfavorable impression on "elements to the left of the zemstvo."[23] Here, the problem for the zemstvo constitutional conference consisted of the fact that most of the members of the deputation were also participants at this conference and thus had to denounce their own actions. Apparently, however, they did so without hesitation. At any rate, they did not attempt to defend themselves, but merely referred to mitigating circumstances. In order to excuse their erstwhile position, they first pointed out that they had to use the opportunity to persuade conservative elements to cooperate with the opposition. In addition, they stressed that one final attempt to turn to the supreme power had to be undertaken to avoid the charge that they had not exhausted every possibility of painlessly bringing about necessary reform in Russia. Finally, they pointed out that they had acted as representatives of the "coalition congress" and thus could not express their own views, but had merely represented what were taken to be the views of the coalition as a whole. Accordingly, the conference adopted a resolution that highlighted that "sending the deputation did not result in any political commitment for the group and that the group takes no responsibility for any words or actions of the deputation."[24]

It is not hard to imagine the impression such zemstvo resolutions and the reports about the atmosphere at zemstvo congresses made on the tsar and government circles. They must inevitably have concluded that the appearance of the zemstvo deputation at the Peterhof Palace had only been a tactical maneuver and that zemstvo circles secretly had no intention of coming to an agreement with state authorities and wanted a revolution. As a result, demands for a representative assembly could only be a trap. It seemed as if *zemstvo* society did not see a representative assembly as a bridge between the tsar and the people. It would create a new situation that would enable the opposition, and indeed even the revolutionary forces, to continue their struggle against the state and the existing order under more favorable conditions. These misgivings, which the attitude of *zemstvo* circles undoubtedly aroused, could easily have put a stop to the preparations for the law to set up a consultative chamber. If this did not happen, it was thanks to the efforts of liberal-minded members in the bureaucracy who actively supported the Bulygin project.[25] This was despite their position being significantly weakened by the fact that they were unable to invoke either the authority of the *zemstvo* or the ideas of its representatives. Maklakov recalls: "In light of what was said at the *zemstvo* congresses, the views of the *zemstvo* representatives could only help the opponents of reform. The *zemstvo* representatives were dangerous allies for the liberal bureaucracy."[26]

It is not certain, incidentally, whether the radical leadership at the *zemstvo* congresses could still be at all described as allies of the liberal bureaucracy. This leadership did not miss any opportunity to distance itself from the liberal bureaucracy. An article appearing in *Liberation* is interesting as an expression of this attitude, in that it was devoted to the "comments by the Minister of the Interior on implementing the directives announced in the rescript of February 18, 1905, by His Imperial Majesty":

> This document is of great interest. It gives us a direct insight into the creative thinking of the bureaucracy. . . . The official who wrote this memorandum had apparently done all in his power to find as generous a solution as possible—within the framework of the rescript and without violating the "Fundamental Laws"—to this difficult problem (of convening a democratic assembly without abolishing the institution of the absolute monarchy).
> . . . This is the same role as was played by the members of the (1860) editing commissions regarding the rescript to Nazimov, in that they tried to prepare the legal basis for a generous solution to the peasant question through a broader interpretation of the same rescript. Those poor liberal bureaucrats and their ungrateful contemporaries! What considerable efforts the former would make to find the common ground on which the monarch and public opinion could meet, although this common ground cannot exist; to pose the constitutional question within the framework of the existing "Fundamental Laws" is to seek to square the circle.[27]

The 1860s were long gone, and the chasm between society and the state apparatus had become virtually unbridgeable. The one person who, without himself belonging to the bureaucracy, helped the liberals in its ranks with their work was the historian Kliuchevsky; he was, however, just as distant from public opinion as he was from the bureaucracy.[28] Although he was a layperson, one can perhaps best describe him as a representative of the church.

The government's plan to create a consultative chamber was an attempt to bridge this gulf more or less in the form envisaged by the Slavophile minority at the *zemstvo* congress of November 1904 and based on the ideas held by this minority. In the August 6, 1905, Manifesto, which was published as a preamble to the Duma statute and the electoral law published on the same day, it states, "The unity and harmony between the tsar and people represent the great moral force with which Russia was created over the centuries." The manifesto points out that the tsar had long been preoccupied with the problem of how to heal the rift between local self-government and the government, which had such a baleful effect on the whole of the state. The manifesto stresses that it was time to call on representatives from the whole country "to actively and continuously participate in the preparation of legislation" and to create a special consultative institution— the State Duma—to work on draft legislation and the state budget.

Despite the resistance of antiliberal elements around the tsar, liberals in the bureaucracy, who were involved in drafting the Duma statute and the electoral law, nevertheless succeeded in having the electoral law based not on social estates, but on the liberal concept of a property qualification (Arts. 12 and 16 of the electoral law of August 6, 1905). The manifesto accordingly described the Duma not as representing the estates, but as representing the country, although the representation of the peasantry was still fundamentally that of an estate (Article 17). According to the laws of August 6, the Duma would be the lower chamber, and the plenary sessions of the State Council took on the function of the upper house. The Duma was given the right to question ministers (Arts. 35 and 58–61 of the Duma Statute), as well as the right to propose legislation (Arts. 34 and 54–57 of the Duma Statute). As far as legislative proposals submitted by ministers to the Duma were concerned, draft legislation could not pass into law, even when ratified by the tsar, if they had been rejected by a two-thirds majority in both the Duma and the State Council. Such legislative drafts had to be referred back to the minister who had proposed it for revision (Art. 49). Although this article in the Duma Statute represents a modest limitation of the tsar's absolute power to legislate, it was unequivocal. This was not lost on the participants at the meeting convened, as stated above, to discuss the draft law. Most of those who expressed support for retaining this article endeavored to demonstrate that Article 49 did not break new ground and followed the State Council's well-established practice. Only Trepov, with his characteristic frankness, said, "The provision regarding referring back rejected draft legislation to ministers without doubt means a restraint on the autocracy; nevertheless a restraint that stems from Your Imperial Highness, which is useful."[29]

If proof were needed, this shows how certain institutions have a particular legal character of their own. Therefore, the establishment of a representative assembly, even with only consultative powers, must necessarily not remain without influence on the unrestricted nature of tsarist power, despite the intentions of the legislator. After all, Article 49 was certainly a departure from the consistent application of the principle according to which the representative assembly should be restricted solely to a consultative function. The essence of a representative assembly restricted to advising the government and reviewing draft laws rests on the idea that the opinion or will of the members of the assembly, regardless whether of the majority or minority, only becomes its will through being ratified by the tsar. It is then recognized as right and the source of law. This corresponds roughly to Rousseau's theory, which is in fact based on the fiction that a view, just because a majority votes for it in an institution, is *la volonté générale,* in other words, that it reflects a will that is recognized as a source of law. That this is a fiction, just like the Slavophile theory, had already been understood by Cicero.[30]

The laws of August 6, 1905, were never applied in practice. Based on them, it had been planned to convene the Duma in January 1906. The move to a constitutional system, however, was announced on October 17, 1905. The State Duma was then convened after a new electoral law, a new statute for the State Duma, and finally new Fundamental Laws were passed on April 3, 1906. The laws of August 6, 1905, are only significant insofar as they made moving to a constitutional system easier for the tsar. Two issues were resolved in a positive way through these laws: creating a representative assembly as a permanent institution and giving this assembly the right to reject draft laws and thus prevent them passing into law. This represented the first modest restriction on absolutism in the field of legislation. After these two fundamental principles of constitutional government had been accepted, it must have seemed much easier to move to constitutional government.

Public opinion was not at all satisfied by the announcement in the August 6 laws that a Duma with consultative functions was to be convened. Possibly only Shipov and his small group of supporters could have been sympathetic to such a project, but they had virtually no influence. They no longer had much of a hearing. Large swathes of public opinion were only interested as to whether to boycott this Duma or exploit it as a new tool to fight the autocracy. The resolution that Kokoshkin put to the September *zemstvo* congress in the name of the *zemstvo* congress-organizing secretariat, and that was adopted in the session of September 12, 1905, stressed that the Duma to be convened on the basis of the August 6 laws could not be seen as a genuine democratic assembly. The value of the Duma consisted in its serving as a staging post for the movement, whose aims were political freedom and a normal democratic assembly.[31] *Liberation* was even clearer: the creation of a consultative Duma, according to the journal, was just a charade. Yet the August 6 law was hugely significant—the creation of the Duma in fact handed the public "a new and extraordinarily valuable battle position."[32]

If anyone spoke out in support of the law of August 6, 1905, it was foreign observers. Maklakov relates that William Stead, who happened to be visiting Moscow at the time, gave a lecture in which he sought to defend the Bulygin Duma against the criticisms of Russian public opinion and to demonstrate that a genuine democratic assembly could gradually evolve from the Bulygin Duma; that it was ultimately an important step to a genuine constitution.[33] It is interesting that among Russian public figures, Miliukov expressed a particularly positive view of the Bulygin Duma. This was quite unexpected, given his general position. It can be explained by the fact that he learned about the meeting chaired by the tsar from his university teacher Kliuchevsky, who attended it. In this way, he gained a better understanding of the views of liberals in the bureaucracy than did the representatives of public opinion in general. Perhaps Kliuchevsky's position also influenced him to a certain degree.[34]

Those who represented public opinion, in other words, the radical majority at the *zemstvo* congresses, did not stop at rejecting the Bulygin assembly. They decided to propose their own version of a genuine constitution in opposition to the government's projects. As early as October 1904, that is, before the first *zemstvo* congress, *Liberation* published the draft of a constitution with the title "The Basic Law of the Russian Empire." The preface to this draft states that "it is the result of long and careful consideration on the part of a group of practitioners and theoreticians."[35] Maklakov noted: "Its content did not bear the mark of any practitioners. The draft resembled the "normal articles of association" of a limited company. As positive law, it would not have survived more than a few months before the regime was overthrown."

We do not know if the *zemstvo* representatives were aware of how weak this draft was, but in any case, they decided to draw up their own version independently. This "Fundamental Law of the Russian Empire" was published before the July *zemstvo* congress in the newspaper *Russkie Vedomosti*,[36] which, as already mentioned, fundamentally supported it. The congress elected a committee that was given the task of further refining the provisions of the draft. Maklakov writes about this draft:

> Without going into details, the draft showed no trace of the practical experience of the *zemstvo* representatives. For example, differences between both chambers even in relation to the budget were supposed to be resolved in a joint session of both chambers by a two-thirds majority. This procedure would have resulted in complete deadlock, as a two-thirds majority could not have been achieved. Among the basic principles of the draft . . . were universal, direct, equal, and secret suffrage and parliamentary democracy. It was generally recognized that "restrictions on the autocracy" were necessary, but transforming the existing unlimited state power into an ornament

and putting government in the hands of a parliament elected by millions of illiterates was not a proposal that any *zemstvo* experience could have justified. . . . Mutatis mutandis, it (the draft) anticipated the Bolsheviks' presumption to catch up and overtake Europe within five years.[37]

Incidentally, it was not just Russian conservative liberals who thought it was reckless to go straight from autocracy to universal suffrage, but also overseas observers, whom one could not possibly accuse of conservatism. When Maklakov visited Clemenceau and discussed the political situation in Russia, he told him that the Kadet Party was resolute in advocating the introduction of universal suffrage, at which Clemenceau shook his head and said in a tone giving away his answer, "What, already?"[38] It is also interesting to note what the delegates at the congress said to justify voting for the draft. For example, de Roberti, in the session on July 7, declared, "The draft is admirable as a whole and can absolutely bear expert scrutiny."[39] Maklakov comments:

> This sort of praise was typical. Only what sort of expert scrutiny did de Roberti have in mind? It is accepted in jurisprudence that states must correspond to the cultural level of their population. That means it is accepted that all constitutions and institutions only have a relative value. Political science might find that progress leads to democracy, that a sound democracy is more stable than an authoritarian regime. It also knows that this only applies in conditions where a country and people are ready for such a democracy. . . . To say that the *zemstvo* draft constitution was good because it was based on political science means either saying something completely meaningless or asserting that Russia's cultural level and its political experience justified choosing the most complex form of constitutional government. De Roberti certainly did not say that. He simply did not think about it. . . . That intellectuals, who took their convictions from books, approached the issue in such a way was excusable, but that *zemstvo* circles thought like that after forty years of *zemstvo* activity and experience was a tragedy.[40]

This was especially tragic as it was precisely from these circles that the members of the prospective representative assembly were supposed to be drawn.[41] It is interesting that both draft constitutions used the term "fundamental laws" and not "constitution." This has to be mentioned here in light of the incomprehensible stubbornness of representatives of these circles in insisting that the law of April 23, 1906, should be called a "constitution," not "fundamental laws," as if it were the name and not the content that gave constitutional laws their genuine constitutional character. Furthermore, it is noteworthy that Miliukov in his negotiations with Witte did not recommend adopting either of these drafts, but gave him some advice that he himself considered practical in order to save time. This was simply to have the Belgian or Bulgarian constitution translated and introduced as the constitution of the Russian Empire. This seems to show that even those who took part in preparing these drafts did not attach much practical value to them.

———————

I have thought it necessary to give a detailed account of both the general *zemstvo* congress and the *zemstvo* constitutional conference in July 1905. Although the elite at these conferences, where it represented the *zemstvos*, did not directly capitulate before the revolution, they did take an uncertain, even ambiguous position vis-à-vis the revolution. As a result, *zemstvo* circles had to abandon their traditional political line; they were simply no longer able to defend and maintain it. In fact, within the Union of Unions, the *zemstvo* group really became the moderate wing of the revolutionary front. The *zemstvo* congresses,[42] however, also lost their identity and turned into meetings of different intellectual circles united around a program of political radicalism. The provincial *zemstvos* were not the only ones to notice this, gradually voicing their opposition to the congresses' assertion that they genuinely represented the *zemstvos*, but it was also highlighted by those who welcomed this development. According to Petrunkevich:

> The inevitable result of the whole situation was that all those who were dissatisfied with the current regime joined the *zemstvo* congresses, where the aims and methods of the struggle were clarified. . . . Not just *zemstvo* members but also others from different professions had access to the congresses. Thus, *zemstvo* congresses actually became an active center for opposition opinion, which had initially appeared fragmented through the various unions and intellectual associations organized by the Liberation Movement.[43]

The fact that two professors, Kovalevsky and Miliukov, were co-opted onto the *zemstvo* congress-organizing secretariat at the *zemstvo* congress in September 1905 is characteristic of this development. When Miliukov joined it, its transformation into a political committee for Russian radicalism was complete.[44]

At this point, it should be pointed out that the unions organized by the Liberation Movement hardly undertook any practical union activity. From the very outset they were not set up to look after the professional interests or defend the rights of their members, but rather to act as cells for the political struggle to bring about a revolutionary situation.[45] This applied to an even greater degree to their federation—the Union of Unions.[46] Belokonsky relates that the Liberation Movement, by striving to establish the Union of Unions, intended that the alliance of all left-wing groups would join it and that its central representative body would take on the role of a preparliament.[47]

In addition, not just organizations but one-off meetings were to be organized and used as a means of revolutionizing Russia. As mentioned above, a series of meetings at the end of 1904 were used to make it harder for *zemstvo* circles and the monarchy to come to an understanding (at the time one could believe that this was still possible).[48] For this very reason, these meetings were to adopt hardline radical resolutions that would discredit public opinion, even of the moderate sort, in the eyes of government circles.[49] The mood of the participants, turning increasingly intolerant and extreme, drove them to it anyway. The tide of revolution carried on rising.

It is therefore all the more incomprehensible that on February 18, 1905, in addition to the antiliberal manifesto, according to which all was to remain as it was, and the liberal rescript to the minister of the interior, Bulygin, promising that a representative assembly would be convened, the government advised the tsar to issue a further decree. This granted a wide-ranging freedom of assembly—the very meetings in which the problems of political reform in Russia were to be discussed. "Whoever advised the tsar," writes Maklakov, "to issue this *ukaz* must have been either very cunning or very naïve."[50] Not the rescript promising a consultative chamber, but rather this *ukaz,* clearly showed that something had changed and that the autocracy had lost its self-confidence.

Contrary to all that had been heard up to then from the authorities, the discussion and elaboration of reform projects in Russia were no longer described as attempts to create unrest, but as praiseworthy efforts (*radenie*) to further the general good.[51] According to the *ukaz,* ministers were no longer allowed to pass such projects on to the public prosecutor's office; instead the Council of Ministers now had the duty to study and analyze them.[52] It was particularly dangerous that on the one hand the wording of this *ukaz* allowed one to conclude that all earlier laws limiting the freedom of assembly and speech no longer applied. On the other hand, no further laws were passed to regulate how meetings were held. Such laws are indispensable even in democracies with deep-rooted traditions of freedom. Maklakov is right to underscore that this *ukaz* brought all previous notions of what was or was not permitted into confusion. He continues, "The supreme authority laid a mine that would blow up the order that up to then it had defended so stubbornly."[53] Although this *ukaz* was soon annulled, on August 6, 1905—no doubt the trouble it might provoke had been realized—its formal repeal did not have much effect. The annulment of this *ukaz* was simply ignored in the increasingly widespread revolutionary atmosphere of the time.

Naturally, the socialist parties and the Liberation Movement immediately grasped the opportunity afforded by this *ukaz;* associations were set up and meetings organized. These meetings, however, even the ones organized by the Liberation Movement, were not at all concerned with the question of reforming the existing regime, but exclusively with how to overthrow this regime and thus secure the victory of the revolution. Certainly, those elements who took part were not going to be satisfied with a constitution proclaimed by the monarchy. It is hardly surprising, therefore, that even on October 18, 1905, that is, on the very next day after the manifesto that brought about the change to a constitutional government was promulgated, the revolutionary tenor of the speeches in these meetings did not change at all. Maklakov attended one such meeting at the music *conservatoire* on the evening of October 18, as an observer. Money was being collected in the foyer under a placard with the slogan, "For the armed uprising." In the hall, someone was giving a lecture on "the advantages of a Mauser over a Browning," a subject that evidently had little to do with constitutional reform.[54]

During the course of the second half of 1905, liberalism hardly obtained a hearing. The more independent minded kept to themselves; those less so trailed along in the wake of radicalism, which in the end turned itself into the right wing of the revolutionary front, and were carried along by the revolutionary tide. It was only later in the following year that liberals attempted to regroup and organize themselves.

It thus happened that the promise to proclaim a constitution was a climbdown in the face of pressure from the forces of revolution and not a concession to the liberals. It is known that the Manifesto of October 17, 1905, was enacted because of the situation created by the mid-October general strike. Nevertheless, Maklakov surmises that the tsar gave way convinced that he was making a concession to the moderate and thus level-headed elements in the country, elements on whose support his grandfather Alexander II had relied against the forces of reaction when implementing liberal reforms.[55]

In any case, it is certain that the tsar's advisers took the view that convening a representative assembly would satisfy moderate elements in the opposition and thus isolate the revolutionary forces. This was Witte's position. That this perception was shared by Sviatopolk-Mirsky is confirmed by Kryzhanovsky in his memoirs.[56]

Those elements who were striving for a constitution, and one proclaimed from above at that, were disorganized, scattered, and lacking in influence. Although their numbers grew as the revolution progressed, as acts of terrorism and signs of anarchy multiplied (they found increasing support among the peaceful and apolitical masses), they certainly remained in the background. This means that the constitution was indeed promised under pressure from those forces that were not interested in it (even though the word often passed their lips) and could not be satisfied by it in any way. Maklakov writes:

> The revolution had a quite different program. At the top of the agenda, as a minimum demand, stood the overthrow of the monarchy—of monarchy per se, and not just absolutism—and the proclamation of full democracy. The end goal was the construction of socialism. . . . The revolutionary parties regarded European liberalism as a retrograde phenomenon. They believed that it was possible to construct a new social order in Russia that was unprecedented in Europe. In one respect, they were not wrong. Nowhere else did demagoguery meet less resistance than in our backward country.[57]

The revolutionaries merely considered the concession of the constitution as a sign of weakness on the part of the state and thus a concession that encouraged them to continue the struggle. In this way, proclaiming a constitution could neither satisfy public opinion nor form the basis for cooperation between it and the state insofar as the former had allied itself with the revolutionary parties. This was the great tragedy at the birth of constitutional government in Russia.

Chapter 22

The Manifesto of October 17, 1905, and the Constitution of April 23, 1906

History of the October Manifesto and the
Constitution—A legal analysis of the Constitution

The most detailed and accurate account of the history of the Manifesto of October 17, 1905, which proclaimed the change to a constitutional system of government, is provided in his memoirs by Witte, the man who masterminded it.

Witte returned to Russia from America on September 16, 1905, after reaching a peace agreement with Japan. He was especially concerned that revolutionary unrest was turning into full-scale revolution, and he recognized that the situation was deteriorating not just by the day, but literally by the hour. This raised the question of how to react. Witte recalls: "From the first days in October 1905, events themselves demanded a response to this question, and from October 6 on, for ten days, pressure from all sides led to that great and significant act, the Manifesto of October 17."[1]

Overcoming the revolution was the first priority. When Witte was received by Nicholas II on October 9, he told the tsar that he thought there were two possible choices. Either someone could be appointed with full dictatorial powers and asked to repress the revolution by violent means, or concessions could be made—in other words, the tsar could proclaim that Russia was to be transformed into a constitutional state.[2]

Witte submitted a memorandum or report to the tsar, which was published in its final version at the same time as the manifesto. We can see from the report that if far-reaching liberal reforms were announced, Witte was relying on the support of public opinion both when it came to implementing these reforms and in the struggle against the revolution. Witte set out the most important measures that were required to create a stable legal order in Russia—that is, to transform Russia into a state with a liberal constitution. Among them, he mentioned "resistance to the excesses that are manifestly a threat to society and the state," stressing that the organization of this resistance had to "be carried out with the support of the sensible majority in society." Further, he stated, "one has to have faith in the political wisdom of the Russian people. It is unthinkable that Russian society wants anarchy."[3] In fact, there is no reason to doubt that at the time, Witte really did believe in the political sense of Russian public opinion.

As we know, Nicholas II chose the path of liberal reforms rather than dictatorship and proclaimed them in the October Manifesto.[4] This manifesto contains three points: (1) it promised to grant freedoms (of speech, assembly, etc); (2) it announced that elections to the State Duma would be democratic; and (3) it declared that the State Duma would have all the characteristics of a legislative institution.[5] It was precisely through this last point that the principle of the separation of powers and thereby the change to a constitutional system of government were proclaimed.

The state authorities, in particular Witte himself (who was appointed chairman of the Council of Ministers on October 19), were thus faced with two main tasks whose successful completion could only be guaranteed by moving to a constitutional regime. First, they had to come to an agreement with the moderate elements in society, and second, they had to flesh out the constitution (to be known as the Fundamental Laws), which the tsar was now obliged to proclaim.

Although negotiations with leading public figures were held before the constitution was proclaimed and the decision arrived at to proclaim the constitution, I think it advisable first to outline the history and content of the constitution, in part at least because of the disappointments experienced during the negotiations. The negative attitude of representatives of public opinion is particularly reflected in their rejection of the constitution proclaimed on April 23 and, indeed, of any proclamation in principle. It is therefore important initially to understand what they rejected.

To begin with, during the first two months of the Witte government, neither Witte himself nor other members of the Council of Ministers had thought it necessary to pass new constitutional laws.[6] Yet it soon became clear that the old Fundamental Laws and the October Manifesto could not simply coexist and that it was necessary to pass a new constitution. Trepov, the palace commandant, was probably the first to grasp that new fundamental laws were needed and pointed this out to the tsar.[7] As soon as that became clear, the question arose whether to draft the new Fundamental Laws with the Duma or to enact the new constitution

before the Duma was convened. This was of course a basic question of considerable significance both in principle and in practice. Witte recounts:

> In fact, I understood that this question amounted to asking whether to
> preserve or overthrow the new system of government. In the former case,
> one had to enact the Fundamental Laws in line with the October Manifesto
> before the Duma was convened, in the latter case to refrain from doing so.
> In this case—and I was quite clear about it—the Duma would have turned
> itself into a constituent assembly, and one would have had to use armed
> force against it, bringing the new regime to an end.[8]

The significance that Witte attached to the publication of the Fundamental
Laws can be seen from a telephone call he made to Trepov after his resignation
(on April 22, 1906). He asked Trepov to convey to the tsar his own, personal opinion as an ordinary citizen: that the Fundamental Laws should be published immediately, because the Duma would convene in a few days' time (on April 27).
Witte stressed: "If in the days before the opening of the Duma, the Fundamental
Laws are not published, and the Duma starts work without being subject to this
legal framework, this can cause a great deal of harm."[9]

It is noteworthy that even when looking back, Witte remained convinced of
this. He concludes the chapter on the constitution in his memoirs with the question of whether, after so many years, he was still of the same opinion:

> Of course, with more time, the Fundamental Laws could have been drawn
> up more thoroughly. Nevertheless, even now I am still convinced that it
> was thanks to my firm insistence that these Fundamental Laws be enacted,
> especially the latest version, that we were not forced to dissolve the Duma
> and withdraw the October Manifesto. According to these laws, the tsar
> retained extensive powers over the exercise of state sovereignty. Since they
> introduced a constitution, albeit a conservative one without full parliamen-
> tary democracy, there was hope that the system of government inaugurated
> on October 17 would become established in the end and that there would
> be no going back to the old regime. Was that a good thing? I believe it was,
> because now in Russia the elements, and above all the psychological condi-
> tions, no longer exist that alone would make unfettered autocracy possible.[10]

After this preliminary issue had been clarified, Nicholas II charged State
Secretary Baron Uexküll with the task of preparing a draft of the Fundamental
Laws.[11] Uexküll's draft was submitted for examination to a special commission,
chaired by Count Sol'sky. Sol'sky approached Witte, asking him to join the commission. Witte, however, resolutely refused because he thought the draft should
go before the Council of Ministers and not the special commission. Accordingly,
the tsar ordered the draft to be put to the Council of Ministers after it had been examined by the special commission. Count Sol'sky had given Witte the first draft

at the end of February, after which it was hurriedly reviewed in relatively few sessions of the Council of Ministers and amended in some places. On March 20, Witte was able to present the tsar with the draft constitution as agreed to by the Council of Ministers. In April, Nicholas II set up a special advisory commission, which he personally chaired, to examine the draft.[12] The advisory commission took the place of the State Council, to which the draft Fundamental Laws would have normally been submitted.

Proceeding to the content of the new Fundamental Laws: Chapter 8 contains provisions on the rights and duties of Russian citizens, although only two of them deal with their duties. Article 70 stipulates compulsory military service for men,[13] and Article 71 the universal duty to pay taxes. Other articles deal with the rights of the citizen and in general correspond to the articles in the *Déclaration des droits. de l'homme et du citoyen* of 1789.

Articles 72–74 lays down guarantees accorded to individuals under arrest or facing prosecution. Article 74 stresses, in particular, that penal law could not be applied retrospectively. Article 75 guarantees the inviolability of the home, and Article 77 the inviolability of private property. This same article states that expropriation was only permissible where it was necessary for the state and then only with adequate compensation.[14] Article 76 recognizes the citizen's right to choose their place of residence freely in Russia and also lifts restrictions on foreign travel.[15] It further grants the right to choose one's employment freely. Subsequent articles (78–80) deal with freedom of speech and the press, the right to organize meetings, and the right to set up associations and societies. Article 81 recognizes freedom of conscience for all citizens.

Chapter 8 of the constitution thus sets out the basics of civil liberty in sufficient clarity and detail. It should not be forgotten, though, that the real effect of these principles depends primarily on laws regulating how these constitutional freedoms are exercised in individual cases and moreover, surely no less so, on the relevant administrative practice. One should certainly not assume that during the brief period when constitutional government existed in Russia, legislation and administrative practice could be completely brought in line with constitutional principle. Nevertheless, even before the First Duma was convened, at a time, therefore, when Witte was chair of the Council of Ministers, three decrees were issued that can be called true successes for liberal ideas, especially when compared with the previous situation, but also generally. These were the decree of November 24, 1905, on the press (P.S.Z. no. 26962); the decree of March 4, 1906, on associations and societies (P.S.Z. no. 27479); and the decree of that same date on the right of assembly (P.S.Z. no. 27480).[16] They were issued as provisional regulations, and it was indicated that definitive legislation was to be left to the representative assembly. The Duma, however, was in no hurry to legislate in this respect. "The Duma has already existed for seven years," Witte writes, looking back, "but no new law has been passed to date—not on the press, nor on associations and societies, nor on assemblies."[17]

The question as to what extent the constitution granted political rights to the citizen has two aspects. First, was the citizen's right to vote genuine, and were too many people excluded from exercising this right? Second, was the elected representative assembly's freedom of expression sufficiently safeguarded, and had the assembly been granted sufficient powers in the area of legislation and scrutiny of the executive?

Suffrage was not universal, yet no section of the population was wholly excluded from the election. The electoral law of December 11, 1905 (P.S.Z. no. 27029), secured the representation of the peasantry and the working class. In the towns, anyone who had rented a dwelling in his own name within the town's boundaries for a whole year was eligible to vote. Thus, electoral rights in the towns virtually approached universal suffrage. (This only applied to men, as women did not have the right to vote.)

Much more important, of course, is the question as to whether the voting rights granted in the electoral law to Russian citizens were genuine. From what we know of communist and fascist dictatorships, which give citizens a formal vote (or impose a duty to vote) but do not allow a genuinely free election, the fundamental significance of this question cannot escape anyone. The answer is quite simple. It can be stated with complete confidence that the voting rights conferred on the tsar's Russian citizens by the constitution enacted on April 23, 1906, amounted to a genuine franchise. The old regime never made concessions willingly, but once it made up its mind to do so (though there may have been conditions attached), it never stooped to the type of sham that socialist dictatorships produce with such "ingenuity." Political parties could now be established legally, and parties that were not authorized—even those like the Social Democrats that were the most hostile to the government at the time—could still put forward their candidates, as these did not necessarily have to be nominated by a party.[18] Each eligible voter could then personally decide to vote (or in the case of an indirect ballot, could vote through an intermediary elector [*vyborshchik*] chosen by him in a free vote) for the candidate of the party of his choice. He was thus able to vote freely and not simply cast a vote, as is the case in one-party states. The ballot was secret, and the election was genuinely free. In the elections to the First Duma, members of the government and the local administration had a completely neutral attitude, more passive than is otherwise the case in Western democracies. Government departments tried to influence the elections to the Second Duma, but without any apparent success.[19]

There is equally no doubt that the members of both chambers, the State Council and the Duma, enjoyed complete freedom of expression. Incidents when deputies misused this freedom, without, however, incurring any negative consequences, are all too well known.

We thus turn to the last and most important question, namely that of the powers of the assembly, especially in the field of legislation. According to the Constitution of April 23, 1906, no government legislative proposal could pass into law without being accepted by the Duma and the State Council. The power of the Russian emperor was thus no longer unlimited. He could no longer issue decrees alone, without the agreement of the representative assembly. This meant the end of absolutism in Russia and the establishment of constitutional government.

It is certainly true that a legislative proposal passed in both chambers could not become law without the tsar's assent. But it would be a mistake to interpret the tsar's right of veto as a sign of the survival of absolutism or at least as a left-over from it. On the contrary, it was a necessary element in a dualistic, that is, not parliamentary, constitution. One can hold the view that a parliamentary constitution is preferable under any circumstance, but one cannot maintain, at least not without abandoning academic objectivity, that a dualistic constitution is a form of absolutism in disguise—a pseudo-constitution. The claims that the April 23 Constitution was a pseudo-constitution have no basis in political theory and are merely an expression of certain political views. It is precisely for this reason that I shall deal with them not in the analysis of the constitution itself, but in the account of relations between the state and society.

In theory, the tsar's veto right was unlimited. However, according to Article 112 of the constitution, the Duma could revisit a draft law even if the tsar had withheld his assent.[20] This gave the representative assembly considerable power, in most cases, to make the tsar back down, and the tsar's advisers were well aware of this. Saburov, for example, stressed in the advisory commission that to avoid creating a dangerous situation, the tsar should absolutely refrain from objecting to resolutions from both chambers. "What situation will your Majesty be in," he said, "if the Duma for a second time passes with a strong majority something you have rejected?"[21] In effect, it would have been very damaging for the monarch's prestige if, during a second reading of a draft law rejected by the tsar, it was shown how useful and sensible it was, and the reasons for its rejection were criticized. The head of state's will can only be decisive in an autocracy or a dictatorship, that is, in regimes that allow no criticism unless it is "self-criticism." If, however, the freedom to criticize—genuine criticism—is guaranteed,[22] it is extremely dangerous, if not impossible in most cases, for the head of state simply to defy it.

Both chambers had the power to turn into law legislative proposals laid before them by the government by voting for them. They could also reject the proposals or work on and amend them, a process that had no limits imposed on it. In addition, both the Duma and the State Council had the power to initiate legislation (Art. 107 of the Fundamental Laws), although this was restricted when it was a question of amending the Fundamental Laws themselves. It was laid down that these could only be amended on the initiative of the emperor. This did not mean that the emperor could change them unilaterally. Changes to the constitution proposed by the government, like all laws, had to be agreed to by both chambers. This limitation only meant, therefore, that the assembly was not allowed to propose such amendments by virtue of its right to initiate legislation. In the advisory commission for reviewing the draft constitution, Witte, in particular, had insisted that the constitution could only be amended on the emperor's initiative. In this case, he used the same arguments as those he had deployed in favor of the need to proclaim the constitution before the Duma was convened. He stressed that if "one allowed the Duma to amend these laws, it would immediately turn itself into a constituent assembly."[23]

There was one further provision that is often interpreted as a restriction on the assembly's power of legislative initiative. Article 57 of the Duma Statute stipulated that the government, if it agreed with one of the Duma's legislative proposals, had to take over the passage of the draft law. This, of course, gave the government the chance to declare its agreement with the Duma and then drag its heels. Apparently, however, nothing like that occurred. Maklakov writes, "Article 57 caused us so little trouble that we did not attempt to amend it on the Duma's initiative, although we were completely within our rights to do so."[24] In fact, the Duma Statute was not part of the Fundamental Laws and could therefore be amended on the initiative of the Duma.

According to the constitution, there were also special areas where the Duma's legislative power was curtailed and the tsar was the sole legislator. Articles 21 and 125, Articles 65 and 68, and Articles 96 and 97, respectively, gave him exclusive power to pass legislation concerning the imperial family, church affairs, and the armed forces. As laws on the imperial family were integral to the constitution itself, this exclusive legislative power was therefore further protected in this specific area of the Fundamental Laws.

There was no opposition to the exclusion of the assembly from legislating on church affairs. "Everyone would have been astonished," writes Maklakov, "if the Duma, like the English parliament, had been given a book of prayer to consider."[25] But the Duma did perceive exclusion of military legislation from its authority as a significant restriction of its powers.

The topic of military legislation is certainly not only interesting but also very important. I think, however, that it cannot be dealt with in more detail here, in the context of a history of liberalism. I wish to add that I share Maklakov's view that the Constitution of April 23 dealt with this issue correctly. At the time, this solution alone was in the interests of the army and the nation and consequently of the constitution itself. A different solution would have run counter to all the feelings and traditions of the army.[26] Military legislation therefore had to be excluded from the Duma's powers, if only to avoid unnecessary conflict with the army. This was made easier as the assembly was not deprived of all influence on military legislation and the affairs of the army in general. It could in fact block any increase in military expenditure during the budget debates and monitor how the resources earmarked for the military in the budget were used. Thus, Article 96 of the Fundamental Laws laid down that the tsar's legislative power was limited exclusively to military affairs and that any military laws enacted by him could not be extended to apply to matters that were regulated by general legislation. The article further stipulated that no expenditure could be incurred in connection with the implementation of measures required by these laws that had not been foreseen in the budget passed by the assembly.[27]

It immediately became apparent that the provision that the tsar was to remain the sole legislator in certain specific areas was contrary to the October Manifesto and the Duma Statute of February 20, 1906. As mentioned above, the manifesto had quite simply declared that, in future, no law could be passed without the agreement of the representative assembly. It allowed for no exceptions, and this was confirmed in the Duma Statute. Opposition circles were not alone in noting that the draft constitution diverged on this point from the October Manifesto. This was one of the first issues raised in the special advisory commission. The head of the State Council Department for Legislation, Frisch, was the first to oppose allowing such special areas to exist after the publication of the October Manifesto.[28] Others who shared this view were Golubev, the head of the State Council Department for Civil and Clerical Affairs; Saburov, a member of the State Council; and the chief procurator of the Holy Synod.

The issues regarding legislation on the imperial family were discussed first. This apparently made it easier in the end to accept the theoretical possibility of such special areas. The interior minister, Durnovo, focused on the article concerning marriage between a member of the imperial family and a person not of the Orthodox faith. According to Durnovo, in a situation where this article had to be amended, and given that the principle laid down in the October Manifesto allowed no exceptions, the respective draft would have to be submitted to the Duma, thus permitting the Duma's intrusion into the private affairs of the imperial family. In Durnovo's view, this was intolerable, as it conflicted with the status of the imperial family in Russia.[29] Moreover, State Secretary Uexküll pointed out that in some constitutional states, the affairs of the ruling family were excluded from the representative assembly's sphere of competence. Thus, it was decided that in matters concerning the imperial family, the tsar alone should have legislative powers.

Golubev put forward an interesting suggestion whose aim was to distinguish between the regulations for the organization of the imperial household and the law regulating the position of members of the imperial family in respect of their property rights and civil law in general.[30] In his view, the emperor should have the right of initiative only in respect of amendments to laws regulating the civil-law situation of members of the imperial family. The scrutiny of such measures should fall within the representative assembly's sphere of competence. Saburov's comment is particularly noteworthy: "The limits and nature of the emperor's property rights have to be defined. It is unacceptable that the emperor himself should act as judge in his own civil affairs."[31] If a seventeenth-century tsar had heard anything of the sort, he would have had absolutely no idea what it meant. Golubev's and Saburov's comments are further proof of the profound impact of the principles of civil society on the ruling elite's outlook. The general validity of the provisions of civil law, which a civil society in essence demands, had become a matter of course. It was no longer possible within this system to justify, on legal grounds, granting a special status to the imperial household, indeed even to the emperor himself.

By acknowledging that it was possible in principle to give the emperor exclusive legislative power over the imperial household, although this was not in line with the October Manifesto, the conditions were created for also extending this exception to church and military legislation. Witte stressed furthermore that *la raison d'État* [an overriding national interest] took precedence over what the law logically stipulated and that, notwithstanding the manifesto and other laws that established constitutional rule, the emperor's legislative and executive powers had to be broad enough and embedded in the constitution to avoid "future instability in the entire state."[32]

In addition, a provision was borrowed from the Austrian constitution to the effect that, in exceptional circumstances, the government could issue legally enforceable decrees on the tsar's authorization when the Duma was not in session. No later than two months after the start of the next session, the responsible minister had a duty to submit to the assembly a draft law corresponding to the decree. If he failed to do this, or if the assembly rejected the draft law, the decree issued during the assembly's recess became void. All this was in the renowned Article 87 of the Fundamental Laws, which also specifically stipulated that the constitution, the State Council, the Duma Statutes, and the electoral law could not be amended by such decrees. The need for this sort of provision is obvious, especially in Russia, where a quick recall for extraordinary sessions was made more difficult on account of the empire's sheer size. Rather than accusing the government of introducing such a measure at all (and radicals frequently made this criticism), it would have made more sense to accuse it of too often using, or even misusing, the powers laid down in Article 87 of the constitution.

The discussion regarding this issue in the advisory commission is noteworthy. Witte pointed out that in the event of extraordinary circumstances, the monarch had to be given powers to declare a state of emergency or state of war in specific regions of the empire, but also to issue decrees dealing with any other severe threat to the state. Such decrees, however, were only meant to remain in force for the duration of the emergency.[33] Saburov opposed Witte's suggestion. "Of course," he said, "governments must be given powers to deal with emergencies, but the limits of these powers must be defined," which, in his opinion, was missing in Witte's proposal.[34] In the opinion of the chief procurator of the Holy Synod, Prince Obolensky, adopting such a sweeping provision in the constitution amounted more or less to potentially abolishing the representative assembly.[35] Witte himself confirmed that Obolensky's interpretation was correct: "There comes a time in all states when a coup d'état is necessary. I hope to God that we do not live to see it. But, if it came to it, it would be better to act on the basis of the law and carry out the overthrow within the law, thus avoiding a coup d'état."[36]

Other members of the commission, however, were not convinced by Witte's argument. Even the thoroughly antiliberal minister of justice, Akimov, declared: "Nowhere in the world are there laws allowing for a coup d'état. . . . It is destructive to adopt a provision in the constitution that could serve as the basis for one. With enough power, one can organize a coup without legal cover, but lacking such power would make a coup impossible even if there were a legal basis for it."[37] When Frisch and Saburov again voiced their opposition to Witte's proposal, the emperor himself spoke against adopting it in the constitution.[38]

After the above discussion of the extent of the legislative powers given to the Duma in the constitution, and the limits of the tsar's remaining legislative power, I shall now turn to the question of the executive. According to Article 10 of the Constitution of April 23, 1906, the full panoply of executive power was held exclusively by the tsar. As far as the highest level of government (*verkhovnoe upravlenie*) was concerned, the tsar exercised this power directly, whereas lower-tier functions of government (*podchinennoe upravlenie*) were carried out by persons and bodies appointed by him as laid down in law.

There was disagreement in the advisory commission on the question of whether the tsar's executive powers were limited by the constitution or whether it was right to continue classifying them as absolute (*neogranichennaia*). Goremykin was of the latter opinion, pointing out that recently promulgated measures had merely changed legislative procedures, but that, on the other hand, not a single restriction on the tsar's executive powers had been introduced. Consequently, he suggested that the constitution should make it clear that the supreme authority had lost its absolute nature only in the field of legislation, not in that of government.[39] This notion was obviously untenable. The fact that the exercise of executive power was the exclusive preserve of the tsar, that he remained responsible for this power and that neither the October Manifesto nor the Duma Statute of February 20, 1906, brought in any restrictions to it, did not mean that the constitution set no limits on these particular powers. Starting with the reign of Alexander I, the principle applied that government rested on a firm foundation of law and was thus bound by it.[40] Of course, as long as the emperor possessed unlimited legislative power, he was still able, if he wished, to change direction in the exercise of his executive power in any specific area, to repeal the relevant laws and enact new ones in their place. Thus, it was not incorrect, prior to October 17, 1905, to describe the tsar's executive powers as unlimited, notwithstanding the abovementioned provision in the Svod. With the Constitution of April 23, 1906, the absolute nature of the tsar's legislative power was fundamentally curtailed, barring the few exceptions described above. The tsar was now no longer able to annul or amend laws without the cooperation of the State Duma and the State Council. This meant that his executive power was circumscribed by laws that did not depend on his own power. Thus, Witte found it easy to refute Goremykin's argument and to show that it was no longer possible to describe the tsar's executive powers as absolute.[41] Article 11 of the constitution was in line with Witte's opinion and stipulated that decrees issued by the tsar had to be consistent with laws; in other words, the exercise of power at the highest level of government was constrained by law.[42]

But immediately there arose the most serious and particularly thorny problem: where to draw the line between the legislative and the executive powers. Witte noted that political science offered no clear guidelines regarding what were laws and what were decrees (dekrety).[43] The experience of earlier times provided even less guidance. As was well known, in Russia there was no clear distinction between the executive and the legislative powers. In theory, it was assumed that the tsar would usually enact laws after consulting the State Council and that therefore draft laws were dealt with initially in the State Council, although this was not required for decrees. In practice, however, some laws never went through the State Council: their drafts were submitted to the emperor by the Committee of Ministers or even individual ministers. On the other hand, it often happened that measures doubtless belonging to the executive sphere were prepared in the State Council. In Frisch's opinion, this had hardly caused any difficulty before, as both executive decrees and laws had always emanated from the tsar, his absolute power being the source for both. As Frisch stressed, it was now vital to define the prerogatives belonging to the highest level of government. Otherwise, each time an issue was dealt with in that framework, the Duma would protest and claim that its legislative powers were being restricted.[44]

Naturally, all the other members of the special commission shared the view that it was extremely important to draw a clear and precise line between the legislature and the executive, although they were all aware that this was virtually impossible in practice. State Secretary Uexküll pointed out that the only likely solution was to set up in Russia a conseil d'état on the French model, whose permanent role was to decide in each case whether a measure to be taken came under the executive or the legislature.[45] For the time being, in his view, the Senate should be given the task of examining whether a decree submitted to it for promulgation encroached on the legislature's prerogatives.[46] Frisch also expressed the view that this demarcation line could only be drawn over time through practical experience. Every time any doubt arose as to whether the government had the right to solve this or that problem by decree, Frisch said: "The legislature will surely ask whether the specific matter did not belong in its sphere of competence. In this way, the correct demarcation line will be automatically established in practice."[47]

This solution, as envisaged by Frisch, did not seem at all satisfactory to Witte. In the months since his appointment as chairman of the Council of Ministers, Witte found his contact with the representatives of public opinion deeply disappointing, and he did not expect anything sensible from them. He thought that if the powers of the executive were not set broadly enough from the outset, the Duma would use the slightest pretext to create a furor, "unless its members themselves become ministers and start governing the Russian empire—then they will agree that everything is permitted."[48] Witte, however, had no better so-lution. Thus, for the time being, the Senate had to decide what belonged to the legislature and what to the executive.

According to the fundamental principles of the constitution, by which full executive power rested with the head of state, that is, in line with the consistently dualistic nature of the constitution, ministers were accountable not to the legisla-ture but to the monarch for "the general business of government."[49] Nevertheless, Article 108 of the Fundamental Laws gave members of the Duma and the State Council the right to question ministers.

It has to be said that Article 108 was not well thought out. It restricted the right of interpellation only to those cases where it seemed that ministers had acted "illegally," and in addition, it laid down that only ministers appearing before the Senate under the law could be questioned. These restrictions, however, were not followed. As Maklakov writes:

> In practice, none of these restrictions had any effect. Ministers were often questioned about malpractice that was not illegal in a formal sense, while those not appearing before the Senate were also asked questions. . . . No one took any notice of these restrictions, because they could not stop the interpellation or deprive it of significance. One has to understand that the effectiveness of an interpellation consisted not in the Duma being able to impose sanctions, but in what was said in the Duma as a result. There was no parliamentary democracy, and thus the Duma could not bring down a minister by a vote. The point of the interpellation procedure was that the Duma had the right, enshrined in the constitution, to expose the actions of the government, to condemn it, to bring it out into the open and demand explanations from ministers.[50]

The crucial significance of such criticism from the assembly has already been mentioned in the above discussion of the possibility of conflict between the Duma and the tsar during the passage of a draft law. Similarly, in the case of an interpellation procedure regarding measures taken by a minister or the Council of Ministers, great weight had to be attached to such criticism and to the fact that it could be done in public, although the situation of ministers, unlike that of the tsar, made it easier for him to be less sensitive to it. Nevertheless, ministers wish-ing to avoid an unnecessary aggravation of the political situation could not ignore this criticism for any length of time.

Everyone was aware that not only the measures taken by ministers but also the decrees issued by the tsar exercising supreme executive power were subject to criticism in the assembly. Therefore, just before the constitution was promul-gated, Article 24 was added, according to which the tsar's decrees and orders, is-sued directly or otherwise through his executive powers, had to be countersigned (skrepliaiutsia) by the chairman of the Council of Ministers or the responsible minister. It is obvious that this provision was added to protect the standing of the monarch, as criticism of the monarch was thus deflected onto the minister. But as it removed some of the inhibitions surrounding criticism, this regulation was also in the interests of opposition opinion, which counted on having its own representatives in the Duma. On the other hand, the requirement of a countersignature was no doubt an unwelcome burden on ministers. It is not surprising, therefore, that the Council of Ministers deleted this article, originally found in the draft prepared by the state secretary. By way of justification, Witte, in the advisory commission, highlighted the fact that in Russia (i.e., in the context of the dualistic constitution) no minister was allowed to resign just because he disagreed with the tsar on any particular issue, but only if he had reached the conclusion that he could no longer lead his department at all. Furthermore, ministers as honorable people were not supposed to inform the Duma or the State Council of their disagreements with the tsar.[51] This meant that a minister could be forced to defend in the assembly a decree issued by the tsar with which he disagreed.

Article 24 was reinstated in the constitution after a last-minute request from opposition circles. Trepov, the palace commandant, had given copies of the draft constitution to representatives of public opinion (V. I. Kovalevsky, Muromtsev, Gessen, M. M. Kovalevsky, Miliukov) and asked them to respond. They produced a critical paper, although only very few of their points found their way into the draft constitution. The most important were demands for the countersignature and for limitation of the executive's sphere in favor of the legislature.[52]

Besides establishing a clear separation between the legislature and the executive, the Fundamental Laws also guaranteed the independence of the judiciary. According to Article 17, the tsar had the power to appoint or dismiss any state official, unless there were legal provisions to the contrary. This qualification was missing from the draft constitution presented to the advisory commission.[53] This immediately attracted the attention of the lawyers on the commission, especially those who were members of the State Council. They explained that if Article 17 of the constitution did not contain this particular qualification of Article 15 of the draft, it would spell the end of the judiciary's life tenure. In their view, this principle had been recognized not just since Alexander II's legal reforms, but also as early as the reign of Catherine the Great. It was thus extremely undesirable to abolish it.[54]

Other members of the special commission noted that judicial tenure had posed no problem as long as the tsar had absolute power. Now that his powers were no longer absolute, recognizing the principle of judicial tenure would only mean a further dangerous weakening of these powers. Because of these considerations, the majority on the commission came out against retaining tenure for judges. To be sure, said the majority, no judge could be dismissed by the justice minister or the Council of Ministers, but the right to dismiss judges had to remain among the tsar's prerogatives. The minority, however, adhered to its position. The conservative minister of justice Akimov stated: "There can be no doubt that only judges with tenure can be independent." He was seconded by his predecessor, von Pahlen: "There can be no justice without tenure. The great principle 'the inviolability of court judgements must be upheld.'"[55] Finally, Frisch pointed out that "the principle of tenure had become lodged in people's consciousness." At that, the tsar declared that he too had nothing against the principle of tenure and added his opinion to that of the minority.[56] The principle of the separation of powers with regard to the judiciary thus also came to be enshrined in the constitution.

Chapter 23

Witte and Public Opinion

Political aspects of the Constitution of April 23,
1906—Its singularity—Russian radicalism's
attitude to the constitution—Witte's efforts
to include representatives of public opinion in
his government—The last *zemstvo* congress in
November 1905—Witte's ultimate failure to secure
the support of public opinion—Collapse of Witte's
political strategy—Violent repression of
the revolution

In his book, Maklakov asks what was new or special about the 1906 constitution, a constitution that was well designed and beneficial for Russia.[1] Surely, its most valuable aspect was that the liberal concept of the separation of powers occupied a prominent place. Furthermore, the fact that in the Constitution of April 23, 1906, this principle was adapted to suit the circumstances prevailing in Russia at the time is especially important. The constitution met the historical and political needs of 1906 and did not apply liberal theory dogmatically.

By basing the constitution on the principle of the separation of powers, it was possible to allocate various roles successfully and to put in place a dividing line between areas of responsibility, which was extremely important not just theoretically but also in practice. This demarcation of areas of responsibility made it possible to give the most important elements active in political life at the time an appropriate sphere of action. Including representatives of public opinion in the legislative process allowed sections of society that had previously been active in local administration, at most, to participate in the affairs of government. By leaving the executive in the hands of the bureaucracy, in other words, those who alone had experience of running the state, the old ruling elite were not excluded from government. Nor were the two spheres wholly insulated from each other. On the one hand, the executive came under the scrutiny of the representative assembly by means of the interpellation procedure. On the other hand, the bureaucracy was not entirely excluded from the legislative process, as the upper house (the State Council) consisted not only of elected members but also of members appointed by the tsar.[2]

This last point was one that attracted especially harsh criticism from Russian radicals. They thought that this provision distorted the true nature of the assembly as a directly elected institution. Even if these charges were not entirely unjustified from a theoretical point of view, and the presence of appointees in the upper chamber regarded as an anomaly that had to disappear over time, one cannot possibly deny that this provision was eminently sensible, particularly at a moment when Russia was in transition from absolutism to constitutional government. Maklakov comments:

> In 1906, the officials serving the old regime did not just represent a considerable political factor; they alone possessed the experience and education for statesmanship. . . . They had, however, no chance at all of being elected—in the eyes of democratic voters they were too tainted by their past. Yet it would have been a form of vandalism, a waste of their skills as statesmen, to exclude them completely from the legislative process. . . . Insofar as what people wanted was not a revolution, but a change from autocracy to constitutional monarchy, the representatives of the old regime with their expert knowledge and experience as statesmen had to be included. It is significant that among the appointed members of the State Council there were not only reactionaries but also men such as Witte, Tagantsev, Koni, and others like them. That by itself shows the real significance and purpose of the appointment system.[3]

The constitution put in place something even more important than this allocation of functions and the appeal to political leaders to fulfill the roles that suited them best. The Constitution of April 23, 1906, created the legal framework that finally enabled that elusive political aim to be achieved: namely, the monarchy adopting liberalism as its own program and public opinion cooperating with the monarchy's traditional forces to implement it, thus achieving a climate of real unity. According to Maklakov, this was the fundamental political significance of the 1906 constitution:

> There were two political forces in Russia. On the one hand, the historical state power with its rich legacy of knowledge and depth of experience was no longer able to govern on its own. On the other hand, there was society, which had understood a great deal correctly and was full of good intentions, but was incapable of ruling anything, let alone itself. Russia's salvation lay in reconciliation, in the alliance between these two forces, in their working together in harmony. The 1906 constitution—and this was its fundamental idea—was not just to make this cooperation possible, but to make it mandatory. Progress, changing something, could only be done by common

consent. Agreement between both political camps had become a necessary condition for the survival of the state.[4]

Maklakov repeats here with regard to a specific situation created by the 1906 constitution what Montesquieu said in general terms about collaboration between *des pouvoirs* in a state where the separation of powers has been established. In fact, the dualistic nature of the 1906 constitution, based on the principle of the separation of powers, made cooperation between the different constitutional powers and an understanding between the political elements that stood behind them a necessity, for without them government would have come to a standstill.

The 1906 constitution's singularity and its fundamental character lay precisely in the fact that a sort of pact (a framework treaty, to all intents and purposes) was concluded between the old monarchy and the new forces in society.[5] This distinguished it from, on the one hand, Speransky's codified fundamental laws for the autocracy and, on the other hand, the parliamentary constitution that was the dream of Russian radicalism. Maklakov writes:

> Previously (before the 1906 constitution) the government machine, at whose head stood the monarch, disposed over the full panoply of power. Society was in no position to resist his will. According to the draft constitution prepared by representatives of public opinion in 1904 and 1905, all of this power would have been transferred to a democratic assembly, that is, to society itself. This would have meant absolute democracy. The 1906 constitution, however, put the two former enemies on an equal footing. Each could obstruct the other or defend the status quo against the other.[6]

In this way, the 1906 constitution in fact embodied genuine constitutional principles. It was intended to bar the way to anticonstitutional revolutionary action on the part of the state as well as society. A revolutionary transformation of Russia as carried out by Peter the Great (and Ivan IV, even earlier) was now impossible without the consent of the representatives of the people. Neither could the revolutionary parties now implement their revolutionary program without the cooperation of the government, even if they enjoyed a majority in the assembly.

Public opinion might have derived some satisfaction from the fact that, thanks to the constitution, the monarch had lost the ability to enact laws as he saw fit. It had become impossible to impose not just despotic laws but also any laws that the representative assembly regarded as harmful for the country or as unjust. Public opinion, however, largely ignored this achievement, as it had no real understanding of the true nature of constitutional government. The essence of such government lies in protecting the existing rule of law and the well-established rights recognized within this framework of law from unlimited arbitrary power standing above the law. In contrast to absolutism, constitutional government makes it impossible for the state to enact or annul laws without being accountable, that is, arbitrarily to overturn the rule of law and violate, even completely abolish, existing rights through new legislation. Russian left-wing radicals of the time ignored and were indifferent to the constitution's significance and fundamental nature, because they were not interested in protecting existing law from the arbitrary exercise of power. On the contrary, they wanted to create an institution with enough power to put new legislation in place of the old laws under a cloak of apparent legality and to abolish existing rights that they thought unjustified from the perspective of their theoretically based program.

The constitution could make cooperation and agreement between the forces of society and the state mandatory, but it could not make them—like the laws of nature—an absolute necessity. Insofar as Russian radicalism did not want such collaboration within the framework of the dualistic constitution, neither could the constitution make it happen by itself. Furthermore, the aim of radicalism was, as mentioned above, to concentrate all state power in the hands of a democratic assembly, where it hoped to have a majority at its disposal. It did not seek a rapprochement with the historic regime, but demanded its unconditional capitulation. Accordingly, radicals disputed the tsar's right to proclaim a constitution. They thought that only a constituent assembly elected by universal suffrage was entitled to enact a constitution based on the principles of a systematic parliamentary democracy. The government should be formed from the ranks of the parliamentary majority and be accountable to it alone. To avoid any obstruction of the will of the lower chamber, the upper chamber was to be abolished. This is the program of absolute democracy, or rather democratic absolutism—*quod maioritati* (the parliamentary majority) *placuit, legis habet vigorem* [what pleases the majority has the force of law].

This approach or mentality posed the principal danger for the establishment of true constitutional government in Russia, for the transformation of Russia into a state under the rule of law. Maklakov writes, "To establish the credentials of a legal order in Russia, the autocracy of the monarchy had to be limited, but not replaced by the autocracy of the State Duma majority."[7]

In contrast to radical opinion at the time, the monarchy's supporters were quite prepared to work with representatives of society. When Witte and other advisers urged the tsar to convene a representative assembly without delay, they assumed that the change to constitutional government and the inclusion of representatives of public opinion in the legislative process would satisfy liberals and their supporters and that these would distance themselves from the revolutionary groups and, moreover, join the government in combating the revolution. They thought this would take the wind out of the revolutionary movement's sails and that it would recede on its own. They believed that military force was no longer necessary and that police action to combat revolutionary excesses would only need to be on a limited scale.

In order to strengthen cooperation with the public even further, Witte decided not to restrict himself to including representatives of public opinion in the legislative process but also to appoint some distinguished public figures, in particular representatives of the *zemstvos,* to the government itself. He turned to one of the moderate representatives from these circles, Shipov, to establish the links with these forces. The negotiations with Shipov and other conservative liberals about joining the government proved fruitless, because they did not want to work with Durnovo. They objected to him not just on political but on moral grounds (it was common knowledge that Alexander III's decision to relieve Durnovo of his post was taken on moral grounds, as the latter had abused the power of his office in a love affair). Witte, however, was convinced that, at a time when revolution threatened, the Ministry of the Interior could only be led by someone with police experience and therefore refused to dispense with Durnovo as the minister. Yet this was just one of the reasons for their reluctance. More important, the moderates from the *zemstvos* were convinced that they did not enjoy the support of large sections of the public. As a result, their joining the government could not lead to reconciliation between society and the state, but only to their being stigmatized as traitors. Partly, it was also that the passage from opposition to being a part of the government proved too difficult for them psychologically, indeed virtually impossible. I do not intend to go into further detail about the negotiations on joining the government between the representatives of public opinion and Witte, as their negotiations with Stolypin—in part even conducted by the same people—were of a similar nature. I can then make the salient points about them when dealing with the negotiations between these leading public figures and Stolypin. This is justified by the fact that some of the issues emerged more clearly in these later negotiations and partly also because they are better elucidated in the sources.

Whether government circles at the time when Witte was chairman of the Council of Ministers seriously considered including members of the radical majority in the government is doubtful, although Witte told Shipov "that he was not afraid of those who are even further to the left. He thought it essential that the representatives of public opinion who were ready to join the government should be resolute, were serious in upholding the interests of the state, and were clearly aware of the necessity of supporting the government and order in the country in the current transitional phase."[8] Whatever may have been the case, nothing was further from the majority's own thoughts than the idea of joining the government. The very fact that Miliukov, in the course of an off-the-record conversation, advised Witte not to appoint any representatives of public opinion to his government, but to choose for his cabinet only those drawn from the ranks of the bureaucracy, clearly demonstrates this.[9]

Nonetheless, Shipov and other representatives of the *zemstvo* congress minority were certainly interested in the idea, precisely because they did not consider themselves empowered to speak for all *zemstvo* opinion. Already at his first meeting with Witte, Shipov advised him, for this very reason, to approach the *zemstvo* congress-organizing secretariat in order to establish links with wider sections of public opinion and to draw them into collaboration. As the secretariat at the time had practically become the political hub for the radical groups, it appointed individuals to negotiate with Witte who were less representative of the *zemstvos* than of radicalism, even though they were members of *zemstvo* circles. The leader of the deputation was Professor Kokoshkin, a typical Russian radical. In his book *Three Attempts,* Miliukov writes with some justification, "Choosing Kokoshkin to negotiate with Witte meant the secretariat rejected any compromise."[10] In fact, the secretariat's deputation did not actually negotiate with Witte; it gave him an ultimatum. The deputation pointed out that a constitution by proclamation was unacceptable and demanded that a constituent assembly representing the sovereign will of the people be convened to prepare a constitution.

This was certainly enough to show Witte that it was inconceivable to expect the representatives of public opinion, least of all those he was dealing with, to help combat the revolution. He had to conclude, on the contrary, that the position that they had adopted favored the revolution. As we have seen, Witte's view was that a conflict between a representative assembly and the crown would be unavoidable, if a constitution was not proclaimed before the assembly was convened, that is, if no firm legal framework was created for its legislative work, but a democratic chamber with all the powers of a constituent assembly was set up. A democratic assembly would inevitably have sided with the revolution in such a conflict. Indeed, it would have appeared to lead the forces of revolution and, because of its character, would have covered it in a cloak of legality. Of course, this would only have strengthened the revolution and favored its progress, as French history had also demonstrated. As an assembly was convened in 1789 without a constitution having been enacted beforehand, the legal basis was missing for cooperation between the Estates-General and the king, thus giving impetus to the revolutionary turn of events. Maklakov comments, "Could anyone really believe that our government would repeat the same mistake 120 years later, especially as this error had been unanimously condemned by all historians?"[11]

It is important to remember that the secretariat's deputation represented the views of not only a small group, but also, in fact, large sections of public opinion. This had become clear at the last *zemstvo* congress, at the beginning of November 1905. This was the first time that a *zemstvo* congress disputed the tsar's right to proclaim a constitution. As, however, moderate elements were also present, it had refrained from calling for a constituent assembly. It demanded that the Duma should prepare the constitution, which would then be ratified by the tsar.[12] Insofar as this compromise resolution included the tsar's ratification, all left-wing groups regarded it as abandoning the principle of the sovereignty of the people and thus indignantly rejected it. At the same time, this formula naturally could not satisfy the government side either. If it had actually been adopted, it would have resulted in the same extremely dangerous conflict between the tsar and a democratic assembly that was to be feared from convening a constituent assembly whose resolutions the tsar would not even have been allowed to ratify. This was clearly understood by Witte in particular, who regarded the *zemstvo* congress resolution as unworthy of serious consideration.

Other recommendations made to the Witte government by this last *zemstvo* congress were equally impractical. It demanded that the government should immediately and unconditionally implement all the freedoms listed in the October Manifesto, annul the emergency powers that were in force in some regions, offer a general amnesty for all political crimes, immediately abolish the death penalty, and so on.[13] This was despite the fact that the wave of revolutionary terror was continuing to spread. How was it possible in all seriousness to consider, Maklakov asked, combating terrorism armed only with "amnesty and freedoms"?

Witte was deeply outraged by the *zemstvo* congress resolutions. He still found it difficult, however, to believe that all *zemstvo* opinion supported these motions. Perhaps he had also heard that a minority at the congress resisted their adoption. Perhaps he knew that *zemstvos* in the provinces were much more conservative in outlook than the congress. Thus, he responded once more to the *zemstvo* congress. When news broke in St. Petersburg of the Sebastopol naval mutiny, shortly after he received the congress decisions, Witte sent Petrunkevich a telegram in which he expressed his conviction that these would have been different if the congress had known what had happened in Sebastopol. He ended the message with these words: "I am turning to you because I believe in your patriotism."[14] The telegram, however, did not have a decisive impact on the delegates at the congress. Although it strengthened a tendency to moderation in some, most believed that it was just a sign of weakness and that the government was prepared to continue negotiations and make concessions. The congress therefore decided to send a new deputation to Witte. The only thing that distinguished this deputation from the secretariat's was probably that it had not been mandated to issue an ultimatum. The position of the congress, however, was all too clear, and the deputation did not have the authority to report to Witte any change of mood in *zemstvo* opinion following the tragic events. Even a conciliatory delegation would hardly have been able to alter the fact that "the *zemstvo* congress had no desire to start propping up the government and remained just as hostile as before."[15] Witte grasped this, refused to meet the delegation, and merely left a brief written reply to be handed to it.

Witte must have realized at that moment that his political hopes and plans lay in ruins. His idea was to achieve reconciliation with liberal opinion and thus to isolate and defeat the revolution. Starting from this position, he had advised Nicholas II to proclaim the transition to constitutional government through the October 17 Manifesto. At the same time, he had frankly told the tsar that there was a different approach, namely, simply to repress the revolution using the police and the army, although he advised against it. Witte now saw that his hopes of finding support among broad sections of public opinion and, in particular, in *zemstvo* circles had come to nothing. He was now faced with having to use methods in the struggle against the revolution that he had unequivocally opposed and did not wish to defend. To avoid using them, he had recommended to the tsar that he should proclaim the constitution. Witte thus gave Durnovo, his minister of the interior, a free hand to use the police and the military to smash the revolution, which was done relatively easily. Even putting down the Moscow armed uprising (in December 1905) only required dispatching a single guards regiment from St. Petersburg. In other cities, the police on their own were able to deal with the revolutionaries.

The proclamation of the constitution, therefore, did not produce the results that Witte wanted. He felt he had misled the tsar and must have felt guilty toward him. However, he must also have repressed these feelings of guilt quickly, as he never admitted his mistakes easily. Perhaps this repressed guilt is the ultimate source for the outbreaks of hostility toward the tsar that occur frequently in his memoirs. What he told Maklakov many years later, which Maklakov repeats in his memoirs, is in my opinion enough to prove that Witte did have a guilty conscience: "If I had thought at the time that all public opinion shared the views of the deputation, I could never have forgiven myself for advising the tsar to grant the constitution."[16]

Ultimately, the question of whether Witte felt guilty toward the tsar is secondary. What is important is only that he was aware of the failure of his entire political strategy. This alone can account for his later attitude. This explains why he often took an antiliberal position in the special advisory commission; why he only spoke of the prospective assembly with the utmost mistrust; and further, why he virtually denied in this commission that the new regime was genuinely constitutional and why he wanted to insert a clause into the constitution that could have legalized a coup d'état. It is also because of this awareness that one can understand why he could not appear as head of the government before the Duma—or even wish to do so—and resigned a few days before its opening. Without the support of public opinion, which he sought but did not find, Witte in fact could only appear before the Duma as just another bureaucrat, or merely as an "expert in statecraft," as it were. Without public support, he was unable to be a figure in the world of politics or to exercise political influence in the true sense—he did apparently play with the idea of such a role, although his personal qualities did not lend themselves to it.[17] It was only the collapse of the hopes he had placed in liberalism, moreover, that explains why he gave Interior Minister Durnovo free rein to repress the revolution and ultimately why he did not intervene more strenuously to counter the increasing acts of white terror perpetrated by the forces of reaction. This last point particularly shocked opposition opinion, although, as Maklakov points out, it largely bore responsibility for that: "Liberal society did not want to grasp that by refusing to lend Witte support, it robbed him of the ground from which to combat reaction."[18]

Public opinion also found it difficult, however, to forgive Witte the ferocity with which the revolution was repressed. It was unable to understand that this barbarity could only have been avoided with its support, as without it Witte had to rely on the help of those who regarded the idea of a constitutional state under the rule of law with contempt. Deprived of this support, Witte had no option but to counter the naked violence of revolutionary terror with the naked force of security measures, if he was not prepared to capitulate to the revolution. This would naturally have meant complete submission on his part and was thus out of the question.

There can be no possible doubt that fighting rather than surrender was the right thing to do not just politically but morally. Maklakov expresses this in his memoirs in his own brilliant and profound way:

> The ferocious acts that the government carried out at the time with such shocking ruthlessness saved Russia from an even greater evil, from revolution. The revolution, which so many anticipated with delight, would have produced the same outcome as Russia is now going through. When history passes judgment, the repressors (*usmiriteli*) of 1905 will thus be seen to be more in the right than those who, from wholly selfless motives, embarked on the uprising,[19] supported it, or were glad that the government had reached an impasse. . . . As long as we are afraid of acknowledging this, we shall not be in a position to assess our past objectively.[20]

Chapter 24

The Constitutional-Democratic Party and the Union of October 17

The minority at the last *zemstvo* congress—
Creation of the Union of October 17—
Comparison between the programs and basic
positions of the Octobrists and the Kadets—On
the eve of the First Duma: the electoral pact
between the Kadets and the socialist parties—
Witte's resignation and Goremykin's appointment
as chairman of the Council of Ministers

At the *zemstvo* congresses of November 1904 and November 1905, there was a distinct minority group alongside the radical majority, except that the minority at the 1905 congress was different from that in 1904. In 1904, the minority came out against constitutional government, while being in favor of it in 1905. This group was composed partly of old constitutionalists like Guchkov, partly also of men like Shipov from the 1904 congress minority, who had been against the constitution at the time but who now accepted it, once it had become a reality.[1] One should not forget, as has been shown earlier, that all the efforts of men like Shipov had always in effect served the constitutional cause and that it was natural for them now to admit to themselves that they supported it. What distinguishes the 1905 congress minority from the majority was not that it ruled out the move to constitutional government, but rather that it approved of the constitution by proclamation and rejected the idea of a constituent assembly as the foundation of a new political order.

Svechin articulated this view with particular clarity.[2] He did not accept that it was possible to have a constituent assembly as long as there was a legitimate government in Russia. In addition, he pointed out that there had been quite different reactions to the October 17 Manifesto. Some wanted to go further, whereas others, by contrast, thought that things had already gone too far. Svechin rejected both these approaches and suggested aligning oneself with the manifesto itself.

This anticipated "Octobrism," while, in Maklakov's opinion, the minority at the last *zemstvo* congress championed liberal ideas just as the Octobrists would do later, in the First Duma.[3]

The minority at the congress advocated views that were opposed to the majority on many other issues besides the question of the constitution. In particular, it unequivocally rejected revolution and vigorously condemned revolutionary terror. Guchkov suggested to the congress that it should include the following clause in the resolution on the abolition of the death penalty: "The congress condemns the use of acts of violence and murder in the political struggle."[4] Nevertheless, even this modest proposal was rejected by the majority. Guchkov's standing was considerably enhanced by taking this independent position. The liberal sociologist M. M. Kovalevsky, who was also at the congress, told Maklakov, "I saw only one person at the congress who thought like a statesman—that was Guchkov."[5]

The Octobrist Party (the Union of October 17) emerged from the minority group at this *zemstvo* congress (November 1905). It was led for a relatively short time by Shipov and then for several years by Guchkov. By contrast, the majority was composed of members of the Constitutional Democratic Party (Kadets), which had been formed a couple of weeks before the congress. The Kadet Party, incidentally, was less identified with the majority at the last congress than the Union of October 17 was with the minority. Some members of the minority, such as Svechin and Maklakov, also joined the Kadet Party. There was always a liberal group within the Kadet Party, whose views were opposed to those of the radical majority. It was, however, not influential enough for its ideas to prevail. At best, it succeeded in getting the party to accept compromise positions, to which it then submitted rather passively, although these were often no less negative than the majority position. In addition to Svechin and Maklakov, mention must be made of two other representatives of this liberal minority in the Kadet Party: N. N. L'vov and Struve. Both men, however, soon left the party.

Soon after October 17, numerous political parties began to be formed that were more right wing than the Kadet Party. Some were openly hostile to the new system of government, and some supported the principles proclaimed in the October 17 Manifesto, while others were groups representing local interests.[6] Shipov and Guchkov, often traveling together between Moscow and St. Petersburg, discussed the necessity of uniting the small groups and parties that shared the aim of implementing the ideas set out in the October 17 Manifesto. After the *zemstvo* congress of November 1905, this became more urgent, as the differences between the radical majority and the liberal minority had become much more acute. The minority added its own "special opinion" to the resolutions passed at the last congress, thus demonstratively distancing itself from the positions adopted by the congress. In particular, the fact that the majority had in mid-October already organized itself as a political party (the Kadets) made opposing it through a more or less organized wider political grouping, representing the ideology of the minority, appear quite natural. As it was, given the impending elections, it was time to form such a group.

Soon afterward, the supporters of this approach held a meeting in Moscow. It was decided to form not a party, but a union that allowed individual parties and groups that wished to join it to retain their independence. It was named the Union of October 17. The term "Octobrist" then attached itself to its members and the parliamentary group in the Duma. The group that had launched this initiative issued a call to public opinion and announced the main points of its program. The appeal highlighted the necessity of uniting all those "who genuinely want a peaceful renewal of the country . . . , who reject both stagnation and revolutionary agitation and recognize the need for a strong government with genuine authority, capable, together with a representative assembly, of bringing about peace in the country through constructive legislation."[7] The appeal was favorably received, and groups of Octobrists began to form throughout the provinces. A central committee was formed in Moscow and Shipov elected leader.

Comparing the main points of the Octobrist program—that is, Russian liberalism's program—with those of the Kadet Party is not without interest. In fact, rather than considering the details of each program, it is probably better to look at its basic ideology and the attitude that sprang from it. The program adopted by the Kadet Party during the congress makes no mention of a constitutional monarchy, but merely the Russian state or empire. Article 13 reads, "The constitutional structure of the Russian state is determined by the Fundamental Laws." Consequently, although the Kadet Party did not demand the establishment of a republic in Russia, neither was it a supporter of the monarchy.[8] They thought it right to retain this leftover from the past for the time being, as long as the sovereign will of the people did not expressly call for its abolition.

By contrast, one of the main aims of the Octobrists, featured in the basic theses of their program, was "to develop and consolidate the principle of constitutional monarchy . . . and to establish unity between the monarchy and the people."[9] One can also gather from the full text of the program and speeches made at their conferences by leading Octobrists, in particular Guchkov, that for them the monarchy embodied a great historic Russian tradition, and thus, looking forward, it alone was regarded as the power that could bring about renewal in Russia. Guchkov, for example, said at the first all-Russian conference of the Union of October 17, which took place from February 8 to 12, 1906: "We cannot dismiss everything created in the old Russia. . . . The principle of monarchy, which has played such an enormous role in Russia, has to be renewed and adopted in the new Russia."[10]

At the same conference, Shipov stressed: "We are sincere, convinced monarchists. We regard constitutional monarchy as an antidote to the tyranny of either an oligarchy or the masses. The monarch stands above all political parties. . . . Therefore, this forms the best framework for safeguarding the individual citizen's freedom and rights."[11] This statement by Shipov formed the basis for the program. It pointed out that although the monarch would henceforward "find his will restricted by the rights of the representative assembly," he would also find his power enhanced because of the curtailment of bureaucratic absolutism and the forging of unity with the people. The monarchy, it continued, would find a new mission as peacemaker, insofar as allowing freedom for political, national, and social struggle would open up extensive opportunities for such a role.[12]

In the same speech, Shipov said, "In common with the parties of the left, we understand that Russia's future lies in far-reaching democratic reform." In contrast to these parties, however, he stressed that the Octobrists thought that these reforms must be based not simply on the concept of liberty but on ethical principles as well. "The basic tenets of the Union of October 17," Shipov concluded, "are respect for the highest principles of liberty, justice, and love."[13] In my view, it is hard to deny that there is a certain affinity between the Octobrists' principles and those of Democrazia Christiana [the Italian Christian Democratic Party, founded in 1943]. Perhaps the Union of October 17 was a party from which an Orthodox Democrazia Christiana could have evolved.

This difference in their basic attitude to the monarchy resulted quite naturally in the Kadet Party rejecting the idea of a constitution by proclamation, while the Octobrists welcomed it.

As part of its program, the Kadet Party demanded universal suffrage. The party was convinced that only a democratic assembly elected by universal, direct, equal, and secret ballot was really worthy of the name. The program demanded the introduction of parliamentary democracy (Art. 19). It did not directly call for the abolition of the upper chamber, but permitted different views within the party on this issue (Art. 14). This meant that the party did not regard the abolition of the upper chamber as undesirable in principle. In any case, the Kadet Party did not see a reformed State Council as the upper chamber, but preferred a chamber elected by democratized local self-government institutions (Art. 14).

In this respect, the Octobrists' position was not at first opposed to that of the Kadets, although the way they expressed it was more moderate and adapted to historical circumstances. Like the Kadet Party, the Octobrists stood for universal, equal, and of course secret elections, although they were not unconditionally in favor of direct elections. The Octobrists advocated that the government should be drawn from the ranks of the majority in the Duma, which is certainly a step toward parliamentary democracy, although they did not insist on its formal and immediate introduction. They opposed turning the State Council into an upper chamber and retaining appointed members, seeing this as an undesirable solution not in keeping with the October 17 Manifesto. However, they did regard an upper house as a necessary and useful institution. The resolution of the Octobrist central committee of March 1906, concerning the legislation of February 20 on the State Council, states expressly that the State Council could not be considered a legitimate representation of opinion in the country. The Octobrist central committee therefore thought that its powers had to be limited. The resolution stressed that the State Council was essential to ensure continuity in legislation and block insufficiently thought-out proposals from the Duma. The State Council's right to reject the Duma's resolutions, therefore, had to be retained. Resolutions rejected by the State Council had to be referred back to the Duma. If, however, the Duma backed the same resolution again, it should not, according to the Octobrists, go back to the State Council, but instead go straight to the tsar, who would then make the final decision.[14]

The following difference is of great importance: the Kadet Party program made no mention of the citizen's property rights in its list of fundamental rights, while the Octobrists included property rights in theirs (point 3 of the fundamental principles). Of course, this does not mean that the latter considered private property inviolable under any circumstances. The Octobrists did allow for the possibility of expropriating large landed estates for the benefit of the peasants to solve the agrarian question. However, they regarded expropriation as a measure only to be undertaken with the utmost circumspection, and then only as a last resort. It was stressed in point 4a of their fundamental principles that the expropriation of large landholdings to expand peasant land ownership was only acceptable with fair compensation and in the general interest. The Kadet Party agrarian program has been analyzed in detail above. It then became apparent that the Kadet Party envisaged the expropriation of private property on a much larger scale than the Octobrists. Furthermore, regarding compensation, they paid little regard to observing the principles of civil law.

The most significant difference between the Kadets and the Octobrists, however, lay not in their programs, but rather in the fact that the Octobrists, in contrast to the Kadet Party, were prepared for the time being to make the best of what they saw as an imperfect constitution. They sought to move forward as quickly and vigorously as possible to prepare liberal reforms in the Duma within the framework of the proclaimed constitution. They were convinced that calm, matter-of-fact work in the Duma and the implementation of liberal reforms would inevitably lead over time to a more democratic constitution. In their program, they stressed that it was extremely important that the Duma convene as quickly as possible and move to a solution of the peasant question in order to give the peasants the same rights as other citizens. The Duma, they continued, also had to address urgently the question of legislation on workers' conditions; prepare legislation to develop local administration; reform the justice system, the bureaucracy, and taxation; and promote education (points 4a–f). For their part, by contrast, the Kadets had no wish to undertake mundane work in the Duma. Miliukov, the Kadet Party leader, said at its April conference in 1906: "The Duma must not be allowed to get involved in practical work. . . . The Duma's task is to do everything to ensure that the entire burden of the struggle and the responsibility for the confrontation with the government fall on the latter's shoulders."[15] According to the Kadet Party and its leader, the government had to be forced to capitulate at the outset and the constitution made completely democratic. Only this would create the conditions for "practical work."

In addition, the Kadet Party acted quite differently from the Octobrists as far as combating the revolution was concerned. It put the blame for revolutionary excesses entirely on the unbending attitude of the government and even refused to condemn the most brutal examples of red terrorism, albeit simply from an ethical perspective. Instead, the Kadets vigorously demanded the immediate abolition of the death penalty and the annulment of laws bringing in a state of emergency or war. The Octobrists, on the other hand, condemned the red terror just as much as the violations committed by the state forces in combating revolutionary disorder.[16] They considered that the government was completely justified in its battle against the revolution. It is significant that the resolution calling for the annulment of laws imposing emergency or war powers—laws in which one could find much to criticize—was only adopted by a slender majority at the Octobrists' conference. There was a powerful group that thought it wrong, at this dangerous juncture, to deprive the government of the legal means to combat the revolution (even if one was aware of their drawbacks).[17]

The Octobrists thus wanted to cooperate with the government in implementing liberal reforms and combating revolutionary turmoil.[18] By contrast, the Kadets were determined not to seek reconciliation with the government. Shipov had highlighted this at the advisory commission in December 1905 in the presence of the tsar: "The radicals are demanding a constituent assembly. They will also take up seats in the Duma to pursue this aim. Those of us in the Union of October 17 want to consolidate the power of the government and the implementation of the reforms announced by Your Majesty."[19]

The Kadet Party's uncompromising attitude to any group more right wing than itself was further reinforced by its refusal to form an electoral alliance with the liberal Union of October 17.[20] This alliance would have been quite natural, as the latter party had emerged from the same *zemstvo* congresses as the Kadets. Instead, they chose an alliance with the socialists, which had only existed up to then as an underground movement. The Kadet Party was implacably hostile to the Octobrists and the other, smaller liberal party, which had been formed at roughly the same time, the "Rule of Law Party," although Miliukov himself had to admit at the party's conference in January 1906 that these parties had now taken over the political role that really belonged to the Kadet Party.[21] In the same speech, Miliukov also expressed the singular hope that notwithstanding such a role, "both these parties, thanks to their support for the government, would take on the colors of the Black Hundreds (reactionary groups)."[22] Miliukov's hopes were largely fulfilled, certainly not because the two parties in question supported the government, but because of the Kadets' own efforts to mount a propaganda campaign, which for once were crowned with success. Even today, many think that the Octobrists were not a liberal but a reactionary party. I hope that my clarification will dispel this attitude and set the record straight regarding this party that did more than any other to consolidate constitutional government in Russia. The alliance with the socialists secured electoral victory for the Kadet Party. It deprived it, however, of freedom, not just during the electoral campaign, but in the Duma itself as well.[23]

If the political position chosen by the Kadet Party made it impossible to work with the government, in general robbing it of the required flexibility, then Witte's resignation and Goremykin's appointment to replace him as chairman of the Council of Ministers made the government's task of cooperating with the representative assembly much harder. There can be no doubt that Witte had honestly sought an agreement with the leaders of public opinion. He attached such importance to this understanding that he attempted at first to avoid putting forward a definitive program. He sacrificed drawing up a clear, distinct government program for the sake of efforts to find common ground with public opinion. This was certainly an error. A clear program would have made it easier, not harder, to reach an understanding with opposition elements—after all, certainty always has its attractions. Witte's attitude was condemned by public opinion, and it aroused the tsar's mistrust. Shipov recounts: "What is most dangerous and destructive is that the government has no definite program based on firm political convictions. It is only with these in place that you can have the trust and support of society. Continual doubts, and the search for compromise that forces concessions, deprive the government of the ability to provide leadership and master public opinion and its movements."[24] Nicholas II said more or less the same thing to Kokovtsov: "My sincere wish is to fulfill the promise I made in the October 17 Manifesto and give legislative power to the people. . . . I am prepared to grant everything that is required, but making concessions at every turn, without knowing where it will all lead, is beyond my strength; and I do not see that my new ministers have a clear program and are prepared to govern the country firmly without continually making new promises."[25] It has to be said in Witte's defense that if he vacillated, it was because he was in fact unable to find understanding or support from any quarter.

Even if one can well understand that Witte had to resign, it is not easy to grasp why Goremykin was appointed in his place. No one from public opinion or among the representatives of the bureaucracy could explain this appointment. Government circles were extremely skeptical about it. When Witte (incidentally a personal enemy of Goremykin) learned from the tsar whom he had appointed to be his successor, he told Kokovtsov that dear old Ivan Logginovich (Goremykin) was probably not the man to get on top of the situation.[26] Even the extremely reserved Kokovtsov thought it his duty to point out to the tsar that appointing Goremykin made the task of finding a modus vivendi with the Duma even harder. He told the tsar that Goremykin's extreme lack of concern, inflexibility, and absolute aversion to any rapprochement with the new elements in the political system would inevitably lead to a hardening of the mood of opposition.[27]

The tsar, however, stuck by his decision. He countered Kokovtsov's objections, saying that Goremykin would probably resign on his own accord if he became aware that his resignation would help foster relations between the government and the Duma. Apparently, Nicholas II was tired of seeing at the head of the government a man who always had an independent view and was able to show some initiative. As far as Goremykin was concerned, one could be absolutely certain that he would never, under any circumstances, develop any independent initiative. Neither, by the same token, could one have expected him to be hostile to the new regime or to the Duma in particular. Maklakov is right to stress that Goremykin's appointment did not in any way signify a departure from the principles of the October 17 Manifesto.[28] The introduction of the new constitutional system, however, surely demanded much more than mere passivity. Goremykin's appointment was thus an extremely unfortunate decision.

Criticism from the public was directed less at Goremykin in person, than at the fact that on the eve of the opening of the Duma, a government was formed that was composed exclusively of bureaucrats and that no consideration had been given to having a government of leading public figures who could have found a common language with the Duma. This was the view not just of the Kadet Party but also of the Octobrists. Even moderate public opinion was not prepared to accept a government by edict on top of a constitution by proclamation.

The reorganization of the government on the eve of the opening of the Duma, set for April 27, proved highly damaging, especially as the tsar had communicated his express wish that no member of the Witte government should be a member of the new Council of Ministers. This meant that a few days before the Duma opened, new men were put in place to head all the ministries. They had no time to find out what their predecessors had done or to come before the Duma with a realistic program. This did not augur well for the encounter with the Duma. The same has to be said about the appointment of men like Stishinsky and Shirinsky-Shikhmatov to ministerial posts. It was generally well known that they did not bring with them any sympathy for constitutional government.

Therefore, it appears that on the eve of the opening of the Duma, no effort was spared by either the government side or the opposition to make cooperation between Duma and government impossible.

Chapter 25

The First Duma

Opening of the State Duma and the reformed
State Council—Opening ceremony at the Winter
Palace—The tsar's address from the throne,
its political content—The First Duma—Plans
to persuade leading public figures to join the
government—Failure of these plans—Goremykin's
resignation and the appointment of Stolypin as
chairman of the Council of Ministers—Dissolution
of the First Duma—Nature of the opposition
from the right in the First Duma—Government
preparations for a new electoral law—Formulation
of a liberal government program

There can be no possible doubt that the tsar really wanted to keep his promise that he was fully determined to implement the program based on the ideas announced in the October 17 Manifesto.[1] The new era in Russia's political life was, according to the tsar's wishes, to be ushered in ceremonially. The opening of the State Duma and the reformed State Council would take place in the form of a reception for the members of both chambers at the Winter Palace. This opening ceremony in fact represented an encounter of two worlds. Kokovtsov, who was present at the reception as a minister, comments in his memoirs, "At that moment the throne room made a singular impression. It had never seen such a spectacle as was created by the throng of guests."[2] On the right stood men in uniform (*mundirnaia publika*): members of the State Council, senators, the Court, members of the imperial family. On the left, "literally crushed together," were the members of the State Duma. Very few wore tails or a frock coat; many, especially those who had pushed forward demonstratively to be near the throne, wore workers' clothes; behind them stood peasants in all sorts of dress, some in national costume; among them were a number of priests. (Later, the dowager empress commented that she had never seen priests like them—such *serye batiushki*, dreary little priests.) Kokovtsov recalls:

> Right at the front, the tall figure of a member of the Duma wearing a
> worker's jacket and large boots particularly stood out, looking round with

scornful, brash curiosity at the throne and all those around it. I could not turn my eyes away. . . . His shameless face was a picture of such contempt and hatred. . . . Stolypin said to me, "Neither you nor I will probably be able to shake off this impression. I am even concerned that the fellow might have a bomb and that something terrible might happen. But I think there is no real danger of that—these people would have too much to lose, and it would be all too clear what we would have to do in the circumstances."

How distant this scene was from the Slavophile dream of unity between the tsar and the people sending its representatives as delegates to the monarch: two hostile camps faced each other implacably.

Politicians were not the only ones to feel that way. When, a couple of days later, Kokovtsov had to introduce himself to the two empresses on his appointment as minister of finance, the dowager empress told him that she was still affected by the impression made by that "terrible reception." "They looked at us," she continued, "as enemies. I could not stop looking at some individuals, their faces so full of a hatred directed against us that seems incomprehensible to me."[3]

The tsar's speech from the throne was completely in line with the spirit and content of the October 17 Manifesto. This speech was short and to the point, setting out very succinctly all the most important parts of the new government's program. Stolypin maintains that Nicholas II himself wrote the speech and that it came as a surprise to the government itself. One can believe it. Its style, in its precision and simple elegance, is reminiscent of the text of the abdication written by the tsar himself.

In this speech, the tsar promised to ensure that the new institutions had a safe future. He announced that an era of reform was dawning with the new political system, "a time for the moral renewal of the Russian nation, the rebirth of its best forces." The main priorities for reform were the solution to the peasant question, the promotion of education, and the development of economic prosperity. These reforms were not to be entirely the work of the government. The tsar invited the representative assembly to participate actively in implementing the reforms, "to identify needs," which was in line with the assembly's power of legislative initiative. He asked for God's blessing for the task that faced him "along with the State Council and the State Duma." The tsar stressed that law was the basis of order—liberty and law were the two pillars on which the new political system rested. Maklakov relates:

> Finally, one more moment from the speech. The very people who were elected to the Duma, had, a short time before, been labeled "enemies of the state and traitors" because of their views. The composition of the Duma had raised a storm of indignation in the right-wing press. No expressions were harsh enough to abuse the deputies. The tsar on the other hand greeted these people as the "nation's best." He was probably not convinced, but he bowed to the "fiction" of the constitution.[4]

Public opinion was distinctly unenthusiastic about the speech from the throne. On April 28, Miliukov wrote in the Kadet Party journal, *Reč* [Speech]: "The government could not bring itself to accommodate public opinion, not even to the slightest degree. . . . The speech from the throne very skillfully went out of its way to avoid every awkward issue."[5] One can say with certainty that public opinion completely ignored the liberal content of the throne speech. Why? Had it closed its mind in advance to anything at all that came from the state, or had it become deaf to the traditional language of the Russian monarchs? As we know, Rodichev once said, "Just as one can't declare one's love in Old Church Slavonic, it is equally impossible to express progressive ideas in the archaic language of imperial manifestos." Certainly, whereas it is doubtful that Rodichev was right in an objective sense, he was actually correct insofar as one reason a progressive program outlined in the traditional language of the Russian monarchs could not be understood by intellectuals was that they had lost the capacity to understand it.

The Duma convened on April 27. Muromtsev, a professor of Roman law, who lost his chair for political reasons and subsequently practiced law in Moscow, was elected as speaker. He belonged to the moderate wing of the Kadet Party. He did not wield any decisive political influence, either at the *zemstvo* congresses or after being elected as speaker, probably because he was a stickler for party discipline, while, however, remaining a member of the minority group in the party. He expressed his views on party discipline in the following way: "Before the decision (by the party) is taken, each party member must defend his position to the bitter end; but after the decision has been made, they must submit to it unquestioningly."[6] Maklakov comments, not without a touch of irony, that Muromtsev hardly defended anything "to the bitter end," in fact submitting, on the contrary, to party decisions unquestioningly. This ensured that he was elected speaker, as the majority could completely depend on him to support their view, even if he did not share it.

As early as his opening speech, Muromtsev gave elegant expression to the majority position. He said that "the Duma's work should be based on the full use of the rights inherent in the nature of representative democracy itself."[7] Thus, the Duma's powers were not rooted in the proclaimed constitution, but in natural law. According to the interpretation of the Kadets and the right-wing socialists, a form of absolute democracy would inevitably be created because of the nature of the democratic assembly, in other words, with all power undivided and concentrated in the hands of the lower house (the Duma) or its majority.[8] This was the program of the revolutionary movement, the aim of the revolutionary forces. Invoking natural law was meant to lend them a veneer of legality.

According to Maklakov, this first speech by the newly elected speaker of the Duma was more or less symbolic of the future role of the Kadets. "In his speech," writes Maklakov, "he managed to give the Duma's revolutionary tendencies the allure of 'natural law.'"[9] The Kadets were in fact not the real representatives of this tendency. Although they rejected the idea of compromise with the government, they lacked genuine militancy. The true militants were the Trudoviks (the Labor group). They wanted a real revolution in Russia, sought confrontation with government, and set about provoking conflict with the state. As the Trudoviks' position was consistent, while that of the Kadets was hemmed in with various qualifications, this quite naturally resulted in the Trudoviks taking over the leadership of the left-wing group and the Kadets being dragged along in their wake. Thus, what happened was exactly the opposite of what the Kadet leadership had expected.[10] The Kadets looked on the Trudoviks with disdain. The Kadet Party was convinced it was destined to play a leading role in the Duma, because of the education and personal talents of its members. In the eyes of the Kadets, by contrast, the Trudoviks were not only a "gray mass," but their parliamentary group was also fragmented, consisting of ten smaller groups without a clear program and unbound by firm party discipline. Maklakov writes: "Yet it was the Trudoviks who were united, rather than the Kadets, with all their party discipline. They were not united around a program, but around a political ethos. That was their strength."[11] The Trudoviks believed the country had been gripped by a profound revolutionary mood and that it was thus the Duma's duty to act as the mouthpiece for the elemental forces of the revolution. As the Trudoviks were the true representatives of these ideas, they were convinced it was now their role to take over the leadership in the Duma with the aim of overthrowing the existing regime and bringing the revolution to a victorious conclusion.[12]

The Duma's demands were determined by the Trudoviks' basic position and the Kadet Party's tactical alliance with them, although less in their content than in their character. The demand to replace the dualistic constitution with a parliamentary democracy, for example, was not a demand for the government to create specific constitutional institutions to consolidate the political system, but actually a demand for the historical state to capitulate to the revolution. One of the leading Kadets, Nabokov, expressed this demand for capitulation quite clearly in his speech in response to the government's declaration, when he solemnly proclaimed, "The executive must be subordinate (*da podchinitsia*) to the legislature."[13] When the Duma also called for the resignation of the government appointed by the tsar and the formation of a government that enjoyed the support of the majority in the Duma, this was just the logical extension of the basic demand for the historical state to surrender. When, in addition, the Duma demanded the abolition of the upper chamber, that too was just a further logical step in the same ultimatum. In so doing, the Duma demanded the removal of a significant obstacle preventing the Duma majority from being fully able to exercise its sovereign, revolutionary will. The same applies to all the other demands made by the Duma. If the First Duma demanded the abolition of the death penalty or the annulment of the emergency powers legislation, evidently this was not merely done because of a principled stand against the death penalty or awareness that the laws in question were inadequate. It was also because it particularly wanted to deprive its opponent, the state, of the means to defend itself. The Duma's demand for amnesty for all political offenses reminds one of the victor's demand that the de-feated immediately release all prisoners of war. When the Duma planned to solve the agrarian question by expropriating large landholdings, this was due less to their understanding that the condition of the peasantry had to be improved, than their wish to ruin the hated reactionary landowning class and deprive the members of this social estate of their civil rights.[14]

Reading the minutes of the First Duma, one cannot help but recall Mme. de Staël's words about the Assemblée Constituante: "It was the most painful of intel-lectual spectacles to see the benefits of civil liberty protected by an unrestrained yet ineffectual political liberty."[15] The first Russian representative assembly, how-ever, was not just incapable of protecting the civil liberty that Russia needed above all else; from the very beginning it set out to violate the principles of civil liberty with regard to a significant section of the population, the landowners.

The government was quite determined not to give way to the Duma on two points. It felt it was impossible to agree either to solving the agrarian question by expropriating large landowners or to changing from the dualistic constitution to parliamentary democracy. All the members of the government were agreed on these two points, including those like Shirinsky-Shikhmatov and Stishinky, who opposed constitutional government, as well as Stolypin and Kokovtsov, who were quite prepared to come to terms with the liberal movement within frame-work of the new Fundamental Laws.[16] These differences between the Duma and the government on basic issues need not necessarily have led to open conflict, as it was not essential to find a solution to them from one day to the next. Conflict need not have broken out if the Duma had initially been content to join with the government in implementing those reforms that were possible under the consti-tution. The Duma, however, had no desire whatsoever to work with the govern-ment. It even refused to approve in full the special credit of fifty million rubles that the government estimated was needed to mitigate the effects of the poor harvest of 1905, reducing this amount to fifteen million rubles, a sum that was certainly inadequate. In defending this decision, the Duma pointed out that the Ministry of the Interior had money at its disposal that it spent on useless, not to mention harmful, purposes, such as the police budget. The ministry could easily use these budgets to provide assistance to the hungry in the afflicted areas; thus, it did not need any additional loans. The Duma knew full well that it was illegal, even contrary to the precise terms of the constitution, to use resources for any other purpose than those set out in the budget. Its position amounted to no more than obstruction. The Duma's systematic refusal to work with the government in the end made a clash between them unavoidable. There was, however, no need to dissolve the Duma immediately because of this, as it was possible to govern for a time without passing new laws and with the old budget.

The fact that the Duma had become a center from which revolutionary sen-timent was transmitted across the whole of Russia meant that the dissolution of the Duma could not be put off for too long. The revolutionary tide, which had ebbed somewhat following the defeat of the Moscow uprising and the arrest of the St. Petersburg Workers' Soviet, began to rise once more; the situation was gradually again becoming menacing. All the reports from provincial governors were unanimous in stressing that the revolutionary mood was growing under the influence of speeches in the Duma. These reports also pointed out that provincial governors did not have the resources to combat revolutionary disorder. They saw a particular danger in the fact that this ferment had taken hold among the lower-ranked administrative officials. It was not clear what position the government would adopt in the event of a clash with the Duma (which all could see coming). Furthermore, they wanted to know what chances the government would have in such a clash, and therefore they did not know what line to take themselves.[17]

This situation made it necessary to dissolve the Duma sooner rather than later or, failing that, to form a government from the Duma majority—that is, in fact, from members of the Kadet Party. The participation of the Trudoviks in the government was, even in the view of the Kadets, out of the question. Miliukov justified this in an article appearing in *Reč* on June 18, 1906, on the grounds that none of their members was sufficiently prepared. Furthermore, in his opinion, the Trudoviks would not want to give up the advantage of being an opposition without responsibility.[18] Both possibilities were weighed in government circles. Trepov, the extremely influential palace commandant at the time, came up with the idea of forming the government from members of the majority in the Duma, or at least giving key ministerial posts to members of the Kadet Party, and started negotiating with Miliukov to this end. On the other hand, both Kokovtsov and Stolypin, the minister of the interior in Goremykin's government, rejected the idea.[19] In answer to the tsar's question of "what should be done to put a stop to what was going on in the Duma and to steer its work in a peaceful direction," Kokovtsov responded: "The political party (Kadets) from whose ranks the author of this plan, who is unknown to me, intends to recruit a new government . . . has promised too much to the extreme left in its eagerness to get hold of power, and in the process has become dependent on them (which cannot be ignored any further). It will be swept away by them, and I cannot see where it will all end. I can see the revolution approaching in all its stark reality."[20] Nearly all the tsar's advisers agreed with Kokovtsov, and the idea of a Kadet government was quickly rejected.

On the other hand, another idea was seized on, namely to form a government with which the Duma might still possibly be able to work, even if it did not consist of members of the majority. A further attempt would therefore be made to arrive at a modus vivendi between the Duma and the state. The plan was to form what was called a "coalition government," insofar as both liberal bureaucrats and moderate public figures, including members of the Kadet parliamentary group, were to join it. The initiative came from both sides. On the government side, Foreign Minister Izvol'sky suggested this solution. In the Duma, N. N. L'vov, a Kadet member, wrote a paper on the same lines. Stolypin took up the idea, and even the tsar gave his approval. Several leading public figures were invited to negotiations with ministers, with the tsar kept in the picture. It was intended that Shipov would lead this "coalition government." The main reason for the failure of this plan was that Miliukov rejected it on his own account and on his party's behalf, even while informing Stolypin that he was ready to form a Kadet government from the Duma majority. Having been misled by his negotiations with Trepov, he was convinced that the tsar approved of a purely Kadet government and that the matter had even been decided.[21] He believed that Stolypin was trying to sabotage the plan to secure the post of interior minister for himself in the new government.[22] He therefore adopted an uncompromising attitude.

It then became clear to Shipov that the whole idea was not going to work. He told Stolypin: "I am certain that even if I managed to form a government solely of people who shared my opinions, such as, for example, Count Heyden and Prince G. L'vov, the Duma would still be just as hostile as it is to Goremykin's government. At the same time, the new government will not be able to rely on the traditions of the old regime. It would very quickly be faced with having to resign, given the inevitable showdown with the Duma."[23] Based on these considerations, the advice Shipov gave to both the tsar and Stolypin was to try to form a government from the Duma majority, in other words, a Kadet government. He thus advocated going back to the plan suggested by Trepov, the palace commandant.

Shipov thought that Muromtsev, the speaker of the Duma, was the most suited among the Kadet politicians to be first minister. Shipov went to see his old friend Muromtsev in order to ascertain whether the latter was ready to take on the post of chairman of the Council of Ministers and convince his party to support a government under his leadership. Muromtsev immediately turned this plan down. For a start, Muromtsev was very unhappy that Shipov had advocated the former's appointment as chairman of the Council of Ministers. This question, he said, had already been decided by the Kadet Party Central Committee, and Miliukov already saw himself as first minister.[24] Muromtsev made it clear that it was presumptuous of Shipov to interfere in the internal affairs of the Kadet Party. Muromtsev's words reveal a curious attitude, according to which not just members of the Kadet Party but also those who did not belong, ultimately even the tsar himself, who had the right to appoint the chairman of the Council of Ministers, would be bound by the decisions of the Kadet Party Central Committee. Much more significant is another of Muromtsev's comments, to the effect that he had considerable doubts that a government of Kadet members could master the situation. Shipov writes:

> Muromtsev thought that no new government, in the circumstances,
> could count on being able to develop its program calmly and productively,
> whatever its composition, given the ferment gripping large sections of
> society and the prevailing negative attitude in society to the state, provoked

by government policy. It would not be able to sustain its position over a relatively longer period. As revolutionary excesses are to be feared, the government would be faced with having to take harsh measures to combat them. This would doubtless provoke more dissatisfaction among the public. The government would then sacrifice the support of society, which it cannot afford to lose.[25]

Only the self-assured Miliukov could still maintain, as an émigré in 1921, in his book *Three Attempts*, that "the Kadet government could have been the first line of defense capable of stopping the course of the revolution."[26] This optimism, however, which not even all the members of the Kadet Party shared (as can be seen from Muromtsev's comments), was alien to Stolypin and the other members of the government. I have already cited Kokovtsov's attitude toward the possibility of a Kadet government. Stolypin thought that forming such a government, especially appointing one of that party to the Interior Ministry, would be an extremely risky undertaking and vigorously opposed it. If a Kadet government had been formed, it is now just a matter of speculation whether Miliukov's optimism or the skepticism of the government and those Kadets like Muromtsev was justified. It is possible, however, to note the following: the Kadet Party had come to the fore on the revolutionary tide; it had ties with revolutionary allies; and there were, even in its own ranks, many members with socialist views who thought the construction of socialism merely premature. These were all factors that would have significantly weakened the Kadet Party in combating the revolution. This was demonstrated again with absolute clarity in 1917.[27]

After the plan to form a Kadet government had been rejected, the decision had to be made to dissolve the Duma. Nevertheless, Goremykin, although he had thought right from the start that the Duma would have to be dissolved, remained quite passive in this matter and waited for the direct order from the tsar.[28] The tsar, on the other hand, thought that it was up to the government to choose the right moment to dissolve the Duma and take the measures necessary to ensure this happened smoothly.[29] This was apparently the immediate cause of Goremykin's resignation and the appointment of Stolypin as chairman of the Council of Ministers.[30] Stolypin, although he initially thought that the Duma should not be dissolved in haste,[31] had in fact reached the conclusion, because of the reports from provincial governors, that delay was no longer possible and reported this to the tsar.[32]

A session of the Council of Ministers was convened at Goremykin's for 8 p.m. on July 7, 1906. The assembled ministers, however, learned that Goremykin was with the tsar and would only arrive later. At nine o'clock, a jubilant Goremykin entered the room where the ministers were waiting and declared: "*Ça y est* [That's it]. You may offer me your congratulations, gentlemen, for the wonderful mercy the tsar has just shown me; I have been relieved of the post of chairman of the Council of Minister and P. A. Stolypin appointed in my place. He will, of course, also remain Minister of the Interior."[33] As the ministers were bombarding him with questions, he answered that they would be told everything by the new chairman of the Council of Ministers and that he himself needed peace and had to go to bed immediately.[34] Stolypin arrived half an hour later and informed the ministers that the tsar had signed the order to dissolve the Duma on July 9.

The appointment of Stolypin cannot, however, be seen as a victory for reaction. On the contrary, it represents a victory for the liberal wing of the bureaucracy. When Stolypin accepted his appointment as chairman of the Council of Minister, he first demanded the dismissal of those ministers who were not sympathetic to constitutional government and their replacement with ministers who supported a liberal course.[35] In addition, he insisted that new elections should be held according to the electoral law of December 11, 1905, and that that law should not immediately be amended, which many had thought unavoidable.[36]

The question that everyone was asking, and that had often been discussed in the past, naturally arose: namely, whether dissolving the Duma would lead to unrest. Stolypin was convinced that there was no need to fear disorder. He was quite sure of this as far as Moscow and St. Petersburg were concerned, but neither did he expect any significant trouble in the provinces. He also thought that moderate elements would not join in any protests, but would in fact quietly accept the dissolution as a sad necessity. Stolypin told Kokovtsov what he had heard from the Duma itself: "Even there, there are many who are beginning to grasp just what a dangerous game the deputies had started to play. Even among the leadership of the Kadet Party, there are some who are not opposed to the dissolution, as it has gradually dawned on them that the beast they have awakened can devour them too when the time is ripe."[37]

In fact, the dissolution of the Duma did not lead to any revolutionary unrest. Even the appeal to the people from the deputies of the dissolved Duma sent out from Vyborg (Finland) found no response. Russia was tired of the stresses of revolution, and among the intelligentsia, at least a few were beginning to realize that the main danger to Russia's development in a liberal direction no longer lay on the right, but on the left. In the world of the *zemstvos*, this awareness was even clearer and more widespread.

Before closing the chapter on the First Duma—whether it was the "people's wrath" Duma, as it was called in left-wing radical circles, or the Duma of "political irresponsibility and unseasoned statecraft," as Witte describes it in his memoirs—mention must be made of opposition from the right in the First Duma, which was quite different from that in the Second Duma. It was not opposed to constitutional government or liberalism, but was made up of representatives of moderate *zemstvo* liberalism.

The dissolution of the First Duma was of the lower chamber alone and in accordance with the provisions of the Fundamental Laws; this government decision could not therefore be described as unconstitutional. The Fundamental Laws, the State Duma statute, and the electoral law all remained in force as before and were not amended in any way.

It was thus decided to stick with the old electoral law for the elections to the new (Second) Duma. It had become clear to most for some time that if the Second Duma also proved unwilling to work with the government and to respect the constitution, this would inevitably lead not just to dissolution, but also to a change in the electoral law, in other words, a violation of the constitution. Preparations for a change in the electoral law were thus set in motion even before the dissolution of the First Duma. Yet this was only undertaken with a heavy heart. Kokovtsov reports that Stolypin asked all his colleagues to keep these plans and preparations completely secret. Kokovtsov writes: "He (Stolypin) stressed that he regarded the amendment of the electoral law as a most unfortunate necessity, only to be undertaken as a last resort, and was still hopeful that it would not come to that."[38] Elsewhere Kokovtsov again reports that Stolypin was most reluctant to consider taking this step, even after the disappointment of the Second Duma:

> Stolypin had to wrestle with himself at length before reaching the decision to amend the electoral law and thus flagrantly violate the constitution that regulated its modification. He did it to save the concept of the representative assembly, albeit by blatantly sacrificing legality. In this respect, the situation of the government, and Stolypin himself in particular, was a tragic one. Stolypin was a firm supporter not just of a representative assembly but also of the principle of the rule of law in general. . . . If he hesitated taking this step (the dissolution of the Second Duma), it was only because he wanted to exhaust every possibility of avoiding a departure from legality. He only wanted to go ahead with it if the Duma refused to help him avoid further conflict.[39]

Stolypin first tried to secure the cooperation of the Second Duma by feverishly preparing a wide-ranging program of liberal legislation, in order to present the Duma from the first day with material for practical work. In addition, he excluded antiliberal members of the bureaucracy from the government and replaced them with men whose sympathies for constitutional government could not be questioned.

Stolypin appeared before the Second Duma with a declaration setting out the government's liberal program. Some measures, however, were being planned that were not in the declaration. In this connection, the intention largely to abolish the existing restrictions imposed on Jews must be mentioned first. The Council of Ministers probably did not intend to grant full equal rights to Jews immediately, but it did plan to abolish a whole range of restrictions as soon as possible. Government resolutions to this end were drafted, and minutes of the Council of

Ministers containing them were submitted to the tsar. These minutes, however, were not ratified by the tsar. In a covering letter that accompanied the minutes sent back to Stolypin, Nicholas II wrote:

> Notwithstanding the wholly convincing arguments in favor of a positive resolution of this matter, an inner voice tells me with more and more urgency not to accept this decision. Up to now, my conscience has never let me down. Therefore, I shall follow its dictates in this case as well. You too believe that "the heart of the tsar is in the hand of God." So be it. I carry a great responsibility before God for all the offices I have established and am ready at any time to be accountable to Him.[40]

"In none of the files that passed through my hands," writes Kokovtsov, "was the mystical sentiment that underlay the way the tsar viewed the nature of his power so clearly expressed as in this letter from the sovereign to his first minister."[41] This came as a huge disappointment to Stolypin.[42]

Chapter 26

The Second Duma

The parties in the Second Duma—Stolypin's
government policy declaration to the Duma—
Reaction of the parties to this liberal declaration—
Inevitable dissolution of the Duma

T he Second Duma was just as reluctant as the First Duma to work with the
government. There was, however, a significant difference between it and
its predecessor, which should not be overlooked. A purely Kadet majority had
been possible in the First Duma, but in the Second Duma, the socialist Left was
strengthened on the one hand, and on the other, a right-wing block, which did
not exist in the First Duma, established itself. The Kadet Party could no longer
single-handedly ensure a moderate course for the Duma, even if it wanted to. It
was no longer in any position to determine the political course of the Duma on
its own, but neither was it possible for the Kadets in the Second Duma to form a
genuine coalition with the parties of the Left or the Right. Since the dissolution
of the First Duma, the gulf between the Kadets and the socialist parties had widened. The Kadets now wanted to avoid the dissolution of the Duma and through
it to achieve whatever was possible. This signaled a clear retreat from the revolutionary tactics to which the left-wing parties still held fast. These tactics, however,
had only exposed the weakness of the revolution and provoked the rise in the
country of the reactionary Right. Perhaps there was even more to it—namely,
the increasing awareness of the dangers that lay in the revolution for freedom
and for Russia's transformation into a state governed according to the rule of law.
Berdyaev was one of the first to warn of this danger. One should not forget that he
was not from the world of the *zemstvos*, but an intellectual and one of the found-

ers of the Union of Liberation. Berdyaev spoke of "the plan to control literature through the police proposed by that most modern of inquisitors—Lenin" and was concerned that intolerance and cowardly thinking prevailed everywhere and that people kowtowed obsequiously to new watchwords like "the proletariat," "the people," "the revolution," and "the uprising."[1]

Relations between the Kadets and the Right are exemplified by the following: when the issue of providing aid to destitute regions was debated, which the Kadets now wanted to deal with in a purely matter-of-fact manner, it so happened that not just the Octobrists but also the whole of the Right voted as a block for the Kadets' proposals. The government too accepted this proposal as the basis for further measures.[2] Maklakov apparently believed a firmer majority of the Right and the center Left could have emerged in this way, with the Kadet Party taking the lead.[3] In Maklakov's view, in fact, many of the reforms proposed by the government in its declaration were acceptable to the moderate Right as well as the Kadets, and there was thus the basis for an alliance. Furthermore, in his opinion, if it had come to an agreement between the moderate Right and the Kadets, the far Right would have had to join this center-right block, if only to avoid voting with the socialists or opposing his Imperial Majesty's government, which would have certainly cooperated with this block. It is hard, however, to attach much credence to any of this. The mutual antipathy between the Right and the Kadets was too strong, while to a certain extent real ideological differences also lay between them. In the view of the Right, the left-wing deputies were not the "best men," as the tsar had publicly called them in his speech from the throne, but rather a gang that should have best been banished to Siberia or at least dispersed as quickly as possible. Even if the Kadets did not belong directly in this "company," they considered the latter respectable enough to maintain relations with them. Furthermore, the Kadets' indifference to the old traditions of the state, even the monarchy, and their republican outlook, so to speak, made them abhorrent to right-wing deputies. Those on the far Right were convinced that only turning back to unfettered autocracy could save Russia from catastrophe, while the moderate Right saw the monarchy as the cornerstone of constitutional government. For their part, the Kadets (with very few exceptions) regarded the government, and all who supported it, as reactionaries and enemies.

A left-wing majority thus emerged in the Second Duma following the pattern set in the Liberation Movement and the First Duma. Now, however, it was just a negative majority, with no common program, and was held together only by criticism of the government and a refusal to cooperate with it. As the only thing that the individual parts of this majority had in common was their shared antagonism to the government, they called themselves the "opposition," which was not fundamentally illogical or incorrect.

The liberal center—in other words, the Party of Peaceful Renewal and the Union of October 17—was very weak in the Duma. On behalf of the Party of Peaceful Renewal's parliamentary group, Konstantinov declared that his party would join neither the Right nor the Left.[4] This party had been formed during the First Duma, when all those deputies who rejected the unconstitutional behavior of the government and the excesses of the revolution in equal measure coalesced around the figure of Count Heyden, who belonged to the Octobrists' left wing.[5] Two fundamental principles underlay this party's position: combating any unconstitutional behavior from whatever quarter and providing an ethical basis for liberation ideology in particular.[6] In the Second Duma, too, this party saw its task as combating all statements and actions in the Duma and the government, whether from the Left "opposition" or the Right, that departed in any way from the principles of the rule of law. It was not prepared to support the Stolypin government, notwithstanding the liberal program it had put forward, because it thought that this government too often violated the constitution and the principles that in general apply in a state under the rule of law. Overall, the Party of Peaceful Renewal stood on the ground of pure liberalism, from which it aimed criticism in all directions. One can thus say that there was a formal resemblance with the Kadets' position, which was entrenched in theoretical radicalism. Both parties based their criticism purely on theory. The difference, however, lay in the fact that the Party of Peaceful Renewal, in contrast to the Kadets, was determined to distance itself equally from both the Left and the Right and to direct criticism without reservation at the anticonstitutional position of the Left. Furthermore, this critique was not based on the ideology of radicalism, but on liberalism.

The Octobrists, by contrast, were prepared to support the government in the Second Duma as well. Accordingly, they often voted together with the Right.[7] They were only a very small group and made up mostly of modest provincials, none of whom was a good enough orator to present and justify the party's position. This explains why it was not made nearly clear enough that they voted with the government for quite other reasons than, for example, the extreme Right— that is, that they wanted above all to support the government's liberal program.

Stolypin thus gained no real support for his liberal program in the Second Duma, not even from the liberals. Some (the Party of Peaceful Renewal) acted like an opposition to his government. Others (the Octobrists) disappeared among the ranks of those supporting the government, whose advocacy Stolypin did not find as acceptable as one might suppose. Of course, he must have welcomed the fact that anyone at all in the Duma was prepared to reach out to the government. It was precisely the support from the Right, however, that held disadvantages for Stolypin, of which he was well aware. First, the support of the Right, especially the far Right, discredited the liberal program in the eyes of the Kadets. The Kadets were able, with some justification, to conclude from the backing for the government's liberal program by the enemies of liberalism in any shape, and constitutional government in particular, that the government's liberal declaration was merely a smokescreen to disarm public opinion, thus making it easier to pursue blatantly reactionary policies.[8] Stolypin, however, regarded the task of winning the support of the Kadets for the government's liberal measures and, in general, encouraging them to cooperate with the government as one of the most important of his immediate political aims. After all, only if this undertaking succeeded could the Duma's dissolution have been avoided. This was something Stolypin primarily wanted to avoid at all costs. In addition, the support for Stolypin from the Right in the Duma and in reactionary circles in general meant that these groups became the Stolypin government's allies. Insofar as not all moderate liberals by far wanted to support this government, the reactionaries turned out to be virtually its only allies. Up to a point, the influence of these circles on the government was just as significant as the socialist influence on the Kadet Party, because of the alliance between them. It was precisely because it was impossible at that moment to count on the nonrevolutionary and nonsocialist elements of public opinion as political allies that the Stolypin government was driven further to the right than he would have liked because of the Right's support. Stolypin later vigorously resisted this influence, after the Octobrists had become a large party in the Third Duma and he was presented with the chance of relying on their support against the Right.

One can therefore state that Stolypin, with his government of liberal bureaucrats and his liberal reform program, was completely isolated vis-à-vis the Second Duma. Here, he encountered either implacable hostility or support that ultimately had to obstruct the implementation of his program.

———————

The liberal program that Stolypin outlined in his great address to the Duma on March 6, 1907, represents one of the most significant advances for liberalism in Russian history. Stolypin, in fact, proposed an extensive and coherent liberal reform package, which is important to study in some detail. It formed the basis for the government's program not just up to Stolypin's death but also under his successor, Kokovtsov. Indeed, one could claim, with some qualification, that it determined government policy until 1917.

In his address, Stolypin presented a whole list of decrees based on Article 87 of the constitution, as well as new legislative proposals. First, he indicated that the government had prepared a series of laws to guarantee religious toleration and freedom of conscience. These were intended to regulate conversion from one faith to another and the foundation of religious communities, as well as to abolish all sorts of restrictions on rights concerning religious denomination.[9] In addition, on behalf of the government, he put forward legislative proposals to guarantee the inviolability of the person. According to these draft laws, arrest, house searches, and the censorship of correspondence could only be undertaken with legal authorization. Where an arrest was made on the orders of the police, a legal authority had to establish within twenty-four hours whether it conformed to the law. Exceptions to this provision were only permitted in time of war or disorder (*narodnykh volnenii*) by virtue of a new law on emergency powers that replaced the three old ones.[10] As far as the administration of justice was concerned, the government thought it desirable that preliminary investigations in political cases should be carried out not by police officers, but by an examining magistrate,[11] and that lawyers should be present.[12] In addition, following the abolition of the office of *zemskie nachal'niki* and the *volost'* courts, it wanted to set up new local courts.[13] The government went on to propose making changes to the rules governing criminal trials that, without violating the principles underlying Alexander II's legal reforms, would introduce what had proved necessary in practice or what was in line with contemporary jurisprudence and had already been adopted in several European states.[14] The whole of the new penal code (the work of Tagantsev) was to come into force and thus replace the old criminal law.[15] Equally, the outmoded *ustav* law on crime prevention and fighting crime was to be replaced by a new police statute.[16]

Stolypin proposed reforms in the area of local self-government that had always been advocated by liberals. These included extending the *zemstvo* system to the *volost'* (these *zemstvos*, in contrast to the old peasant *volost'* institutions, would not be based on the estate system);[17] increasing the roll of eligible voters in *zemstvo* elections; expanding the *zemstvos'* areas of responsibility; limiting the administrative institutions' powers of control over *zemstvo* business solely to legal supervision; and finally, introducing local self-government in Poland and the Baltic regions.[18]

As far as administrative reform was concerned, plans to unify the structure of the whole of the civil administration were outlined in the speech. The creation of administrative courts, in particular, was seen as one of the most important aims. A *nachal'nik* was to be appointed to head each district administration, creating an office that was akin to the German *Landrat* [a district chief executive]. (As we know, many of the functions of this office had up to then been performed by district marshals of the nobility on a voluntary basis.)[19]

The declaration then went on to outline measures to solve the peasant question that have already been dealt with above and need not be reiterated here.[20] One should just mention at this point Stolypin's justification, based on Article 87 of the constitution, for the need to speed up the implementation of the agrarian laws. First, he stressed that the peasantry was threatened by a process of disintegration (*sovershennoe rasstroistvo*) and went on to point out that the government, by thwarting from the outset any direct action on the part of the peasants, had assumed responsibility for immediately offering them a legal way out of their hardship.[21] As far as labor legislation was concerned, the speech mentioned different forms of social insurance for workers that the government intended to introduce. In addition, economic strikes were to be legalized.[22]

Finally, Stolypin outlined a series of measures that his government thought were essential to develop the education system. He particularly stressed that the government did not intend to depart from the principle of university autonomy recognized in the decree of August 27, 1905.[23]

Stolypin did not just present the Duma with a list of draft laws; he also pointed out the fundamental principle that all this proposed legislation had in common:

> There is one key idea behind all the draft laws that the government is presenting to the Duma and that will govern all its future activity as well. The idea is to establish substantive norms that should embody the new legal relations arising from the recent reforms. Our fatherland, reformed according to the will of our sovereign, should be transformed into a constitutional state. . . . These legal norms must therefore also be clearly formulated in law, as otherwise life will inevitably lead to conflict between the new foundations of state and society approved by the sovereign and the old institutions and laws opposed to them.[24]

Here, Stolypin says that the new legal relations resulting from the reforms had not merely to be reflected in appropriate legislation and thus protected from violation by the executive.[25] He also maintains that new legislation was required to annul the old institutions and laws inconsistent with the new foundations of state and society created by the passage to constitutional government, that is, to bring all law in the Russian Empire in line with the principles of constitutional government.

At the beginning and end of his speech, Stolypin stressed the government's determination to work together with the Duma. At the beginning, he spoke of "action in concert with the Duma." In his conclusion, Stolypin described the government as the Duma's partner and declared: "Only by introducing the new principles of government in a considered and determined fashion can the highest legislative institutions ensure reconciliation and rebirth in our great fatherland. The government is prepared to do its utmost to achieve this: its efforts, goodwill, and experience will be at the Duma's disposal."[26]

Even after hostile and aggressive speeches from the Social Democrat deputies, Tsereteli and Ozol, Stolypin once more stressed that "it would be desirable for the government to find common ground with the Duma."[27] In so saying, nothing was further from Stolypin's mind than the idea that the Duma would merely play a passive role in this cooperation and that it was only there to rubber-stamp the government's program: "I am convinced that the views of that section of the Duma that wants to get on with the job . . . will prevail, even if they oppose the views of the government. I can go further. I say that the government welcomes every public exposure of misrule or abuse of any kind."[28]

One gains the impression from his daughter's memoirs that Stolypin did in fact initially entertain hopes of getting the Duma to cooperate and that he tried to prevent its dissolution.[29] In any case, his attempts to put out feelers to at least some individual members of the Kadet Party, as reported by Maklakov, seem to support this.[30]

One could not reasonably deny that Stolypin announced a far-reaching liberal reform package in his address to the Duma. (Only totally biased socialists such as, for example, Tsereteli could do so.) In a lecture given on March 28 (i.e., three weeks after Stolypin's great speech), Miliukov said, "No European could understand that a vote of no-confidence was possible following such a declaration."[31] Yet the Left majority, even those belonging to the majority who might have agreed with the content of the declaration, did not think it was possible to adopt a positive attitude to the speech. This was because it was the product of a government that used methods to combat the revolution that were incompatible with the principles of the rule of law, indeed, with the policies announced in the October 17 Manifesto and the constitution of April 23, 1906.[32]

Maklakov, in particular, asserted this last point of view in the Duma. In his book on the Second Duma published in the 1940s, Maklakov again maintains that in the time between the dissolution of the First Duma and the opening of the Second, when the government was able to make use of its powers (according to Art. 87 of the constitution) to issue decrees with legal force, Stolypin, instead of using the old emergency powers, should have enacted a decree in line with the principles of the new constitution. This would have been in contrast to the old legislation that allowed the bureaucracy to act arbitrarily. Maklakov stresses that in that particular period, Stolypin, under pressure from certain influential groups, amended only one of these laws, which merely gave the bureaucracy even more scope to act in a highhanded manner.[33] As a result, it was possible to misuse these laws to serve the government's counterrevolutionary terror. Stolypin certainly understood that it was impossible to defend these laws from a legal point of view. He justified their retention (but not their being tightened up, which in all probability was a concession on his part) on grounds of necessity. In Stolypin's view, if the state faced an existential threat, it could not be bound by law, not even by the constitution. Maklakov makes the point that given such an attitude, the government could justify anything it wanted, calling this ideology the "great lie of the present moment."[34] Maklakov regrets that Stolypin adopted this crude position. One should highlight here that those who took this point of view and condemned Stolypin were not only liberals like Maklakov, belonging to the Kadet Party, but also, as mentioned above, the Party of Peaceful Renewal and some Octobrists—in other words, a range of deputies in the Duma who did not belong to the left-wing majority. The fact that the Union of October 17 did not criticize the government from this perspective with sufficient vigor was one reason why Shipov broke with Guchkov, left the Union of October 17, and joined the Party of Peaceful Renewal.[35]

Those unable to vote for Stolypin's liberal program solely because of their disapproval of his methods must surely have found it difficult to justify this rejection. Furthermore, neither did such people, indeed even some socialists, want to provoke a confrontation with the government, which would have led to the immediate dissolution of the Duma. They decided therefore to refrain from any criticism of the government and to propose a formal direct move to the order of business, a tactic developed by the Kadets in particular to save the Duma. Naturally, the government was not in the dark as to what this reticence meant, especially as the left-wing press hastened to enlighten the public about it. Miliukov, for example, pointed out in *Reč* that this silence was meant to tell the government that "the Duma wants nothing to do with you."[36]

The Duma majority, however, did not keep up this tactic consistently, while the Social Democrats did not join in. Tsereteli, one of the Social Democrats' best orators, responded to the declaration on behalf of his party with a speech that can only be described as a call to revolution. A closer analysis of this speech lies outside the scope of this book, which can only deal in passing with the extremely interesting history of the Second Duma, belonging as it does in a general political history of Russia and not in a history of liberalism in Russia, especially as liberals were not strongly represented in the Duma. It suffices to say here that the general tenor of this speech and its true meaning were demonstrated just by Tsereteli's reworking of Nabokov's phrase used in the First Duma and already quoted above: "We don't say, 'The executive should submit to the legislature.' We say, 'The legislature, standing in unity and solidarity with the people, should bring the executive to heel.'"[37] Thus, it is clear how ambiguous the silence of the other left-wing parties, especially the Kadets, must have seemed after this speech. This silence could now justifiably be interpreted as tacit support for the Social Democrats' call to revolution and to some extent was indeed interpreted like that. From Kokovtsov's memoirs, it emerges that he regarded Tsereteli not just as a spokesman for the Social Democrats alone, but for all the parties of the Left. Stolypin himself, however, did not make the same mistake, probably being better informed about the shades of opinion within the left-wing parties. His continued efforts to find common ground with the Kadets in the Duma testify to this.

By contrast, the Right, even the far Right, greeted Stolypin's speech with enthusiasm. Maklakov is quite correct to explain this by the fact that the Right accepted the government's program not because of its content, but because it was the program of His Imperial Majesty's government, a government, furthermore, resolutely and successfully fighting the revolution.[38] That the Right was quite unsympathetic to the content of the government's program is made clear in the memoirs of Tikhomirov, who was very critical of the declaration.[39] Although Tikhomirov was not a deputy in the Duma, he was one of the few reactionary ideologues, so one can consider his views as representative of the far Right in the Duma.

After a formal move to the order of business, a question arose that life itself posed—whether there was a majority in the Duma that could get down to business in collaboration with the government. It is evident that the Stolypin government was interested in the formation of such a majority. When it came down to it, even some Kadets, despite their reservations, thought it necessary to form such a majority. In order to achieve this, the Kadet Party was prepared to vote with the

Right on certain issues, but without, of course, entering into a formal alliance with it. They were ready to do this to "spare" the Duma, that is, to prevent its otherwise unavoidable dissolution.

The speaker of the Duma, Golovin, probably prompted in this respect by Kokoshkin, maintained that this was how the Kadets could secure their influence. He added that there were two majorities in the Duma: the Kadets had one on policy matters with the Left, another with the Right regarding the use of tactics. Joining forces with the Right on tactical grounds was meant to make it possible for the Duma to get down to work.[40]

In addition, one should not forget that the most antiliberal deputies on the Right did not seek a confrontation with the government either, but rather thought of themselves as its allies. Thus, they had no intention of undermining the work of the government in the Duma, not even when the government tabled liberal legislation in the Duma, which was not to their liking. As a result, they had to accept the necessity of voting with the Kadets, when the latter supported the government's measures.

In Maklakov's view, the Second Duma increasingly found a way to work constructively within the framework laid down for it by the constitution. Right from the start there were, as he reports, two tendencies. Some wanted to follow the First Duma's revolutionary example, while others wanted to go down a constitutional road. There was hardly a debate on any issue without a dispute between these two camps. Furthermore, Maklakov asserts that "it became increasingly evident that the supporters of the constitutional path were carrying the day."[41] He maintains that some Kadet deputies thought this was the correct approach, advocating it with some success, and that the Duma's legislative work was progressively developing.[42] In my opinion, however, as I have stated above, this judgment is far too optimistic. Maklakov himself acknowledges that "policies and tactics were more interconnected than they (Golovin and Kokoshkin) thought."[43] One cannot really accept that the Duma was capable of constructive work insofar as it did not have a stable majority, and then only one reached on a case-by-case basis after the Kadets' maneuverings. In addition, only a few in the Kadet Party seriously considered the possibility of working with the government. As already mentioned, Stolypin tried on his own initiative to approach individual members of this party. Most in the party, however, were so hostile to any contact with the government that those who did meet Stolypin had to keep it secret from their fellow party members, for fear of being denounced as traitors.[44] The majority in the Kadet Party was wholly in favor of a stable alliance with the Left and thus took a consistently negative view of anything that stemmed from the government.

Maklakov is anyway quite alone in his optimism about the chances for constructive work in the Second Duma.[45] All the other reliable sources considered it incapable of functioning. Most were convinced that conflict between the government and the Second Duma and its dissolution were inevitable. Shipov, for example, comments:

The Left gained even more seats in the Second Duma. The Kadet Party lost many of its most influential (and in part precisely its moderate) members, as these were being prosecuted because of the Vyborg appeal and were barred from participating in politics. Right from the opening of the Duma, it was clear that establishing normal relations between the representative assembly and the government would be impossible. It could only be a matter of time before the inevitable confrontation took place.[46]

Kokovtsov also took a very negative view of the Second Duma. In his opinion, Duma sessions were unbelievably chaotic: "It was clear that constructive work in the Duma was impossible. Neither was anyone interested . . . because the whole Duma, with few exceptions, was nothing but a rag-bag of revolutionaries."[47]

It is interesting that Bulgakov, too, sitting as an independent deputy with the Left in the Duma (he later described himself as a Christian Socialist in his autobiographical sketches), was profoundly disdainful of "its weakness, ignorance, and incompetence."[48] He stated that it was so weak that it was not even capable of noticing that it was absolutely unsuited for any work and drowning in endless talk: "I have never been anywhere where the atmosphere was as unwholesome as in the chamber and the corridors of the Second Duma." He adds:

> Go out into the street, take any passersby, add an assortment of well-intentioned but powerless men, convince them that they are the saviors of Russia . . . and there you have the Second Duma. By contrast, how knowledgeable, statesman-like, and down-to-earth was the impression made by the "bureaucrats." . . . Stolypin made a strong impression on me through his personality, his courage, and the remarkable power of his address to the Duma. I did not support his policies at all, but I nourished the hope that he loved Russia and would not lie. With this last hope, I left the Tauride Palace.[49]

Chapter 27

The Coup of June 3, 1907, and the Third and Fourth Dumas

Dissolution of the Second Duma and changes to the electoral law—Significance of the coup of June 3, 1907—Historical role of the Octobrists— Consolidation of constitutional government during the Third and Fourth State Dumas

The Second Duma was dissolved on June 3, 1907. As a pretext, the government used the circumstance that the Duma had hesitated too long in lifting the immunity from prosecution of Social-Democrat deputies who were allegedly involved in a plot. However, this pretext in itself was of little interest. Whether or not the plot actually existed, and whether or not ministers really believed in its existence, is surely of secondary importance, because the real reason for the dissolution lay elsewhere. In fact, it was impossible for the government and the representative assembly to cooperate and, in particular, to work together to bring about agrarian reform.[1] On the eve of the dissolution, when Stolypin "secretly" received four representatives of the Kadet Party, Struve asked why the government had decided to dissolve the Duma at precisely the moment when it was ready to get down to constructive business. In reply, Stolypin pointed out that there was one issue on which they could not agree, namely the agrarian question, and that a showdown was therefore inevitable.[2]

Thus Stolypin, on whom Bulgakov pinned his hopes, and of whom Maklakov said that he had the impression that he was a man with whom one could reach an understanding,[3] took the huge responsibility on his shoulders of not only dissolving the Duma but also this time changing the electoral law,[4] in other words, violating the constitution and carrying out a coup d'état.

The imperial manifesto announcing the coup strongly emphasized the fact that it was only the electoral law that was being altered and that, by contrast, all the other rights granted by the October 17 Manifesto and the Fundamental Laws remained in place.[5] This was a victory for Stolypin. The reactionary camp's plans to use the dissolution of the Second Duma to put an end to constitutional government itself were thus thwarted.[6]

Changing the electoral law to restrict the numbers eligible to vote was a return to constitutional thinking that more than anything had its roots in the world of the *zemstvo*, that is, the predominant view of the 1860s and 1880s and largely of later times as well. The electoral law of December 11, 1905, was an attempt, one could say, to leapfrog this *zemstvo* stage and put the constitution on a wider, more democratic footing. Now, one had to conclude that this experiment had failed. Even if this conclusion were correct, such a return to earlier thinking had its disadvantages, like all backward-looking steps. Democratic ideas had taken a much firmer hold compared to the 1860s, and indeed even the 1880s; ignoring them, even if there was no alternative, was not without its dangers.[7] In any case, it was natural and positive that precisely the traditional view of popular representation would come to the fore, after it was decided to alter the electoral law of December 11, 1905. This law had given peasants as well as intellectuals the decisive influence in elections.[8] The ensuing composition of the Duma made it impossible to put into practice constitutional government based on the Fundamental Laws.

There was a view in Russia that only the *zemstvos* could provide the historical foundation for future constitutional government, and it was believed that the representative assembly would somehow crown the *zemstvo* institutions. Elections to both chambers of the representative assembly, it was thought, did not simply represent an extension of the elections to *zemstvo* assemblies. The world of the *zemstvos* was also the sole milieu able to provide a social basis for constitutional government, because it alone was mature enough to understand the challenges of power.

Although Stolypin endeavored to build constitutional government on the foundations of the *zemstvo* world by way of changes to the electoral law, he did not use the *zemstvo* institutions as the basis for the representative assembly, as was thought in the 1860s and 1880s.[9] Nevertheless, he did ensure that representatives from the *zemstvos* would predominate in the Duma; in other words, this milieu became the social mainstay of the representative assembly. Stolypin knew well that there was still a willingness in the provincial *zemstvos* to cooperate with the government. He was also aware that the *zemstvo* world would support the government in meeting the two main challenges it faced, namely implementing the liberal reform program and combating revolution, which would help consolidate constitutional government in Russia. Stolypin knew this much better than Witte, because he had emerged from this world and not from the ranks of the bureaucracy and, ultimately, because as a provincial governor he had much more experience dealing with *zemstvo* people than members of the St. Petersburg civil service. In general, one cannot properly appreciate Stolypin's political personality unless one bears in mind that as governor he was less a representative of the bureaucracy in the provinces than a representative of the provinces in St. Petersburg. He was aware of this himself, something also highlighted by Kokovtsov, a typical product of St. Petersburg officialdom. When the tsar offered Stolypin the post of chairman of the Council of Ministers, he tried to refuse, citing his lack of experience and in particular his ignorance of St. Petersburg, with its web of secret influences.[10] Elsewhere Kokovtsov reports that initially in the Council of Ministers some things Stolypin said were not taken quite seriously, because they betrayed a certain provincialism and insufficient familiarity with the way things were done in the St. Petersburg bureaucracy.[11]

In fact, by the time of the last *zemstvo* congress in November 1905, some *zemstvo* assemblies had already distanced themselves from its radical position. The mayor of Kiev, for example, sent a telegram to this congress with the message that the Kiev city duma had not authorized its members to attend the congress and that in general, it did not support the actions of the congress.[12] There were other examples of this gulf between the radical ideas of the *zemstvo* congress and sentiment in the provincial *zemstvo* assemblies, as highlighted by the Kiev mayor's telegram. The Tula *zemstvo,* for example, expressed its gratitude to the tsar for the October 17 Manifesto and sent a delegation to meet Witte to assure him of their support. This was more or less at the very time that Prince L'vov, representing the Tula *zemstvo* at the congress, presented, along with other members of the congress deputation, an ultimatum to the Witte government to convene a constituent assembly.[13] The increase in revolutionary excesses accelerated a natural shift in sympathy from left to right in *zemstvo* circles, especially as some incidents clearly showed that the revolution was a threat not just to individuals but also to *zemstvo* institutions. There were instances of workers' strike committees demanding that town dumas or *zemstvos* should hand over their functions and especially their funds.[14]

These changes in sentiment in the world of the *zemstvos* were reflected in the 1906 and 1907 *zemstvo* elections. Many *zemstvo* assembly members and members of *zemstvo* institutions were not reelected, and their place was taken by more conservative people.[15] Following these elections, the gulf between opinion in *zemstvo* circles and the radical-opposition opinion that predominated in the First and Second Dumas became more and more apparent. It emerged that there was, in fact, a preponderance of people in the *zemstvos* prepared to support and work with the government.

Whether *zemstvo* circles would move too far to the right was an issue that now posed a danger for Stolypin. In several *zemstvos,* downright reactionary elements had come to the fore. These blamed constitutional ideas for the revolution and entirely rejected constitutional government. Nevertheless, liberal ideas were too well established in the world of the *zemstvos* for them to succumb simply from the painful shock of revolutionary upheaval. Thus, in most *zemstvos,* Octobrists, or independents sympathetic to moderate liberalism and against reaction, prevailed. It was possible to conclude from this that an Octobrist majority was guaranteed in the Third Duma, following the changes to the electoral law. This is how things turned out and was without doubt a success for Stolypin. After all, what would have become of his liberal program if a reactionary Duma had been elected following the new electoral law? He could only implement his policies with the support of the Octobrists. Furthermore, Stolypin made it unequivocally clear in the Third Duma that he intended to rely on support from the Octobrists and not the parties of the Right.[16]

It had already become clear, even before the Second Duma opened, that for their part the Octobrists were prepared to support the Stolypin government, precisely because it was a liberal government. At the time, Guchkov, the Octobrist leader, had already warmly welcomed Stolypin's program. The content of Stolypin's declaration had been set out in outline form in a government communiqué in August 1906, soon after the dissolution of the First Duma.[17] Shortly after the publication of the communiqué, Guchkov, who rightly saw it as a policy declaration, explained to a correspondent from the newspaper *Novoe Vremia* [New Times] that he agreed with its content:[18]

> I must acknowledge my deep satisfaction that the government has not abandoned the principles it advocated when negotiating with the opposition. . . .[19] I take it from this that the government does not intend to exploit its victory. It could have enjoyed its triumph and put off the reforms, even come to believe it could govern without the Duma. The government, however, has avoided this pitfall, promising instead to draft a series of reforms even before the Duma convenes and then to work with the Duma, even though the declaration only offers the prospect of progress that is all too cautious and slow. . . . Even the government's reference to the resolute measures in the fight against revolution gives hope to those who prefer peaceful means that they will find in the government a firm bastion of power that will protect our youthful political liberty.

Finally, Guchkov emphatically declared that the establishment of military field tribunals was a cruel necessity and that even on this issue the Octobrists would not make life difficult for the government.[20]

The Octobrists' support for the government's declaration is not surprising insofar as the liberal reforms it announced were similar to their own program. It should not be forgotten, however, that even those who agreed with the content of this declaration often enough withheld their support, as they abhorred the methods the government used to combat revolution. Guchkov's announcement that he also supported these measures was by no means a matter of course and thus highly significant. As the Octobrist majority was secure, this was, after all, the only chance for the Stolypin government to work with the Duma and to rely on it not just in implementing liberal reforms but also when it came to combating revolution. The question arose, however, whether the Octobrists would take a different position in the wake of the June 3 coup. As stated above, the Octobrists were prepared to accept those aspects of the Fundamental Laws and the electoral law with which they disagreed from a theoretical point of view, in order to assist the implementation of liberal reforms and thus consolidate constitutional government. Their program included a demand for universal suffrage, and the Octobrists, not without reluctance, accepted the electoral law of December 11, 1905, which did not fully meet this demand. Now, after significant antidemocratic changes were made to the electoral law through the June 3 coup, it remained to be seen whether the Octobrists, so as not to abandon their chosen path of cooperation with the government, would also swallow this amendment, this further departure from their principled demands, especially the illegal procedure that brought about this change. This was by no means a foregone conclusion. One should not forget that later, Guchkov demonstratively resigned as speaker of the Duma following a constitutional dispute with Stolypin. Nevertheless, the Octobrists resolved to take this step. No doubt, their experience of the elections for the First and Second Dumas made their decision easier. Thus, Shidlovsky writes in his memoirs: "A necessary condition for secret ballots is that voters should not be illiterate. This is because if not all voters are able to fill in their ballot paper by themselves, there can be no question of a secret ballot. Given the current level of education in Russia, there is a choice to be made between universal suffrage and secret ballots. The two are not compatible in Russia."[21]

This experience, however, was not the most important factor. What was decisive was that the Octobrists, and Guchkov in particular, grasped that the only way to secure constitutional government and prevent a return to absolutism, whether in a traditional or a modernized form, was through genuine cooperation between the Duma and the government and that, on the other hand, only changes to the electoral law could guarantee this cooperation. Overall, the Octobrists understood that the June 3 coup was an attempt to save the liberal course on which Russia had embarked.[22] This interpretation of the June 3 coup as an act in the interest of Russia's liberal transformation challenges the accepted view and appears paradoxical, and yet it is the only correct one. We now know, as mentioned above, that Stolypin and his colleagues hoped to use the changes to the electoral law as a means to ensure the survival of constitutional government. The following quotation from an important passage in Kokovtsov's memoirs can serve to underline the point once more: "The new electoral law was enacted precisely with the aim of saving the representative assembly, which had been endangered by a too broad electoral law in December 1905 that was ill-suited to the needs of the country."[23]

Whether the Duma electoral law was more or less democratic was not in fact the issue at the time. The most important thing then, from a liberal point of view, was the preservation of constitutional government and the implementation of the government's liberal program. This alone could lend some practical relevance to and breathe real life into this political system. All this, however, was only possible if the government and the Duma worked together. Insofar as changes to the electoral law made such cooperation possible, the coup of June 3, 1907, prevented the disruption of Russia's transformation into constitutional state. Ultimately, the coup served the interests of liberalism, not reaction.[24]

Without doubt, the fact that the Octobrists understood this and worked unstintingly with the government in the Duma, where they enjoyed a majority, in implementing the liberal reforms announced by Stolypin was their great service to constitutional government in Russia. This was something new in the history of politics in Russia. According to Maklakov:

> Sentiment in society (he means that it was irreconcilable) was shaped by our history. This was the price paid for the achievements and qualities of our state. Since Peter the Great, the state was much more advanced than society or the people. It could only improve their conditions through coercion. The achievements of the state, for which Russia should have been grateful, were alien to the people, who failed to understand them. This explains why for a long time there were only two extremes in the people's relationship to state power: servile subservience or secret resistance. History only forged two types of people in society: the "devoted servant" or the "agitator." Life did not nurture any autonomous independent individuals who were also loyal to the state.[25]

Maklakov's assertion possibly sounds much too dogmatic. There were independent but loyal people in Russia throughout its history, especially in the top ranks of the aristocracy. It is true that these were the exceptions, but in the context of *zemstvo* self-government, this type was seen more often. Constitutional government now brought with it new opportunities for more of them to develop. For this potential to be realized, cooperation between the bureaucracy and prominent public figures had to amount to more than an isolated episode. That it turned out like that was to the Octobrists' credit, but of course also to Stolypin's. After the state and public opinion had been for a while, in Maklakov's words, "reminiscent of a pair of irreconcilable foes wrestling on the edge of an abyss," Stolypin and Guchkov shook hands and attempted to work together.[26]

Constitutional government was consolidated during the Third and Fourth Dumas.[27] As Maklakov recalls:

> Those who lived through this period witnessed how the constitution began to educate both state and society. One can only marvel at its success, considering that the constitution only survived for eight years under normal conditions (as the war years really cannot be included). During those eight years, Russia's economy began to grow,[28] and Russian society began to develop politically. A new type of bureaucrat emerged who understood the value of cooperation with the State Duma; our "politicians" learned to find

common ground with the government. . . . Joint rule by government and society was an irreplaceable school for both camps, and for Russia it marked the beginning of its rebirth.[29]

The picture Maklakov paints is fully confirmed in Kokovtsov's memoirs:

> The Third Duma was opened on November 20, 1907. . . . From that day on, for six long years, all my work as minister of finance, and from September 11 as chairman of the Council of Ministers, was inextricably linked first to the Third and then to the Fourth Duma. One could say that my fourteen-hour working day was equally divided between the rostrum in the State Duma and my office in the Ministry of Finance. . . .[30] This time cost me a lot of work and nervous energy; I had many difficult moments, although my work in the Duma also gave me not a little moral satisfaction.

Kokovtsov recalls his work in committee with even greater satisfaction. This work was no less strenuous than appearing in plenary sessions, but it was much more productive. In the Duma's Finance Committee, Kokovtsov writes, "there were neither long speeches nor was the public present. . . . Here, everyone got on with the business in hand." As Kokovtsov observes, even arguments with the opposition, the Kadets in particular, were mostly not too caustic, although in his opinion the Kadet opposition had adopted, right from the opening of the Third Duma, an uncompromising position, which it maintained unswervingly up to the outbreak of war in 1914, not taking even a single step to accommodate the government.[31] One can also name individual deputies in the Duma who put in huge amounts of detailed work on government legislation, as, for example, Shidlovksy, the *rapporteur* for the Agrarian Committee, or Maklakov.

That the October 17 Manifesto and the Fundamental Laws of April 23, 1906, laid the foundations of a new political system is irrefutably proven, in my opinion, by the fact that a new type of man began to emerge in the context of this system. That the Russian constitution was a genuine one and not a pseudo-constitution (*Lzhe-konstitutsia*) is borne out by this sociological phenomenon. Furthermore, the political motives that lay behind assertions that the April 23, 1906, constitution was a pseudo-constitution were so transparent that they could not to be missed. They strip this contention of any serious significance. Reactionaries held the view that the Fundamental Laws were not a constitution in order to prove that they did not restrict the tsar's power. Radicals asserted that without universal suffrage and greater parliamentary democracy, that is, the abolition of the upper chamber, there could be no genuine constitution, as they wanted to make the parliamentary majority (insofar as this concerned the First and Second Dumas, i.e., themselves) the sole holder of state power. Neither, according to the radicals, was the constitution genuine because it was by proclamation, and the tsar had not sworn allegiance to it. Incidentally, as was only to be expected, this last point was given even greater weight in the arguments from right-wing opponents of the constitution. They thought, no doubt, that the tsar could break his promise without further ado, that is, annul the new Fundamental Laws, because he was not bound by oath.

My attempt to show that the constitution was genuine through a legal analysis of the Fundamental Laws does not need reiterating. It suffices here to recall that Tagantsev, one of Russia's foremost legal minds, summed it up in the Special Advisory Commission preparing the Duma Statute (February 11–16, 1906), when he said that the Fundamental Laws contained the true essence of a constitution: "One can never reduce the constitution to the oath (of the tsar). It is distinguished above all by the participation of three elements (the lower and upper chambers and the monarchy) in the legislative process. And we have that in Russia."[32]

Struve, a member of the Liberation Movement, recognized, in contrast to most of his colleagues, that genuine constitutional government had been established in Russia in 1905. During the Third Duma, however, he thought that instead of developing, constitutional government was in decline. He set out this idea in an article with the title "Stolypin and Guchkov."[33] His views were probably based on the otherwise correct observation that Stolypin did not make any effort to speed up the passing of legislation to guarantee the exercise of liberty and the inviolability of the person, focusing all his attention instead on his agrarian policies. Maklakov too highlights this.[34] Maklakov points out that Stolypin probably proposed legislation to that end in the Duma above all to appease the educated minority in society, but that he was not by any means prepared to confront the Right for the sake of these draft laws. This was not, however, in any way opportunism on Stolypin's part or a capitulation to influential antiliberal circles (as Struve believed), but a logical outcome of his overall strategy.

In fact, Stolypin was deeply convinced that Russia could only become a free state under the rule of law if the peasantry, in other words, the great mass of the population, understood the value of liberty and law. On the other hand, there could be no hope of this unless the agrarian reforms began to bear fruit, that is, unless the peasants were granted such a fundamental right as the private ownership of land and such a basic liberty as the right to dispose freely of their goods and chattel and their labor. It seemed a meaningless exercise to Stolypin to proclaim basic rights, without creating the conditions that alone could guarantee that they could be exercised. Without these conditions, which could only be generated through the successful implementation of his agrarian reforms, these fundamental rights, even the constitution itself, were, in the words of Stolypin cited by Maklakov, merely like "putting makeup on the corpse."[35]

It is not easy to explain why Struve, of all people, did not appreciate that Stolypin's policy was not the outcome of capitulation, but on the contrary, arose logically from his basic outlook, particularly as Struve correctly understood the true nature of absolutism, as well as the problem of how to overcome it. The following comments that he made in 1903 are of great interest:

The first volume of the Svod is usually regarded as autocracy's legal canon. This, however, contains only dry abstractions on autocracy, compiled relatively skillfully by the constitutionalist Speransky. Autocracy's real law is found in Volume 14 of the Svod, in the *ustav* on crime prevention and the fight against it, as well as many other laws, which cannot in any way be described as "fundamental" law. Furthermore, as long as this actual law survives . . . all the reforms planned by representatives of the *zemstvo* world . . . must remain "senseless dreams."[36]

Considering these comments, Struve ought to have understood that what he had aptly characterized as the real law of autocracy could have only been overcome if the peasants too, in the wake of Stolypin's agrarian reforms, had become genuinely subject to law within the framework of civil society. They had to become subject to a genuine property law and the requirements of the law of obligations that would have applied to them when they began to participate in free transactions under civil law. For only when the peasants too had become subject to such law would the broad masses have developed a feeling for personal autonomy, making it impossible for the autocracy's actual law to survive and ensuring the enforcement of fundamental rights and the constitution.

I have stressed on several occasions that it is a mistake to describe the April 23, 1906, constitution as a pseudo-constitution. If, nevertheless, it were possible to assert this, it would certainly not be because there was no parliamentary democracy or universal suffrage, or because the tsar had not sworn an oath on the constitution. It would simply be because in Russia constitutional government was not built on the foundation of a developed civil society, which, in general, is a necessary condition for any truly liberal—that is, genuine—constitution. As stated at the end of part 2, it was precisely, in fact, the underdeveloped state of civil society and liberty that led to the extinction of political freedom and the collapse of constitutional government in Russia.

NOTES

FOREWORD

This originally appeared as the preface to the Russian edition, published by YMCA Press in 1979 and translated by Parmen Leontovitsch from the French edition.

INTRODUCTION

1. Translator's note: "legal subject" is a literal translation of the German term *Rechtssubjekt*. This denotes the individual as the "subject of law," not the object, i.e., an individual with rights and obligations in law.

2. Hauriou, *Droit constitutionnel*, 2nd ed. (Paris, 1929), p. 139.

3. Translator's note: The author quotes the French in the original: "Le but de toute association politique est la conservation des droits naturels et imprescriptibles de l'homme" (*Déclaration des droits de l'homme et du citoyen*, Art. 2 [1789]).

4. De Ruggiero, *Storia del liberalismo Europeo* (Bari, 1925), p. 25.

5. Ibid., p. 57.

6. Hauriou, *Principes de droit public* (The Principles of Public Law), 2nd ed. (Paris, 1916), p. 386

7. We shall disregard here, of course, the meaningless distinction between civilization and culture.

8. Cf. Hauriou, *Principes*, p. 603ff.

9. Ibid., 601ff., 612.

10. Ibid., p. 610. This observation is particularly important for a correct understanding of some of the factors in the political and constitutional development of Russia in the second half of the nineteenth century and the beginning of the twentieth century.

11. Ibid., p. 612.

12. Sadly, I must refrain from dealing with a range of other extremely interesting aspects of constitutional government, e.g., that constitutional government reinforces the public nature of the state; that it allows public opinion to emerge as a new form of sovereignty; or that the adoption of a written constitution creates, in a way, a statute for the state, giving the latter the status of a legal person.

13. Cucumus's observations can serve as an example of this view. In his work *Lehrbuch des Staatsrechtes der konstitutionellen Monarchie Bayerns'* (Textbook on Constitutional Law in the Kingdom of Bavaria), which appeared in 1825, and thus at a time when unadulterated liberalism predominated, he wrote, "All citizens are entitled to enjoy civil liberty" (p. 130). (Significantly, Cucumus calls this a "requirement flowing directly from the aims of the state.") Without, however, the existence of political freedom for the people, the former has no firm foundation or guarantee.

14. Cucumus (*Textbook*, p. 86), e.g., highlights this in respect of the Bavarian constitutional declaration of May 26, 1818. He writes, "The Bavarian constitution does not directly set out to define the aims of the state. The statute as a whole, however, does contain an acknowledgment of the only possibility, which consists of the primacy of law and the security of the citizen. The introduction to the constitutional declaration already mentions the aims of the state in general, although more specific details are found in Section IV, paragraph 8, of the constitution, where it states, 'The state guarantees each inhabitant the security of his person, his property and his rights.' This text is sufficiently explicit about what this aim consists of, what the state strives to achieve, and what demands the governed can make of the state. This repudiates all those ridiculous demands made in brilliant but practically useless theories that actually promote despotism. Here is a practical acknowledgment that the state must manage the external conditions required for the development of national life, but that it should not intervene to control it." Cucumus therefore asserts that the actual purpose of the state is to guarantee each citizen the security of his person, his property, and all his other acquired individual rights, and not to desire to determine the development of national life. This aim constitutes the internal limit to the exercise of legislative state power on the one hand and the political freedom of the citizens on the other.

15. Translator's note: All the quotations translated into English of Rousseau's "Contrat Social" are taken from the G. D. H. Cole translation, which is in the public domain.

16. I am indebted to Professor Otto Vossler for pointing out that it is possible to interpret the sovereignty of the *volonté générale* not to mean the sovereignty of decisions of the *communauté*, but the sovereignty of the categorical imperative. I assume that this interpretation takes the abovementioned problem as its starting point.

17. Hauriou, *Principes*, p. 613.

18. Hauriou, *Droit constitutionnel*, p. 140.

19. It is one of Hauriou's greatest achievements to have pointed out that the individualistic liberal social order does not depend just on the separation of powers as defined by Montesquieu, but on separations of power that are found even deeper in the social fabric of the state. For example, religious freedom in the narrow sense is based on the separation between spiritual and secular power. The division between the civilian bureaucracy and the military plays a large role in maintaining political liberty. Finally, as stated above, the separation between economic and political power that is now of such particular interest is an essential component of liberal order, as civil liberty is based on it.

20. Victor Leontovitsch's article "Abhängigkeit und Selbständigkeit bei der Gewaltenteilung" (Dependency and Independence in the context of the Separation of Powers) appeared in *Schriften der Soziologischen Abteilung des Forschungsinstituts für Sozial- und Verwaltungswissenschaften* (Cologne, 1951), vol. 1, pp. 394ff, published by Leopold von Wiese.

21. Hauriou, *Principes*, pp. 368ff.

22. Ibid., p. 140.

23. Hauriou, *La science sociale traditionnelle* (Paris, 1896), p. 412.

CHAPTER I. CATHERINE II

1. Translator's note: "P.S.Z." is the abbreviation for *Polnoe Sobranie Zakonov* (The Complete Collection of the Laws of the Russian Empire).

2. This *ukaz* is interpreted, however, in a diametrically opposite way by Romanovich-Slovatinsky; see *Dvorianstvo v Rossii ot nachala 18-go st. do otmeny krepestnogo prava* (The Nobility in Russia from the Beginning of the Eighteenth Century to the Abolition of Serfdom). [Translator's note: No publication information is provided in the original.]

3. The "Rassuzhdenie" was published in *Russkii Arkhiv* in 1865. This printed text, however, is not complete. A. Florovsky was able to find two handwritten versions of the same. The printed text corresponds to about two-thirds of the manuscript. For exact details of the manuscripts, refer to A. Florovsky, *K istorii economich. idei v Rossii v 18-om st.* (On the History

of Economic Ideas in Eighteenth-Century Russia), *Nauchnye Trudye,* University of the Russian People in Prague, vol. 1, p. 83, n. 1

4. See also Florovsky for the manuscripts containing these notes by Catherine (ibid., p. 84, n. 3).

5. All Catherine's comments cited above are taken from ibid., pp. 88ff.

6. *Sbornik Russk. Istor. Obshch.,* vol. 43, p. 209.

7. Ibid., vol. 36. [Translator's note: This translates to "statute on the rights of the citizen" or "of people of middle rank."]

8. Translator's note: See J. Donnelly, *The Concept of Human Rights,* Croom Helm International Series in Social and Political Thought (London, 1985), pp. 24–25. The German text contrasts "subjective" rights with "objective" law, terms that appear to be largely absent from English-language jurisprudence.

9. Translator's note: The author quotes the French in the original: "Lorsque le public a besoin du fonds d'un particulier, il ne faut pas agir par la rigueur de la loi politique, mais c'est là que doit triompher la loi civile qui, avec des yeux de mère, regarde chaque particulier comme toute la cité même. Si le magistrat public veut faire quelque édifice public, quelque nouveau chemin, il faut qu'il indemnise."

10. "Zhalovannaia gramota dvorianstvu," Apr. 21, 1785 (P.S.Z. no. 16 187). Guarantees of the property rights of townspeople were also included in the Charter to the Townspeople ("Gramota na prava i vygody gorodam russkoi imperii"), Apr. 21, 1785 (P.S.Z. no. 16 188—see esp, Arts. 4 and 88). Some of the regulations of the draft "Prav sredniago roda liudei" [legal statute for the middle class] were used in this charter.

11. Manifesto of June 28, 1782 (P.S.Z. no. 15 447); decree of Sept. 22, 1782 (P.S.Z. no. 15 518).

12. This is also confirmed by her legislation aimed at making the penal code more humane, which was enacted in various decades of her long reign.

13. K. Zaitsev, *Leksii po adm. pravu* (Lectures on Administrative Law) (Prague, 1923), p. 157 [hectographed copy].

14. M. Vladimirsky-Budanov, *Obzor istorii russkogo prava* (History of Russian Law) (Kiev, 1915), p. 237.

15. Catherine, *Instruktion* (German translation of the *Nakaz'*) (Riga, 1769).

16. Translator's note: The author uses French in the original: "Pour adoucir la servitude des paysans."

17. Catherine, "Materialy dlia Nakaza," introduction to *Nakaz,* published by Chechulin (Petersburg, 1907), p. lxxvi.

18. Ibid., p. xii.

19. Ibid., p. xi.

20. Evidence that at the time when the Commission on Laws was convened, much significance was attached and attention paid to the problem of peasant property is provided by the fact that the Free Economic Society awarded a prize for the best paper on the following question: "Which is more useful for the state: whether a peasant should also own land or just goods and chattels, and what are his rights in respect of the one and the other?" The best paper was by Polenov, who was also awarded a gold medal. Polenov (1738–1816) went on a study trip abroad after graduating from the St. Petersburg Academic University. He studied at the universities of Strasburg and Göttingen See A. Korkunov, *Istoriia filosofii prava* [History of the Philosophy of Law] (St.Petersburg, 1908), p. 255. Despite this prize, the paper, in which the author resolutely expresses his opposition to serfdom, was not published at the time, as some of the members of panel, insofar as "they were judging not just the content but also the style of the paper, found it to include excessively strong and improper language taking into account the conditions and context of the times." The paper was only published in 1865 as a historical document in the *Russkii Archiv* (1865, no. 3).

21. See Kotoshikhin, *O Rossii v tsarstvovanii Alexeia Michailovicha* [On Russia under Tsar Alexei Mikhaelovich], pp. xi, 3; Pososhkov, *O skudosti i bogatstve* [On Poverty and Wealth], p. vii,

both quoted in A. Gradovsky, *Nachala russk. gosud. prava* [Outlines of Russian Constitutional Law] (St. Petersburg, 1892), vol. 1, p. 239, n. 126; p. 240, n. 129.

22. Even so, the establishment of local government based on ideas of self-administration is an indication of a move toward political freedom.

23. Benjamin Constant, *De l'esprit de conquête et de l'usurpation* (German translation, Bern, 1942), p. 97.

24. Ibid., p. 97.

25. Taine also mentions these words of Napoleon.

26. V. Maklakov, *Vlast' i Obshchestvennost' na Zakate Staroi Rossii* (*Vospominaniia Sovremennika*) (State Power and Public Life before the Decline of the Old Russia: Memoirs of a Contemporary) (Riga, n.d.).

27. As is well known, Catherine predicted the caesaristic outcome of the revolution: "When the Gauls in Caesar's time were tearing themselves apart, just like today," she noted, writing to Grimm in Feb. 1791, "Caesar conquered them. When will this Caesar appear? He will come, of that you can be certain!" She raised this point several times in the same lines, in particular in Feb. 1794, when she wrote, "Should France emerge from her present predicament, it will be stronger than ever; it will be as obedient and meek as a lamb, but it needs a superior and courageous man who can dominate his contemporaries and perhaps the whole of the century. Has he been born? Will he come? Everything depends on it." Catherine is quoted in Stählin, *Geschichte Russlands von den Anfängen bis zur Gegenwart.*, 5 vols. (Berlin: Ost-Europa-Verl., 1923–39), vol. 2, pp. 729ff.

28. The arguments that Burke put forward in order to strengthen her in her antirevolutionary stance are interesting. Burke writes, "The debt, which your Imperial Majesty's august predecessors have contracted to the ancient manners of Europe, by means of which they civilized a vast empire, will be nobly repaid by preserving those manners from the hideous change, with which they are menaced. By the intervention of Russia the world will be preserved from barbarism and ruin" (letter of Nov. 1, 1791).

29. Radishchev too—in *Puteshestvie*—considered that only a gradual emancipation of the serfs was possible. See Radishchev, *Sochinenija* (St. Petersburg, 1907), vol. 1, p. 156; this is missing from the German translation published by Stählin. Like the empress, he conceives of the liberated peasants as small independent landowners. See Radishchev, *Reise von Petersburg nach Moskau*, German translation (Leipzig, 1922), p. 108. [Translator's note: This can be translated as "Journey from St. Petersburg to Moscow."]

30. Radishchev, "Reise," p. 148

31. Catherine, *Sobranie Sochinenii* (Collected Works) (St. Petersburg, 1907), vol. 12, p. 615.

32. Savigny, *Vom Beruf unserer Zeit für Gesetzgebung und Rechtswissenschaft* (Of the Vocation of Our Times for Legislation and Jurisprudence) (Heidelberg, 1814), pp. 4ff.

33. V. Sergeevich, "Otkuda neudachi Ekaterininskoi Zakonodatel'noi Komissii" (Causes of the Failure of Catherine's Law Code Commission), *Vestnik Evropy* (1878): vol. 1, p. 198.

34. Catherine, *Collected Works*, vol. 12, p. 617; cf. the following from the Instruction: "Laws that are intended to do all too much good often do a great deal of harm" (Art. 65). Further on: "By making illegal what is naturally allowed or otherwise inevitable, all that is achieved is to dishonor people who act that way" (Art. 344). [Translator's note: The author uses the French in the original: "La chose qui la plus sujette à des inconvenients est de faire quelque nouvelle loi."]

35. Author's note: The French is preferable here, as the idea is less clearly expressed in the Russian and German translations.

36. Translator's note: The author uses the French in the original: "Les lois sont des institutions particulières et précises du législateur; les mœurs et les coutumes, des institutions de la nation en général. Ainsi quand on trouve qu'il est nécessaire de faire des grands changements dans une nation, pour son plus grand bien, il faut réformer par des lois, ce qui est établi par des lois, et changer par des coutumes, ce qui est établi par des coutumes. C'est une très mauvaise politique de vouloir changer par des lois ce qui doit être changé par des coutumes."

37. Catherine repeatedly expresses the idea that legislation must be in tune with the general character (*l'esprit*) of the nation, because in the first place, "we do nothing well unless we undertake it voluntarily, and not through compulsion, but following our inclination" (Art. 57), and second, because "laws are most natural when their specific form accords with the disposition of the people for whom they have been created."

38. In Russia the Senate has the function of guardian of the law (Art. 26).

39. Author's note: In the Russian version "gosudarstvennye pravitel'stva," and in the French "corps politiques."

40. Translator's note: The author uses the French in the original: "qui sont contraires à l'ordre établi dans l'État."

41. Radishchev, "Reise," p. 78.

42. Corpus Jur. Can., *Decreti Prima Pars.*, C.2, Dist. IV. [Translator's note: The author uses the Latin in the original: "Erit autem lex . . . secundum consuetudinem patriae."]

43. Hauriou, *Principes*, p. xvii. See also Pertile, *Storia del Diritto Italiano* (Rome, 1896), vol. 5, pp. 387ff. Pertile is concerned with the less interesting case, in which statute laws take on the properties of common law following the collapse of the state in which they were enacted—i.e., the situation in which the laws (statutes) of a state that has disappeared continue to survive as common law under a new state that replaced the former. In contrast, Hauriou analyzes the possibility that laws, even when they remain in force and are respected as such, also become common law by the fact of their long survival. This means that the annulment of such laws, which have deep roots in the legal tradition of a nation, by a revolution or through a radical reform is not just the abolition of laws, but at the same time also the abolition of a common-law tradition.

CHAPTER 2. ALEXANDER I

1. K. Waliszewski, *Le fils de la Grande Cathérine, Paul I* (Paris, 1912), p. 230. [Translator's note: The author uses the French in the original: "la chimère de l'Etat-Providence universelle."]

2. Waliszewski emphasizes the fact that Paul I's patriarchal despotism was in essence similar to the revolutionary tyranny of the Jacobins. He writes, "Le despotisme de Paul, sa façon d'intervenir jusque dans la vie intime de ses sujets ont pour source principale l'idée essentiellement patriarcale qu'il se fait de sa fonction et qu'il rattache à la doctrine de l'Etat-Providence, professée aussi en commun, sans qu'il y prenne garde, avec des Jacobins qu'il a en abomination" [Paul I's despotism, his way of intervening in the private life of his subjects, derived mainly from his essentially patriarchal conception of his role. He combines this with the doctrine of the providential state, without realizing he had this in common with the Jacobins, whom he abominated]. It is certainly not unlikely that Catherine's rejection of Radishchev's ideas was based on her recognizing in them a reflection of the tyrannical tendencies of Jacobinism. In any case, this is supported by a series of notes in the margin of Radishchev's book, in which she points out the affinity between his views and Jacobin thinking.

3. V. Ikonnikov, *Count Mordvinov* (St. Petersburg, 1873), p. 28, footnote.

4. There are three versions of the draft of this declaration—two Russian (1 and 2) and one French (3). Version 2 differs from version 1 in that three articles from version 1 have been left out. These first three articles deal with the nature of the tsar's powers (Art. 1); the law of the succession to the throne of Apr. 5, 1797 (Art. 2; this law was confirmed by this article); and the situation of the Senate—in other words, the basic institutions of the state (Art. 3). Apparently, it was thought illogical to include these three individual, rather disparate articles in the declaration, which was about the basic rights of the subject. Otherwise version 2 only differs from version 1 as a result of a few, mostly stylistic corrections. (The text of the declaration is reputed to have been written by Radishchev, who had been reinstated in government service under Paul I and was then corrected by Speransky, particularly from a stylistic point of view. Radishchev, as we know, wrote in a style that was dated at the time: Pushkin described his style as barbaric.) This version appears in Semennikov's book *Radishchev* (Moscow, 1923), pp. 180–94. The first three articles from version 1 are also included: pp. 431ff. The French version

3 was published together with Vorontsov's Observations of Aug. 12, 1801, in a supplement to the journal *Russkii Archiv* (1908): vol. 2, pp. 7–13. These observations were regarded as a joint memorandum by Vorontsov, Kochubei, and Novosil'tsev, although Vorontsov was probably the real author. Version 3 leaves out some of the demands of version 2, apparently those that were seen as particularly "radical." In essence, however, the content is the same as version 2. Particularly significant is the alteration to the title of version 3. While both the first two versions were directly called *Gramota*, the heading of the French version is "Articles ou matériaux qui peuvent servir à la confection d'un édit ou manifeste de privilèges, franchises etc." [Articles or materials that could serve to produce a text or manifesto of privileges, franchises, etc.]. This title sounds as if the author no longer counted on the declaration being published in the foreseeable future. In fact, neither the third version nor the first two were adopted by Alexander.

5. Translator's note: The author quotes the French from the source text.

6. This memorandum is also printed in the supplement to the journal *Russkii Archiv* (1908): vol. 2, pp. 18–20.

7. A. Makarov, "Proekt osnovnych Zakonov ross. imperii 1804 goda" (Draft of the Fundamental laws of the Russian Empire in the year 1804), in *Zapiski russk. nauchn.* (Belgrade: Inst., 1937), no. 15. The Russian text of this draft (abridged) was published by Makarov; see ibid., pp. 157–64. The German text was published as a supplement to his larger German study: *Entwurf der Verfassungsgesetze des Russischen Reichs von 1804. Ein Beitrag zur Geschichte der Kodifikation des russischen Rechts'* [Draft of the Fundamental Laws of the Russian Empire, 1804. A Contribution to the Codification of Russian Law] (Jahrbücher für Kultur u. Geschichte der Slawen, N.F., vol. 2, no. 2, 1926), pp. 201–366.

8. Ikonnikov, *Count Mordvinov*, p. 4.

9. Korkunov, *History*, pp. 261ff.

10. M. Korf, *Zhizn' grafa Speranskogo* (The Life of Count Speransky) (St. Petersburg, 1861), vol. 1, p. 191.

11. Ikonnikov, *Count Mordvinov*, p. 72ff.

12. The members of the "Unofficial Committee" were V. P. Kochubei, N. N. Novosil'tsev, Prince Adam Czartoryski, and Count p. A. Stroganov.

13. Ikonnikov, *Count Mordvinov*, p. 31.

14. *Polnoe Sobranie Zakonov*, vol. 26, no. 20075. The "many people" mentioned by Stroganov must surely also include Vorontsov. The following appears in the notes to the draft declaration of rights, which he wrote in Aug. 1801 in collaboration with Kochubei and Novosil'tsev: "Ne pourrait-on pas accorder tant aux paysans de la couronne qu'à ceux des propriétaires le droit d'acheter des terres sans habitations. . . . Ce que nous entendons sous la dénomination de 'pustosi,' leur permettre pour cela de passer des actes par devant les tribunaux en leur propre nom sans qu'ils ayent besoin d'avoir recours à un prêtenom, comme ils le font toujours et enfin de leur garantir cette propriété qui en seroit une foncière comme celle de tous les autres membres de la société. Cette mesure qui ne paraît pas impracticable, produirait dans un pays tel que la nôtre un bien infini: car outre l'encouragement. . . À défricher la quantité de terres incultes que nous avons et à tirer le meilleur partie possible de celles qui leur appartiendroient en propre; outre que cela augmenteroient beaucoup la masse de nos productions annuelles cela offiroit l'avantage de faire connoître mieux encore que tous les préceptes possibles ce qui constitue la nature d'une propriété, chose dont la plupart des paysans n'ont aucune idée. Il est cependant aisé de voir combien il est essentiel qu'ils sachent distinguer le propriétaire du tenancier ou fermier et qu'ils commencent à sentir un intérêt à respecter la propriété; car c'est en cela seul que consiste tout le danger de les rendre libre ou de se précipiter de faire beaucoup en leur faveur" ("Observations" on Art. 9, in *Russkii Archiv* [1908], vol. 2). As can be seen, Vorontsov goes further than Mordvinov and the *ukaz* of Dec. 12, 1801. He recommends that not only state peasants but also serfs should be granted the right to own land.

[Would it not be possible to grant to state peasants and those on private estates the right to buy land without dwellings—what we understand by the term *pustosi*—to allow them to go before the courts on their own account for this purpose, without having to use a pseudonym, as they always do, and finally to guarantee that this property would be the same as that belonging to other members of society? This measure, which does not appear impractical, would produce infinite benefits in a country such as ours. For besides the motivation to open up areas of uncultivated land and making the best of those that would belong to them; besides greatly increasing our annual production, it would also offer the advantage that they would get to know better than from any teaching the nature of property, something about which the peasants have no idea. Nevertheless, it is easy to see how essential it is that they learn to distinguish a proprietor from a tenant or leaseholder and start to feel that it is in their interest to respect property; for in that lies the only danger of emancipating them or hastening to do much for their benefit.]

15. The Nepremenny Soviet (Permanent Council) presided over by the tsar was founded by Alexander I on Mar. 30, 1801, following a proposal from Troshchinsky. It comprised twelve members, and its role was to review all the important affairs of state and legislation. It replaced the Vremennii Soviet (Provisional Council) (Ikonnikov, *Count Mordvinov*, p. 37, n. 1).

16. Ibid., pp. 37, 39, 38, 52.

17. In German research, it is customary to call the Gosudarstvennyi Soviet the Imperial Council [*Reichsrat* in the original]. I prefer to use the exact translation, in other words, the expression "State Council" [*Staatsrat* in the original]. There was nothing in the function of the State Council that particularly related to the existence of Russia as an Empire (Imperium). On the other hand, the State Council was set up in the context of efforts to draw a line between the legislative power and the executive and to establish a balance between these two branches of the state.

18. There were four departments in the State Council: (a) for legislation, (b) for military affairs, (c) for civil and cultural affairs, and (d) for economic affairs. Speransky was appointed as secretary of state. The collaboration between Speransky and Mordvinov resulted from their position on the State Council. They had, however, known each other well before then and had worked together on, e.g., the preparation of the draft financial system (Ikonnikov, *Count Mordvinov*, p. 77).

19. Mordvinov drew up the draft statutes for private and state banks (ibid., p. 202).

20. See ibid., pp. 95, 102.

21. Cf. his article "Some Considerations on Manufacturing in Russia and on Tariffs" (1816). It is interesting that in connection with the necessity of finding a market for the resulting excess Russian production, he thought not of "old" Europe but of "new" Asia. Trade with the East seemed to him to be the peaceful and "elegant" way to secure Russian interests on that continent (Ikonnikov, *Count Mordvinov*, p. 104).

22. This supposition is justified, however, because Mordvinov's and Speransky's views otherwise display many remarkable similarities even in points of detail.

23. Mordvinov held the same opinion as Catherine in her Instruction (derived in the final analysis from Montesquieu) that Russia's large size necessitated the retention of the absolute monarchy. This seems to be an uncritical reiteration of a traditionally held view (Ikonnikov, *Count Mordvinov*, p. 122, n. 1).

24. The following passage from Speransky's letter to his friend Stolypin is well known: "Epurez la partie administrative. Venez ensuite à établir les lois constitutionelles, c'est à dire la liberté politique et puis ensuite et graduellement vous viendrez à la question de la liberté civile, c'est à dire la liberté des paysans. Voilà la véritable ordre des choses" (quoted in Gradovsky, *Outlines*, p. 246, n. 162).

[Purge the administration. Then establish constitutional laws, that is to say, political liberty, and gradually the question of civil liberty will arise, that is, the liberty of the peasants. That is the way things are ordered.]

25. Quoted in ibid., p. 247, n. 164.

26. Ibid., p. 246.

27. Translator's note: The author uses the French title in the original: "La Russie et les Russes."

28. Quoted in Ikonnikov, *Count Mordvinov*, p. 236.

CHAPTER 3. SPERANSKY

1. M. Speransky, *Vvedenie k ulozheniiu gosudarsvennykh zakanov* [Introduction to the Codification of the Laws of the State] (1809). V. Semevsky's edition is used here.

2. That this is the essence of constitutional government was shown at length by Hauriou in his *Principes de droit public.*

3. This idea can also be found in a somewhat different form in the report (May 1, 1804) of the Commission for the Draft Constitution, headed by Lopukhin and Novosil'tsev: "These basic principles of law are for the most part found in Catherine's Instruction. . . . They are scattered in other decrees . . . enacted by the autocratic power of the Russian monarchy and blessed by the hand of time, that judge who decides impartially as to the strengths and weaknesses of laws" (p. 20).

4. Speransky, *Druzheskie pis'ma k Masal'skomu* (Friendly Letters to Masalsky) (St. Petersberg, 1862), p. 34.

5. Incidentally, this danger had been recognized earlier; some analyzed socialist ideas and socialist programs before the attempts to put socialist principles into practice (Chicherin, Hauriou); others looked at the effects of the antiliberal legislation in the 1890s in Russia. See Struve, *Na raznye temy* (On Diverse Topics) (St. Petersburg, 1902). Struve's article "Pravo i prava" (Law and Rights), which first appeared in the journal *Prav* in 1901, reproduced here on pp. 522–25, deals with this subject.

6. Translator's note: The author uses the French in the original: "Le plus grand novateur est le temps."

7. In 1810, thirty-five members were appointed to the State Council; by 1890, the council had increased to sixty.

8. Accordingly, the old wording, cited above, used when the tsar confirmed the resolutions of the State Council, was not renewed in the law of 1842, but was replaced by wording in line with the new decree.

9. Thus Witte records that this was the case with the enactment of Minister of the Interior Pleve's anti-Semitic decrees: "The legislators . . . knew that the State Council (the old one [i.e., prior to the reform undertaken after 1905], made up exclusively of bureaucrats, to use the fashionable term) would either express its opposition through its majority, or would let the proposal 'run into the sand,' or at least would speak many unpleasant truths to the ministers who were responsible for the new restrictive measures against Jews. Such legislative proposals were thus not put before the council, as would have been required by law, but were laid before the tsar with the help of the Committee of Ministers and, in cases in which opposition was expected even there, through special audiences or simply personal reports from the responsible minister." See Witte, *Vospominaniia* (Memoirs) (Berlin, 1922), vol. 1, p. 189.

10. It is wholly inconceivable that it would have been possible with such personalities to organize the unanimous affirmative votes seen in the assemblies of totalitarian states. In any case, it has to be said that the tsars were hardly interested in such votes. What they were interested in was the expert opinion of experienced members of the government and senior civil servants, not their agreement or approval. The legitimate absolute monarch of a country without a tradition of liberty or developed public opinion could easily dispense with such approval. Most if not all tsars in the nineteenth century, as far as we know, would have been temperamentally hostile to such organized, insincere acclamation.

11. M. Korf, *Memoirs* (St. Petersburg: Russkaia Starina, 1899), pp. 280ff. See also Kisevetter, *Istorich. ocherki* (Moscow, 1912), pp. 451ff.

12. Korf, *Memoirs*, pp. 19ff.

13. Ibid., p. 20.

14. Meshchersky, *Vospominaniia* (Memoirs) (St. Petersburg, 1912), vol. 3, p. 288.

15. Ibid., vol. 3, p. 289.

16. Ibid.

17. Interesting details about the State Council before the 1906 reforms, as well as about some of its famous members, can be found in V. I. Gurko, *Features and Figures of the Past Government and Opinion in the Reign of Nicholas II*, Hoover Library on War, Revolution and Peace, Publication No. 14 (Stanford: Stanford University Press, 1939), chaps. 2, 9. Chap. 3 deals with the chancellery, which was closely connected with State Council.

18. Speransky, *Friendly Letters*, p. 35.

19. Translator's note: The author only provides the German translation of the first title. The original Russian title for this work is found in M. Raeff, *Michael Speransky—Statesman of Imperial Russia* (The Hague, 1957), 369.

20. Speransky only rarely uses the term "authentic monarchy" (e.g., *Friendly Letters*, p. 25); mostly he just writes "monarchy." It is always clear that what he means by this is an "authentic" monarchy, i.e., a constitutional monarchy, and that he regards this as the antithesis of despotism.

21. It is clear that here Speransky means institutions and not estates when he uses the term *soslovie*.

22. This whole passage was deleted by Speransky and omitted from the final edition.

23. The poet Vyazemsky called Speransky a "gigantic clerk."

24. Barsukov, *Zhizn' i trudy Pogodina* (Life and Works of Pogodin) (St. Petersburg, 1896), vol. 10, p. 111.

25. G. Florovsky, *Puti russkogo bogosloviia* (The Routes of Russian Theology) (Paris, 1937), p. 139.

26. Staroverov to Pogodin, in Barsukov, *Pogodin*, vol. 10, p. 109.

CHAPTER 4. KARAMZIN

1. Incidentally, constitutionalists can also believe that the extensive implementation of liberal measures while still under an absolute monarchy is a necessary condition for the transition to a constitutional monarchy.

2. Karamzin, *Istoricheskoe pokhval'noe slovo Ekaterine* (Historical Eulogy to Catherine II), in *Sochinenia* (Collected Works), (St. Petersburg, 1835), vol. 8, p. 41. See also p. 42.

3. Ibid., p. 40.

4. "The sovereign must fulfill his own duties no less than any subject." Karamzin, *Zapiska o drevnei i novoi Rossii* (Memorandum on Ancient and Modern Russia), an appendix to Pypin's *Istoricheskie Ocherki* (Historical Sketches) (St. Petersburg, 1885), p. 496. The memorandum was presented to the tsar by Karamzin in 1811.

5. Karamzin, *Collected Works*, vol. 8, pp. 29–77.

6. Karamzin, *O Tainoi Kantseliarii* (The Secret Chancellery), 1803, in *Collected Works*, vol. 8, pp. 131ff.

7. This repeats Article 511 of the Instruction.

8. Karamzin, *Pis'mo sel'skogo Zhitelia*, (Letter from a Country Dweller), in *Collected Works* (St. Petersburg, 1834), vol. 7, pp. 238–52.

9. The fact that "the serfs of a reasonable landowner . . . are better off than state peasants" demonstrates this (*Memorandum*, p. 513).

10. In my opinion, this would have meant the demise of all *pouvoirs intermédiaires* as understood by Montesquieu, of all nonstate, and thus independent, services, even if these were only on a modest scale. One should not forget that in the country at the time in the context of serfdom, all administrative functions, the police, the courts, recruitment to the army, tax collection, and economic relief were undertaken by landowners.

11. It has to be said that ultimately the whole failure—or to put it more cautiously, the basic shortcomings of the emancipation of the serfs in 1861—was a direct consequence of the fact that at the time—in 1861—these conditions had not been put in place. This will be taken up in the relevant chapter later.

12. Translator's note: The author uses the Italian in the original: "la legge è fatta, si troverà anche il rimedio."

13. Karamzin, "Osvobozhdenie Evropy" (The Liberation of Europe), in *Collected Works* (St. Petersburg, 1834), vol. 1, pp. 253ff. In this edition, pp. 241–53 are wrongly numbered, having been double counted.

14. Translator's note: The author quotes Sallust, the Roman historian (86 B.C.E.–35 B.C.E.), in the Latin original: "Quae homines arant, navigant, aedificant, virtuti omni parent" (Sallust, *Bellum Catilinae [Catiline's War]*, chap. 2).

15. Author's note: This is in spaced type in the original (Karamzin, "Liberation," p. 258).

16. Karamzin, "Letters of a Russian Traveller" (Moscow: Pis'ma Ruskago Puteshestvennika, 1797).

17. Karamzin, *Pis'mo k Dmitrievu* (Letters to Dmitriev) (St. Petersburg, 1866), letter dated Aug. 17, 1793.

18. Ibid., p. 412.

19. Ibid., p. 411.

20. Ibid., p. 299.

21. Quoted in M. Volkonsky, *Die Dekabristen* (The Decembrists) (Zürich, 1946), p. 74 (author's emphasis).

22. Cf. Bestuzhev's words cited above.

23. A. Fateev, *Le problème de l'individu et de l'homme d'état dans la personnalité historique d'Alexandre I, empereur de toutes les Russies* (Prague, 1938), vol. 4, p. 3.

24. Cf. Alexander's letter to Speransky of 1818 in which he expresses his religious resignation.

25. G. Vernadsky, introduction to *La charte const. de l'Emp. Russe de l'an 1820* (Paris, 1933), p. vii; see also p. 47.

26. Quoted in ibid., p. 26. [Translator's note: The author uses the French in the original: "L'organisation qui était en vigueur dans votre pays a permis l'établissement immédiat de celle que je vous ai donnée, en mettant en pratique les principes de ces institutions libérales, qui n'ont cessé de faire l'objet de ma sollicitude et dont j'espère, avec l'aide de Dieu, étendre l'influence salutaire sur toutes les contrées que la Providence a confiées à mes soins."]

27. Karamzin reports this in a letter to Dmitriev of Sept. 2, 1825.

28. Vernadsky analyzes Novosil'tsev's draft in the work already cited above. I can therefore restrict myself to citing only the most important articles. The final article (Art. 191) declares that the *Ustavnaia Gramota* carries the significance of a constitution; that its aim is "to provide a foundation for the inviolability of the person and property and to secure the inviolable nature of civil and political rights." For example, the inviolability of the person is grounded in Arts. 81, 82, 87; that of property vis-à-vis the state in Arts. 97 and 98. Art. 90 is interesting as it grants the right to citizens of the Russian Empire to emigrate with all their property, as is Art. 93, which allows all foreigners the right to move to Russia, to leave it, and to maintain immovable property there. Novosil'tsev's draft therefore goes further than the 1801 draft declaration quoted in chap. 2, which only mentions the right of the gentry and the townspeople to move abroad. Incidentally, the first attempts to give this right a legal basis came in the Time of Troubles. This certainly represented a reaction against the policies of Ivan IV that aimed, as Kurbsky put it, to keep people inside his empire as if in hell. As far as political rights are concerned, their exercise was based on the establishment of a representative assembly. This assembly would consist of two chambers. According to Art. 101 (see also Arts. 13 and 31), the tsar can only exercise his legislative power with the participation of the representative assembly. The two chambers would not be given legislative power of initiative. The assembly could only express opinions on legislation laid before it by the tsar through the State Council, where draft laws were normally prepared (Art. 42). (According to the draft, the State Council is a branch of the executive, while the Senate is the Upper Chamber.) Overall, this draft has many features in common with the 1818 Bavarian constitution and the one in Baden. What distinguished the draft was the way Russia was divided into large regions (*Namestnichestva*). Each of these

regions had a constitution that reflected that of the whole empire. For each region there would be a small provincial parliament, which would elect candidates, of whom half would be confirmed as members of an Imperial Assembly by the tsar. In Vernadsky's opinion, the aim of the draft constitution's federalist tendency was to ensure the unity of the empire. He writes, "Le fédéralisme tel qu'il ressorte de la Charte, ne signifiait pas une division de la Russie, mais sa consolidation" [The federalism such as emerges in the Charter does not entail the division of Russia but its consolidation] [ibid., p. 46]. B. Nolde stresses this aspect of the draft even more. He believes that the reason Novosil'tsev drafted the constitution of the Russian Empire along federalist lines was to solve a quite concrete problem, namely how to do away with Polish autonomy. Nolde cites the draft of an *ukaz* connected to Novosil'tsev's draft constitution. According to this *ukaz*, Poland was to be incorporated into the Russian Empire. The justification for this move, contained in the *ukaz*, was that "the existence of two constitutions in one empire did not contribute to and was downright detrimental to the need for a unified and successful government." See B. Nolde, *Dalekoe i blizkoe* (Paris, 1930), p. 15. It is also interesting that Nolde doubts it is possible to claim, like Vernadsky, that the draft represented a moment "in the development of the whole of Tsar Alexander's political system." In Nolde's opinion, the draft was based not on Alexander's ideas, but on Novosil'tsev's views and administrative experience.

29. Fateev, *Probleme*, p. 2.

CHAPTER 5. THE CODIFICATION OF THE LAW

1. Karamzin, *Priiatnye vidy, nadezhdy i zhelaniia nyneshniago vremeni* (Pleasant Views, Hopes, and Wishes of Our Times), 1802, in *Works* (St. Petersburg, 1835), vol. 9, p. 94.

2. Ibid., p. 95.

3. M. Korf, *Zhizn' Grafa Speranskogo* (The Life of Count Speransky) (St. Petersburg, 1861), vol. 1, p. 146.

4. Ibid., vol. 1, p. 147. Cf. also Makarov in the article cited above about Rosenkampf's constitutional project.

5. In Russia at the time there was a similar development to the West, about which Savigny wrote, "A sense of history is awakening everywhere, next to which that incredible arrogance (the expectation that the present time can be perfected) has no place. See *Vocation of Our Times*, pp. 5ff. It comes as no surprise that Karamzin, the father of Russian historical studies, became the representative of this school of thought in Russia.

6. This assertion is historically incorrect, as Peter the Great did in fact have some foreign laws translated. However, this is of no importance here, because it is not the historical fact that is significant, but Karamzin's views.

7. This is an allusion to the fact that during the eighteenth century there were nine commissions entrusted with working on a new law code.

8. Bacon, *De argumentis Scientiarum* (The Advancement of Learning), book 8, chap. 3, aphorism 59. [Translator's note: The whole of this aphorism is worth citing here: "But if laws heaped upon laws swell to such a vast bulk, and labour under such confusion as renders it expedient to treat them anew, and reduce them into one sound and serviceable corps, it becomes the work of the utmost importance, deserving to be deemed heroical, and let the authors of it be ranked among legislators, and the restorers of states and empires." See *The Advancement of Learning in the Physical and Metaphysical Works of Lord Bacon*, trans. Joseph Devey (London, 1856), p. 358.]

9. Bacon, *De argumentis Scientiarum*, aphorism 64: "'Twere to be wished that such a recompilement of the laws might be undertaken in such times as excel the ancients (whose acts and works they model anew) in point of learning and universal knowledge." See *Advancement of Learning*, p. 359.

10. Quoted from Latkin, *Uchebnik istorii russk. prava* (Handbook of the History of Russian Law) (St. Petersburg, 1899), p. 92. [Translator's note: Latkin's work focuses on the eighteenth and nineteenth centuries.]

11. The first time, as stated above, the first two parts of the draft were checked by the State

Council in 1810, in other words, at a time when Speransky was still director of the commission; the third part was put to the State Council in 1813, during Speransky's exile. This part of the Civil Code was, however, never dealt with by the State Council, as in June 1814 an order was issued by the highest authority to revise the first two parts of the code, together with this third part. This revision was suspended in 1815 after objections from the minister of justice, Troshchinsky, who was extremely critical of the draft. Troshchinsky was particularly critical of the draft because it was based on foreign models and was alien to the spirit of the Russian people. As a result, the State Council decided that the laws in the draft should be compared to existing legislation and that a start should be made on producing a systematic edition of existing legislation (Korf, *Life of Count Speransky*, vol 1, pp. 168ff).

12. Ibid., vol. 2, p. 277. Latkin is of the same opinion.

13. Ibid., vol. 2, pp. 278ff.

14. A. Fateev, *Svod Zakonov i ego tvorets* (The Law Code and Its Creator), in *Zapiski russk. nauchn. Instituta v Belgrade* (1932), vol. 7, p. 66.

15. Korf, *Life of Count Speransky*, vol. 2, p. 211.

16. Speransky had not known Karamzin before 1812. They met for the first time in 1812 at Nizhni-Novgorod, when Speransky stayed there as an exile and Karamzin as a refugee.

17. Korf, *Life of Count Speransky*, vol. 2, pp. 298ff.

18. For more details, see Latkin, *Handbook*, pp. 98ff.

19. See M. Vinaver, *K voprusu ob istochnikakh X-go toma* (On the Question of the Sources of the Tenth Volume of the Svod), in *Zhurnal Min. Just.* (Oct. 1895).

20. Korf, *Life of Count Speransky*, vol. 2, pp. 324ff.

CHAPTER 6. NICHOLAS I

1. *Sbornik Imp. Ross. Istor. Obshch*, vol. 74, pp. 171ff. The comment was also made that only a few words should be added, for the same reasons, about the serf-owning rights of landowners.

2. Zaitsev, *Lectures*, p. 177.

3. Ibid., p. 161.

4. A. Kizevetter, "Emperor Nicholas I as a Constitutional Monarch," in *Istorich. Ocherki* (Historical Sketches) (Moscow, 1912), p. 417. Cf. *Sbornik Imp. Ross. Istor. Obshch.*, vol. 131. This volume contains correspondence between Tsar Nicholas I and his brother Constantine.

5. A. Zablotsky-Desiatovsky, *Graf P. D Kiselev i ego vremia* (Count P. D. Kiselev and His Times) (St.Petersburg, 1882), vol. 2, p. 2; see also vol. 2, pp. 208ff.

6. The feeling of disappointment that spread through the country following the defeat of 1855 served only to accelerate the formation of this awareness.

7. D. Miliutin, *L'abolition du servage en Russie*, extract from *Journal des Economistes* (June 1863) : p. 2.

8. Gradovsky, *Outlines*, pp. 249ff.

9. *Sbornik tsirkuliarov i instruksii Min. Vn. Del.* (Collected Circulars of the Ministry of the Interior from Its Foundation to October 1, 1853), 8 vols. (St. Petersburg, 1854), vol. 1, paragraph 234.

10. In 1816, a start was made during the reign of Alexander I with the emancipation of serfs in the Baltic regions. This reform in the Baltic provinces proved to be a deterrent for the Russian heartlands. In fact, the serfs were emancipated in the Baltic regions without giving them land. Even the land that the peasants had cultivated before remained the property of the landowners. The serfs became day laborers, and their economic situation deteriorated rather than improved.

11. The chairperson of the committee was Count Kochubei; the other members were Count Tolstoy, Prince Vasil'chikov, Prince Golitsyn, Baron Dibich, and Speransky; the secretary was Bludov.

12. Kizevetter, "Emperor Nicholas I," pp. 445ff. The question as to what legal status such contracts would have is not without interest.

13. Quoted in ibid., p. 481.

14. Quoted in ibid., p. 484; cf the law of Apr. 2, 1842 (P.S.Z. no. 15462).

15. It is obvious that the solution put in place by the law of Apr. 2, 1842, was not only impractical but also a non sequitur from a legal point of view. An agreement freely entered into by two free parties is possible, but not between masters and serfs in the context of serfdom.

16. Gradovsky, *Outlines*, p. 252.

17. My assertion here is apparently contradicted by the fact that the Provincial Committees of 1858–59 had almost unanimously supported the retention of the administrative powers of the landowners in the villages. The formal resolutions and subjective feelings do not necessarily have to match one another. Besides, this was only meant to apply to the years of transition.

18. Quoted in Kizevetter, "Emperor Nicholas I," p. 485.

CHAPTER 7. NICHOLAS I (CONTINUED)

1. The tsar later repeatedly made statements along the same lines as the speech to the State Council cited above; these statements are quoted in Latkin, *Handbook*, p. 211.

2. Nicholas's long-serving minister of finance, Kankrin, set out his ideas on economics in the following publications: *On Wealth and the National Economy* (1821) and *On the Economy of Human Society* (1845). Ikonnikov writes that "in Kankrin's opinion (absolutely in line with liberalism), which he sets out in these publications, the government's aim must be to improve the well-being of the individual and not to increase the income of the state" (*Count Mordvinov*, p. 450). He stresses that in practice Kankrin adhered strictly to his theoretical views. Other ministers held similar views. When a draft of the new statute on trade was presented in 1856 to the minister of the interior and the minister for estates by the minister of finance, they again came out against any restrictions on free trade. See *O Prave na Torgovliu* (On the Right to Trade) (St. Petersburg, 1860), esp. pp. 9, 57.

3. Translator's note: this French term denotes a mechanism whereby constitutional checks are available "above" legislation. Here the author is by analogy describing the tsar's pastoral duties as a form of check on his legislative duties.

4. *Sbornik tsirkuliarov i instruksii Min.Vn. Del.*, vol. 4, paragraph 98.

5. Miliutin, *L'abolition du servage*, p. 3, n. 1; see also Schnitzler, *L'empire des tsars au point actuel de la science* (1862), vol. 2.

6. Translator's note: One *desiatin* is only slightly larger than a hectare, or 2.5 acres.

7. Zablotsky-Desiatovsky, *Graf P. D Kiselev*, vol. 2, p. 27.

8. This term was not used at that time. There were many categories of individuals in the rural population who were not serfs, but who were all given the status of state peasant by the decrees of 1714 and 1724.

9. Zablotsky-Desiatovsky, *Graf P. D Kiselev*, pp. 25ff.

10. Ibid., p. 28.

11. Ibid., p. 30.

12. Cf. Latkin, *Handbook*, p. 169.

13. Zablotsky-Desiatovsky, *Graf P. D Kiselev*, pp. 31ff.

14. Quoted in ibid., p. 10.

15. Cf. *Sbornik Russk. Ist. Obshch.*, vol. 74, p. 310.

16. Zablotsky-Desiatovsky, *Graf P. D Kiselev*, pp. 18ff.

17. Quoted by Zablotsky-Desiatovsky, who cites Count Kiselev's report of Oct. 6, 1836 (ibid., p. 21).

18. Report by Count Kiselev of May 17, 1837, quoted in ibid., p. 59.

19. Quoted in ibid., p. 108.

20. Quoted in ibid., p. 62.

21. Cf. *Svod Zakonov* (1833), vol. 12, *Svod postanovlenii . . . o blagoustroistve v kazennych seleniiakh*, and the 1826 *Polozhenie* on the administration of agriculture in the provinces of St. Petersburg and Pskov.

22. Quoted in Zablotsky-Desiatovsky, *Graf p. D Kiselev*, p. 62.

23. Quoted in ibid., p. 64.

24. Quoted in ibid., p. 78.

25. Ibid., p. 51.

26. Ibid., p. 50.

27. Ibid., p. 171.

28. Ibid., p. 167.

29. Ibid., pp. 175ff; cf. also p. 32.

30. The response of the deputy minister for state domains was typical. He was at pains to demonstrate that the new ministry's offices had ensured that aid had not been kept in the hands of those responsible for distributing it, and that neither had it been passed on exclusively to the kulaks. The minister pointed out, however, that it would have been wrong of the *popechitel'stvo* (trustees) to agree to all the peasants' wishes, which were "always exaggerated and unjustified," "which would give them the dangerous idea that the government had the duty to feed them when their own supplies ran short" (quoted in ibid., p. 84).

31. Ibid., p. 165.

32. Ibid., pp. 155ff. It should not be forgotten that at the time one thought of the emancipation of the serfs as giving the serfs the status of state peasants.

33. Cf. Kiselev's 1849 report to the tsar, which is in this spirit, in ibid., p. 199.

34. Ibid., p. 49.

35. Ibid., pp. 45ff.

36. All these details have been taken from the jubilee edition of *The Department of Agriculture and Its Work over Seventy-five Years (1837–1912)* (St. Petersburg, 1914), pp. 26ff.

37. Kizevetter, "Emperor Nicholas I," pp. 456ff.

38. Ibid., p. 419.

39. B. Chicherin, *Moskva sorokovych godov* [Moscow in the 1840s] (Moscow, 1929), p. 27.

40. *Moskovskii Nabliudatel* no. 3 (May 1838): pp. 250–77, quoted in Barsukov, *Pogodin*, vol. 5 (St. Petersburg, 1892), pp. 135ff.

41. B. Chicherin, *Moscow in the 1840s*, pp. 84ff.

42. Ibid., p. 31.

43. Ibid., p. 6.

44. Ibid.

45. Ibid., 7.

46. Ibid., pp. 20ff.

47. Ibid., pp. 260ff.

48. Ibid., p. 19.

49. Ibid., p. 225.

50. Chicherin, *Puteshestvie za granitsu* (Travels Abroad) (Moscow, 1932), pp. 22ff.

51. Ibid., p. 72.

CHAPTER 8. THE EMANCIPATION OF THE SERFS

1. These words have been used quite unfairly to criticize Alexander. They were supposed to show that he was no friend of the emancipation, only embarking on it out of fear of a popular revolution. Interpreting his words like this, however, is somewhat arbitrary. When addressing the nobility, he had to use arguments that would make an impression on them. Why draw the firm conclusion that this was his only reason for justifying the necessity of reform?

2. Gradovsky, *Outlines*, p. 258, n. 206.

3. Ibid., p. 259, n. 207.

4. It was also called the Department for the Economy.

5. Popov was an official of the Codification Department in H.I.M.'s Privy Chancellery.

6. L. Kulczycki, *Geschichte der Russischen Revolution* [History of the Russian Revolution] (Gotha, 1910), vol. 1, pp. 292ff.

7. Quoted in ibid., vol. 1, p. 285.

8. Chicherin, *Moskovskii Universitet* (Moscow University) (Moscow, 1929), p. 22.

9. Quoted in ibid., p. 21. Tsitovich makes the same point in "Explanations" regarding the "Review of Internal Affairs" in *Vestnik Evropy* 12 (1878) (Odessa, 1879), pp. 12, 8ff.

10. Kulczycki, *Geschichte*, vol. 1, p. 328.

11. Chicherin, *Moscow University*, p. 21.

12. Chicherin, *Kurs gosudarstvennoi nauki* (A Course on Political Science) (Moscow, 1896), vol. 2, p. 30.

CHAPTER 9. THE EMANCIPATION LAWS AND THEIR LATER INTERPRETATION

1. *Usad'ba* refers here and elsewhere to the peasant farmstead.

2. A. Skrebitsky, *Krest'ianskoe delo v tsarstvovanii Imp. Aleksandra II* (Peasant Affairs in the Reign of Emperor Alexander II) (Bonn, 1863), vol. 2/1, pp. 451ff.

3. Ibid., vol. 2/1, p. 453, n. 11.

4. Ibid., vol. 2/1, p. 452, n. 6.

5. Ibid., vol. 4, p. 794.

6. Ibid.

7. Ibid., vol. 4, p. 798; see also vol. 4, pp. 259ff.

8. Ibid., vol. 4, p. 846.

9. Ibid., vol. 2/2, p. 986.

10. The Olonets and Smolensk committees, in ibid., vol. 2/2, p. 985, n. 17.

11. The Moscow Committee, in ibid., vol. 2/2, p. 985.

12. The Smolensk Committee, in ibid., vol. 2/2, p. 986. It is interesting to note that the factory owners in Perm' demanded that the peasants should only be allowed to keep their *usad'ba* on condition that they continued working in the factories (ibid., vol. 2/2, p. 986).

13. Ibid., vol. 2/2, p. 988.

14. The Taurien committee, in ibid., vol. 2/2, p. 987, n. 24.

15. Ibid., vol. 2/2, p. 991.

16. Ibid., vol. 2/2, p. 986, n. 22.

17. Quoted by Witte in *Zapiska po Krest'ianskomu Delu* (Memorandum on the Peasant Question) (St. Petersburg, 1904), p. 24

18. K. Zaitsev, *Die Rechtsideologie des russischen Agrarwesens und die russische Agrarrevolution* (The Ideology of Law in Russian Agricultural Life and the Russian Agrarian Revolution) (Berlin, 1925), vol. 19, p. 58.

CHAPTER 10. PEASANT LAW

1. The Senate itself did not distinguish clearly enough between farmstead ownership and communal ownership. It is noteworthy that Senate rulings on this issue were not unambiguous. In a ruling of Mar. 12, 1899, of the Senate Second Department on farmstead ownership, land was also described as belonging to the commune. On the other hand, rulings in the First and Second Courts and the Court of Appeals, of Nov. 27, 1895, no. 20 and others, take the opposite view.

2. Zaitsev, *Lectures*, pp. 201ff.

3. Overall, I have based my explanation on Zaitsev, but I do not believe that it is right, as Zaitsev does, to qualify "the right to land" as a right under public law. The peasant's entitlement to an allocation of land is an entitlement to a state benefit, which is completely alien to the nature of "rights."

4. Quoted in Zaitsev, *Lectures*, pp. 196ff.

5. Quoted in the unofficial edition of the weekly legal journal *Pravo* (St. Petersburg, 1899).

6. Quoted in ibid.

7. Zaitsev, *Lectures*, p. 200.

8. Ibid., pp. 201ff.

9. In *Archiv für Rechts- und Wirtschaftsphilosophie* (Berlin, 1925), vol. 19, pp. 59ff.

10. The recognition of the village communes as a legal entity probably arose because they

were able to buy and own land that was not part of the common land bank, in accordance with the provisions of general civil law, and thus possibly in this case did act as a legal entity (but only within these limits and only in relation to this property). The statement to the effect that the family, i.e., the farmstead, was a sort of "legal, economic association, which is related to the concept of a legal entity" (from the 1899 ruling of the First Chamber and the Court of Appeals, no. 1) is worthy of note.

11. Zaitsev, *Lectures*, p. 197.

12. Rulings of the Civil Court of Appeals (no. 88, 1894, and no. 91, 1893); cf. the ruling of the First and Second Courts and the Court of Appeals, no. 41 (1892).

13. Quoted in Zaitsev, *Ideology*, p. 60.

14. Ruling of the Civil Court of Appeals, no. 99 (1911).

15. For more detail about this, see Zaitsev, *Ideology*, p. 60.

16. Witte, *Memoirs*, vol. 1, p. 469.

CHAPTER II. THE PEASANT QUESTION IN THE REIGN OF ALEXANDER III

1. Quoted in Zaitsev, *Ideology*, p. 238.

2. Art. 15, section 2, of the Law on State Peasants states, "The transfer of plots of land belonging to the agrarian commune to individual heads of farmsteads is only permissible on a decision agreed by two-thirds of those members of the commune with voting rights; the taxes that fall on the transferred plot are then also calculated." For the wording of Art. 165 of the law on land buyouts, see p. 141.

3. The *Svod zakl. gub. soveshchanii po voprosam otnosiashch. k peresmostru zakonodatel'stva o krestianakh* (Collected Decisions of the Special Gubernatorial Advisory Committee on Questions Concerning the Review of Peasant Legislation), 4 vols. (St. Petersburg, 1897), does not name the provincial governor in question. I assume, however, that Akhlestyshev was the governor of Tver' at the time. See Petrunkevich, *Iz zapisok obshchestvennago dieiatelia; Vospominaniia* (Memoirs) (Berlin, 1934), p. 251. [Translator's note: The Russian title of Petrunkevich's work does not appear in the original.] It is important to note that according to Petrunkevich, Akhlestyshev was appointed governor of Tver' at the same time as Ivan Durnovo became minister of the interior. One can suppose that he shared Durnovo's views and expressed the views of the government of the day in his memorandum.

4. *Svod zakliuchenii gub. soveshchanii* (St. Petersburg, 1897), vol. 3, p. 214.

5. Ibid., vol. 3, p. 194.

6. Ibid., vol. 3, p. 148.

7. Witte still defended the rural commune in a memorandum in 1894. Extracts from this were published in the anthology *Osvobozhdenie* (Liberation) (Stuttgart, 1903), pp. 72ff.

8. Witte, *Memoirs: Vospominaniia: Tsarstvovanie Aleksandra II i Aleksandra III* (*The Reigns of Alexander II and Alexander III*) (1849–94; Berlin, 1923), vol. 1, pp. 374ff. [Translator's note: The Russian title does not appear in the original.]

9. *Svod zakliuchenii gub. soveshchanii*, vol. 3.

10. Witte, *Memorandum*, p. 59.

11. Ibid., pp. 27ff.

12. M.V.D., *Trudy redaktsionnoi kommissii po peresmotru zakonopolozhenii o krest'ianakh* (Ministry of the Interior, Work of the Editing Commission for the Revision of Legislation on the Peasantry) (St. Petersburg, 1903), vol. 1, pp. 64ff.

13. Ibid., vol. 1, p. 63; Witte, *Memorandum*, p. 72.

14. Witte, *Memorandum*, p. 72. Only minor cases involving up to fifteen rubles were heard by the so-called *raspravy*, which existed in the state peasant *volosti*. As far as I am aware, there was no ban on rulings being based on the provisions of general civil law.

15. Ibid., p. 27.

16. Ibid., p. 73.

17. Ibid., p. 76.

18. Ibid., pp. 75ff.

19. Ibid., p. 74.

20. Ibid., p. 44; cf. also pp. 42ff.

21. The committee reports from 1894 also record that not just land sales but also the division of land was carried out illegally.

22. Witte, *Memorandum*, p. 74.

23. Ibid., pp. 77ff.

CHAPTER 12. THE PEASANT QUESTION IN THE REIGN OF NICHOLAS II BEFORE 1905

1. M.V.D., *Trudy redaktsionnoi kommissii*, vol. 1, p. 7.

2. Ibid., vol. 1, p. 9; Witte, *Memoirs*, vol. 1, p. 478. This revision was put in place by the Supreme Order of Jan. 14, 1902, already mentioned above. The section of the Ministry of the Interior dealing with the peasantry was really only involved in this work after the appointment of Pleve. Gurko writes about this: "When Pleve was appointed Minister of the Interior in May 1902, this preliminary work had gone no further than an exchange of correspondence with the Ministry of Finance on the subject of money to be allocated for this work, and, if my memory serves me right, the rather large sum of some 120,000 rubles a year for five years had been requested. The Ministry of Finance had considered this amount excessive and indulged in lively arguments with the Ministry of the Interior. The only other start had been made by the Peasant Section, which had compiled a rough project on village taxation (*mirskie sbory*)" (Gurko, *Features and Figures*, pp. 131ff). On the whole, Gurko's memoirs contain interesting details about the revision of peasant legislation in the Ministry of the Interior. [Translator's note: Gurko is quoted in English in the original.]

3. Witte, *Memoirs*, vol. 1, p. 479.

4. This prompted Maklakov, who was otherwise well informed, to assume that the *osoboe soveshchanie* had already been officially ended by then. See Maklakov, *State Power*, p. 303.

5. The Special Advisory Committee (*osoboe soveshchanie*), chaired by Witte, was officially wound up by a decree on Mar. 30, 1905. At the same time, a new advisory committee chaired by Goremykin, who was renowned for his antiliberal views, was set up. Most of the members of this committee shared the conservative views of the chairman. This committee achieved nothing, as Witte commented, not without irony (*Memoirs*, vol. 1, p. 482). It too was ended after Witte was appointed chairman of the Council of Ministers after Oct. 17, 1905.

6. M.V.D., *Trudy redaktsionnoi kommissii*, vol. 1, p. 12.

7. Insufficient account has been taken of the fact that the restrictive measures against Jews also derived essentially from the same anticapitalist sentiments. It is plain that these measures did not arise from racial discrimination. At the time in Russia, the concept of race was of little interest to anyone outside specialist ethnological circles. It was more possible that these measures might have been taken on religious grounds, although at least in the nineteenth century even these were no longer crucial in this respect. What was decisive was the fear of the rise of capitalist elements, who might exploit the peasants and indeed all working people. There is evidence for this assertion in numerous sources. Take, e.g., the discussion of these measures by the Committee of Ministers in Apr. 1882. The minister of the interior who proposed these measures, Count Ignatiev, did not say that the Jews were the enemies of Christ or something along those lines, but he called them "leeches, sucking the blood of honest working people." In particular, he advocated banning Jews from selling or leasing goods. The measures proposed by the minister of interior were opposed by the minister of finance, Bunge, and the state controller, Count Solski. The latter demanded that the rights of Jews should be protected against any infringements, just like those of any other subjects. Reutern, the chair of the Committee of Ministers, supported him and declared, "Everyone has to be protected from illegal attacks. Today the Jews are being harassed and plundered; tomorrow people will turn against the so-called kulaks, who from a moral point of view are the same Jews, but of

the Orthodox Christian faith. Then it will be the turn of businesspeople and landowners. In a word, given such inactivity on the part of the authorities (who do not protect the Jews enough), one can only expect the development of the most disastrous socialism in the near future" See Peretz, *Dnevik* (*Diary*) (Moscow, 1927), pp. 130ff. This observation is extremely interesting. It is a warning that it does not matter which ethnic group first has its civil rights infringed and is deprived of its liberty. The outcome will always be the same—the abolition of liberty and the inauguration of socialism. The German experiment of 1933–45 confirms what Reutern said.

8. Certainly, but especially because nothing that Catherine II and Karamzin had considered desirable had been enacted in the nineteenth century.

9. Maklakov, *State Power*, pp. 275ff.

10. Witte, *Memorandum*, p. 4.

11. Quoted in Izgoev, *Obshchinnoe Pravo* (Rural Communal Law) (St. Petersburg, 1906), p. 136.

12. Witte, *Memoirs*, vol. 1, p. 441.

13. Ibid., vol. 1, p. 444.

14. Ibid., vol. 1, p. 444. Witte points out in his *Memorandum* that the internal relations in the *obshchina* were subject more and more to state control and oversight by the *zemskie nachal'niki*, which meant they increasingly lost their character of an association under private law (pp. 88ff).

15. Witte, *Memorandum*, p. 86.

16. Witte, *Memoirs*, vol. 1, pp. 439, 443.

17. Ibid., vol. 1, pp. 453ff.

18. Ibid., vol. 1, p. 479.

19. The conversation between the minister of the interior, Sviatopolk-Mirsky, and the tsarina, as reported by Witte (ibid., vol. 1, p. 296), is characteristic in this respect.

CHAPTER 13. THE AGRARIAN PROGRAM OF THE LEFT-WING PARTIES

1. P. Katenin, *Ocherki Russk. Politich. Techenii* (Russian Political Currents) (Berlin, 1906), p. 85. By contrast, the Social Democrats were at the time in favor of repealing all legislation that limited the peasant's right of disposal over his land—not to strengthen civil society in country areas, but because they expected that this would result in more economic differentiation and hence a flare-up in the class struggle in rural areas (ibid., p. 71).

2. Chernov, *Konstruktivnye Sotsialism* (Constructive Socialism) (Prague, 1925), vol. 1, p. 292, cited in Zaitsev, "The Legal Ideology of Russian Rural Society, etc.," in *Archiv für Rechts- und Wirtschaftsphilosophie* (1925), p. 68.

3. The French ambassador Bompard writes in his interesting memoirs, "The Russian peasant, held back within the confines of rural communism by a blind government, eventually became accustomed to it and demanded its extension to all of Russia's land, instead of demanding its abolition." See Bompard, *Mon ambassade en Russie (1903–1908)* (Paris, 1937), p. 232.

4. For more detail about the Union of Liberation and the Kadet party, see the next section.

5. I. V. Gessen, "Osnovy pravoporiadka" (Foundations of the Rule of Law), in *Nuzhdy derevni* (Needs of the Countryside) (St. Petersburg, 1904), p. 47. [Translator's note: This was cited in German in the original text: *Grundlagen der Rechtsordnung*.]

6. Translator's note: The author uses the French in the original: "Les pays ne sont pas cultivés en raison de leur fertilité, mais en raison de leur liberté."

7. It is significant that part 1 of the Kadet Party's program, which lists fundamental rights, omits private property.

8. What the Kadets understood by fair compensation was not compensation based on market values, but compensation based on a lower, specially calculated price.

9. Maklakov, *Vtoraia Gos. Duma* (The Second State Duma) (Paris, 1942?), p. 37.

10. A. Stolypin, "P. A. Stolypin" (Paris, 1927), p. 17. For the text of the speech, see State Duma, transcribed reports, 2nd leg., 2nd sess., col. 438.

11. See the collection of articles *Agrarnyi vopros* (Agrarian Questions), published by the Kadet Party, pp. 333ff.

12. Ibid., pp. 303ff.

13. Ibid., p. 321. It is noteworthy that Manuilov is here giving an opinion diametrically opposed to that of Catherine II (see above).

14. Ibid., p. x.

15. See the newspaper *Reč*, no. 57, 1906, reprinted in Miliukov, *God bor'by* (The Year of Struggle) (St. Petersburg, 1907), p. 336.

16. Miliukov, *Year of Struggle*, p. 336.

17. Ibid., p. 341.

18. Ibid., p. 415.

19. Ibid., p. 439.

20. Ibid., p. 416.

21. Ibid., p. 339.

22. Ibid., p. 416. Here Miliukov's position approaches that of Catherine, except that he put it forward 150 years after the empress.

23. *Reč*, no. 88, June 1, 1906, reprinted in Miliukov, *Year of Struggle*, p. 437.

24. Miliukov, *Year of Struggle*, p. 438.

25. Ibid., p. 438.

26. Ibid.

27. Ibid., p. 439.

28. Ibid., pp. 437ff.

CHAPTER 14. THE PEASANT QUESTION AFTER 1905

1. Journal of the plenary State Council, Dec. 30, 1902, published in German by the editorial board of *Osvobozhdenie* (Liberation) (Stuttgart, 1903), p. 7.

2. The positive content of this manifesto is meager, and what it announces is not free of inconsistencies, but Witte immediately grasped that it signified the triumph of those forces that were hostile to him. He must have certainly been aware of the motives and influences that were behind the manifesto. In fact this antiliberal tendency, hostile to Witte, later emerged more clearly and more consistently in the decree of Jan, 8, 1904 (P.S.Z. no. 23860), which was enacted with reference to the Manifesto of Feb. 26, 1903.

3. C. V. Dietze, *Stolypinsche Agrarreform und Feldgemeinschaft* (The Stolypin Agrarian Reform and the Peasant Commune), Quellen und Studien des Osteuropa-Instituts (Breslau, 1920). Further references can be found there.

4. After later editions of Art. 12.

5. Cf. A. Kaufmann, in "Ezhegodnik," '*Reč* (1912): p. 189.

6. Where these amendments are significant, their content will be outlined here as the arguments for and against them are presented.

7. State Duma, transcribed reports for 1909, 3rd leg., 2nd sess., part 3, cols. 2950ff.

8. Shingarev approvingly described the Senate's practice as cautious, that is, the Senate rulings that were analyzed above (ibid., col. 2855).

9. State Duma, transcribed reports for 1909, ibid., cols. 616ff. We shall refer again to columns from part 3 after this point.

10. Translator's note: If two Duma deputies had the same name, they were ranked according to length of service.

11. The commission had elected two spokesmen, Krasovsky and Stishinsky, as no group within it enjoyed a clear majority. The commission consisted of thirty members, of whom fifteen belonged to the Center, that is, to Stolypin's supporters; three belonged to the Progressive group (also called the academic group, as most representatives of the academy and the universities belonged to it), that is, the left opposition; and the remaining twelve belonged to the right opposition.

CHAPTER 15. THE PEASANT QUESTION AFTER 1905 (CONTINUED)

1. State Council, shorthand reports of 1909–10, 5th sess., col. 1180.

2. Olsufiev certainly meant that Jews could not be granted equal rights, as they were exploiters, i.e., stronger, while labor legislation was essentially based on the principle of the protection of the weak.

3. Krasovsky said, "At first sight it appears . . . that not much is left of the decree of November 9, so numerous are the amendments and additions that have been adopted by the Duma and the State Council's commission, yet it is easy to see that it retained its main provisions and principles without amendment" (ibid., col. 1133).

4. Even Stishinsky, who under Pleve, when the Interior Ministry's editing commission drafted peasant legislation along antiliberal principles, was one of the most determined advocates of the land commune and household ownership in particular, and now only voted with reservation in favor of the draft law, had to concede that the efforts of the peasants to leave the land communes were not just based on the wish, as he previously believed, to be free of the burden of the *krugovaia poruka*, but on the natural desire to own property (ibid., cols. 1126ff).

5. Why should the peasant necessarily be seen as weak, as someone in need of state benefit? Does not the fact "that the Russian peasantry has managed to buy 24 million *desiatin*, not counting its land allocation, during the fifty years that have passed since the emancipation" (Krasovsky's report, in ibid., col. 1239) argue clearly enough against this?

6. Stolypin highlights that household ownership had two disadvantages: (1) Each member of the family, even a family member who had been resident in a town for years, enjoyed the right to demand to be taken into the household at any time. (2) On the division of the household, each family member could demand to be left not an equivalent amount of money, but a plot of land *in natura*, which could sometimes badly affect the viability of a farm (ibid., col. 1624). Furthermore, if the form of farmstead sales was to take the same form as that for any other Russian citizen, that is, if they would be completed with the participation of a solicitor, retaining family household ownership would lead to countless problems. "No solicitor," said Stolypin, "would commit themselves to completing a sale on the declaration of the head of household alone" (ibid., col. 1625), on learning that it was not a case of the private property of the head of household, but collective family property. Thus, in practice, the peasant would be unable to exercise his right to dispose freely of his land, a right that is theoretically recognized as his.

7. Witte stressed that it was a great mistake, in general, not to consider regional differences and to want to seek a single schematic solution for the whole of the enormous empire.

8. Voting figures are taken from Stählin, vol. 4.2, p. 855, which in turn quotes Polovtsev.

9. Gurko too, in his memoirs, which he wrote as an émigré in Paris after the revolution, claims that the groundwork for the revision of peasant legislation, which he completed as head of the department for peasant affairs at Pleve's behest, served as the basis for Stolypin's decree of Nov. 9, 1906 (*Features and Figures*, p. 131). According to Gurko, this was possible because he was even then, in 1902, contemplating the abolition of land communes (ibid., p. 157) and was able to push through the adoption in the bill of a provision by which a peasant could leave a land commune and demand to be given his allotted land in a single plot. He maintains that at the time, the only reason he justified this provision on purely technical grounds was to avoid provoking unnecessary and possibly insurmountable opposition against this measure. Insofar as, on the whole, the land commune was not so much threatened as protected by the drafts for revising peasant legislation prepared by the Interior Ministry, one can assume that the true purpose of Gurko's claims was to show that he had always been consistent and that his participation in preparations for the decree of Nov. 9, 1906, did not amount to abandoning his original position. Be that as it may, it has to be conceded that Witte was absolutely right on this point. The decree of Nov. 9, 1906, has no organic link with the work of the Department of Peasant Affairs in the Ministry of the Interior, but rather with the material put together by the Special Advisory Committee led by Witte himself.

10. Maklakov, *Pervaia Gosud. Duma* (The First State Duma) (Paris, 1939), p. 139.

11. Ibid., pp. 140ff.

12. C. von Dietze, *Die Stolypinsche Agrarreform und die Feldgemeinschaft* (The Stolypin Agrarian Reforms and the Land Commune) (Leipzig and Berlin, 1920), p. 71.

13. Ibid., p. 71.

CHAPTER 16. THE HISTORY OF POLITICAL LIBERALISM IN THE REIGN OF ALEXANDER II

1. Hauriou, *Principes*, p. 607. Hauriou states, "La liberté politique, c'est le citoyen libre dans la nation libre, grâce à une décentralisation et à une répartition de la souveraineté, grâce à la rédaction d'un statut" [Political liberty consists of the free citizen in a free nation, thanks to decentralization and a division of power, thanks to the framing of a constitution] (p. 608). By "decentralization of power," Hauriou means "la décomposition de la souveraineté en plusieurs formes et plusieurs pouvoirs répartis entre plusieurs éléments de la nation" [the breakdown of sovereignty into several forms and powers divided among several elements in the nation] (pp. 607ff).

2. Ibid., p. 608.

3. Ibid., p. 609.

4. Hauriou writes, "Il y a eu en France, au XIX siècle, deux poussées constitutionelles successives, celle qui a duré de 1814 à 1848 et celle que a repris en 1871; or, d'une part, ces deux poussées constitutionelles succédaient chaque fois à un régime impérial de centralisation administrative contre lequel elles avaient l'intention de réagir; d'autre part, chaque fois, leur programme contenait des réformes de décentralisation administrative destinées à compléter les réformes gouvernementales. Il est de même à remarquer que, si dans la période 1814-1848, les réformes gouvernementales ont précédé de quinze ans les mesures de décentralisation départementale et communale, à raison des résistances de la Restauration, au contraire, en 1871, la loi décentralisatrice du 10 août sur les conseils généraux a passé avant les lois constitutionelles, tellement les hommes de l'Assemblée Nationale étaient persuadés qu'il fallait refaire l'édifice constitutionel en commençant par en bas, parce que l'esprit public du pays ne pouvait être régénéré que dans l'administration locale" [In France in the nineteenth century, there were two successive periods of constitutional progress: the first lasting from 1814 to 1848 and the second following in 1871. On the one hand, in each case these two periods of constitutional progress followed an imperial centralized bureaucratic regime as a reaction against it. On the other hand, each time their program contained reforms to decentralize the administration to accompany the reforms of government. At the same time, it should be noted that if in the 1814–48 period, reform of government preceded the decentralization of the administration and local government by fifteen years because of resistance during the Restoration period, by contrast, in 1871 the decentralizing law of August 10 on departmental assemblies was passed before the constitutional laws, so convinced were the members of the Assemblée Nationale that it was necessary to rebuild the constitutional framework from the bottom up, because the nation's civic spirit could only be regenerated in local government] (ibid., p. 610).

5. Meshchersky, *Vospominaniia* (Memoirs) (St. Petersburg, 1897), vol. 1, p. 292.

6. Ibid., vol. 1, p. 414.

7. This plan was only published later in *Vestnik Prava*, no. 9 (1905): pp. 225–69; this journal was unavailable to the author. The best account of this plan can be found in an article written by Miliukov about the Manifesto of Aug. 6, 1905, which was published in the periodical *Pravo*, no. 31, and reprinted in *God bor'by*, pp. 55ff.

8. Stankevich, *Granovsky* (Moscow, 1869), p. 158.

9. Ibid., p. 161.

10. Ibid., p. 147 (from Granovsky's letter to members of his audience).

11. Ibid., p. 235.

12. Translator's note: The Russian title of Herzen's work does not appear in the original.

13. Ibid., p. 297. Cf. also Chicherin, *Moscow in the 1840s*, p. 44. Chicherin, concerning

the antagonism between Granovsky and Herzen, writes: "If Herzen, . . . having seen that democracy, to which he was devoted heart and soul, was impossible in 1848, expounded an extreme anarchist position, by contrast, Granovsky, a true historian, painted a sober and accurate picture of the political development of the nations, a picture that was equally untainted by radical impatience or reactionary thinking, that was colored by a deep sympathy for liberty, although it nevertheless took account of the conditions that were necessary to achieve it in human society" (p. 75). Dostoevsky famously tried to portray Granovsky in the character of S. T. Verkhovensky. Chicherin justly remarked (without naming Dostoevsky) that it was shallow to depict such an unusually painstaking scholar, a "tireless reader," as a superficial and idle windbag (p. 42).

14. Ibid., p. 120.

15. Ibid., p. 58.

16. Chicherin, *Voprosy politiki* (Political Questions) (Moscow, 1904), p. 27.

17. Translator's note: The Russian title of Valuev's work does not appear in the original.

18. P. A. Valuev, "Zapiski" (Observations), *Russk. Starina* (May 1891): p. 357. [Translator's note: *Duma Russkovo* was written by Valuev in 1855, but published in 1891.]

19. This fact was also highlighted by Korkunov in his work *Russkoe Gosudarstvennoe Pravo* (Russian Constitutional Law) (St. Petersburg, 1893).

20. Members of the peasant electoral college were chosen by *volost'* assemblies.

21. Rural inhabitants and townspeople who did not meet the qualification were represented by delegates elected by them.

22. Translator's note: The *conseil du départment,* or Departmental Council, is the council in each of France's one hundred local administrative areas.

23. The 1890 legislation, prepared by the State Council, represents a compromise solution. This law did not extinguish all the liberal leanings of the 1864 decree. Minister of the Interior D. Tolstoy had intended to replace the elected *zemstvos* with government commissions. His plan could not be implemented, as he died in 1889.

24. I. Belokonsky, *Zemskoe dvizhenie* (The *Zemstvo* Movement), 2nd ed. (Moscow, 1914), pp. 2ff.

25. Translator's note: The author uses the French in the original: "Comment voulez-vous qu'un ministre de l'intérieur ait le temps de penser à vous répondre, quand il s'agit de fermer le zemskoe sobranie."

26. Meshchersky, *Memoirs,* vol. 1, pp. 414ff. He reports that Bezobrazov, Count Suvalov, and Platonov were cited as the most active in pursuing these efforts in St. Petersburg.

27. According to Meshchersky, the following in particular were mentioned: the Samarin brothers, Golokhvostov, and Prince Shcherbatov. Chicherin also names Uvarov and Musin-Pushkin.

28. Meshchersky, *Memoirs,* vol. 1, p. 138.

29. Chicherin, *Moscow University,* p. 67. This, however, seems to contradict his views in another part of his memoirs (*Moscow in the 1840s,* p. 103), where he points out that constitutionalism sprang from a genuine love of freedom.

30. Chicherin, *Moscow University,* p. 164.

31. Ibid., p. 112.

32. The Russian title of Chicherin's work does not appear in the original.

33. Chicherin provides extracts from this memorandum in ibid., pp. 113ff.

34. Chicherin defines conservative liberalism in the article "Raznye vidy liberalizma" (Different Forms of Liberalism), which appeared with others under the collective title *Neskol'ko sovremennykh voprosov* (Some Contemporary Questions). Struve points out that the term "liberal conservatism" was first coined by Prince P. A. Viazemsky. See P. Struve, *Sotsial'naia i ekonomicheskaia istoriia Rossii* (Social and Economic History of Russia) (Paris, 1952), p. 328.

35. Chicherin first developed these ideas in two letters to his brother in Oct. 1864. See Chicherin, *Moscow University,* pp. 24ff, 28ff.

36. Ibid., p. 70.

37. That serfdom was not removed from one day to the next on Feb. 19, 1861, but that the long process of its abolition was only initiated in 1861, can be seen in part 2 of this book.

38. Chicherin, *Moscow in the 1840s*, p. 162.

39. Belokonsky, *Zemstvo Movement*, p. 15.

40. An interesting account that fully illustrates the disarray prevailing in government circles is to be found in the memoirs of Prince Meshchersky, the publisher of the radical right-wing newspaper *Grazhdanin* (St. Petersburg, 1898), vol. 2, pp. 424ff. After the attempted assassination of Alexander II by the village schoolteacher Solov'ev at the beginning of 1879, the emperor appointed Valuev, the minister of state domains at the time, as chair of a committee to consider measures to combat revolutionary activities. Other members of the committee included the minister of the Interior, Makov; the finance minister, Greig; the minister of defense, Miliutin; the justice minister, Nabokov; the minister of education, Tolstoy; and the chief of police, Drenteln. Valuev reported on the emperor's command to the Committee of Ministers, which was more or less composed of the same people as the special committee set up under his chairmanship. The view of the Committee of Ministers was that it was inopportune and even dangerous to examine such issues, for fear that if it ever became public knowledge, it would only intensify the animosity to the existing order. Alexander II, however, did not share this view and reiterated his command, and thus the committee, chaired by Valuev, commenced its deliberations. The committee made a number of proposals: to withdraw the right of magistrates to issue court orders to the police; to make the appointment of secretaries to local government bodies (*upravy*) dependent on the approval of the provincial governor; to reinforce the police by increasing the number of rural policemen (*uriadniki*) at the district level—i.e., in areas where terrorists were not normally found; to relax the restrictions on "Old Believers," as it had been shown that they remained impervious to socialist propaganda; and to abolish the burdens imposed on the Poles in the aftermath of the 1864 uprising. Finally some measures relating to education were proposed—e.g., to strengthen the influence of the clergy in schools. Meshcherksy, who lists these measures, was surely right to comment that this was a case of the elephant giving birth to a mouse. In Meshchersky's opinion, this approach could only paralyze the fight against the revolutionaries. He added that it would only distract from the only important and most urgent question, i.e., regarding what action the police should undertake to destroy the revolutionaries' organization. Meshchersky held that anarchy could only be brought to an end if the committee decided on a series of remorselessly stringent and resolute measures, i.e., "to fight revolutionary terror (the *kramola*) with legal terror" (ibid., p. 430). In effect, the illusion that there was a political theory or a political system that could have prevented the rise of destructive revolutionary forces could only be a diversion from the real tasks and methods of combating the revolutionary movement.

41. Quoted in G. Dzhanshiev, *Epocha velikich reform* (The Epoch of the Great Reforms), 8th ed. (Moscow, 1900), p. 37, n. 2.

42. Ibid.

43. Belokonsky, *Zemstvo Movement*, p. 10.

44. Presniakov, introduction to Peretz's diary: Peretz, *Dnevnik* (Diary), 1880–83 (Moscow, 1927), p. iv.

45. For details of this proposal, see Loris-Melikov's report to Alexander III of Mar. 6, 1881. The text of this report can be found in a booklet called "Konstitutsiia Loris-Melikova," published in London in 1893 (pp. 36–44) by the Fund of the Russian Free Press.

46. Peretz, *Diary*, pp. 32–46.

47. Valuev, *Dnevnik* (Diary), 1877–84 (Petrograd, 1919), pp. 151ff.

48. According to Valuev's diary, "the procurator of the synod made an intolerable speech in which he called all the proposals and everything European [*sic*] a great lie and then trotted out all the usual phrases about the unity of the tsar and the people (all the time meaning only the so-called 'common' people)."

49. Valuev, *Diary*, p. 154.

50. For example, twelve experts from various regions of Russia were consulted when the

issue of the abolition of the redemption payments was dealt with; in another instance (that of alcoholic drinks) there were thirty-two experts.

CHAPTER 17. THE PERIOD FROM 1881 TO 1902

1. Meshchersky, *Memoirs,* vol. 3, p. 2.

2. Shipov, *Vospominaniia i dumy o perezhitom* (Recollections and Thoughts on My Experiences) (Moscow, 1918), p. 132.

3. Maklakov, *First State Duma,* pp. 15ff.

4. Meshchersky, *Memoirs,* vol. 3, p. 287; cf. also Pobedonostsev, *Pis'ma Aleksandru III* (Letters to Alexander III) (Moscow, 1926), vol. 2, pp. 203ff. Pobedonostsev expressed his distrust of the gentry, e.g., at the conference on Bulygin's Duma proposal (July 19–26, 1905). See *Petergofskoe soveshchanie o proekte Gos. Dumy* (Petrograd, 1917), pp. 201ff.

5. Meshchersky, *Memoirs,* vol. 3, p. 336. It is noteworthy that Witte repeatedly calls Pobedonostsev a nihilist in his memoirs.

6. Ibid., pp. 27ff.

7. Ibid., p. 130.

8. Ibid., p. 27.

9. Ibid., p. 24.

10. Shipov and Maklakov agreed on this point (ibid., p. 131)

11. Ibid., p. 272.

12. Ibid., pp. 132ff.

13. Ibid., p. 134.

14. Ibid., pp. 135ff.

15. Shipov, *Recollections,* pp. 66ff.

16. It is symptomatic that in those increasingly reactionary times, government departments took measures described as socialist in an article with the title "Mysli o sovremennom polozhenii Rossii" (Thoughts on the Current Situation in Russia), signed "Zemets" (a *zemstvo* man), in the anthology *Osvobozhdenie* (Stuttgart, 1903), p. 168. [Translator's note: The original article title does not appear in the original.] It contains the following: "Socialist measures are being carried out on the orders of the mayor of Moscow, and *Mokovskie Vedomosti* has begun to proclaim, in the guise of a government program, that the autocracy can solve the world's problems and transport Russia up over the heads of European bourgeois regimes, directly into the future era of the great socialist ideal." The former socialist Tikhomirov also repeatedly highlighted how extreme right-wing organizations, which glorified the autocracy, rejected a constitution and championed extreme nationalism, and anti-Semitism in particular, had a pronounced leaning to socialism. A well-known representative of the bureaucracy, Kryzhanovsky, who distanced himself from all political organizations in general and even from all the political salons in St. Petersburg, made the same point. He writes, "The extreme right wing of this movement (the Union of the Russian People) adopted almost the same social program and almost the same propaganda methods as the socialist parties. The only difference was that the former promised the masses the forcible redistribution of property in the name of the autocratic tsar who acted in the interests of the people and protected them against the oppression of the wealthy, while the latter did so in the name of the workers and peasants organized under a democratic, proletarian republic." See *Vospominaniia* (Memoirs) (Berlin, n.d.), p. 153. It is noteworthy that Witte also saw that the surest way to finish off liberalism would have been to divide the large landed estates among the peasants, which would have destroyed the social class from which liberalism largely emerged. He also said as much with striking candor to Petrunkevich, although he was quick to add that the government did not intend doing anything of the kind nor even thought it possible. "Do you think," asked Witte, "that the government has shown its impotence and is incapable of dealing with the ferment in public opinion without the help of the public? I must tell you that the government has means at its disposal not just to crush this ferment but also to deal it a knockout blow once and for all. It would suffice to promise the peasants that each family would be given an area of twenty-five *desiatin*—which

would sweep away all your great landowners forever. Of course, the government would not use such methods, but you should not ever forget it" (Petrunkevich, *Memoirs*, p. 429).

17. Shipov, *Recollections*, p. 80.

18. Ibid., pp. 79, 68.

19. Hauriou, *Précis de droit administratif*, 8th ed. (Paris, 1914), pp. 71ff; Hauriou, *Principes*, p. 19. [Translator's note: The author quotes the French in the original: "Gouverner c'est diriger; les gouvernants s'appellent couramment les dirigeants; d'autre part, il s'agit bien de diriger à travers les événements, c'est-à-dire à travers tous les imprévus de la vie sociale nationale et internationale, à travers les nouveautés; le rôle essentiel du gouvernement est de résoudre constamment les difficultés nouvelles qui se présentent et qui intéressent le groupe; quant aux difficultés anciennes déjà résolues, si on les rencontre une seconde fois, si on repasse par les mêmes chemins, ce n'est plus affaire de gouvernement mais plutôt d'administration."]

20. Shipov, *Recollections*, pp. 132, 80ff.

21. Maklakov, *First State Duma*, pp. 298ff.

22. See ibid., pp. 291–97.

23. Shipov, *Recollections*, p. 134.

24. It is not important that Shipov thought it would be wrong to see him as a Slavophile. There is no doubt that his political ideas were based on the worldview of Slavophilism.

25. Shipov, *Recollections*, p. 154.

26. Ibid., p. 153.

27. Ibid., p. 158.

28. Ibid., p. 169.

29. Maklakov, *First State Duma*, pp. 317ff.

30. Shipov, *Recollections*, p. 174.

31. Ibid., p. 174.

32. Maklakov, *First State Duma*, p. 317.

33. Shipov, *Recollections*, p. 206.

34. Ibid., p. 234.

35. Ibid., p. 237.

36. Maklakov, *First State Duma*, pp. 317ff.

37. Shipov, *Recollections*, p. 194.

38. Ibid., p. 199.

39. Ibid., p. 225.

40. Ibid., p. 223.

41. Ibid., p. 214.

42. Ibid.

43. Ibid., p. 237.

44. Ibid.

45. Maklakov, *First State Duma*, pp. 318, 300.

CHAPTER 18. THE LIBERATION MOVEMENT

1. Petrunkevich, *Memoirs*, p. 337.

2. Ibid., p. 337.

3. Ibid.

4. Ibid.

5. This was in July 1903, according to Miliukov. See *Vospominaniia* (Memoirs) (N.J., 1955), vol. 1, p. 238.

6. Petrunkevich, *Memoirs*, p. 339.

7. Maklakov, *First State Duma*, p. 147.

8. *Osvodozhdenie* (Liberation), no. 1, p. 10.

9. Maklakov, *First State Duma*, p. 148.

10. Ibid., p. 154.

11. Ibid., p. 155.

12. Ibid., p. 153.

13. Ibid., p. 151.

14. Ibid., p. 150.

15. Ibid., p. 161.

16. Ibid., p. 163.

17. Translator's note: The Russian title of the *Liberation* article does not appear in the original.

18. Quoted in ibid., pp. 163ff.

19. Quoted in ibid., p. 164.

20. Translator's note: The Russian title of the *Liberation* article does not appear in the original.

21. Ibid., p. 158.

22. *Osvobozhdenie* (Liberation), no. 5, cited in ibid., pp. 176ff.

23. Ibid., p. 177.

24. Ibid.

25. Cf. Miliukov, *Memoirs,* vol. 1, p. 243.

26. Maklakov, *First State Duma,* p. 188.

27. Ibid., p. 466.

28. Quoted in ibid., p. 407. It is hardly necessary to add that even attempts to flee can be interpreted as a form of resistance.

29. Ibid., p. 194.

30. Ibid., p. 191.

31. This countermovement found its ideological expression above all in the collected edition *Vekhi.* For more on *Vekhi,* cf. L. Shapiro, "The Vekhi Group and the Mystique of Revolution," *Slavonic and East European Review* 34, no. 82 (Dec. 1955).

32. Maklakov, *First State Duma,* p. 198.

CHAPTER 19. LIBERALISM IN 1904

1. Witte, *Memoirs,* vol. 1, p. 436. Witte wanted to show in the memorandum mentioned here that *zemstvo* institutions were incompatible with autocracy. What practical considerations lay behind this theoretical exposition is in fact difficult to judge and is the subject of debate.

2. Maklakov, *First State Duma,* pp. 140ff.

3. Ibid., p. 141.

4. Ibid.

5. Petrunkevich, *Memoirs,* p. 403.

6. Maklakov, *First State Duma,* p. 320.

7. Witte, *Memoirs,* vol. 1, p. 288.

8. Ibid., vol. 1, p. 321.

9. Shipov, *Recollections,* p. 239.

10. Maklakov, *First State Duma,* pp. 320ff.

11. Shipov, *Recollections,* p. 240.

12. Maklakov, *First State Duma,* p. 324.

13. Translator's note: The Russian title of the *Liberation* article does not appear in the original.

14. Quoted in ibid., p. 323.

15. Shipov, *Recollections,* p. 242.

16. Ibid., p. 241.

17. Ibid., p. 249.

18. Ibid., p. 258. The minister said only that he would post a police guard in front of the houses where meetings were to take place. This was not, however, to watch over the work of the conference, but to prevent any possible demonstrations by workers or students. In fact, the police were very friendly toward the delegates at the conference and even showed them the entrances to the houses.

19. Ibid., p. 260.

20. Ibid., pp. 261–65.

21. Ibid., pp. 267ff.

22. Ibid., p. 271.

23. Ibid.

24. Ibid., p. 309. Shipov's ideas here are closely related to those of the Slavophiles and are rooted extensively in the same philosophical thinking. Shipov himself stresses that he greatly admired the members of this school of thought, such as V. I. Kireevsky, Khomiakov, and J. Samarin. In particular, he shared the Slavophiles' conviction that the progress of society is not based on the improvement of social and political forms, but on the "inner structure of the personality." There are, however, points on which he takes issue with the Slavophiles. "I did not entirely share," he writes, "the Slavophile position on the slogan 'Orthodoxy, Autocracy and the People.'" The salient point here is that Shipov denied the superiority of the Orthodox Church over other Christian denominations and thought that different churches could work together. He also rejected the concept of the divine origin of state power in general and thus the idea of a divine source for the power of the Russian autocrat (cf. ibid., pp. 269ff).

25. Ibid., p. 273.

26. Ibid., p. 274.

27. Ibid., p. 275.

28. This delegation was composed of five people: the congress chairman, Shipov; two deputy chairmen, Prince G. E. L'vov and Petrunkevich; and two specially elected delegates, Count Heyden and M. V. Rodzianko (ibid., p. 278).

29. Ibid., p. 278.

30. Ibid., p. 280.

31. This memorandum is printed as an appendix to Shipov's memoirs; see ibid., pp. 581–87.

32. Ibid., p. 583.

33. Trubetskoy repeats this once more (ibid., p. 585). He is certainly echoing Chicherin here.

34. Ibid., p. 582.

35. Ibid.

36. Ibid., p. 584.

37. Ibid., p. 281.

38. Ibid., p. 287.

39. The tsar said that he had repeatedly convened such conferences, but they were always fruitless (ibid., p. 287).

40. This account of Witte's position is based on Maklakov. He writes, "I have heard this idea so often from Witte that I am in no doubt as to his perspective" (*First State Duma*, p. 336).

41. Shipov, *Recollections*, p. 147.

42. Maklakov, *First State Duma*, p. 253. How little Witte's thinking was understood at the time is shown by an article by Struve in *Osvobozhdenie*. Struve describes Witte's efforts to put the peasant question in the foreground as a diversion, in order to stabilize the autocracy, at least temporarily. See his editorial in *Osvobozhdenie*, Dec. 18, 1904, cited in ibid., p. 338.

43. Ibid., p. 259.

44. Ibid., p. 260.

45. Ibid., p. 262.

46. Ibid., p. 257; see also Petrunkevich, *Memoirs*.

47. Maklakov reports that Witte was horrified just by the idea that the art of polemics and a gift for oratory could be taken for the skills of a statesman.

48. This is the key idea of his famous memorandum on the *zemstvos*, so brilliantly set out and interpreted by Maklakov (ibid., pp. 256ff).

49. Ibid., p. 256.

50. Ibid., p. 265.

51. Ibid., p. 263.

52. The draft law referred directly to the results of the work of the committee set up by the Special Advisory Committee on the Needs of Agrarian Industry. The planned laws concerning the peasantry were thus based on the program advocated by Witte (ibid., p. 334).

53. Pobedonostsev, the minister of justice, Muraviev, and Grand Duke Sergei Alexandrovich were resolutely opposed to Art. 9, while Count Sol'slkii and Frisch were unhesitatingly for it, Kokovtsov less so (Shipov, *Recollections*, pp. 288ff).

54. Ibid., p. 290.

55. Maklakov, *First State Duma*, p. 337.

56. Ibid., pp. 338ff.

57. Ibid., p. 334.

58. Ibid., p. 341.

59. The great success he enjoyed at the peace negotiations in Portsmouth seems to contradict this view. Nevertheless, this was a foreign policy success and is anyway an isolated case.

60. Ibid., p. 274.

61. Ibid., p. 440.

62. Ibid., p. 261.

CHAPTER 20. THE *ZEMSTVO* CONGRESSES

1. Witte, *Memoirs*, vol. 1, p. 319.

2. The reasons why the legislative work of the Duma often stalled and produced no satisfactory results will be dealt with below.

3. Witte, *Memoirs*, vol. 1, p. 323.

4. Translator's note: This is the equivalent in St. Petersburg of an institution like the British Library.

5. Ibid., vol. 1, p. 323.

6. Ibid., vol. 1, pp. 325ff.

7. Ibid., vol. 1, p. 327.

8. Ibid., vol. 1, pp. 330ff.

9. Ibid., vol. 1, pp. 319, 331, 334.

10. Maklakov, *First State Duma*, p. 330.

11. Witte, *Memoirs*, vol. 1, p. 336.

12. Maklakov, *First State Duma*, p. 339.

13. Ibid., p. 340.

14. L. Takhotsky, *G. Petr Struve v Politike* (Mr. Peter Struve and Politics) (St. Petersburg, 1906), p. 15.

15. Maklakov, *First State Duma*, p. 352.

16. Ibid., p. 349.

17. Ibid., p. 353; cf. also L. Tikhomirov, *Dnevnik* (Diary). [Translator's note: No publication details are available for Tikhomirov.]

18. Maklakov, *First State Duma*, p. 371.

19. Petrunkevich, *Memoirs*, p. 369.

20. These propositions are printed in Shipov, *Recollections*, pp. 304–8.

21. Maklakov, *First State Duma*, p. 373.

22. Ibid., p. 356.

23. Shipov, *Recollections*, p. 294.

24. The text can be found in Belokonsky in *Zemstvo Movement*, pp. 263ff.

25. Shipov, *Recollections*, pp. 296ff.

26. Cf. ibid., p. 297.

27. Maklakov, *First State Duma*, p. 374.

28. Ibid., p. 376.

29. Ibid., p. 377.

30. Shipov, *Recollections*, pp. 317ff.

31. Ibid., p. 318.

32. Soon afterward, he had to travel to the Far East front as a *zemstvo* representative. He only returned to Moscow at the end of Sept. Unfortunately, his memoirs cannot then serve as an historical source for the middle part of 1905.

33. The text of the petition is printed in *Osvobozhdenie*, no. 72, p. 365. It reads, "We entreat His Majesty to convene the representatives of the people without delay. . . . May these representatives together with Your Majesty decide the vital questions of war and peace . . . and present to all other nations a Russia no longer divided and exhausted by internal conflict, but healed and standing strong in its renewal." In addition, a resolution was adopted that condemned the bureaucratic system even more strongly than the petition did and laid the blame for internal unrest and defeat in the war at the feet of the government. It demanded that a representative assembly be convened, all laws restricting freedom repealed, and the highest officials replaced. The most interesting point is neither the petition nor the resolution itself, but how the editors of *Osvobozhdenie* interpreted these documents. The petition was published under the headline "Poslednee Slovo Zemskoi Rossii k Tsariu" (*Zemstvo* Russia's Final Word to the Tsar). It seems that the petition was indeed an ultimatum, in other words, exactly the opposite of what some had been determined to avoid. Even more telling is the editorial comment on the resolution: "This obviously incompetent government must capitulate before the nation; if it refuses, the nation will no longer see itself as bound and will overthrow a government that refuses to go." The minority at the congress itself, led by Shipov, could stop the adopted resolutions from sounding like a call for revolution. It was not, however, in a position to prevent them from being subsequently interpreted in this sense.

34. Both are printed in Petrunkevich, *Memoirs*, pp. 378ff.

35. Ibid., pp. 377ff.

36. Only a few days after the reception of the *zemstvo* congress deputation, the tsar received two further deputations: the Kursk gentry on June 20 and the Orel gentry on June 21. Included in the Orel deputation were S. D. Sheremetev, A. A. Bobrinsky, and Naryshkin, all genuine representatives of *zemstvo* public life. The first deputation expressed the wish that a consultative chamber should only be comprised of members of two estates, the nobility and the peasantry. The Orel deputation stressed that convening a representative assembly should not signify a move to a democratic system, as in Russia, from time immemorial, sovereignty had rested with the tsar and not with the people. In addition, the deputation cautioned the tsar against regarding the deputation from the *zemstvo* congress as the sole representative of all public opinion. Certainly, the tsar's reply to the deputations from Orel and Kursk had exactly the same general and noncommittal character as that given to the *zemstvo* congress deputation. Petrunkevich writes, "The tsar received the deputations from Orel and Kursk in the same friendly manner and promised them no less than he did to us." What the tsar said in reply was determined by what the deputations had said. In his reply to the Kursk deputation, Nicholas II said that he was aware of the usefulness of convening a consultative assembly and of the presence in it of the two main rural estates, the gentry and the peasants (ibid., pp. 384ff).

37. Ibid., p. 376.

38. *Osvobozhdenie*, no. 73, p. 370.

39. Translator's note: *Kramola* means "sedition" or "mutiny"; see H. Leeming, "The Etymology of Old Church Slavonic Крамола," *Slavonic and East European Review* 52, no. 126 (Jan. 1974): pp. 128–31. Here it appears to mean the revolutionary movement as a whole.

CHAPTER 21. FURTHER *ZEMSTVO* CONGRESSES AND THE AGGRAVATION OF THE REVOLUTIONARY SITUATION

1. Petrunkevich, *Memoirs*, p. 383.

2. *Osvobozhdenie*, no.75 (1905): pp. 418ff.

3. After the *zemstvo* congress had voiced its agreement with the draft constitution, it asked the *zemstvo* congress secretariat to send copies of it to *zemstvo* institutions, local self-govern-

ment offices in towns, and competent individuals for information and feedback. It would then present the draft together with all this supplementary material at the next congress in Sept. (Belokonsky, *Zemstvo Movement*, p. 297).

4. *Osvobozhdenie*, no. 75 (1905): p. 433.

5. Petrunkevich, *Memoirs*, p. 384.

6. Trubetskoy's death, which occurred during a meeting in which he was defending university autonomy against ministerial representatives, was greeted by Lenin with *schadenfreude*.

7. *Osvobozhdenie*, no. 75 (1905): p. 427.

8. Ibid., p. 426.

9. One of the *zemstvo* congress–organizing secretariat's resolutions demanded that these bodies take the initiative themselves to introduce the rights necessary to hold elections (ibid. p. 434; cf. also p. 425).

10. Ibid., p. 427.

11. Ibid., p. 426.

12. Ibid., p. 419.

13. Petrunkevich, *Memoirs*, p. 393.

14. *Osvobozhdenie*, no. 76 (1905): p. 455.

15. Petrunkevich, *Memoirs*, pp. 393ff.

16. *Osvobozhdenie*, no. 75 (1905): p. 434.

17. Maklakov, *First State Duma*, p. 487; cf. also p. 416.

18. Ibid., p. 165.

19. Quite apart from the delegates from the extreme Right, who left the congress anyway.

20. *Osvobozhdenie*, no. 76 (1905): p. 456.

21. Ibid., p. 455.

22. *Osvobozhdenie*, no. 75 (1905): p. 434.

23. Ibid., p. 434.

24. Ibid., p. 435.

25. Maklakov, *First State Duma*, pp. 389, 394. Gurko bears witness to the fact that some members of the bureaucracy "increasingly realized the need for popular participation in the government" as "the State apparatus had virtually ceased to function as a factor of national life. It had become a mere mechanism serving current public needs" (*Features and Figures*, 359). In particular, "the event of January 9 . . . had also created a certain panic among bureaucrats convincing them that things could not go on as they were much longer and that a reform of the government was inevitable" (ibid., p. 351). This explains why some members of the bureaucracy supported the Bulygin Duma project so vigorously.

26. Maklakov, *First State Duma*, p. 390.

27. *Osvobozhdenie*, no. 75 (1905): p. 419.

28. Maklakov, *First State Duma*, p. 390.

29. Quoted in ibid., p. 394.

30. Cf. V. Leontovitsch, in *Abhängigkeit und Selbständigkeit bei der Gewaltenteilung* (Dependency and Independence in the Context of the Separation of Powers), *Schriften des Soziologischen Abteilung des Forschungsinstitut für Sozial- und Verwaltungswissenschaften in Cologne*, p. 396.

31. Belokonsky, *Zemstvo Movement*, p. 366.

32. Editorial, *Osvobozhdenie*, no. 77 (1905): p. 465.

33. Maklakov, *First State Duma*, p. 392.

34. A reprint of Miliukov's article along these lines published in *Pravo* and *Syn otechestva* (Son of the Fatherland) immediately after Aug. 6 can be found in *God borby* (A Year of Struggle). Cf. Miliukov's observations in *Russ. Zapiski* 11 (Nov. 1938): p. 148, and his *Memoirs*, vol. 1, p. 299.

35. Quoted in Maklakov, *First State Duma*, p. 387.

36. The reprint can be found in Belokonsky, *Zemstvo Movement*, pp. 297ff.

37. Maklakov, *First State Duma*, pp. 387ff.

38. Ibid., p. 535.

39. *Osvobozhdenie*, no. 76 (1905): p. 452, from the minutes of the *zemstvo* congress session of July 7, 1905.

40. Maklakov, *First State Duma*, pp. 388ff.

41. Ibid., p. 387.

42. Two further such congresses took place—one in Sept. and one on Nov. 6–8, i.e., exactly a year after the famous congress of Nov. 1904. Maklakov writes that it is difficult to say whether it was a coincidence that the congress was convened exactly one year later to the day or whether it was intentional.

43. Petrunkevich, *Memoirs*, p. 392.

44. Belokonsky, *Zemstvo Movement*, p. 373. Particularly interesting is Belokonsky's comment that the *zemstvo* congress arranged for Oct. 12, 1905 (i.e., the next one after the Sept. congress) was "no longer a nonparty congress but had turned into a founding conference of the Kadet party" (ibid., p. 388).

45. Cf. Maklakov, *First State Duma*, pp. 365ff, 368.

46. Ibid., p. 361.

47. Belokonsky, *Zemstvo Movement*, pp. 210ff.

48. These meetings, incidentally, were not specifically organized for this purpose. They were to be set up in the wake of the Liberation Movement's decision generally to stimulate political activity, i.e., the activities of the opposition groups. The Liberation Movement had in fact decided on Oct. 20, 1904, before the *zemstvo* congress of Nov. 6–8, 1904, "to organize banquets on the occasion of the fortieth anniversary of the law reforms (November 20, 1904), to set up professional associations and their federation—the Union of Unions, to campaign to get the *zemstvo* assemblies and congresses to embrace the demands for the introduction of democratic constitution in Russia."

49. *Osvobozhdenie* carried a report of one such gathering (on the occasion of the fortieth anniversary of the introduction of the liberal law reform of Nov. 20, 1864), held in St. Petersburg and chaired by the writer Korolenko. A lawyer, I. V. Gessen, and a historian, Semesky, appeared as speakers. The meeting put forward the following demands: freedom of conscience, speech, the press, assembly, and association; total amnesty for political and religious crimes; and finally the convening of a constituent assembly. See "Listok" (Bulletin), *Osvobozhdenie*, no. 21 (Dec. 9, 1904). The bulletin reported not just large gatherings but also smaller meetings; e.g., one evening there were two meetings held at the Technical University, a liberal one and a "social-democrat" one. The participants at the social-democrat meeting burst into the main hall, where a ball was taking place, singing revolutionary songs. In the hall they hung a large red banner with the slogan "Down with the autocracy!" over a large portrait of the tsar. By itself, the behavior of the revolutionaries was not unexpected. What was significant, however, was that no one in the entire great hall protested against it, a fact that the *Osvobozhdenie* bulletin particularly highlighted. It also came to street demonstrations that one can also read about in *Osvobozhdenie*.

50. Maklakov, *First State Duma*, p. 360.

51. Ibid., p. 357.

52. Ibid.

53. Ibid., p. 358.

54. Ibid., p. 406.

55. Ibid., pp. 146ff.

56. Kryzhanovsky, *Vospominaniia*, p. 16.

57. Maklakov, *First State Duma*, p. 405.

CHAPTER 22. THE MANIFESTO OF OCTOBER 17, 1905, AND THE CONSTITUTION OF APRIL 23, 1906

1. Witte, *Memoirs*, vol. 1, p. 500.

2. Ibid., vol. 2, p. 8.

3. Ibid., vol. 2, pp. 4ff.

4. The tsar doubtless had no choice but to make this decision, particularly because he was advised to do so not only by liberal officeholders, like Witte and Count Sol'sky, among others, but also by people like Grand Duke Nicholai Nicholaevich and the deputy minister of the interior P. N. Durnovo. Without their support, he could not have contemplated the violent repression of the revolution. Witte reports that Durnovo referred in conversation with him to wide-ranging liberal reforms as the only option. According to Witte, Durnovo's opinion carried particular weight not least because he was deputy minister of the interior under four interior ministers and had previously held the office of Head of the Police Department (ibid., vol. 1, p. 499).

5. The wording for points 2 and 3 is based on the legislation of Aug. 6, 1905, on the Bulygin Duma. Point 3 stipulates that no draft legislation could pass into law without the Duma's endorsement.

6. Ibid., vol. 2, p. 257.

7. Ibid., vol. 2, p. 259.

8. Ibid., vol. 2, p. 259. This thought is worded in the following cautious manner in the minutes of the Council of Ministers meeting where the council presented the draft fundamental laws to the tsar: "It is impossible to postpone drafting the fundamental laws until the Duma meets and to complete its revision in cooperation with the Duma. Thus the newly convened representatives of the people might not get down to productive business but become entangled in dangerous and fruitless debates about the limits of their powers and the nature of their relationship with the supreme power" (quoted in ibid., vol. 2, p. 260).

9. Ibid., vol. 2, p. 266.

10. Ibid., vol. 2, p. 268.

11. Witte calls Baron Uexküll a "well-disposed (*blagonamerennyi*) liberal" and says that he considered him to be a very respectable, highly cultured, and very experienced civil servant and that, in his opinion, he was no opportunist, although he was given to irony and lacked grand ideas (ibid., vol. 2, pp. 258, 263). Uexküll was joined by his deputy Kharitonov, who, in Witte's view, was a good-natured opportunist, but also an experienced official and a clever, cultured man.

12. The minutes of the meetings of this advisory committee were published in the journal *Byloe*, no. 4 (1917). [Translator's note: This was the monthly journal of the Liberation Movement.]

13. Articles of the fundamental laws are cited from the *Svod Zakonov*, vol. 1, part 1 (1906 ed.).

14. It is precisely for this reason that one could say that the Socialist and Kadet parties' draft agrarian laws presented in the Duma were unconstitutional, a point that was also maintained by Duma member Sul'gin in the Second Duma (shorthand record, 1907, vol. 1, col. 1133). Equally, Maklakov points out that according to these draft laws, property belonging to members of the gentry estate had to be expropriated for the benefit of the peasant estate— i.e., for the benefit of another estate, not for the benefit of the state as a whole. However, it might also be said that improving the lot of one estate can be, at the same time, in the general interest. Witte too had made this point in the special commission. He criticized Goremykin's proposal that Art. 77 should state that expropriation should only be permitted for the benefit of state institutions, saying, "How can the emperor say it would only be admissible to meet the needs of state institutions, and not the needs of the peasantry, when that would likewise be in the public interest?" (*Byloe*, no. 4 [1917]: p. 234). Thus, if one is critical of Kadet agrarian policy, one has to show that implementing it would have had, in the end, an adverse effect on the peasantry itself, because it would have resulted in the destruction of civil society, which alone could have made the peasants free. This is something I tried to show in the section of this book on the peasantry.

15. At the end of Art. 76, however, there is mention of special legislation that set out restrictions on the right to choose one's residence freely. The most important of these laws were

those forbidding Jews in general, apart from some exceptions, from being residents outside a certain area (*cherta osedlosti*). Witte explained that it was necessary to include a mention of these special laws, because if this was omitted, he said in the advisory commission, the entire press would maintain that the fundamental laws gave Jews total freedom of movement (*Byloe*, no. 4 [1917]: p. 233). It was, however, obvious to everybody that these restrictive laws would soon have to be repealed. This is clearly indicated by the final words of Art. 76 in the draft of the fundamental laws, to the effect that these restrictions would remain in force "until their amendment."

16. Cf. Witte, *Memoirs*, vol. 2, pp. 280ff.

17. Ibid., vol. 2, pp. 280ff.

18. If the Bolshevik wing of the Social Democrats officially had no representatives in the First Duma, this was not the result of government action, but of Lenin's decision to boycott the elections.

19. Ibid., vol. 2, p. 298.

20. There was admittedly one limitation in this regard. The Duma was not able to return to a rejected draft law in the course of the same session. This restriction, however, cannot be described as significant. If the session was not coincidentally the last one of the legislative period, then the Duma with the same composition could continue the struggle for its draft law.

21. Quoted in Maklakov, *First State Duma*, p. 587.

22. This freedom of the Duma was safeguarded by the constitution (Art. 79) and by Arts. 43 and 45 of the State Duma statute. It guaranteed not only freedom of expression in the Duma but also the publication of reports about the criticism voiced in the Duma.

23. *Byloe*, no. 4 (1907): p. 189.

24. Maklakov, *First State Duma*, p. 586.

25. Ibid., p. 570.

26. Ibid., pp. 571, 573. Cf. also Shulgin, *Dni* (Belgrade, 1925), p. 7.

27. It was also pointed out here that preparing military laws was a matter for the Army Council or the Admiralty Council and that therefore the possibility of the tsar enacting arbitrary laws even in this area was essentially excluded.

28. *Byloe*, no. 4 (1907): pp. 191, 193, 195ff.

29. Ibid., p. 196.

30. Ibid., pp. 195ff.

31. Ibid., p. 224; cf. also Arts. 20, 21, 217, 218, of the Fundamental Laws.

32. Ibid., p. 194.

33. Ibid., p. 225.

34. Ibid.

35. Ibid., p. 226.

36. Ibid., p. 227.

37. Ibid., p. 227.

38. Ibid., p. 228.

39. Ibid., p. 205.

40. This legal principle was introduced by Speransky in the law setting up the State Council. From there Speransky added it to the *Svod zakonov*, from which it went into the Apr. 23, 1906, constitution (Art. 84).

41. *Byloe*, no. 4 (1907): p. 206.

42. The phrase stating that decrees issued at the highest level of government must be consistent with laws also meant, incidentally, that the supreme power was not allowed to exceed the budget limits set by the assembly when implementing measures set out in these decrees (Frisch, in ibid., p. 215).

43. Ibid., p. 214.

44. Ibid., p. 203.

45. Translator's note: The *conseil d'état* is the Council of State, the organ of the French constitution advising the executive on legal issues.

46. Ibid., p. 216. According to Art. 24 of the constitution, decrees issued by the executive were published by the senate.

47. Ibid., p. 215.

48. Ibid., p. 215.

49. In cases of malfeasance, ministers were answerable under the relevant provisions of civil or criminal law.

50. Maklakov, *First State Duma*, p. 598.

51. *Byloe*, no. 4 (1907): p. 228.

52. Witte, *Memoirs*, vol. 2, pp. 267ff.

53. *Byloe*, no. 4 (1907): p. 219. Art. 17 of the constitution corresponds to Art. 15 of the draft.

54. Ibid., pp. 221ff—comments made by von Pahlen and Frisch.

55. Translator's note: This is in French in the original text: "la force de la chose jugée."

56. Ibid., pp. 220ff.

CHAPTER 23. WITTE AND PUBLIC OPINION

1. Maklakov, *First State Duma*, p. 561.

2. The number of appointed members was not allowed to exceed the number of elected members—there could only be fewer.

3. Ibid., p. 591.

4. Ibid., p. 585.

5. Ibid., p. 445.

6. Ibid., p. 585.

7. Maklakov, *Second State Duma*, p. 8; cf Maklakov, *First State Duma*, p. 18.

8. Shipov, *Recollections*, p. 335; cf. p. 341.

9. Miliukov, *Tri popytki* (Three Attempts) (Paris, 1921), p. 24.

10. Quoted in Maklakov, *First State Duma*, p. 437.

11. Ibid., p. 551.

12. Ibid., p. 461.

13. Ibid., p. 464.

14. Quoted in ibid., p. 470.

15. Ibid., p. 471.

16. Quoted in ibid., p. 439.

17. Ibid., p. 419.

18. Ibid., p. 420.

19. This refers to the armed uprising in Moscow in Dec. 1905.

20. Ibid., pp. 429ff.

CHAPTER 24. THE CONSTITUTIONAL-DEMOCRATIC PARTY AND THE UNION OF OCTOBER 17

1. Shipov himself did not participate in this congress, but several of his political allies did.

2. Svechin joined the Kadet Party, belonging to its right wing.

3. Maklakov, *First State Duma*, p. 469.

4. Ibid., p. 466.

5. Ibid., p. 469.

6. Shipov, *Recollections*, p. 402.

7. Ibid., p. 404.

8. Of the nonsocialist parties, only one small relatively unknown party called the Radical Party openly called for a republic.

9. Quoted in ibid., p. 405.

10. Quoted in ibid., p. 413.

11. Ibid., p. 419.

12. *Polnyi sbornik platform vsekh russk. politich. partii* (Complete Collection of Party Programs of all Russian Political Parties), 3rd ed. (St. Petersburg, 1906), p. 114.

13. Shipov, *Recollections*, p. 420

14. Ibid., pp. 423ff.

15. Quoted in Maklakov, *First State Duma*, p. 549.

16. Stakhovich spoke on these lines at the Octobrist conference; cited in Shipov, *Recollections*, p. 415.

17. Ibid., p. 421.

18. The Octobrist program stressed that the Union of October 17 insisted on the government rapidly implementing the principles of the October Manifesto, but that it was prepared "to lend support to the government on the path to beneficial reforms" (*Party Programs*, p. 112).

19. *Byloe*, no. 3 (1917): p. 242. This special advisory committee was set up to discuss the draft electoral law proposed by the Council of Ministers. It met on Dec. 5, 7, and 9. The Octobrists were accused not just of supporting the government's program of reforms, but of indiscriminately justifying all the actions of the Stolypin government. Bulgakov (*Memoirs*) regarded this party as pure opportunists. By contrast, Gurko (*Features and Figures*, p. 513) stresses the independent attitude of the Octobrists vis-à-vis the government. One can find criticism of this party in the memoirs of one prominent Octobrist, Shidlovsky, and especially in Maklakov (*Second State Duma*, pp. 52ff). Kizevetter gives a pertinent account of the differences between the Kadets and the Octobrists; see *Na rubezhe dvuch stoletii* (At the Turn of the Century) (Prague, 1929), p. 406.

20. Struve advocated this coalition in the journal *Poliarnaia Zvezda*, no. 4 (Jan. 5, 1906).

21. Quoted in Maklakov, *Second State Duma*, p. 500.

22. Ibid., p. 500.

23. See ibid., p. 544.

24. Shipov, *Recollections*, p. 374.

25. Kokovtsov, *Iz moego proshlogo* (From My Past) (Paris, 1933), vol. 1, pp. 132ff.

26. Ibid., vol. 1, p. 166.

27. Ibid., vol. 1, p. 169.

28. Maklakov, *First State Duma*, pp. 33ff.

CHAPTER 25. THE FIRST DUMA

1. Cf. Maklakov's comments about this in *First State Duma*, p. 20.

2. Kokovtsov, *From My Past*, vol. 1, p. 173.

3. Ibid., vol. 1, p. 174.

4. Maklakov, *First State Duma*, pp. 50ff.

5. Quoted in ibid., p. 51

6. Quoted in ibid., p. 54. Muromtsev's comment is reminiscent of a comment (quoted elsewhere) made by Count Panin, after he was appointed chairman of the editing commission preparing legislation for the emancipation of the serfs, on the citizen's duty to submit unquestioningly to the will of the monarch.

7. Shorthand minutes of the Duma for 1906, vol. 1, p. 3.

8. Maklakov, *Second State Duma*, pp. 7ff.

9. Maklakov, *First State Duma*, p. 57.

10. Ibid., pp. 41ff.

11. Ibid., p. 42.

12. Cf. T. Lokot' (a member of the Trudoviki parliamentary group in the First Duma), *Pervaia Duma* (The First Duma) (Moscow, 1906), p. 142.

13. Quoted in Kokovtsov, *From My Past*, vol. 1, p. 186.

14. Cf. Maklakov, *First State Duma*, pp. 146, 148.

15. Mme. de Staël, *Considérations sur. . . la Révolution Française* (Paris, 1818), vol. 1, chap. 23, "Acceptation de la Constitution appelée 'Constitution de 1791,'" p. 431. [Translator's note: The author quotes the French in the original: "C'était donc le plus pénible des spectacles intellectuels que de voir les bienfaits de la liberté civile mis sous la sauvegarde d'une liberté politique sans mesure et sans force."]

16. Kokovtsov, *From My Past*, vol. 1, pp. 183ff.

17. Ibid., vol. 1, pp. 182, 188.

18. Quoted in Maklakov, *First State Duma*, p. 192.

19. Cf. Kokovtsov, *From My Past*, vol. 1. pp. 201ff.

20. Ibid., vol. 1, p. 199.

21. This was certainly an error. On the contrary: the tsar in all probability either had no idea about the negotiations between Trepov and Miliukov (Trepov's initiative was probably a personal one) or did not authorize it.

22. Maklakov, *First State Duma*, pp. 201ff.

23. Quoted in Miliukov, *Three Attempts*, p. 31.

24. Ibid., p. 38.

25. Quoted in ibid., p. 38.

26. Ibid., p. 40.

27. Cf. Maklakov, *First State Duma*, p. 409.

28. Kokovtsov, *From My Past*, vol. 1, pp. 203, 205.

29. Ibid., vol. 1, pp. 203, 209.

30. Ibid., vol. 1, pp. 212ff.

31. Ibid., vol. 1, p. 188.

32. Ibid., vol. 1, p. 204.

33. Ibid., vol. 1, p. 210.

34. Ibid., vol. 1, pp. 218ff; cf. also Witte, *Memoirs,* for the story about the alleged withdrawal of the order to dissolve the Duma (vol. 2, p. 319).

35. Kokovtsov, *From My Past*, vol. 1, pp. 214ff.

36. Ibid., vol. 1, pp. 175, 232.

37. Ibid., vol. 1, p. 204.

38. Ibid., vol. 1, p. 235.

39. Ibid., vol. 1, pp. 259ff.

40. Quoted in ibid., vol. 1, pp. 238ff.

41. Ibid., vol. 1, p. 239.

42. Cf. Stolypin to Nicholas II, Dec. 10, 1906, in *Byloe*, nos. 5–6 (1917): pp. 3ff. Stolypin then suggested to the tsar that he make it clear in his resolution that he accepted the solution proposed by the Council of Ministers in principle, but that he thought it proper to take the relevant measures not on the basis of Art. 87, but through the normal legislative process. Interestingly enough, some public figures feared that the government could abolish the restrictions without the Duma's agreement. Of course, there is no doubt that they held the abolition to be necessary and right, but they thought that this would reduce the Duma's powers. Cf. Shipov, *Recollections*, pp. 180ff.

CHAPTER 26. THE SECOND DUMA

1. Berdyaev, "Revoliutsiia i kul'tura," *Poliarnaia Zvezda*, no. 2 (Dec. 22, 1905).

2. Maklakov, *Second State Duma*, pp. 101ff.

3. Ibid., p. 104; Tikhomirov also allows that such an alliance was possible (*Krasny Arkhiv*, vol. 61, p. 100). He writes, "Perhaps the Kadets, in union with the Right, will tame the Left, and thus lead to the consolidation of constitutional government here in Russia." His comment that the tsar would not hear of the abandonment of constitutional government is also noteworthy (p. 110).

4. Shorthand reports of the Duma, 1907, vol. 1, col. 37.

5. Shipov, *Recollections*, p. 513.

6. Ibid., p. 515.

7. At the same time, the Octobrists did not always vote with the Right—e.g., they voted against military tribunals. This can be explained by the fact that by chance Professor Kapustin became leader of the parliamentary group, not Guchkov (he had not been elected to the Second Duma), who, as is well known, thought that the military tribunals were a necessity.

8. One must not attach too much weight to this factor. Even without the irksome support of the Right that might frighten off the moderates, Stolypin's government would probably not have received any backing from the Kadets, even from those elements that stood between the Kadets and the Octobrists.

9. Shorthand reports of the Duma, 1907, vol. 1, col. 110.

10. Ibid., vol. 1, col. 110.

11. Ibid., vol. 1, col. 113.

12. Ibid., vol. 1, col. 114.

13. Ibid., vol. 1, col. 113.

14. Ibid., vol. 1, col. 114.

15. Ibid.

16. Ibid., vol. 1, col. 113.

17. Ibid., vol. 1, col. 111.

18. Ibid., vol. 1, col. 112.

19. Ibid., vol. 1, col. 113.

20. Ibid., vol. 1, cols. 114, 116.

21. Ibid., vol. 1, col. 108.

22. Ibid., vol. 1, col. 116.

23. Ibid., vol. 1, col. 118.

24. Ibid., vol. 1, col. 107.

25. Maklakov is right to point out that Speransky's codification had also had this aim (*Second State Duma*, p. 87).

26. Shorthand reports of the Duma, 1907, vol. 1, col. 120.

27. Ibid., vol. 1, col. 167.

28. Ibid., vol. 1, col. 169.

29. M. Bock, *Vospominaniia o moem otse* (Memories of My Father) (New York, 1953), p. 222.

30. Maklakov, *Second State Duma*, pp. 227ff.

31. Miliukov, *Vtoraia Duma* (The Second Duma) (St. Petersburg, 1908), p. 197.

32. Certainly many members of the left majority only opposed these methods because they were directed at themselves, but were prepared to employ even worse methods against their own enemies.

33. Maklakov, *Second State Duma*, p. 20.

34. Ibid., p. 26. Overall, the whole of chap. 2 of this book is devoted to some extremely interesting reflections on the methods used to combat the revolution used by Stolypin, or at least tolerated by him.

35. Although Shipov approved of the liberal content of the government's declaration, he felt he could not support the Stolypin government, insofar as he believed that the government's practice did not match its program. He accused Stolypin of not intervening energetically enough against the brutal and illegal actions carried out by the authorities in the fight against revolutionary disorder and stated that he did not quickly enough have legislation prepared and laid before the Duma to regulate the exercise of rights granted in the constitution. Shipov was convinced that Stolypin only widened the gulf between the state power and the public through this policy, reducing the chances of cooperation between the Duma and the government.

36. Quoted in Maklakov, *Second State Duma*, p. 85.

37. Shorthand reports of the Duma, 1907, vol. 1, col. 126.

38. Maklakov, *Second State Duma*, p. 89.

39. L. Tichomirov, memoirs, published in *Krasnyi Arkhiv*, vol. 61, p. 95.

40. It is noteworthy that the socialist parties also had an interest in the Kadets joining forces with the Right. They were keen that the Kadets should save the Duma in this way, thus giving them the opportunity to exploit it for revolutionary purposes. (See Miliukov, *Second Duma*, pp. 144, 161ff.)

41. Maklakov, *Second State Duma*, p. 116.

42. Ibid., pp. 122, 229.

43. Ibid., p. 165.

44. Ibid., pp. 231, 247, 254.

45. Despite this optimism, even Maklakov has to acknowledge that the level of culture in the Second Duma was extraordinarily poor and that it was poorly equipped to deal with the enormous task that faced it (ibid., p. 254).

46. Shipov, *Recollections*, p. 498.

47. Kokovtsov, *From My Past*, vol. 1, p. 257.

48. It is difficult to ascertain whether Bulgakov was in fact independent or whether he joined the Kadets' parliamentary group in the Duma, without otherwise belonging to the Kadet Party. (See Maklakov, *Second State Duma*, p. 231.)

49. Bulgakov, *Avtobiograficheskie zametki* (Biographical Sketches) (Paris, 1946), pp. 80ff.

CHAPTER 27. THE COUP OF JUNE 3, 1907, AND THE THIRD AND FOURTH DUMAS

1. Maklakov, *Second State Duma*, pp. 246, 254.

2. Ibid., p. 246.

3. Ibid., p. 231; see also pp. 250, 255ff.

4. See Kryzhanovsky, *Memoirs*, pp. 90, 107, for the changes to the electoral law of Dec. 11, 1905, and the drafting of the electoral law of June 3, 1907. Kryzhanovsky drafted the electoral law of June 3, 1907, as well as, incidentally, the law of Dec. 11, 1905.

5. The text of this manifesto can be found in the legal weekly journal *Pravo*, no. 23 (June 10, 1907).

6. Maklakov, *Second State Duma*, p. 225.

7. It is widely held that Russia might well have been spared these disadvantages and risks, had the plan to use the *zemstvo* institutions as a foundation for a gradual and cautious development of constitutional government not been rejected in the 1880s.

8. One should not suppose that favoring the peasantry in the electoral law of Dec. 11, 1905, was inspired by genuinely democratic thinking. On the contrary, it was largely advocated by the supporters of the autocracy, who still saw the peasants as a bastion of conservatism.

9. Nevertheless, some of the provisions of the electoral law of June 3, 1907, bear a close relationship to the *zemstvo* electoral system, although Kryzhanovsky's alternative draft that went even further in this respect was rejected. The draft that was adopted was based extensively on the principles underlying the electoral law of Dec. 11, 1905 (Kryzhanovsky, *Memoirs*, pp. 108, 111).

10. Kokovtsov, *From My Past*, vol. 1, p. 213.

11. Ibid., vol. 1, p. 231. Gurko says the same in his memoirs (*Features and Figures*, pp. 462ff). It is possible that Stolypin was especially able to establish a working relationship with the Octobrists in the Third Duma to some extent, because most of the Octobrists were men like him, from the provinces.

12. Maklakov, *Second State Duma*, p. 467.

13. Ibid., pp. 455ff.

14. Ibid., p. 399.

15. Shipov, *Recollections*, p. 519.

16. Maklakov, *Second State Duma*, p. 31.

17. The text of this communiqué can be found in the weekly journal *Pravo*, no. 34 (1906), cols. 2697ff.

18. This interview with the correspondent was published on Aug. 27, 1906.

19. Guchkov refers here to Stolypin's negotiations with representatives of public opinion about the formation of a "coalition government," which is discussed above.

20. Quoted in Shipov, *Recollections*, pp. 493ff.

21. Shidlovsky, *Vospominaniia* (Memoirs) (Berlin, 1923), p. 100.

22. It is often asserted that the Octobrists voted for the new electoral law for purely selfish

reasons, as they knew that they stood to benefit from it. This may be true in part, although overall this explanation is too crude and unfair to the Octobrists.

23. Kokovtsov, *From My Past*, vol. 1, p. 277.

24. All of Maklakov's commentary in his book on the Second Duma regarding the coup d'état of June 3, 1907, supports this view. Maklakov stresses much more forcefully the positive significance of this event in the introduction to his memoirs published later in New York. Nevertheless, Maklakov also correctly recognized the disadvantages of the coup (*Second State Duma*, pp. 254ff).

25. Ibid., pp. 603ff.

26. Ibid., p. 246.

27. Representatives of quite different schools of thought agree that it was precisely during the Third and Fourth Dumas that constitutional government took root. See, on this question, Kizevetter, *At the Turn of the Century*, p. 466; Miliukov, *Memoirs*, vol. 2, p. 16; Maklakov, *Second State Duma*, p. 28; Gurko, *Features and Figures*, p. 511.

28. Kokovtsov's memoirs give an idea of Russia's economic progress in this period; see Kokovtsov, *From My Past*, vol. 2, part 4, chap. 5.

29. Maklalov, *Second State Duma*, p. 601; see also Miliukov, *Memoirs*, vol. 2, p. 18.

30. Kokovtsov, *From My Past*, vol. 1, pp. 287ff.

31. Ibid., vol. I, pp. 290ff.

32. *Byloe*, nos. 5–6 (1917): p. 308. It is noteworthy that such an eminent authority as Max Weber agreed that the 1906 constitution was a pseudo-constitution. This may be explained by the influence of his Russian friends in the Kadet Party.

33. Struve, *Patriotika* (St. Petersburg, 1911).

34. Maklakov, *Second State Duma*, pp. 29ff.

35. Ibid., p. 30.

36. Struve, second foreword to Witte, *Samoderzhavie i zemstvo* (The Autocracy and the Zemstvo) (Stuttgart, 1903), p. lxx.

INDEX OF NAMES

Abaza, A. A., finance minister (1880–81), 201–3

Akimov, M. G. (1847–1914), justice minister (1905–6), 278, 281

Alexander I (1801–1825), 31–38, 46, 50, 54, 59, 66–69, 76, 79–80, 98–100, 191, 207, 236, 278, 337n15, 342n10

Alexander II (1855–1881), 25, 37, 66, 79, 87, 103, 107, 109, 111–12, 120, 137, 152–53, 161, 196, 199–202, 204–8, 212, 227, 267, 281, 315, 353n40

Alexander III (1881–1894), 47–48, 63, 123, 133, 136–37, 143, 195, 199, 202–3, 205, 207–8, 240, 287

Azef, Evno, terrorist and provocateur, 216–17

Bacon, Francis, 34, 43, 71, 75, 77, 341n8

Balugiansky, M. A. (1769–1847), 34, 77

Belokonsky, I., 265, 360n3

Bentham, Jeremy, 34, 76

Bestuzhev, A. A. (1797–1837), Decembrist, 66, 340n22

Bulgakov, S. N., member of the Second Duma, 320–21, 365n19, 368n48

Bulygin, A.G., minister of the Interior (1905), 248, 255, 260, 263, 266

Bunge, N. Kh., (1823–1895), finance minister (1881–86), 143, 347n7

Burke, Edmund, 26, 334n28

Catherine II (1762–1796), 17–33, 35, 53–54, 57–60, 62, 79, 81, 84, 86–88, 92–93, 98–99, 101, 113, 135, 137, 159, 207, 281, 334n27, 335n37, 335n2 (chap. 2)

Chernov, V. M., leader of the Socialist-Revolutionary Party, 156, 348n2

Chernyshevsky, N. G. (1828–1889), 111, 258

Chicherin, B. N. (1828–1904), philosopher and constitutional lawyer, 99–103, 112–13, 153, 155, 191–92, 196–97, 338n5, 351n13, 352n34

Chicherin, V. N. (1829–1884), diplomat in Paris, 112–13

Constantine Pavlovich, Grand Duke, 26, 80

Cucumus, Konrad von, 331n13, 332n14

Dmitriev, I. I. (1760–1837), 64–65

Dolgorukov, P. D., Prince, member of the First and Second Duma, 214, 254

Durnovo, I. N. (1830–1903), minister of the Interior (1889–95), 143, 346n3

Durnovo, P.N. (1845–1915), minister of the Interior, 143, 243, 276, 287, 290, 362n4

Fateev, A., 66–67

Florovsky, A., 18–19, 332n3

Frederick the Great, 69, 72–73

Frisch, E. V. (1833–1907), chairman of the State Council, 276, 278–79, 282, 358n53

Gessen, I. V., member of the Second Duma, Kadet, 281, 348n5, 361n49

Gessen, V. M., member of the Second Duma, Kadet, 156–57

Golovin, F. A., speaker of the Second Duma, Kadet, 217, 229, 319

Goremykin. I. L. (1839–1917), minster of the Interior (1895–99), chair of the Council of Ministers (May–July 1906; 1914–16), 209–12, 230, 278, 298–99, 305–7, 347n5, 362n14

Gradovsky, A., 37, 45, 81, 87

Granovsky, T. N. (1813–1855), Westernizer, 100, 191–92, 351n13

Guchkov, A. I., speaker of the Third Duma, Octobrist, 292–94, 317, 324–26, 328, 366n7

Gurko, V. I. (1862–1927), deputy minister of the Interior, 161, 185, 347n2, 350n9, 360n25, 365n19

Hauriou, Maurice (1856–1929), French constitutionalist, 2, 4–6, 8,11–12, 29, 62, 189–90, 211, 332n19, 335n43, 351n1, 351n4

Herzen, A., 100, 111, 191, 220, 351–52n13

Heyden, P. A., member of the First Duma, Octobrist, 306, 313

Hume, 49, 76

Ikonnikov, V., 33–34

Ivan IV (1533–1584), 20, 53, 57–58, 285, 340n28

Kankrin, E. F. (1774–1845), finance minister (1823–44), 46–47, 68, 93, 343n2

Karamzin, N. M. (1766–1826), 24, 31, 48, 55–65, 67, 69–75, 77, 130, 135, 137

Katkov, M. N. (1818–1887), 101, 112, 137, 192–93, 205, 225

Kavelin, K. D. (1818–1865), 99–100

Khomiakov, A. S. (1804–1850), Slavophile, 100–101

Khomiakov, N. A., speaker of the Third Duma, Octobrist, 213–14, 247

Kiselev, P. D. (1788–1872), minister of State Domains (1837–56), 81, 83–84, 93–94, 96–97, 116

Kizevetter, A. A. (1867–1933), historian, member of the Second Duma, 80, 90, 98

Kliuchevsky, V. O., 214, 260, 263

Kochubei, V. P. (1768–1834), minister of the Interior (1802–12; 1819–25), 32, 35

Kokoshkin, F. F., member of the First Duma, 213, 233, 262, 288, 319

Kokovtsov, V. N., finance minister (1906–11), 298–301, 304–5, 307–10, 314, 318, 320, 323, 325, 327

Koni, A. F. (1844–1927), lawyer, member of the State Council (from 1907), 242, 284

Korf, M. A. (1800–1876), member of the State Council, 46, 54, 70, 76–78, 96

Korkunov, A., 34, 77

Koshelev, A. I. (1806–1883), 117–18

Krasovsky. M. V. (1851–1911), member of the State Council (after 1906), 178–79, 182–85, 350n3

Kropotov, A. E., peasant, volost' clerk, member of the Third Duma, Trudovik, 172–73

Kryzhanovsky, S. E. (1862–1934), deputy minister of the Interior (1906), 267, 354n16, 368n4, 368n9

Kutaisov, I. P., favourite of Paul I, 35–36

L'vov, G. E., Prince, 306, 323

L'vov, N. N., member of First–Fourth Dumas, 221, 233, 293, 305

La Harpe, F. C. (1754–1838), 26, 35

Lenin, 186, 226, 258, 312, 360n6, 363n18

Loris-Melikov, M. T. (1825–1888), minister of the Interior (1880–81), 190, 199–203, 214, 218

Maklakov, V. A., member of Second–Fourth Dumas, 26, 156, 158, 185–86, 204–8, 213, 215, 219, 221–23, 225, 227–29, 231, 234, 236–41, 245–48, 250, 257–58, 260, 263–64, 266–67, 275, 280, 283–86, 288–91, 293, 299, 301–3, 312, 316–19, 321, 326–28, 362n14, 368n45, 369n24

Makov, L. S., minister of the Interior (1878–80), 200, 202

Mandelstamm, Kadet, 257–58

Manuilov, A. A., member of the State Council (after 1906), 159, 161, 178

Meshchersky, V. P., Prince, publicist, 47, 190, 196, 204, 353n40

Mikhailovich, Alexei (1645–1676), 54, 59, 73

Miliukov, P. N. (1859–1943), member of the Third and Fourth Dumas, 159–63, 169, 220–21, 229, 263–65, 281, 287–88, 296–97, 302, 305–7, 317–18

Miliutin, D. A. (1816–1912), minister of Defense (1861–81), 81, 91, 137, 200

Miliutin, N. A. (1818–1872), member of the Editing Commission (1859–60), 108, 197

Montesquieu, 7–10, 17, 27, 32, 71, 74, 135, 157, 285, 339n10

Mordvinov, N. S. (1754–1845), chairman of the Economic Affairs Department of the State Council (1810–13; and from 1816), 33–38, 68, 236

Muromtsev, S. A., speaker of the First Duma, Kadet, 255–56, 281, 302, 306–7

Nabokov, V. D., member of the First Duma, Kadet, 244, 255–56, 303, 318

Napoleon, 25, 53, 55, 65, 70, 72

Nicholas I (1825–1855), 46, 65–66, 68, 77, 79–84, 87–91, 93, 98–100, 107, 110–12, 117, 191–92, 204–5, 207

Nicholas II (1894–1917), 143–44, 153, 207, 235, 238–40, 243, 252, 269–72, 289, 298–99, 301, 310, 359n36

Novosil'tsev, N. N. (1761–1836), representative of the Russian government in Warsaw (1812–31), 32, 67, 70, 340–41n28

Obolensky, A. D., Prince, procurator of the Holy Synod, 235, 277

Panin, V. N. (1801–1874), minister of Justice (1859–62), 108, 198–99

Paul I (1796–1801), 31–33, 35, 57–58, 207, 335n2

Pazukhin, Simbirsk, marshal of the nobility, 47, 204

Peretz, E. A. (1833–1899), secretary of State (1878–83), 199–200, 347–48n7

Perovsky, L. A. (1792–1856), minister of the Interior (1841–52), 85, 135

Peter I (1689–1725), 27, 43, 54, 59, 69, 71, 92, 101, 193, 285, 326

Peter III (1762), 17, 24

Petrunkevich, I. I. (1844–1928), member of the First Duma, Kadet, 220, 228–29, 239, 247, 250–52, 255–58, 265, 289, 346n3

Pleve, V. K. (1846–1904), minister of the Interior (ca. 1902–4), 144–45, 157–58, 164, 213, 215–19, 228–29, 239, 338n9, 347n2

Pobedonostsev, K. P. (1827–1907), 164, 190, 200–1, 204–6, 211, 235, 244

Polovtsov, A. A., secretary of State (1883), 47–48

Pushkin, 27, 34

Radishchev, A. N. (1749–1802), 25–30, 334n29, 335n2, 335n4

Redkin, P. G., professor at Moscow University, 99–100

Reutern, M. Kh., chairman of the Committee of Ministers (1881–86), 158, 347n7

Roberti, E. V. de, 225, 264

Rodichev, F. I., member of the First–Fourth Dumas, Kadet, 159, 207–8, 251, 302

Rosenkampf, Gustaf A. (1764–1832), secretary to the Law Drafting Commission (1804–8), 33, 70, 72, 76

Rousseau, J. J., 8–10, 262

Ruggiero, Guido de, 2, 4

Saburov, A. A. (1838–1916), top civil servant in the Ministry of Education, 201, 274, 276–78

Samarin, Y. F. (1819–1876), Slavophile, 100, 102, 108

Savigny, 27, 62, 71–75, 77, 341n5

Sergeevich, V. I., historian of law, member of the State Council (after 1906), 27, 182

Sergei Alexandrovich, Grand Duke (1864–1905), governor of Moscow, 208, 217, 245

Shakhovskoi, D. I., Prince, member of the First Duma, Kadet, 213, 220–21

Shidlovsky, S. I., member of the Third and Fourth Dumas, Octobrist, 118, 170–72, 179, 325, 365n19

Shingarev, A. I., member of the Second–Fourth Dumas, Kadet, 169–71

Shipov, D. N, leader of union of Oct. 17th, chair of Moscow Province zemstvo executive committee (1906), 204, 208–11, 213–19, 228–35, 246–47, 249–51, 262, 287, 292–95, 297–98, 306, 317, 319, 357n24, 359n33, 367n35

Shirinsky-Shikhmatov, A. A., Prince (1862–1929), 299, 304

Skrebitsky, A., 116–17

Smith, Adam, 34, 76, 192

Sol'sky, D. M. (1833–1910), member of the State Council (after 1899), 201–2, 271

Speransky, M. M. (1772–1839), 32, 34–36, 38–46, 48–55, 58, 68, 70, 72, 75–78, 83, 87, 93, 137, 285, 329, 337n18, 339n20, 363n40

Staël, Mme de, 2, 25, 304

Stakhovich, M. A., Orel marshal of the nobility, 213–17, 247, 258

Stishinsky, A. S. (1851–1920), head of Department of Peasant Affairs, Interior Ministry (from 1893), 145, 147, 174, 184–85, 299, 350n4

Stolypin, P. A. (1862–1911), minister of the Interior (1906), 10, 37, 145, 158, 163, 165, 167–69, 172, 176, 179–82, 184–86, 212, 229, 243, 287, 301, 304–10, 313–26, 328–29, 350n6, 367n35

Stroganov, A. G. (1795–1891), governor general of New Russia and Bessarabia, 117, 200–202

Stroganov, S. G. (1794–1882), curator of Moscow University, 99, 101

Struve, P. B. (1870–1944), editor of *Osvobozhdenie* (Liberation), member of the

Second Duma, 159, 220–21, 224, 293, 321, 328–29, 357n42

Svechin, A. A., member of the First Duma, Kadet, 292–93

Sviatopolk-Mirsky, P. D., Prince (1857–1914), minister of the Interior (1904–5), 164, 213, 228–30, 233–35, 238, 240, 245, 267

Tagantsev, N. S. (1843–1923), author of the State Criminal Code, member of the State Council (from 1906), 242, 284, 315, 328

Tikhomirov, L., 318, 354n16

Tolstoy, D. A. (1823–1889), minister of education (1866–80), minister of the Interior (1882–89), 47–48, 204

Trepov, D. F. (1855–1906), governor of St.Petersburg, Imperial palace commandant, 261, 270–71, 281, 305–6

Troshchinsky, D. P. (1754–1829), minister of Justice (1814–17), 337n15, 341–42n11

Trubetskoy, P. N., Prince, Moscow marshal of the nobility, 246–47

Trubetskoy, S. N, Prince, rector of Moscow University (1905), 214, 224, 233–34, 251–56, 259, 360n6

Tsereteli, I. G., member of the Second Duma, social democrat, 316–18

Uexküll, Y. A. (1852–1918), secretary of State (1904–9), 271, 276, 279, 362n11

Uvarov, S. S. (1786–1855), minister of education (1833–49), 99–101

Valuev, P. A. (1814–1890), minister of the Interior (1861–68), 190, 193, 196, 200–202, 206, 353n40, 353n48

Vasil'chikov, I. V., Prince (1777–1847), member of Commission of Dec. 6th, 46, 119

Volkonsky, N. S., Prince, member of the Second and Third Dumas, 170, 174

Voltaire, 26–27

Vorontsov, A. R. (1741–1805), chancellor (1802–4), 32, 335n4, 336n14

Witte, S. J. (1849–1915), finance minister (1892–1903), chair of Committee of Ministers (1903–5), 37, 131, 134, 137, 139–45, 150–54, 156–57, 161, 164–65, 167, 169, 180, 182–85, 190, 205, 207, 217, 227–28, 234–41, 243–45, 247, 264, 267, 269–72, 275, 277–81, 284, 286–91, 298–99, 308, 322–23, 338n9, 349n2, 354n16, 356n1, 357n42, 357n47, 362n14

Zablotsky-Desiatovsky, A. P. (1808–1881), 92, 95–96

Zaitsev, K. O., lawyer, 21, 123, 127, 345n3 (chap. 10)

Zavadovsky, P. V. (1738–1812), chair of commission for new legislation (1802), 32, 69